Fodor's

E X P L O R I N G

SINGAPORE & MALAYSIA

FODOR'S TRAVEL PUBLICATIONS, INC.
NEW YORK • TORONTO • LONDON • SYDNEY • AUCKLAND

Published in the United States by Fodor's Travel Publications, Inc.
Published in the United Kingdom by AA Publishing.

Fodor's and Fodor's Exploring Guides are registered trademarks of Fodor's Travel Publications, Inc.

ISBN 0-679-02666-5
First Edition

Fodor's Exploring Singapore & Malaysia

Author: Fiona Dunlop
Series Adviser: Ingrid Morgan
Joint Series Editor: Susi Bailey
Cartography: The Automobile Association
Cover Design: Louise Fili, Fabrizio La Rocca
Front Cover Silhouette: Bob Krist

Special Sales
Fodor's Travel Publications are available at special discounts for bulk purchases for sales promotions or premiums. Special editions, including personalized covers, excerpts of existing guides, and corporate imprints, can be created in large quantities for special needs. For more information, contact your local bookseller or write to Special Markets, Fodor's Travel Publications, 201 East 50th Street, New York, NY 10022.

Manufactured in Italy by LEGO SpA, Vicenza
10 9 8 7 6 5 4 3 2 1

Fiona Dunlop lives in Paris, where she has reported on the city's cultural life for newspapers and magazines such as *The (London) Times* and *Sunday Times* the *European, Art International, Vogue Décoration*, and *Elle Decoration*. She is author of the *Paris Art Guide* and *Exploring Paris*, and has contributed to several other guides, including the *Time Out Guide to Paris*.

Pulau Pinang's spectacular Kek Lok Si Temple

How to use this book

This book is divided into five main sections:

❏ Section 1: *Singapore and Malaysia Are*
Discusses aspects of life today, from economics to cuisine.

❏ Section 2: *Singapore and Malaysia Were*
Places the nations in their historical context and explores those past events whose influences are felt to this day.

❏ Section 3: *A to Z Section*
Breaks down each nation into regional chapters, and covers places to visit, including walks and excursions. Within this section fall the Focus-on articles, which consider a variety of topics in greater detail.

❏ Section 4: *Travel Facts*
Contains practical information vital for a successful trip.

❏ Section 5: *Hotels and Restaurants*
Lists recommended establishments in Singapore and Malaysia, giving résumés of their attractions.

How to use the star rating
Most of the places described in this book have been given a separate rating:

▶▶▶ **Do not miss**

▶▶ **Highly recommended**

▶ **Worth seeing**

Not essential to see

Map references
To make the location of a particular place easier to find, every main entry in this book has a map reference to the right of its name. This comprises a number, followed by a letter, followed by another number, such as 176B3. The first number (176) refers to the page on which the map can be found; the letter (B) and the second number (3) pinpoint the square in which the main entry is located. The maps on the inside front cover and inside back cover are referred to as IFC and IBC respectively.

Contents

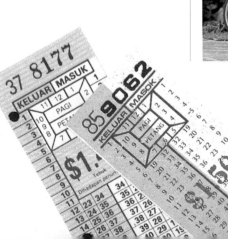

Quick reference

This quick reference guide highlights the features of the book you will use most often: the maps; the introductory features; the Focus-on articles; the walks and the excursions.

7

Fishing boats at Marang

Terry Tan is a former broadcaster, feature writer and, latterly, food and travel writer for the *New Straits Times* publications section. He is currently a restaurateur, food consultant, food magazine editor, and cookbook writer.

My Singapore

by Terry Tan

The sleepy hollow of my childhood has grown up into a rambunctious city state full of serious business and serious fun. But although the back lanes of my youth are now soaring expressways and ribbons of asphalt, the streets still spill over with friends taking in the cool evening air. At the same time, my taste buds still find much promise in food stalls on every street corner, each one providing the chance of a gustatory sojourn.

Sometimes the well-oiled machinery of Singapore frightens me, but although the shops and boutiques still beckon I find I can pass them by without a blink when I'm anticipating the camaraderie of renewed friendships in coffee shops and in the cool atriums of a dozen and one hotels. The stretches of coast continue to promise languid escape—come here for the cool caress of tropical breezes, but try the seafood as well!

Singapore stimulates the soul if the watchword is moderation—in food, shopping, and work, for they can be very addictive in this pulsating little island.

My Malaysia

by Zaharah Othman

My fondest memories of Malaysia tend to find their setting on the delightful island of Pinang. I was born in nearby Alor Setar in the state of Kedah, but it was in Pinang that I spent an enjoyable stint as a journalist, and it now remains a must on my itinerary on every trip home.

The blend of the urban and the rural, the delightful colonial architecture, drawing from both exotic and local influence, the lush greenery and the variety of cuisines all add up to an experience which is quintessentially Malaysian.

I can think of no better way of introducing my children to the fascinating charm of this bewitching isle than by a ride around town in trishaws, or kings of the road as they are locally known. With the sea breeze in our hair, we race along the Esplanade, home to hundreds of little food stalls at night and a hunting ground for seafoodlovers like me.

We always top this with a trip up Pinang Hill, a nostalgic journey for me and a thrilling ride for the children on the funicular train that goes up and down this cool peak.

Nature has blessed Malaysia with some of the most beautiful islands in the region, and I would be failing my duty therefore if I did not mention my other favorite place, Langkawi, with its crystal-clear waters, scenic beaches, and swaying palms. I first biked around this island when I was a student, and I am sure you will be impressed by the warmth and friendliness of its people.

Each trip that I make back to Malaysia provides me with physical and spiritual rejuvenation, and rekindles my love affair with my home country.

Zaharah Othman is a freelance journalist and broadcaster with the BBC's World Service, and also writes for the Malaysian newspaper, the *New Straits Times*. She is married to another journalist and has four children.

SINGAPORE AND MALAYSIA ARE

■ **Spiked with state-of-the-art high-rises, Singapore's urbanized skyline is a far cry from East Malaysia's scarred but still dense rain forest, and Peninsular Malaysia's pitted tin-mining region, limestone outcrops, palm-oil plantations, and jungle. Towns, lakes, rivers, waterfalls, blindingly white beaches, and turquoise horizons may intervene, but finally nothing can alleviate the visitor's overwhelming impression of a green landscape. .....■**

Singapore's chrome and glass
When Singapore and Malaysia parted federated company in 1965, few could foresee the face that the island would present to the world barely 25 years later.

Industrialized at a speed unheard of, much of Singapore's jungle, grasslands and mangrove swamps have disappeared under public housing estates and industrial zones. Malay fishing *kampungs* (villages) will soon only be fond memories; their wooden stilt houses have become anachronisms in an age

Malaysia's east-coast islands boast pristine white-sand beaches and coconut palms

when hundreds of Singaporean families are packed into high-rise apartment blocks.

Land reclamation may continue apace on the island, but the city continues to encroach on the shrinking rural landscape. Exceptions are in the northeast, where shipyards mingle with a few surviving mangrove swamps, rubber trees, and coconut groves, and in the northwest, where a wetland coastal site has been transformed into a bird sanctuary—a sign that Singapore is clinging desperately to what little nature it has left.

Peninsular Malaysia Stretching over an area of 50,612 sq miles from the Thai border down to the causeway

leading to Singapore, Peninsular Malaysia's population of over 14 million is concentrated mainly along its west coast. A combination of immigration, tin mining, plantation agriculture, and industrialization has transformed this region over the last century, and today Kuala Lumpur's urban sprawl is comparable to that of any thriving Asian city. Yet head across the central mountain range to the east coast, and the landscape pans out into its natural jungle state, nurtured by Malaysia's constantly hot and wet climate.

Viewed from the populated and cultivated lowlands, the forest-clad hills and mountains (occupying about half of the land area) seem to sleep in a peaceful blue haze. However, this belies their often treacherous nature, more fully appreciated by the thousands of indigenous insect, bird, and mammal species than by man.

To the north, limestone spurs tufted with vegetation and riddled with caves border a rugged, unspoiled region now overflowing with man-made lakes, while immediately west Kedah's paddy fields unfold gently toward the coast. Interspersed with some beaches and ports, mangrove swamps fringe the west coast. In contrast, the east coast is practically one long, hedonistic expanse of white sand. Dotted with coconut palms and casuarina trees, the peninsula's eastern seaboard is often fronted by outlying islands, each more enticing than the next—that is if no oil rig looms on the horizon.

Last wilderness About 15,000 years ago the island of Borneo is thought to have been joined to Peninsular Malaysia by Sumatra and Java. Today the two parts of Malaysia still share physical characteristics—this being especially true of Sabah. Its 28,350-sq-mile area shifts from cultivated western plains into forested uplands—the Banjaran Crocker and Gunung Kinabalu. This highland area is broken up into a succession of hill ranges and valleys that descend into the partly forested, partly cultivated eastern side.

Occupying 47,863 sq miles, Sarawak possesses Malaysia's

Dramatic Gunung Santubong in Sarawak, East Malaysia

11

❏ "The forests, somber and dull, stood motionless and silent on each side of the broad stream. At the foot of big, towering trees, trunkless nipa palms rose from the mud of the bank, in bunches of leaves enormous and heavy, that hung unstirring over the brown swirl of eddies. In the stillness of the air every tree, every leaf, every bough, every tendril of creeper and every petal of minute blossoms seemed to have been bewitched into an immobility perfect and final."
From: *Tales of Unrest*, Joseph Conrad (1898). ❏

greatest remaining wilderness tracts, with over 70 percent of the state lying under jungle cover of some sort. Flat coastal plains and peat swamps rise into densely forested hill ranges riddled with rivers that drain into the South China Sea. Pepper, which tolerates the high rainfall, grows on fertile slopes, while rubber, coconuts, palm oil, cocoa, coffee, and tea are cultivated on a lesser scale. However, in all East Malaysia it is the rain forest that dominates the landscape.

■ **Steered by business mandarins perched in the glass skyscrapers that crowd Singapore's prosperous business district, the economic fortunes of this diminutive nation are legendary. A showcase of almost alchemical talents, the island with no natural resources or agriculture has transformed itself in under 25 years from an Oriental bazaar into a fully industrialized nation. But is the momentum finally slowing down?** .....■

Singapore's political leaders are directly responsible for the radical socioeconomic transformation of the last few decades. Unique in this field is Lee Kuan Yew, leader of the governing PAP (People's Action Party) from 1959 to 1990. Still an outspoken senior statesman, Lee's benign dictatorship was ironically considered dangerously left wing by the West when he first swept to power. After independence was won in 1965, Singaporeans were catapulted by the PAP along a path paved with the Chinese work ethic. For almost 20 years the average economic growth rate fluttered around the 9 percent mark—one of the highest rates of constant growth the world has ever seen.

Recipe for boom time But what was the recipe for this miraculous growth? Economic analysts have pointed to the stereotypical traits of the Chinese, who hold full sway in a nation where they make up 78 percent of the population: a will to succeed, a sense of community, a respect for authority, and an undeniable gift for business. But plenty of other factors contributed to the relentless trajectory, and these were carefully engineered by the PAP: limited labor union power and tough legislation against strikes; strict wage controls; open doors to foreign investment; an absence of import and export duties; targeted industrial development; and long-term economic planning—all under the watchful eye of the Monetary Authority of Singapore (MAS), a

Lee Kuan Yew

powerful financial market regulator.

Much influenced by the Japanese model, Singapore also keeps a constant eye on the evolution and status of Hong Kong, emulating its business initiatives while constantly trying to outperform this rival Asian dragon. Following the vagaries of political change, foreign investors shift their headquarters between the two economic centers. Initial fear of 1997, the date when Hong Kong reverts to Chinese sovereignty, benefited Singapore, but recent trends show renewed confidence in Hong Kong's future and yet another flux eastward.

Goals of the economic dragon At the heart of Lee Kuan Yew's strategy was a determination to base Singapore's economy on manufacturing rather than on the more volatile sectors of banking, tourism, and

trade. With an automated port that is the world's busiest, a major petro-chemical processing role, over 5 million visitors a year and no foreign debt, Singapore has easily surpassed its initial goals. Almost half of Singapore's visitors come from Japan and ASEAN countries (Association of South East Asian Nations—Thailand, Malaysia, Singapore, Brunei, Indonesia, and the Philippines), while 55 percent come for conventions—an expanding sector in which the island is ranked seventh in the world and first in Asia.

Behind the boom lie numerous social achievements: full employment; available and affordable housing for married couples (90 percent are homeowners); high standards of education (there is 90 percent literacy) and health care (a lower infant mortality rate than in most Western countries); and an enviable public transportation system.

Negative signals However, signs that all is not golden in the state of Singapore are beginning to appear. Economic growth has slowed to 4.7 percent and in many fields neighboring Malaysia is dangerously competitive, while the other Asian dragons—Hong Kong, Taiwan, and South Korea—go from strength to strength. Since 1990 Prime Minister Goh Chok Tong has led the PAP, but the 1991 general elections proved that the ruling party's popularity was on the wane. In the constituencies that it contested, the opposition SDP (Singapore Democratic Party) obtained 48–49 percent of the vote,

despite the fact that SPH (Singapore Press Holdings) has strong PAP ties and supports the government.

So, is enough enough? Now highly educated, prosperous, and comfortably housed, Singaporeans may be thirsting for something other than the trappings of economic success.

❑ Shopping in Singapore continues to be the favorite activity for visitors—more than 87 percent indulge and they spend an estimated annual S$2.75 billion (US$1.7 billion). ❑

Singapore's business district

■ **Keeping a low world profile, Malaysia is following an apparently untroubled path toward full industrialization. Blessed with rich natural resources and a liberal economy, which have been joined by a booming industrial sector and energetic foreign investment, the country seems poised to take off. However, a few skeletons rattle in the closet of this multi-ethnic society as it races toward the 21st century. .....■**

14

The catchwords of Malay society and politics at the end of the 20th century are "*Bumiputra*" and "*Vision 2020.*" Neither can be missed and both have their significance, implying Malay nationalism on the one hand and an ambitious socioeconomic goal on the

Malaysia's Prime Minister, Dr. Mahathir Mohamad

other. Seated firmly in the driving seat of this new Asian powerhouse since 1981, Prime Minister Mahathir Mohamad is an outspoken, confrontational politician whose strongest opposition comes from within his own party. Political stability and forward planning have played major roles in Malaysia's rapid economic development, with Mahathir's party, UMNO (United Malays National Organization), sailing through every election since Independence in 1957 and currently holding a two-thirds parliamentary majority. Years of investment in infrastructure and manufacturing

equipment are now bearing ripe fruit, and the country seems on the verge of reaching economic maturity.

Skeletons Meanwhile, lurking in the shadowy wings are a few ethnic problems that this strongly Islamic country has yet to resolve. The word *Bumiputra* (meaning "sons of the soil") was coined after the bloody intercommunal riots of 1969. At that time only a tiny slice of company assets was owned by Malays, who lagged far behind Chinese-Malaysians in terms of per capita income and still do. New guidelines brought out at the time stipulated obligatory participation by *Bumiputras* in any company, and these, combined with controls on political liberties, left about 45 percent of the population feeling resentful. Was it pure chauvinism, or a last-ditch attempt to stave off complete takeover by the Chinese community?

Even more extreme and a constant thorn in the government's side is the state of Kelantan, ruled by a fundamentalist opposition party hand-in-glove with its sultan.

Economic diversification Twenty years ago the Malaysian economy was heavily reliant on the products of plantations and tin mines. This dependence on rubber and tin left the country at the mercy of fluctuating commodity prices. In the early 1970s, however, the first timid steps were taken toward diversification by encouraging foreign investment in electronics. But it was not until after the full easing of restrictions on for-

Malaysia's economy was heavily based on rubber until 20 years ago

country where labor costs are low and natural resources plentiful. Taiwan currently leads the investment field—it poured in RM2.2 billion (US$870 million) in 1990—followed closely by Japan and the USA. As a result of this investment, annual growth now hovers at an impressive 8–9 percent.

Meanwhile, the government focuses on much-needed social and employment-training programs, and on improving the country's infrastructure.

❑ Southeast Asia's first successful carmaking venture was Malaysia's homegrown car, the Proton Saga, which has been rolling off the production lines at booming Shah Alam since 1985. The car is now exported to Singapore, New Zealand, and the UK, and a second model—the Iswara—was launched in 1993. ❑

eign investment in 1987 that the economy moved into top gear.

Many of the world's industrial giants leapt at the opportunity to establish manufacturing and regional export bases in this stable, strategically located

The Proton Saga

■ The tangled tropical wilderness that once blanketed Malaysia is fast disappearing, and the country's recent rate of deforestation has become a prime target for environmentalists. Where primary rain forest vanishes, so too does indigenous wildlife. Increasingly conscious of the "green" isssue, the federal government is making efforts to forestall further losses, but pessimists predict that soon after the year 2000 Malaysia will be a net importer of timber. ....■

16

Possessing some of the richest commercial forests in the entire humid tropics, Malaysia is strongly aware of the influence of the logging issue on its world profile. Half the tropical timber on the world market is exported from Malaysia. After two decades of forest conversion to rubber and oil-palm plantations, as well as destruction from logging, Malaysia now holds up the banner of sustainable forest management. During the 1980s the country claimed an annual deforestation rate of only 1.5 percent (down from 4 percent) in the peninsula.

But what is so precious about this merciless jungle environment?

Wild Malaysia—the green hell
Malaysian forests are categorized in the following way: coastal mangrove and nipa (palm trees); freshwater swamp; dipterocarp forest (lowland hardwoods); heath forest; and montane forest.

Humid lowland conditions are perfect for luxuriant growth, and trees, lianas, epiphytes (parasitic plants such as ferns), palms, and herbaceous plants flourish all year round in the unchanging tropical climate to form the most

❑ Peninsular Malaysia is thought to have originally been cloaked in 46,150 sq milesof primary forest, of which 22,690 sq miles remain today. Sabah's original forest area of 25,000 sq miles probably stands at 15,380 sq miles today, while about half of Sarawak's almost total original rain-forest cover has been logged. In Malaysia overall, 59 percent of land remains under forest (although independent estimates vary from 48 percent to 50 percent), of which 82 percent is now permanent forest reserve (in other words, used for selective logging only), national park, or wildlife sanctuary. ❑

complex ecosystem on earth.

This intricate balance is contributed to by about 8,500 species of flowering plants and ferns in the peninsula and 11,000 in East Malaysia, many of them rich in medicinal properties that the West has yet to discover. Described as a "green hell" by those who had to withstand rain-forest conditions during World War II, the dark, rotting undergrowth shaded by a thick canopy nurtures a vast range of fungi and insects—from cicadas to scorpions and leeches—as well as increasingly elusive wildlife.

Jungle insect life: the Atlas beetle

Remaining wildlife Although still rich in species, the rain forest is now home to a relatively small number of animals, and ongoing deforestation is depriving even these creatures of their natural habitats. Elephants, tigers, and leopards do exist in the peninsula but are rarely seen, although salt licks in the Taman Negara attract wild cattle (seladang), tapirs, deer, and wild pigs.

Eastern Sabah claims the greatest remaining concentration of elephants in the country, along with specifically East Malaysian species such as orangutans, proboscis monkeys, pangolins, and bearded pigs. The Sumatran rhinoceros (immutable for the last 30 million years) teeters on the brink of extinction—partly because its horn is prized by the Chinese as an aphrodisiac.

Visible throughout Malaysia are monkeys—including leaf monkeys and the coconut-climbing, nitpicking long-tailed macaques of coastal forests. And as night falls, a flying reddish blur in the gloom will usually prove to be a flying squirrel.

Logging or sustainable forest management? Any rain forest cleared of vegetation is immediately carpeted by shrubs and grasses, and

Over 40 percent of Malaysia's rain forest has been logged

You may see, or rather hear, gibbons in the rain forest

eventually—after 60 years or so—by secondary forest. The object of selective logging is to fell the valuable hardwood trees on a rotational basis, thus allowing time for the logged area to regenerate before the next harvest (usually 25 to 60 years later). It has been estimated that 110 to 375 years are needed for the original, tall forest to be replaced, although the counter-argument states that the removal of mature trees gives younger trees more room and light for unencumbered growth.

SINGAPORE AND MALAYSIA ARE *Architecturally diverse*

■ **Malaysian and Singaporean architecture covers an incredible range, from wooden houses on stilts to ruined forts, luxurious Chinese mansions, planters' bungalows, imposing colonial relics, riverside longhouses, onion-domed mosques, lavish red and gold temples, and steel-and-glass skyscrapers. These symbols of numerous races and eras pepper the tropical landscape with a bewildering array of styles. .....■**

18

Mosque and temple architecture and colonial styles are explored in more detail on pages 94–95 and on page 98 respectively, but Malaysia also has a unique and diverse range of domestic architecture.

Longhouse mode Terrain, agricultural habits, and defense were the factors governing Borneo's indigenous architecture until very recently.

Apart from labyrinthine **Bajau** water-villages, Sabah's styles are less remarkable than those of Sarawak. Longhouses only remain in the north among the dramatic **Rungus** people, the high sloping roofs inspiring the stylized form of Kota Kinabalu's museum.

In Sarawak, the **Iban** have lined the banks of most of the state's rivers

Today East Malaysia's longhouses often have corrugated-iron roofs

with their sprawling longhouses. Traditionally built of chopped timber tied with creepers and thatched with leaves, longhouses have inevitably moved with the times and now display planks and corrugated iron.

Quite different in style from the longhouses are the conical thatched-roof bamboo huts of the **Bidayuh**, designed to cling to steep hillsides in western Sarawak. Further into the interior and up in the highlands, the **Kayans**, **Kenyahs**, and **Kelabits** built their longhouses to last using solid ironwood, but sturdiest of all East Malaysia's dwellings are those of the **Melanau**. Members of this small coastal group were easy prey for marauding pirates, and as a result their traditional houses were massive affairs, raised nearly 50 ft. above the ground with slits in the floor so that their assailants could be scalded with boiling water.

Kampung styles

Harmonizing with the extremes of their environment, *kampung* (village) houses are traditionally raised on stilts to improve ventilation, and to avoid monsoon waters and wild animals. Each region claims its own style, but all are made of timber and have prominently sloping *attap* (thatched palm) or tiled roofs shading the house. Shutters and verandas are common, often embellished with fine decorative fretwork and carving.

East coast homes reveal Thai and Cambodian influences, the older ones with elaborately carved gables and ventilation grilles. Roofs peak dramatically in Negeri Sembilan where the Minangkabau style shoots gables skyward, and in the Melaka region houses have painted walls and decorative tiled staircases.

Chinese shophouses

Typical of every urban shopping street in Singapore and Malaysia, the narrow, terraced Chinese shophouse evolved from early one-story versions with wooden pillars and *attap* roofs—still visible in northern Malaysia. The arcaded fronts were declared public walkways and had to measure five colonial feet (hence the name, five-foot ways). Interiors followed traditional Chinese layout, but by the

Above: Chinese shophouses
Below: Architectural contrasts in Singapore

1870s facades increasingly reflected colonial influences—whether Portuguese or British—as well as proudly proclaiming commercial

success. Omnipresent from Sabah to Pinang, the most elaborately restored versions can be found in Singapore's conservation districts.

■ **While other nations are torn apart by racial strife, Singapore and Malaysia present a relatively serene multiracial face to the world. Bugis, Minangkabau, Achinese, Thai, Indian, and numerous other influences have contributed to Malaysia's melting pot, while in Singapore the Chinese population has expanded faster than those of the Malays, Arabs, and Indians. Both societies are highly conscious of their racial balance and harmony which, despite past hiccups, they hope will remain trouble-free. .....■**

Singapore makes more effort to accommodate multiethnicity than does Malaysia, where Malays are favored with numerous privileges to regulate the "economic imbalance." In 1969 this provoked violent race riots between Chinese and Malays in Kuala Lumpur, but the bloody aftermath actually resulted in a stepping-up of Malay economic quotas and the imposition of Bahasa, the Malay language, as the official tongue. Since then, the rapid rise in the standard of living has gained the upper hand over abstract notions of equality, and each race seems content to remain within its own socioeconomic sector.

Malays The *Bumiputras* of Malaysia, or "sons of the soil," are composed of Borneo's indigenous peoples and the Muslim Malays. A carefree, courteous, tolerant race, essentially rural in spirit, Malays have only drifted into urban living over the last century and still represent an overwhelming majority in less industrialized east coast areas of the peninsula. Since Independence in 1957 they have flourished, increasing their share in the nation's wealth, which was previously monopolized by the Chinese.

Fishermen today may use outboard motors and businessmen mobile phones, but the humid equatorial climate ensures that the Malay password *tidak apa* (meaning "never mind") prevails. Nor will their 600-year-old respect for Islam change, a religion whose theoretical aim is to attain the peace the Malays relish.

Singapore's Indian community clings firmly to its traditions

Chinese Relentlessly hard-working, the Chinese have fashioned the economies of Singapore and Malaysia. Mostly Cantonese-, Hakka- or Hokkienese-speaking southern Chinese, their dialects may disappear in Singapore where Mandarin Chinese is now imposed beside English, Malay, and Tamil as one of the national languages.

Although some Straits Chinese families can trace their presence back over 400 years, massive Chinese immigration really only

began in the mid-19th century to man Singapore's port and work Malaysia's tin mines. On the peninsula, Chinese communities flourish wherever urban profits are to be made, and they outnumber Malays in both KL and Pinang. Chinatowns from Melaka to Kuching throng with ornate temples, clan houses, and, above all, wonderful gastronomy.

Indians Despite their strong early imprint on Malay culture, the Indians form barely 7 percent of Singapore's population and less than 10 percent of Malaysia's. Mainly Hindu Tamils, they were brought in by the British to work the coffee and rubber plantations, and to build Singapore's roads and monuments. Professionals followed, and Indian teachers and lawyers now form an integral part of the Malaysian middle classes. Indian communities are concentrated in the

states of Selangor, Perak, and Pinang, where you will find sari-clad women, banana-leaf curries and riotously colorful temples.

Indigenous peoples Malaysia's native peoples form a multiplicity of

Chinese communities flourish in Singapore and in Malaysia's towns and cities

communities on the Malay Peninsula and in Borneo, each limited to its own region and with its own agriculture, crafts, and lifestyle. These are the original people (*orang asli*) of Malaysia, comprising the Negritos, Senois, and Proto-Malays. Despite being categorized with Malays as *Bumiputras*, the indigenous tribes of Sabah and Sarawak inhabit another world where forest gods vie with river levels for the well-being of the people.

Tattooed Iban tribesman

Religions and festivals

■ **Religious festivals, the inescapable celebrations of spiritual beliefs, monopolize
much of the calendar in both Singapore and
Malaysia. A sensual riot of costumes,
music, incense, performances, and rituals
draws the outsider straight into the heart
of the culture in question, and provides an
opportunity to see concentrations of ethnic
groups that are otherwise diffuse in these
multireligious societies. .....■**

Year in, year out, the dates of festivals shift according to Buddhist and
Hindu lunar-based calendars or the
Islamic version, but once a year all
denominations unite during National
Day parades—August 9 in Singapore
and August 31 in Malaysia.

Chinese/Buddhist Kicking off the
year is **Chinese New Year**, which
falls in late January or early February.
Although essentially family oriented,
celebrations spill on to the streets
with spectacular lion dances,
firecrackers (banned in Singapore)
and a profusion of pungent delicacies
and rituals. After two weeks festivities culminate in **Chap Goh Meh**,
celebrated with pulsating energy in
Pinang and in Kuching. The latter is
also the only place to hold the superb

and traditional accompanying
Lantern Festival.

In the seventh lunar month, the
Festival of the Hungry Ghosts
marks a period of suspicion when it
is believed that the souls of the
dead—especially those ignored by
relatives—return to roam the earth.
Wary of their revenge, pious Chinese
make religious offerings while reso-
nant *wayang* (Chinese opera) swings
into action near temples. *Wayang*
also appears during the **Festival of
the Nine Emperor Gods**, when
processions honor each of the nine
sons of Guan Yin (the goddess of
mercy).

The more poetic **Mooncake
Festival** held in mid-autumn marks
the overthrow of Mongol rulers in
14th-century China, but in reality it is

*A remnant from the days of imperial China, the Mooncake Festival honors
the dead with fruit and cakes*

an excuse to troop out with the family by lantern light, gaze at the moon, and eat sweet mooncakes.

Twice a year Singaporean Chinese celebrate the **Monkey God Feast**: seekers of mediums' powers skewer their cheeks and tongues in a compelling though painful performance.

Malay/Muslim The highlight of the Malay year is the feast of **Hari Raya Puasa**, held in March or April at the new moon at the end of the fasting month of Ramadan. Like Chinese New Year it is largely a family occasion, when forgiveness is sought for sins committed and special prayers are held at mosques. Two months later **Hari Raya Haji** is a quieter celebration involving all those who have accomplished the essential pilgrimage to Mecca, the hadj. During Ramadan itself, a tantalizing display of edible Malay specialities materializes by major mosques ready for those breaking their fast with a vengeance at sunset.

Indian/Hindu Concentrated in Singapore, Kuala Lumpur, and Pinang, Hindu festivities are among the most spectacular, peaking at **Thaipusam** in January or February. At this time devotees, their bodies pierced with skewers in a trance-inspired homage to Lord Muruga, trudge beneath highly decorated wheel structures (*kavadis*). An electrically charged atmosphere of incense, chanting, drumming, and songs follows the penitents' arduous route to the temple. In Singapore this culminates at the Chettiar Temple, in Kuala Lumpur it ends at the Batu Caves and in Pinang it finishes up at the Waterfall Road temples.

The Hindu "Christmas" is **Diwali**, celebrated in October or November to mark the end of Rama's exile.

23

Fire-walking during the Hindu festival of Thaipusam at Singapore's Sri Mariamman Temple

Every Little India is festooned with lights, while temples are filled with flower garlands, offerings, and oil lamps symbolizing the triumph of good over evil. Determined devotees also push their luck by fire-walking during this period.

Indigenous harvest festivals In East Malaysia the rice harvest inspires frenetic and colorful celebrations. Sabah's Kadazans let loose at the end of May, while Sarawak's Dayaks hold **Gawai Dayak** on the first and second days of June. Feasting is the focal point, with plates of roast pork and free-flowing *tuak* (rice wine), accompanied by storytelling, singing, and dancing in elaborately feathered and beaded costumes. Each ethnic community holds its own *gawai* (festival) at different dates, the most joyful and widespread being the **Gawai Kenyalang** (Iban Hornbill Festival). The many Christians of this region also celebrate Easter.

■ As tourists tread Malaysian paths demanding souvenirs, so handmade artifacts do a disappearing act. Manufactured handicrafts abound, enthusiastically promoted in every resort or major town and displacing the labor-intensive products of the more leisurely past. Yet whether machine or handmade, Malaysia's batik cloth, metalwork, weaving, pottery, and woodcarvings all have distinctive styles, these being unaffected by the nation's diverse historic influences. .....■

24

Weaving Apart from the princely brocade *songket* (see page 206), Malaysia produces a fantastic variety of pandan-weaving. Woven and plaited from the dried and split leaves of the nipa palm or the *Pandanus* (screw pine), mats, baskets, dish covers, fans, bags, paddy-farmers' sunhats, and numerous other items geared to contemporary needs are deftly created in rural areas. Motifs range from basic checks and stripes to intricate patterns reproducing ethnic symbols or totemic animals.

Unique to Sarawak is the laboriously produced *pua kumbu* (handwoven covers). Each subtle design (depicting deities, weapons, animals, or plants) has immense symbolic significance and the most intricate can take months to complete—hence their elevated prices. *Ikat* warp tie-dyeing on the loom was traditionally

A Mah Meri mask carved by Orang Asli tribespeople on Pulau Carey

Kain songket, *a rich silk brocade once reserved for royalty*

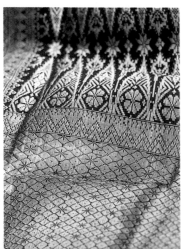

limited to vegetable dyes, but today synthetic-dyed threads are common.

Batik Originally from Java, batik caught on rapidly in Malaysia and is now the material of the national rural costume. Still handmade in Kelantan and Terengganu, patterns are produced by repeated stages of waxing areas of cotton or silk, thus protecting them from the color dyes. Hand-painted or metal-stamped, Malaysian batik patterns are finer and more conservative than the bold Indonesian variety. Markets all over the country abound with sarong

lengths from both countries, and shops sell shirts, skirts, ties, table-mats, purses *et al.*

Pottery Although less sophisticated than the Chinese ceramics that infiltrated Borneo 1,000 years ago, Malaysian pottery has its own distinctive style. Major pottery centers exist near **Kuala Kangsar**, where the renowned black Sayong pots and water bottles have regained popularity; at **Ayer Hitam** in Johor where the Aw Pottery Works churns out traditional and modern designs; and in East Malaysia in **Kuching** and in **Tuaran**, where Chinese techniques are combined with local decorative patterns.

Metalwork Silverwork was traditionally linked to rajahs and sultans, and royal museums throughout Malaysia display superb examples—sadly no longer produced. *Kris,* the fearsome Malay weapons, have lost their skilled artisans, as have many other unique creations. However, Kelantan's thriving cottage industry uses filigree and repoussé (beaten in reverse) methods to create jewelry and commemorative plates.

Brasswork continues in Kelantan and Terengganu, mainly reproducing Islamic calligraphy, while in Sarawak the Maloh people are renowned for their metalwork skills. Brass and silver have always been popular with the indigenous peoples, reaching extremes when heavy brass earrings drag earlobes to the shoulders. Fine antique jewelry, belts and

headdresses are still found, while brass or bronze gongs, although no longer pounded at the approach of every stranger, continue to ring out during riotous festivities.

Woodcarvings Little remains of the Malays' talent for decorative wood-carving, so spectacular on many old buildings. Masks and carvings by the Mah Meri of Selangor (on **Pulau Carey**, see page 148) are entirely geared to the tourist trade, but the most elaborate and intriguing wood-work is found in Sarawak.

Intricate songket *designs are still woven on the peninsula's more traditional east coast*

■ **Few tourist destinations offer such varied cuisine or food so expertly prepared. Chinese, Malays, and Indians all cling to their culinary traditions, relying on local ingredients as a base. Fish, caught fresh from the sea, indigenous tree-ripened fruit, and aromatic herbs and spices are standard fare, served up daily at quayside restaurants and local eating-houses, where the bill is always pleasantly modest. .....■**

Malay Past interaction with Thailand, Indonesia, China, the Middle East, and India has left a very palatable mark on Malay cuisine, but the basic ingredients are immutable: rice, fish, coconut, chicken, and beef.

Nasi (steamed rice) is a constant companion to meals, at breakfast presented in a neat upturned mound or cooked in coconut milk to accompany fried anchovies, eggs, peanuts and cucumber (*nasi lemak*). Lunch

Which dried fish?

often means *nasi padang*, steamed rice with a selection of curried meat, fish, and vegetables. Lunch can also consist of Malaysia's national dish, *satay*, skewers of marinated meat barbecued over a charcoal fire and served with a spicy peanut sauce, cucumber, onion, and *ketupat*, rice cakes steamed in palm-leaf envelopes. Equally popular is *laksa*, a deliciously spicy fish soup with noodles that assumes different flavorings from state to state.

Salads of raw vegetables topped with peanut sauce (*rojak* or *gado gado*), beancurd with fresh beansprouts (*tahu goreng*), stir-fried noodles with vegetables and meat (*mee goreng*), or a spicy dry curry (*rendang*) all contribute to the Malay enthusiasm for *makan*—eating! And to cool the chili fires there is always a streetside "ABC" stall churning out fluorescent mountains of grated ice, syrup, corn, and beans.

Chinese West coast Malaysia, Kuching, and, above all, Singapore are havens for anyone who enjoys the wide range of Chinese food. Dishes range from simple Hainanese chicken rice, to subtle Cantonese *dim sum* (steamed seafood or vegetable dumplings), *won ton mee* (soya noodle soup with prawn

Chilies are an integral part of Malaysian dishes—including Chinese mee (noodle) soup

dumplings, roast pork, and vegetables) or the full three courses of Peking duck.

The demands of Singapore's prosperous Chinese community have led to a proliferation of restaurants specializing in exotic and recherché dishes (duck smoked over tea-leaves and camphor? Szechuan drunken chicken? frogs' legs sautéed with chili? shark's-fin soup?), all balancing health-giving properties with an aesthetic blend of textures, colors, and flavors.

Indian Although the Indian community mainly originates from south India, where Hindu Tamil food is strictly vegetarian, Kuala Lumpur and Singapore both offer an enticing spread of north Indian Muslim food. The latter is considered more sophisticated and less chili-hot than that dished up in the south, being more subtly spiced and often served with creamy sauces. Tandoori (clay-oven baked) dishes and Punjabi or Kashmiri cuisines are usually accompanied by crisp wheat *chapatis* or unleavened *naan,* spiced with garlic, herbs, or dried fruits. Rice comes back into its own in southern Indian

banana-leaf restaurants, where piles of different curried vegetables, fish, and sometimes meat are eaten with the right hand. *Roti canai,* a thin pancake tossed with exhibitionistic dexterity, becomes *murtabak* when stuffed with meat, eggs, and onions. Found all over Malaysia, this dish has been enthusiastically assimilated into national breakfasts.

Nyonya Unique to Singapore, Melaka and, to a lesser extent, Pinang, this sophisticated cuisine combines Chinese pork dishes and soups with Malay herbs, Indonesian black nuts, fruit, and liberal doses of garlic, chilies, onions, pepper, limes, and ginger. The Straits Chinese glutinous black rice pudding is one of many laboriously prepared but delicious desserts based on rice and coconut—certainly not for those watching their waistline!

Buah keluak, *a Nyonya delicacy that includes black nuts*

■ **Despite the inroads of television, video and karaoke (jukebox singalongs), traditional music, dance, and drama still flourish in Malaysia.** Usually only mounted for ceremonial occasions or after the rice harvest, these events plunge each state into the customs, costumes and rhythms of its past, reaffirming a cultural identity that is otherwise fast disappearing under the universal blanket of an industrialized society. .....■

28

Instruments In Malaysia music is all-important, the 20 or so traditional percussion instruments ranging from the *rebana besar* (a gigantic drum), to the *rebab*, a three-stringed viol probably of Persian origin. Wind instruments are rarer, but include the *serunai* (an oboe, whose sounds resemble a peacock) and the *seruling* (a bamboo flute).

In Johor, *ghazal* (musical parties) feature sitars, harmoniums, and—more recently—guitars to provide recitations with a haunting background melody. Meanwhile, in Melaka quartets urge audiences to participate in romantic songs (*dondang sayang*) which are rife with Straits Chinese influence.

Dance drama *Sandiwara* (Malay theater) and *bangsawan* (Malay opera) are based on traditional and contemporary themes, the latter introduced from Persia in the 19th century.

The most sophisticated of all Malay performances is the *Mak Yong*, a dance drama that incorporates opera and comedy, and which probably came to Malaysia from Thailand several centuries ago. Similar in form except that it is performed by males, the *Manohra* reveals strong Buddhist influences. Originating in Thailand and only performed in Kelantan and Kedah, the 12 acts of this play tell of a prince who confounds ogres and demons to win his princess.

Dances Most popular of all throughout Malaysia is *joget,* performed during cultural celebrations and Malay weddings and one of the few "unisex" Malay dances. The male and female dancers avoid touching each other in an upbeat pace, said to have its origins in Portuguese Melaka.

More graceful are the royal court dances such as *tarian asyik,* evolved in Kelantan to appease a queen for the loss of her pet bird. Often visible on the tourist circuit is the beautiful *tarian lilin* (candle dance), a fluid, dextrous dance from Sumatra relating the sad tale of a maiden's nocturnal search for her lost engagement ring. Peculiar to Johor is the *kuda kepang* based on the activities of nine evangelizing Javanese Muslims. Dancers astride decorative two-dimensional horses enter a semi-trance as they reenact Islamic battles to a rich percussion accompaniment.

Dances for the land and sea Rural activities give rise to some colorful dance interpretations. Terengganu and Kelantan's *payang* was once performed on the beach by village girls awaiting the return of the fishing boats. The *jala ikan* actually interprets the movement of the fishermen hauling in nets, and dancers are dressed in fishermen's clothes. In Kedah the more stylized *tarian cinta sayang* symbolizes the community's wish for the fishermen's safe return.

Sabah's Kadazans appease the spirits of the paddy fields after the harvest with the *hala*, while the Biduyuhs welcome harvest guests to their longhouses with a rhythmic imitation of the flapping wings of an eagle. Most spectacular of all, however, is the *ngajat lesong* dance of Sarawak's Ibans—dancers lift a 40-pound rice-pounding mortar with their teeth during the performance!

SINGAPORE AND MALAYSIA WERE

■ **Singapore's past may be slim, but it is certainly not uneventful.** Inextricably linked to the activities of neighboring Malay states Java, and Sumatra, and surrounded by pirate-infested seas, it was long an obscure little island that experienced a short high in the late 14th century before sinking into oblivion for more than 400 years. It was not until the British administrator Stamford Raffles set foot there in 1819 that Singapura (City of the Lion) entered the mainstream of history. .....■

Commercial Square – now Raffles Place – at the turn of the century

Early years Singapore's original name of Temasek (Dan Ma Xi) first appeared in the 14th-century chronicles of the Chinese merchant mariner, Wang Da Yuan. Pirates controlled the narrow strait between Singapore and Sentosa, and Chinese maritime charts compiled in 1415 by Admiral Cheng Ho clearly show this passage as "Dragon's Teeth Gate."

After a period of rule under the Javanese-based Hindu Majapahits during the 14th century, Temasek's Malay inhabitants returned to piracy and trade, their settlement centered on Bukit Larangan (Forbidden Hill), later to become Fort Canning Hill. Foreigners came again in the form of the Sumatran Prince Parameswara, who renamed the island Singapura in 1392. However, after holding court

there for five years he was chased north to Melaka by the Javanese.

New faces Power changed hands again in the 18th century when the Bugis of Celebes gained control of Johor and Singapura, and left local rule in the hands of a *temenggong* (chief minister). When Raffles disembarked in 1819 he soon realized the strategic potential of the island and began negotiating annual stipends for Sultan Hussein Shah of Johor and the local *temenggong* in exchange for exclusive trading rights.

Island lifeline The Singapore river became the lifeline of this rapidly booming entrepôt trading center. Godowns lined its banks while sampans, twakows, tongkangs, proas, and pukats ferried goods from these vast warehouses to sailing vessels anchored at the river mouth.

By 1900 Singapore had become one of the busiest ports in the world, positively humming with activity and commerce, and accommodating the new oceangoing steamships. Oxcarts transported goods through the thriving town, while Chinese coolies dragged local merchants and colonials in rickshaws to dine at the Hotel de l'Europe or Raffles. Conditions for many were appalling, but for others they were luxurious, as Singapore held the commercial purse strings for all Southeast Asia.

Storm clouds of World War II
Obstinately believing that the Japanese would arrive in Singapore from the sea, the British were totally unprepared when, in December 1941, Japanese troops landed at Kota Bharu in northeast Malaysia. Within two months the attacking forces had cycled down the Malay Peninsula to Singapore, sweeping aside all resistance and besieging Singapore across the Selat Johor to enforce British capitulation. After seven days' fighting nearly 140,000 Australian, British and Indian troops

had been killed or captured. The island was renamed Syonan-to (Light of the South) and Operation Clean-Up began—the elimination of all anti-Japanese elements. This operation focused mainly on the Chinese, and between 6,000 and 20,000 were executed during the war years.

This tragic period finally came to an end in September 1945, when Lord Mountbatten officially accepted Japanese surrender of Singapore and the Union Jack once again fluttered over the Padang. For the next 20 years Singapore moved slowly toward self-government, entering and then being expelled from union with Malaysia. It finally became an independent republic in August 1965, with Lee Kuan Yew ambitiously occupying the driver's seat.

Right: Allied prisoner of war at Changi Prison
Below: Evacuation boats leaving Singapore harbor

■ **Recent evidence shows that while Stone Age man chipped happily away in Peninsular Malaysia, "Niah man" sheltered in majestic caves in Sarawak and other early settlers lived around an enormous volcanic lake in Sabah. Thus long before any Malay had set foot on these shores, the fruits of its tropical climate were being enjoyed by Paleolithic and Neolithic inhabitants. Embedded in the depths of limestone caves, Malaysia's prehistory remains an enigma. .....■**

32

❏ Carbon dating of the "death ships" discovered in Niah's Painted Cave place them between A.D.1 and A.D.780. These small canoe-like wooden structures possibly served as coffins and were placed in the burial site of the Painted Cave, whose cave-drawings illustrate related death rituals. ❏

Sarawak's Niah Caves

First arrivals Early man is presumed to have spread from mainland Asia southward to Australia, and it is probable that the Negrito aborigines of the hilly northern parts of Peninsular Malaysia are his descendants. During Paleolithic times sea-levels were much lower than today, and Borneo would have been joined by swamps and dry land through Sumatra to mainland Asia. Over the millenia peoples and cultures spread to the region by land and sea in an uneven process. Relics of their presence are

few as most evidence has been destroyed by the tropical climate.

For the moment it is Borneo that claims the earliest inhabitants in Malaysia. An excavated human skull is startling proof of man's presence in the **Niah Caves** nearly 40,000 years ago and constitutes Southeast Asia's first representation of *Homo sapiens*. The earliest signs of human activity in the caves are coarse chopping tools, which by 10,000B.C. had been replaced by more advanced and versatile flaked pebble tools. By 2500B.C. stone axes appeared, presumably designed for cutting forests to plant crops and for building boats and shelters. These were accompanied by nets, decorated pottery (including burial urns), and mats. By about 150B.C. Bronze Age culture had spread to Borneo, eventually providing the metals used in blowpipe manufacture.

Other Stone Age finds
Stone tools show that early man was also developing in southeastern Sabah about 20,000 years ago, first on the shores of a lake at **Tingkayu** and then at the nearby **Baturong Caves** before disappearing for unknown reasons around 10,000B.C. In the same region, the **Madai Caves** later became home for mesolithic man, but again the caves were inexplicably

Above: Stone Age tools from Kota Tampan Ayer

abandoned—around 500B.C. Various hypotheses abound as to the reasons for this.

Meanwhile, in the **Lenggong Valley** of upper Perak on the Malay Peninsula, Stone Age man was not idle. Important finds at **Kampung Kota Tampan Ayer** reveal that this

Precision blowpipes first appeared in Malaysia during the Bronze Age

region was inhabited about 34,000 years ago. The discovery of a Stone Age workshop containing thousands of tools has forced archaeologists to revise their previous theories—based on 8,000-year-old finds from Gua Musang (Kelantan)—and to rewrite the story of Malaysia's origins.

33

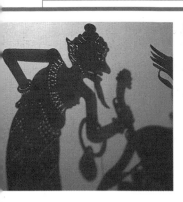

■ **Multiethnicity is no new facet of Malaysia. For centuries the country's rich resources attracted invaders by both sea and land who brought with them the latest innovations of their own cultures, whether concrete artifacts or abstract religions. Even the Malays themselves were once invaders, a northern race intermarried with Chinese, Cambodians, Bengalis, Arabs, and Siamese. Tracing their diverse and overlapping origins reveals an astonishing racial web built up through contact with most of Asia. .....■**

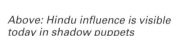

Above: Hindu influence is visible today in shadow puppets

34

Forming the southernmost tip of Asia, Peninsular Malaysia was a prime target for invaders from the north, south, east, and west. In prehistoric times two waves of Proto-Malays arrived from northern Asia, first the forefathers of today's Senois peoples and finally, about 4,000 years ago, the antecedents of the Malays. Of Mongoloid stock but intermarried over the centuries with Indochinese races encountered on the way south, these sophisticated hunters, cultivators, and sailors forced the ancestors of today's Negritos into the hills and central jungle, where many still lead nomadic lives today.

In Borneo the ancestors of the headhunting Ibans, Muruts, and rice-growing Kadazans settled along the coasts and rivers, while nomads (related to today's Penans) roamed the jungle. The final ethnic mix was provided by the Orang Laut or Proto-Malay sea-gypsies, who rode the waves off the coasts of the Malay Peninsula and eastern Sabah.

Indian inroads By the 1st century A.D., improved navigational techniques using the force of the southwest monsoon brought inveterate traders from India. Stopping over on their way to China, they soon dis-

Borneo's coastal tribes first settled in Malaysia about 4,000 years ago

covered the riches of the peninsula—gold, spices, and aromatic woods—and many chose to settle. Close on their heels came brahmin and Buddhist priests, eager to impart their religious philosophies to the pagan animist inhabitants.

The Indian system of law, politics, and religion was adopted by the ruling classes, while the ordinary people assimilated the polytheist beliefs of Hinduism into their animism. Remnants of this powerful religious force survive today in Hindu epics enacted by *wayang kulit* (shadow

❑ The Terengganu Stone, the first evidence of Islam in Malaysia, was found 20 miles inland from Kuala Terengganu. Dating from A.D.1303, this rough granite monolith inscribed with Islamic law in a mixture of Sanskrit, Malay, and Arabic script proves that Islam had already permeated the east coast by that time. Further evidence shows that by about 1400 the Idahan people of the Madai area in Sabah were convinced Muslims. Presumed to have been brought to Malaysia by Muslim Indian traders, Islamic influence eventually spread to the use of the title "sultan" by local rulers and the adoption of the Jawi script—Malay written in Arabic. ❑

extended to west Borneo and Java. Kedah's **Bujang Valley** flourished in a constant exchange of trade and culture with Pallavan India (of which impressive relics remain), while Sarawak underwent parallel development, as evidenced in numerous artifacts found in the **Santubong** area—including a 12th-century Buddhist shrine, Borneo's oldest known evidence of worship. Both civilizations disappeared at about the same time, but were soon replaced by a Muslim powerhouse based in Melaka.

Chinese trade Although Chinese contacts with Malaysia continued for centuries, often through intermediary Indian and Arab merchants, they never left as strong a sociopolitical imprint as did the Indians. More concerned with the benefits of trade and the area's gastronomic delicacies, they exchanged porcelain, silk, and ornaments for goods such as birds' nests, turtles' eggs, and hornbill ivory.

It was in the Sung and Yuan dynasties (11th to 14th centuries) that Chinese junks began to dominate the South China Sea, and it was then that close links developed with the Melakan sultanate.

plays) and certain tantric rituals used by the few remaining Malay medicine men.

Between the 7th and 14th centuries, the west coast was dominated by the Indianized Sri Vijaya Kingdom, a Malay Buddhist empire based in Sumatra, whose control

■ **Dominating both sides of the Selat Melaka for a century, the Melakan sultanate marked the zenith of classical Malay culture, bequeathing rituals, customs, and, above all, Islam to contemporary Malaysia. Hinduism and Buddhism went rapidly out of fashion, Melaka became Southeast Asia's trading crossroads, and wealth poured into the port. Melaka's rise from obscurity to supremacy was meteoric, but its fall was equally so when the first Europeans appeared on the horizon. .....■**

Melakan culture flourished in the 15th century, peaking during the reign of Sultan Mansur Shah (1459–1477) when his holdings encompassed Kedah, Terengganu, Pahang, Perak, Selangor, and Johor, as well as the coastal states of Sumatra. Forming a gateway to the Islamic states in the west and China and the Spice Islands in the east, Melaka's location was everything. The Melakans themselves hardly needed to lift a finger. They grew and made nothing, only offering for sale a few resins, gums, and precious woods the Orang Asli collected in the jungle.

All the resources of the Melakans were instead focused on creating warehouse space for the hundreds of trading ships and junks that steered toward the deep harbor. Northeast monsoon winds brought Chinese, Siamese, Javanese, and Bugis traders, while later in the year the southwest winds blew Indian and Arab vessels across the Indian Ocean to this new powerhouse.

Founding prince Astute founder of what was to become a vital cultural center, the Sumatran Prince Parameswara (said to be descended from Alexander the Great) arrived in Melaka in the early 1400s. He initially chose the island of Temasek (today's Singapore) as his base, but was soon forced to flee from there by Javanese invaders.

Legend has it that Parameswara's choice of Melaka as a new home was inspired by the plucky behavior of a local mouse deer. The deer kicked a hound that pursued it in a scene witnessed by the prince from the shade of a melaka tree. So Melaka—or Malacca—it was to be.

Embracing Islam, the prince changed his name to Iskandar Shah and thus became Malaysia's first Muslim ruler. Sensitive to the dangers of invading hordes, he immediately set about assuring the safety of his new settlement by enlisting the aid of the Orang Laut (sea-gypsies) to fend off pirates. He also formed an alliance with the Chinese against belligerent Siam.

Straits Chinese in traditional costume, 1901

Chinese bonds Official recognition of Melaka by China's Ming emperor came via the great Admiral Cheng Ho, who first arrived as trade ambassador in 1403. A eunuch from the province of Yunan, Cheng Ho pitched his tent on the hill now known as Bukit China and set about establishing a diplomatic and trading relationship that took Prince Parameswara himself on a visit to China in 1411.

The Malay–Chinese axis was further cemented in 1459 under Sultan Mansur Shah when Princess Hang Li Poh and her glittering dragon-court retinue sailed to Melaka for her marriage to the sultan. Electing to live on Bukit China, her 500 beautiful handmaids became the "Eves" of Peranakan culture when they all eventually married Malays.

Detail from Peranakan inlaid blackwood staircase

Exoticism and absolutism
Meanwhile, Melaka's port grew fast. At its peak, the city's multiracial population numbered 40,000 and the area had already assumed its contemporary layout, with the palace and Malay *kampungs* to the south of the river and the merchants' houses and stores to the north.

The Melakan court was a sumptuous blend of cultures. The Jawi script (Malay written in Arabic) evolved, and rulers were called "sultans," had absolute power, received commoners' petitions in the *balai* (audience hall), wore royal yellow and were shaded by white parasols while riding bejeweled elephants. A palace was built of previously unheard-of proportions and richness—described in the *Sejarah Melayu* (Malay Annals) written in the 16th century it has been re-created in Melaka's Cultural Museum—and a formidable national guard was developed by the remarkable chief minister, Tun Perak. Particularly distinguished warriors were honored with the title "Hang," while their exploits and disputes

became legendary—notably those of Hang Jebat and Hang Tuah.

But as in every prosperous absolutist court, intrigues flourished, and Mansur Shah's successor, Alauddin

37

Melaka's Sam Po Kong Temple (1795) is dedicated to Cheng Ho

Riayat Shah, died of poisoning at the age of 26. Melaka's reputation for wealth had also reached Portuguese ears. Eager to break the Muslim monopoly on the spice trade and to impart the tenets of Christianity, the Portuguese soon set sail for Melaka.

■ **A new century, a new ruler. This became Malaysia's inadvertent habit for 400 years: the sultans in the 15th century, the Portuguese in the 16th century, the Dutch in the 17th century, and the British in the late 18th century.** Malaya bowed to colonial forts, churches, and law courts, at the same time facing infiltration from Sumatra's Minangkabaus and Bugis from the Celebes. European invaders inevitably concentrated on the west coast, and once again Melaka became the focal point for foreign interests. .....■

38

Portuguese During Melaka's "Golden Age" Portugal had been riding the waves during its "Age of Discovery." From Brazil to East Africa, its maritime influence was rapidly spreading and the Portuguese were ready to take on two new trading posts: Goa in India and Melaka.

Pinang's Fort Cornwallis is on the site of Light's wooden stockade

At the helm was the empire-building commander, Alfonso de Albuquerque. In 1511, with one eye on Melaka's lucrative spice trade and the other on revenge (the Melakans had captured some Portuguese sailors two years previously), he attacked the port. Sultan Mahmud fled with his followers to Johor and Melaka's streets were taken over by swash-buckling Portuguese adventurers.

Concentrating his garrison on the hilltop fortress of **A Famosa**, Admiral d'Albuquerque established a walled medieval city around the slopes of the hill to enclose the administration and Portuguese homes. Outside the walls the Malays carried on as before, bartering with itinerant traders and multiplying profits on spices.

For 130 years the Portuguese waged trade and military wars from their impregnable hilltop site, forcing all ships passing through the straits to obtain a permit and imposing arbitrary dues on port activities.

Clog time However, other eyes soon started to focus on the East.

Admiral Alfonso d'Albuquerque captured Melaka in July 1511

The first to appear on the Malay horizon were the Dutch, who already controlled most of neighboring Indonesia and who were intent on monopolizing not only the distribution but also the production of spices. Formed in 1602, the Dutch East India Company profited from a power vacuum created by British involvement in their own civil war and Portuguese struggles to maintain their independence against Spain.

In 1640 the Dutch turned their cannons on A Famosa, blockaded the port, and after a seven-month siege that forced the Portuguese inhabitants of this gilded fortress cage to eat rats and snakes, stormed in to victory in January 1641. However, for the Dutch the conquest of Melaka represented a merely defensive move as their economic power was concentrated in Batavia (Jakarta) in the Dutch East Indies. Like the Portuguese, the Dutch enforced permits on Indian and British traders, a practice that did not make for allies.

In Melaka the new masters rebuilt the ruins in the form of a Dutch town, renovating the fort and adding sturdy administrative buildings around the base of the hill. Yet despite the 150-year presence of the Dutch, their influence spread no further. By 1795 conflicts in Europe resulted in the transferral of Melaka to English "caretakers."

And then there was Light Although it was happy to concentrate on trade with India and to leave control of Southeast Asia to the Dutch, the English East India Company was nevertheless interested in gaining a trading post in Malaysia so that its ships could be replenished on the tea route from China to India. The sheltered east side of the Bay of Bengal seemed eminently suited to this purpose, and the attention of the British soon became focused on the island of Penang (now known as **Pulau Pinang**).

In 1786 Captain Francis Light acquired Pinang from Kedah's sultan in return for protection and an annual stipend (still paid by the federal government today!). More commercially astute than the protectionist Dutch, Light declared the island a free port and by 1800 around 10,000 workers had settled there. This was Melaka's final death blow, and when Singapore appeared on the scene 20 or so years later, its Oriental supremacy had been lost for ever.

Although most of A Famosa fort was later destroyed by the British, the Porta de Santiago was saved by Raffles' intervention

■ From the mid-19th century onwards, Borneo's history was rich in British adventurers and traders when it was not ruled by the Sultan of Brunei. Worthy of Hollywood (Errol Flynn nearly took on the role), the Rajah Brookes' epic Sarawak saga lasted exactly a century. In neighboring Sabah, the British North Borneo Chartered Company's impact was less widespread, mainly confined to trading ports. However, both protectorates terminated abruptly with the Japanese invasion in 1941. .....■

Above: Fort Margherita in Kuching was built by Rajah Charles Brooke in the 1870s

Parangs flashed and poisoned darts found their targets as, over the centuries, northern Borneo's independently minded peoples fought against marauding pirates and European traders. Quietly paddling their dugouts along Borneo's rivers, Ibans or Muruts would ambush the members of other tribes to lop their heads. These heads were then used in fertility and death rites, and also constituted a significant symbol of Iban male valor. But change was on the way in the form of James Brooke, a wealthy adventurer only too willing to aid the Sultan of Brunei in quelling a Dayak rebellion in 1839.

The first white rajah "It is a grand experiment...If by dedicating myself to the task I am able to introduce better customs and settled laws, and to raise the feeling of the people so that their rights can never in future be wantonly infringed, I shall indeed be content and happy."

Sarawak's first white rajah, James Brooke

Such were James Brooke's words when, in 1841, the Sultan of Brunei showed his gratitude by proclaiming Brooke Rajah of Sarawak, then a small territory around Kuching.

A charming if eccentric dictator, Brooke was astute enough to enlist the help and advice of Malay nobles, the *datus* or local chiefs who had been overpowered by Brunei, and who were to participate in the

40

supreme council and court. Owing allegiance to no one, Brooke was free to fashion his own government and maintain any existing laws and customs that seemed reasonable to him (including Muslim traditions).

Increasing evidence shows that both James Brooke and his successor, Charles, were masters of the divide-and-rule game, setting one river community against another in order to abolish headhunting. Brooke installed governors (later to become inspiring subject matter for Somerset Maugham's short stories) at strategic forts along the river, but internal conflicts were far from over. Although many Bidayuhs rallied to Brooke's cause, the more resilient upriver Ibans were still an unpredictable element inspiring his lament: "I have at last a country, but oh, how ravaged by war, how torn by dissention and ruined by duplicity, weakness and intrigue."

A dedicated nephew At James Brooke's death in 1868, he was succeeded by his nephew who reigned until 1917. Blind in one eye and deaf, Charles Brooke nevertheless managed to get things done. Although opposed to industrial developments, he encouraged agriculture and education, formalized government, built a railway, and structured Kuching. Not least, by 1905 he had extended Sarawak to its present boundaries at the expense of Brunei, professing his dictum: "Sarawak belongs to the Malays, the Sea Dayaks, the Land Dayaks, the Kayans and all other tribes, and not to us. It is for them we labor, not for ourselves."

The third and last rajah, Charles Vyner Brooke, was not of the same mold, his main interest lying under women's skirts or sarongs. Despite this, he put an end to the absolute power of the rajah in 1941 by proposing a new democratic constitution governed by the Council Negeri. Too late. On Christmas Day 1941 Japanese forces captured Kuching, and in 1946 Brooke handed over Sarawak to the British government.

Meanwhile, in North Borneo After 18th-century fits and starts, British colonial presence in North Borneo rematerialized in 1846 at Labuan, and 20 years later the American Trading Company (owned by two American businessmen) controlled Sabah's west coast. Short lived, their interests were superceded by an Austrian consul, Overbeck, who together with a British commercial syndicate obtained sovereignty over all Sabah.

In 1881 Overbeck withdrew and the British North Borneo Chartered Company was formed, first based at Kudat and then at Sandakan. By 1888 the country had become a British protectorate.

From 1895 to 1905 recurring local resistance was led by Mat Salleh, a Sulu prince who was finally killed by the British in 1900 (see side panel on page 249). Then came the Japanese, and in 1942 both Sandakan and Kota Kinabalu were bombed in a last-ditch Allied attempt to prevent them from being used as naval bases.

■ **First Pinang and then Melaka fell under the sway of the British, who brought with them the resources and structures of the Industrial Revolution. One by one the sovereign states of the peninsula fell into the colonial net, and the process of their political integration into a modern nation began. By 1914 all the states of present-day Malaysia had, in one form or another, permanent British representatives who inexorably increased their spheres of influence until the sultans found themselves mere puppets. .....■**

The 19th century marked the zenith of colonial power, with the Europeans and the United States carving up the world between them. In true colonial spirit, the Anglo-Dutch Treaty of 1824 finally clarified these two nations' conflicting interests, giving the Dutch freedom of action in Sumatra and the British uncontested access to the Malay Peninsula. For 50 years British power was content to remain within these strategic boundaries, with commerce radiating from the Straits Settlements of Singapore, Melaka, Pinang, and Labuan.

Frank Swettenham, British Resident of Selangor

In 1874, Andrew Clarke, the new Straits Settlement governor, moored off the island of Pangkor, where he set about negotiating with local Malay chiefs. The result was the Pangkor Treaty, which settled the disputed Perak throne and imposed a British Resident, thus ensuring an element of stability for commercial interests. By 1896 the Federated Malay States had been created, encompassing Perak, Selangor, Negeri Sembilan, and Pahang, later joined by Johor in 1914. Meanwhile, the northern states of Kedah, Perlis, Kelantan, and Terengganu were bartered away from Siam by Britain in 1909 to become the Unfederated Malay States.

Pangkor Treaty Canned food was the prosaic genesis of the Federated Malay States. Developed in the United States in the 1860s, this industry led to an increased demand for tin, which had been mined in the peninsula since the days of the Melaka sultanate. Prolific tin mines existed in Perak and Selangor, but both states were plagued by internal power disputes and the secret societies of Chinese tin miners.

Residents' housewarming Unified government with its capital in Kuala Lumpur, a structured civil service, judiciary, law, and tax enforcement systems sugared the pill that the Malay states had to swallow, the sultans' power being confined to religion and customs. British Residents or advisers moved into newly built neo-

classical mansions, pristine white in the glare of the tropical sun. Planters built bungalows in isolated plantations, fortune-seeking Chinese flooded to the mines and expanding towns, and Tamils were brought from southern India and Ceylon to tap the free-flowing rubber.

By the late 19th century, the Federated States supplied 55 percent of world tin and in 1920 over 50 percent of world rubber.

Resistance The colonial path was, however, by no means smooth as the Malays were not always keen to bow to foreign overlords.

First to rebel on the peninsula were the Minangkabaus based in Naning, a district inland from Melaka. Rejecting British imposition of annual tithes in 1831 they rose up, forcing the British troops to struggle through dense jungle to put down the rebellion.

Equally bloody, the Pahang War was a direct result of communication problems between the British and Pahang's Sultan Ahmad in 1891. The murder of an Englishman and British fiscal intransigence triggered a long-drawn-out and costly war. Dato' Sahaman, a defiant local chief heading a fearsome band of guerrilla fighters, captured police stations, small towns, and even launched a massive dual assault on Kuala Lipis and Tembeling. Although the remaining rebels eventually surrendered in 1895, one of the most resilient warriors, Mat Kilau, remains a Malaysian national hero to this day.

More direct action took place in 1875 when James Birch, Perak's first British Resident, was assassinated in his bath house. Epitomizing a certain British superciliousness, he had handled the local sultan tactlessly and attempted to bulldoze through British policies with no consideration for local custom. Surprisingly, a memorial to him still stands in Ipoh.

This resentment of the colonials continued to rumble below the surface until, after World War II, it finally developed into direct action.

The grave of James Birch, Perak's unpopular first Resident, who was assassinated in 1875

■ As World War II raged in Europe, Japanese forces gradually spread through China and then Indochina, Malaya appearing to be a sitting duck. Yet the swiftness of the Japanese occupation took everyone by surprise, not least the British officers and intelligence who were convinced of their military superiority. Then commenced a period of hardship and brutality under the Japanese conquerors. Illusions of British supremacy were shattered and the country that emerged in 1945 possessed a very different psychology. .....■

"The Japanese are very small and short-sighted and thus totally unsuited physically to tropical warfare. They have aeroplanes made from old kettles and kitchen utensils, guns salvaged from the war against Russia and rifles of the kind used in films about the Red Indians." Such was a British intelligence officer's appreciation of the enemy prior to 1941.

Mistakenly believing Malaya to be buffered by neutral Siam to the north and protected by Singapore to the south, the British held limited troops in Malaya and only obsolete fighter

One of the few Japanese tanks destroyed by Allied troops

planes that operated from scattered and defenseless airfields.

Surprise, surprise In the early hours of December 8, 1941, contrary to all military expectation, Japanese troops landed on the beaches of Kota Bharu on the peninsula's east coast. By nightfall the town had been taken and within days Japanese tanks and bicycle-mounted forces spread through northern Malaya.

Poorly trained in jungle warfare, and lacking ammunition and numbers, the beleaguered Commonwealth troops staggered from defeat to defeat, unable to prevent the fast-peddling Japanese infantry from entering Kuala Lumpur on January 11, 1942. On January 31 the remaining Allied forces retreated to Singapore across the causeway, blowing it up in their wake. Meanwhile, North Borneo had fallen at an even greater speed. General Yamashita's Malayan campaign was over in seven weeks.

Occupation Not easy on the Malays but even tougher on the Chinese, the Japanese occupation polarized Malaya's population. Apart from the widespread raping of young Malay girls, many of whom blackened their faces and hands to diminish their desirability, the brunt of Japanese brutality was directed at the Chinese. Resentful of the occupation of mainland China, many Chinese were actively hostile toward the Japanese in Malaya. Pockets of guerrilla resistance continued throughout the war,

❏ A relic of wartime guerrilla activities and intent on forming a republic, the Communist Party turned its postwar attention to disrupting the economy. A state of emergency was declared in 1948 as the Communist insurgents, led by the redoubtable Chin Peng, attacked villages and plantations. The Emergency was declared officially over in 1960, although the last fighters were rounded up near the Thai border as recently as 1989. ❏

Malaysian flags at Merdeka Square, Kuala Lumpur

led by stranded Allied troops or by Chinese, many of whom were communists. Despite the resistance, torture centers and squalid POW camps, executions, death marches and forced labor—notably on the infamous Burma railway—all took their tragic toll.

When the British returned in 1945, the forces of incipient nationalism had been unleashed and the road to Independence was laid.

Independence Britain's initial offer of limited self-government was predictably so unpopular that in 1948 it was revoked and replaced by the Federation of Malaya, which left the sultans their power and promised full independence. By then a national movement had been formed under the banner of UMNO (United Malays National Organization) which, strengthened by Chinese and Indian parties, presented an influential and popular united alliance.

In 1955, Malaya's first national elections propelled Tunku (Tuanku) Abdul Rahman to power and finally, on August 30, 1957, the cry of "*Merdeka!*" (freedom) rang out all over the peninsula. Six years later the Federation of Malaysia came into being, encompassing Sabah, Sarawak, and Singapore, although the latter was forced out in 1965.

SINGAPORE

STEVENS ROAD

Newton Ⓜ

BUKIT TIMAH ROAD

CAVENAGH ROAD

KAMPONG JAVA RD

E

SCOTTS ROAD

CENTRAL EXPRESSWAY

BUKIT TIMAH ROAD

■ Istana

Mount Emily Park

Botanic Gardens

TANGLIN ROAD

ORCHARD ROAD

ORCHARD ■ Orchard Ⓜ

ROAD

CLEMENCEAU AVE

ORCHARD ROAD

ORCHARD

PATERSON ROAD

BOULEVARD

Emerald Hill ■

■ Peranakan Place

D

Somerset Ⓜ

SOMERSET ROAD

EXETER ROAD

PENANG ROAD

DHOBY GHAUT

Ⓜ Dhoby Ghaut

GRANGE ROAD

RIVER VALLEY ROAD

OXLEY RISE

National Museum & Art Gallery ■

KIM SENG ROAD

Chettiar Temple ■

RIVER VALLEY ROAD

Keramat Iskandar Shah ■

Fort Canning Park

Armenian Church ■

C

ZION ROAD

GANGES AVENUE

CLEMENCEAU AVENUE

Van Kleef Aquarium ■

HILL

Singapore

■ Clarke Quay

HAVELOCK ROAD

ROAD

OUTRAM ROAD

EU TONG SEN STREET

NEW BRIDGE ROAD

UPPER CROSS ST

PICKERING ST

Ⓜ Tiong Bahru

TIONG BAHRU ROAD

Bird Café ■

Pearl's Hill City Park

CROSS

LOWER DELTA ROAD

Monkey God Temple ■

B

CENTRAL EXPRESSWAY

CHINATOWN

Wak Hai Cheng Bio Temple ■

OUTRAM ROAD

Ⓜ Outram Park

Chinatown Centre ■

SOUTH BRIDGE ROAD

Thian Hock Keng Temple ■

JALAN BUKIT MERAH

■ Singapore General Hospital

NEW BRIDGE ROAD

CANTONMENT ROAD

TANJONG PAGAR ROAD

MAXWELL ROAD

CECIL STREET

JALAN BUKIT MERAH

LOWER DELTA ROAD

A

AYER RAJAH EXPRESSWAY

KAMPONG BAHRU RD

NEIL ROAD

Kim Lan Chinese Temple ■

Tanjong Pagar Ⓜ

SHENTON WAY

ANSON ROAD

Spottiswoode Park

■ Singapore Railway Station

AYER RAJAH EXPRESSWAY

1   2   3

Leong San
See Temple
Sakya Muni Temple
(Temple of a
Thousand Lights)
Sri Sreenivasa
Perumal Temple
New
World
Park

Farrer
Park

LAVENDER STREET

Angullia
Mosque

SERANGOON ROAD

BESAR

Jalan Besar
Stadium

SYED ALWI ROAD

LITTLE INDIA

JALAN

KALLANG ROAD

CRAWFORD ST

Lavender

Zhu Jiao
Centre

Rochor

SELEGIE RD

Sim Lim
Tower

ROCHOR CANAL ROAD

Jama-Ath
Mosque

JALAN SULTAN

Hajjah Fatimah
Mosque

Crawford
Park

OPHIR ROAD

Sim Lim
Square

ROCHOR

Sultan
Mosque

BEACH ROAD

NICOLL HIGHWAY

MIDDLE ROAD

STREET

New Bugis
Streeet

VICTORIA STREET

ROAD

Bugis

NORTH BRIDGE

ROAD

REPUBLIC
AVENUE

BENCOOLENE ROAD

BRAS BASAH ROAD

East Coast
Park

Raffles
Hotel

NICOLL HIGHWAY

TEMASEK BLVD

STAMFORD ROAD

STREET

BEACH ROAD

RAFFLES BOULEVARD

BENJAMIN SHEARES BRIDGE

RAFFLES AVENUE

City Hall

Marina
Centre

St Andrew's
Cathedral

City
Hall

HIGH STREET

Padang
Park

CONNAUGHT DRIVE

Marina
Park

RAFFLES AVENUE

Victoria Memorial
Hall &Theatre

Raffles
Statue

Merlion

Clifford Pier

CHURCH ST

COLLIER QUAY

Raffles
Place

*Marina
Bay*

North
Pier

ST

RAFFLES QUAY

Festival
Market

*Marina
City Park*

Marina Bay

EAST COAST PARKWAY

Singapore
Conference
Centre

Finger Pier
*Marina
Wharf* 4

5

0   200   400   600   800 m

Population

Only numbering a few hundred when Sir Stamford Raffles stepped ashore in 1819, Singapore's population is now almost 3 million. Throughout the 1970s birth control campaigns were so successful that by the 1980s the population was actually shrinking. A government volte-face created the present policies of tax incentives to boost the size of families. Today 78 percent of the population is Chinese, 14 percent Malay, 7 percent Indian and the remaining 1 percent a mixture of Eurasians, Arabs, and expatriates. The manual workforce is brought in on two-year contracts from India, Sri Lanka, Indonesia, and Thailand. No foreign worker is allowed to marry in Singapore, thus preempting any potential immigration problems— although the doors have recently opened to an influx of Hong Kong Chinese.

One of Singapore's 3 million inhabitants muses on the island-state's future

Singapore Singapore is quite simply a flagrant success story. Effortlessly channeled through the symbols of its high-tech boom, visitors can't fail to be impressed by its efficiency, even if they only stay here an average of three days. Gone are the degenerate characters and atmosphere of the Oriental bazaar and bustling port that monopolized the maritime crossroads of Asia. In more than three decades of extraordinary growth, Singapore has smoothed out every unharmonious edge to present a prosperous, orderly, and westernized face to the world. Yet this one-way trajectory has not been without a price: many visitors are disappointed by the lack of old-world authenticity, or stifled by the sterility and overwhelming regimentation of society, while many inhabitants are only too aware of dissenters lying in the shadows.

Singapore is hardly an idyllic island where time stands still. Of its 247 sq mile surface area, only 11 sq miles of forest remain. The rest is an urban sprawl, criss-crossed by freeways, a patchwork of industrial suburbs and housing developments, all interconnected by a super-efficient public transportation system. Its port, now the world's busiest, is lined with automated loading systems. Old godowns are converted into discothèques, and the picturesque sampans and bumboats that used to animate the river and harbor landscape are today used for ferrying tourists. Historic shophouses of **Chinatown** have been bulldozed, chaotic street markets have been structured and the nocturnal decadence of Bugis Street has been transformed into a theater set. Yet for some visitors the positive factors outweigh the negative: crime is virtually nonexistent, hotels are superlative and service is impeccable, English is spoken everywhere, food is bewilderingly varied and plentiful, parks and gardens spring out of the urban fabric, conservation areas now blossom, and, of course, shopping hails from every street corner.

Dragon of the Orient Much favored by tourists from neighboring Asian countries, Singapore is, with Taiwan, Hong Kong and South Korea, one of the four economic "dragons" of the Orient and a blatant symbol of what an enterprising society is capable of. High-rises are designed by top international architects, the MRT (Mass Rapid Transit) system is the envy of any major Western city, and education and health standards are high by any criteria. Japanese, Korean, and Chinese visitors crowd one of the world's best zoos and file through the shopping malls of **Orchard Road**. More than half the visitors come for business conventions: already Asia's number one convention venue, Singapore is now targeting a world market. A major new business landmark, **Suntec City** (located opposite Raffles Hotel), will accommodate no fewer than 13,000 people in one hall, yet another example of Singapore's bigger-and-better goals.

Despite its frenetic reputation, Singapore is an ideal family destination, offering theme and recreation parks, offshore island beaches, nature reserves, and resorts such as **Sentosa** where every amusement is offered. Thinking adults may, however, find themselves slightly short on stimulation. Despite plans to create five new

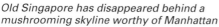

Old Singapore has disappeared behind a mushrooming skyline worthy of Manhattan

museums in and around Fort Canning, Singapore has neglected the arts. The authorities seem belatedly aware that happiness does not necessarily lie in full employment, 6 percent mortgage rates, and karaoke lounges. In a recent *cri de coeur* they called for more indigenous culture, mortified that Hong Kong and Malaysia monopolize local film and music industries. After decades of concentrating on the external trappings of economic success, Singapore is thus waking up to the need for intellectual nourishment and creative input. Yet this cry may have come too late for a spoon-fed generation brought up in such controlled conditions that self-expression has been lobotomized. Much depends on the direction Lee Kuan Yew's governmental successors will take during the 1990s. One thing is certain: one of Singapore's talents has always been a willingness to correct mistakes so this, combined with the commercial astuteness of its people, could lead to a new, open era.

Feng shui
The art of geomancy, or *feng shui*, is an integral part of any Chinese architecture, no less so in Singapore. Whether concerning the position of buildings or the layout of furniture within a room, correct orientation is considered essential to avoid bad influences (negative energy or *chi*) and to attract the good. Water is an important element and buildings are carefully designed to allow its positive energies to flow unimpeded from the sea. One of Singapore's more recent landmarks, The Gateway, a stunning construction designed by I. M. Pei which mirrors two prism-shaped towers, had to be reoriented—luckily while still on the drawing board—in order to accommodate positive flow from the nearby harbor. *Feng shui* geomancers are often called in if a business is in the doldrums: the result of their analysis may merely mean that furniture is rearranged, but could lead to a massive new fountain in the lobby.

SINGAPORE

▶▶▶ Arab Street 61B2
MRT: Bugis

The maze of streets leading off Arab Street provide a whistle-stop tour through the Islamic world. The district, dominated by the gold-domed Sultan Mosque, retains a distinct Muslim identity that is expressed in the costumes of many locals and further accentuated by the goods on sale. Carpets, textiles, leatherware, jewelry, basketware and alcohol-free perfume have a Middle Eastern quality, as do the shady old coffee shops where gemstone dealers peer at their riches. Meanwhile, a traditional Malay gravestone carver chips away at flat-fronted female stones or three-dimensional male versions—easily transported to the Muslim cemetery across Victoria Street. Streets bear names such as Kandahar, Muscat, Baghdad, Jeddah or Haji, and much of the original architecture remains.

▶▶ Armenian Apostolic Church of St. Gregory 47C4
Hill Street
MRT: City Hall

Built in 1835 and considered one of the finest of architect George Coleman's designs, this exquisite little church and garden is today encircled by fast roads and highrises. The circular internal structure is a reminder that the church was originally crowned by a dome and not the present 1853 spire.

▶▶ Botanic Gardens IBCC4
Corner of Cluny Road and Holland Road
Bus: 7, 14, 106, 174

These superbly landscaped gardens should be a priority for anyone interested in tropical flora. Almost half a million plant specimens are said to grow here, in patches of primary jungle, in elegant flower beds, around ornamental lakes, and in the pavilions and greenhouses. The pure Victoriana orchid pavilion is an obvious highlight, attracting more than a million tourists annually. Although Singapore's first Botanic Gardens date from 1822, the present 23-acre site opened in 1859 and claims "Mad" Ridley, the propagator of the rubber seed (see page 126), as one of its early directors.

The sights of the Botanic Gardens, recently revamped, cover most variants of tropical nature

►► Bugis Street   47D4

MRT: Bugis

In 1991, six years after decadent Bugis Street was bull-dozed by the Singaporean authorities, New Bugis Street emerged in a conciliatory attempt to re-create the original setting on a nearby site. Visually identical and integrating some original features, today's theater-set Bugis Street still attracts tourists and has lively bars, restaurants, and an outdoor night market, although its notorious trans-vestites are long gone. Original features from pilasters to grillwork and shop signs were salvaged and reinstalled, "atmospheric" washing is hung from windows where nobody lives, and one wall is designated as the only place in Singapore where posters can "freely" be stuck. However, Singapore's authorities have failed to re-create old Bugis Street's spontaneous decadence, a human trait that could not be planned on paper.

► Central Sikh Temple   IBCC5

Serangoon Road

Bus: 97, 101, 103, 131

An example of contemporary architecture that also encompasses more traditional features, this pink-granite temple was completed in 1986 for the 518th anniversary of the first Sikh guru. The air-conditioned prayer hall is crowned by a 43-foot-high mosaic dome and enshrines the Sikh holy book.

Indian temple sculpture
As most of Singapore's Indian community hailed from the southern part of the subcontinent, the city's temples are in the same elaborately carved Dravidian style. The Chettiar Temple is an excellent example of the current style, and also acts as a focal point for the Thaipusam and Navarathri festivals (see pages 22–23).

51

►► Chettiar Temple   46C3

Tank Road

MRT: Dhoby Ghaut

In 1984 the present temple replaced an earlier building financed by the Chettiars, moneylenders from southern India. The *gopuram* (pyramidal gateway) leads to a court-yard of shrines covered by a spectacular ceiling with engraved glass panels angled to catch the light.

The original Chettiar (moneylender) founders may have blanched at the extravagance of today's new Chettiar Temple

Money and mortality
Joss paper, often folded to resemble gold ingots, is a common Chinatown sight burning by the roadside or in clay urns in temple compounds. The Chinese believe that the ashes will rise to the gods or the souls of their departed family and be received as material wealth. Effigy-makers still working in Temple Street create paper and cane representations of comforts for the afterlife: cars, televisions, lanterns, and fake paper-money eventually go up in smoke to contribute to a more comfortable heavenly existence and prevent any potential return of the departed.

Right: Offerings on family altars, a common sight in Chinatown

Chinese souvenirs

► ► ► **Chinatown**   *46B3*

MRT: Raffles Place, Outram Park, Tanjong Pagar

Although undergoing extensive and often excessive renovation, Chinatown still has pockets of its former character where the Oriental will to work (and succeed) is evident everywhere. Bounded by Pickering Street to the north, Cecil Street to the east, Cantonment Road to the south, and New Bridge Road to the west, it is today a heady mixture of incense-clouded temples, concrete shopping complexes, industrious specialist workshops, and pungent eating-houses. Washing suspended from bamboo poles emerges from richly stuccoed shophouse facades that are thrown into relief against a skyline of rapidly encroaching skyscrapers. Craftsmen chisel at temple idols while the local community consumes noodle soups and businessmen clinch deals in the dark interiors of clan clubs.

A world unto itself, Chinatown was originally developed in the 1840s for Cantonese, Fukienese, and Hokkien coolies brought in to build the new city. Thousands lived in appallingly crowded conditions, opium being their only diversion, until they worked their way up to become food-hawkers, tailors, traders or specialized craftsmen. Parallel to this upward mobility, Chinatown's architecture evolved from simple, brightly painted two-story shop and lodging-houses to more elaborate turn-of-the-century constructions, whose molded plasterwork, tile decorations, pediments, and arches reflected the increasing wealth of the local inhabitants.

Since 1987 conservation projects have been rampant, creating the showcase of **Tanjong Pagar** with its restored shophouses. This has been followed closely by the areas of Kreta Ayer and Telok Ayer Street (once the sea front before land reclamation).

A project is also afoot to preserve Ann Siang Hill—once a nutmeg plantation, and still a charming enclave of winding streets where many Chinese clubs and clans are based.

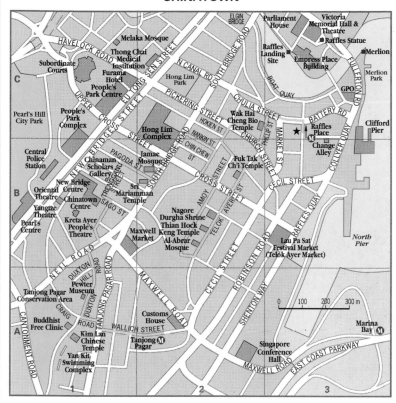

CHINATOWN

Walk Temples, craft shops and herbalists

To feel the pulse of Chinatown, meander through its heart to take in temples, traditional craft shops and coffee shops, shopping complexes, and conservation areas.

From Raffles Place MRT, walk through the office blocks of Chulia Street to discover the surprising roof decoration of the Taoist **Wak Hai Cheng Bio Temple** in Phillip Street. China Street and Pekin Street propel you into authentic Chinatown, and toward the remaining temples on Telok Ayer Street: the charming **Fuk Tak Ch'i Temple** and, farther down, the flamboyant **Thian Hock Keng Temple**. In between is the simple **Nagore Durgha Shrine**, built by Tamil Indians between 1828 and 1830. Farther down, enter the restored **Al-Abrar Mosque** before turning into Amoy Street, once a Hokkien lodging district.

Back in bustling China Street, follow Nankin Street to a footbridge leading across the roaring traffic of South Bridge Road to a Chinese shopping complex. Pass the **Jamae Mosque** to reach the technicolor splendors of the **Sri Mariamman Temple** before turning down Pagoda Street, lined with tourist-oriented shops—as is Trengganu Street. In between are traditional barbers, herbalists, tailors, tea emporiums, and anything else smacking of the Orient. Cross Neil Road to the renovated **Tanjong Pagar Conservation Area**, a gentrified stretch of shops and restaurants, before ending at Tanjong Pagar MRT.

53

SINGAPORE

What's in a bumboat?
Singapore's bumboats (also sampans or tongkangs) were once the mainstay of port activity. Before the days of containerized shipping they were used to ferry cargo back and forth between ships moored at sea and the rows of godowns (warehouses) lining the river banks. Today visitors can take bumboat river cruises from Parliament House landing steps, Clifford Pier, or Clarke Quay.

▶ **Chinese and Japanese Gardens**   *IBCD3*
Yuan Ching Road, Jurong
MRT: Chinese Garden
Favorite settings for local wedding photos, these adjacent gardens on Jurong Lake are connected by a 213-ft.-long bridge. The Chinese Garden is inspired by Sung Dynasty traditions whereby ornate features complement a formalized nature. The more meditative Japanese Garden, "The Garden of Tranquillity," is built around a carp pond, with minimalist 15th-century Japanese landscaping.

▶▶ **Chinaman Scholars Gallery**   *53B1*
14b Trengganu Street
MRT: Outram Park
Climb up a narrow wooden staircase of a Chinatown shophouse to discover the atmosphere of a Chinese scholar and merchant's home of the 1930s. Set up by an enterprising antique dealer, this living museum presents a typical Cantonese lifestyle, from the tea ceremony to embroidery. (Tel: 222 9554 to check opening times.)

Copied from Beijing's Summer Palace, the Chinese Garden comes alive at Chinese New Year

▶ **Clarke Quay**   *46C3*
MRT: Raffles Place
The latest stage in Singapore's resurrection of its past, Clarke Quay's old riverside warehouses have been developed into an ambitious shopping, food, and entertainment center.

▶▶▶ **Empress Place Building**   *53C3*
Empress Place
MRT: Raffles Place
This elegant neoclassical building overlooking the river was built in 1865 as a courthouse, and after extensive restoration reopened in 1989 as a museum. Its lofty interior now forms a superb background for a series of long-term exhibitions concentrating on Chinese heritage.

Watch out!

Penalties are exorbitant for any misdemeanor in a country intent on preserving a squeaky-clean society where every footstep is steered, and every utterance is controlled to correspond to rigid moral standards and the political status quo. This is as visible in the MRT (Mass Rapid Transit) as in any heavily censored Western film: when the courting couple finally makes it to the bedroom, the screen jerks nervously and cuts to... coffee the next morning!

All is forbidden Most obvious is the ban on smoking. The standard fine is S$500 (US$312), and the noxious weed is outlawed in all air-conditioned establishments (offices, restaurants, and so on) and any public space. Prohibitory and eclectic signs abound in all MRT stations: no smoking, no eating, no drinking, no durians (these fruit have an extremely unpleasant odor), and no skateboarding.

Above ground, street behavior is also strictly regimented. No littering (S$1,000 or US$625), no crossing against a red pedestrian light and no jaywalking (although this is sometimes ignored—witness those crossing Orchard Road to Dhoby Gaut MRT station in reckless, joyful pedestrian abandon). Meanwhile, hidden cameras photograph traffic offenders and posters are forbidden. And beware! If you forget to flush a public toilet you could be up for S$150 (US$93).

Nor do public housing blocks escape the moral majority. An insidious move to keep elevators clean led to the installation of urine-detectors. As the offender commits his heinous crime an alarm goes off and, to celebrate this invention in its early days, press photographers were called in to record the dastardly rogues as they emerged! Less overt is the government's control of local community services, which mysteriously grind to a halt in areas where an opposition candidate is elected.

Big Brother The government is omnipresent; certain foreign publications have restricted circulation (even the *Asian Wall Street Journal* was banned for a time) and seven out of eight of Singapore's dailies are government controlled. Drugs, of course, have always been out of the question (a death sentence or 30 years in prison is the penalty for those caught possessing large quantities), but Singapore's latest ban takes some beating: if you must smuggle something in make it chewing gum, now a prohibited substance!

Up in smoke...
However radical Singapore's drug laws are today, it is ironic to recall that until the mid-1920s 50 percent of the island's revenue derived from opium. An essential and lucrative element in the British East India Company's trade with China, opium was grown in India and shipped via Singapore to be exchanged with vast quantities of Chinese tea demanded by an increasingly thirsty British population. The potent narcotic was a favorite with Singapore's struggling coolies and rickshaw *pullies*, many of whom would suddenly abandon their customers and dive into a den for a quick fix. Far-gone addicts would even eat it from the leaf (without preparation), thus reducing their life expectancy to 35 to 40 years.

► Fort Canning *46C3*

Canning Rise
MRT: City Hall
For the early Malays Fort Canning Park (once named Bukit Larangan, or Forbidden Hill) was a sacred royal burial ground, but this was ignored by Raffles, who cleared the jungle to build his first residence on the summit. In 1859 the simple *attap* construction made way for Fort Canning; all that remains of the fort today is an 1833 neo-Gothic gateway, two cannons and a Christian cemetery. In the Fort Canning Center it is possible to visit the Underground Command Bunker where British military operations were coordinated during World War II.

High above the traffic, Fort Canning's gateway leads into one of Singapore's three nature parks

►► Fuk Tak Ch'i Temple *53B2*

76 Telok Ayer Street
MRT: Raffles Place
This shadowy, intimate Shenist temple (combining Confucianism, Buddhism and Taoism) is one of Singapore's oldest. Built in 1825, its name means Temple of Prosperity and Virtue, and it is dedicated to Tua Peh Kong, the god of wealth, whose sackcloth-shrouded figure stands to the left of the entrance.

► Guinness World of Records *IBCB4*

World Trade Center
Bus: 65, 143
Another of Singapore's blockbusting children's destinations, this center features world record-breaking feats with separate Singaporen and Asian showcases. Spectacular human endeavors and natural phenomena are represented by three-dimensional replicas and audio-visuals, and a computerized sports databank pops up the names of the latest champions.

Hajjah Fatimah Mosque   47D5

Beach Road
MRT: Lavender
Although not an outstanding building in itself, this mosque near Arab Street is a synthesis of Singaporean cosmopolitanism. It was built in 1845 by a British architect using classical themes, and financed by a Malay woman, Hajjah Fatimah, who was married to a Bugis sultan and whose daughter married an Arab. Chinese architects, French contractors, and Malay craftsmen later worked on its reconstruction. One curiosity is the Melakan-style tiered minaret which leans at an angle of six degrees. Hajjah Fatimah, a successful business-woman, is buried in the graveyard behind.

► **Kong Meng Sang Phor Kark See Temple Complex**   IBCD4

Bright Hill Drive
MRT: Bishan, then taxi
Also known as Bright Hill Temple, this vast hillside complex covers 29 acres and is Singapore's largest. The modern, richly decorated buildings contain countless statues and shrines. One of the annexes is an old people's home, a continuation of the Chinese tradition of sending terminally ill relatives to "death houses," as any death at home is considered bad luck. From here it is but a short trip to the crematorium where funerals are accompanied by the curling smoke of smoldering paper effigies. These effigies—often fake paper money, cars, and houses—are made and then burned so that the dead will be able to take some practical comforts on their journey to heaven.

► **Lau Pa Sat Festival Market**   53B3

18 Raffles Quay
MRT: Raffles Place
Dismantled to prevent damage during construction of the nearby MRT station, then reconstructed and reopened in 1992 in the heart of the financial district, the octagonal-shaped Lau Pa Sat Market is a superb example of ornamental Victorian cast-ironwork and is crowned by a 65-ft. clock tower. Cast in Glasgow, it functioned as a wet market (dealing in "wet" goods—fresh fish and meat) from 1894 until the 1970s. Now an upscale food center arranged around souvenir and clothes stalls, Lau Pa Sat's activities continue well into the evenings when hawkers set up their stalls along Boon Tat Street.

►► **Leong San See Temple**   47E4

Race Course Road
Bus: 23, 64, 65
Founded in 1917 by a Buddhist monk and built in the Chinese palace style, the temple saw its decoration spoiled by alterations made in the 1960s. However, some lovely frescos have survived, as has the central altar dedicated to Guan Yin (the goddess of mercy). Her 18 hands symbolize mercy and compassion, and are beautifully carved with birds, flowers, and the mythical phoenix. Two lions guard the entrance, while fine ceramic dragons and chimeras decorate the roof.

World of Aquarium
At the back of Fort Canning Hill and accessible from River Valley Road is the Van Kleef Aquarium. Some 71 landscaped tanks create a liquid living museum of more than 6,000 of these creatures—a pleasant escape from the above-water world.

57

■ **More than a concrete jungle, Singapore offers a surprising number of nature reserves to the high-rise-haunted tourist. Its 243 sq miles of low-lying equatorial land may be increasingly criss-crossed with highways and invaded by public housing blocks, but pockets of nature have been protected valiantly for stressed Singaporeans who are ever-thirsty for the outdoor life .....■**

Nature tours
For those interested in a more specialized introduction to Singapore's nature, some fascinating tours are organized by a committed and entertaining bird and nature specialist, Subharaj. Most nature tours are designed for a minimum of ten people, but tailor-made itineraries can be organized. Contact: R Subharaj, 8 Jalan Buloh Perindu, Singapore 1545 (tel/fax: 442 9774).

View from the summit of Bukit Timah over the Central Catchment Nature Reserve

When Raffles disembarked in 1819 he found a hilly, thickly forested island, 80 percent of which was clothed in lowland jungle, another 13 percent in mangrove swamp, and the rest in freshwater marshes. Soon after, spice and crop plantations, quarries, and settlements had radically transformed the horizon, while picturesque coastal bays were ironed out in the wake of land reclamation. Today, Singapore—now sensitive to green issues—is actually increasing the area of its nature reserves and taking steps to protect what remains of its wildlife.

Bukit Timah Apart from the central national parks—Fort Canning and the Botanic Gardens—the most accessible nature reserve (just 8 miles from the city center) is at Bukit Timah (meaning "Hill of Tin"). Established as a reserve in 1884, it has since revealed many previously unknown specimens of Malay plants and is a surprisingly rich enclave of botanical diversity.

Troops of long-tailed macaques crash through the branches, but squirrels are less obtrusive, the rare flying lemur may only be a distant blur and the last tiger was shot there in 1933. Bird specialists may spot the racket-tailed drongo and hear the stripe-throated titbabbler.

Whether you reach the summit by trail or along the easier private road, the views over the Upper Peirce Reservoir and forest make the effort worth while. Access is by Bus 171 or 182 from Orchard Road to Courts, where Hindhede Drive leads to the information center.

Pulau Ubin To experience the landscape of Singapore as it was 50 years ago, head for the island of Pulau Ubin (see page 74), easily accessible by bumboat from Changi Point. There primary mangrove swamps, mudflats, old rubber plantations, prawn ponds, and secondary jungle harbor wildlife that has long disappeared from the mainland. You may spot monitor lizards and the scarlet-plumed jungle fowl, an endangered species. Hire a bicycle at the nature house and spend a day exploring.

Pasir Ris Park Mangroves are an essential part of tropical coast ecology. As the spiky, tangled roots silt up, new land is created naturally, gradually advancing into the sea. The backwaters of mangrove creeks nurture fish and crustaceans, while the silt deposits harbor tiny fiddler crabs, mud lobsters, small-clawed otters, and mud skippers. To spot these creatures, go to Pasir Ris Park (at the eastern MRT terminal) where a sturdy plankwalk leads through one of the coastline's last mangrove forests, now conserved as a bird and nature reserve.

The reservoirs From Bukit Timah it is possible to hike down to **Upper Peirce Reservoir,** one of the four reservoirs in the Central Catchment Nature Reserve. This area of mainly secondary forest hides some surprising patches of freshwater swamp, havens for ornithological rarities such as the white-bellied woodpecker and the moustached babbler. The Nee Soon Swamp Forest at **Seletar Reservoir** (accessible from Mandai Road) claims the most welcoming environment for snakes, swamp forest frogs, and cream giant squirrels. Follow the path around **MacRitchie Reservoir** (enter from Lornie Road) for a peaceful walk through mature secondary forest that is enlivened by troops of monkeys.

The best aquatic area, however, is found at **Kranji Reservoir** (further to the northwest) where freshwater marshes on its southern shores are home to a variety of tortoises, toads, and fish. Close by is the **Sungei Buloh Bird Sanctuary** (see page 72), a 763-acre wetland site of swamps and coconut groves that forms the habitat for more than 120 species of birds.

Bird-watcher's special
Although not officially a nature reserve, Senoko (at Jalan Kedai, off Canberra Road in the north of the island) is home to perhaps the largest variety of birds in Singapore. Its diverse habitats—grasslands, mangroves, ponds, and riverbanks—are a feeding and breeding ground for thousands of seasonal migrants. Rare migrant waders include the red-wattled lapwing and the greater painted snipe. You may also spot the endangered Chinese egret on its annual migration from Central Asia, the straw-headed bulbul or the copper-throated sunbird.

A cattle egret, common to Singapore's coastal marshlands

▶▶▶ **Little India**   *47E4*

Bus: 64, 65, 92, 106, 111

The exotic sights, smells, and sounds of southern India are easily absorbed in the streets leading off Serangoon Road, starting at the Zhujiao hawkers' center and market, leading east to Rochor Canal and north to Kitchener Road. Although dating from the 19th century, when Buffalo Road was a dairy farm and cattle-traders' center, Little India was mainly developed in the 1920s and the architecture

Auspicious dates are calculated by a Serangoon Road fortuneteller

reflects that period's predilection for ornate detailing. Much is now earmarked for conservation (Roberts Lane, for example), but Singapore's public housing department has also left its indelible high-rise mark in the vicinity.

The Indian community, mainly Tamils, played an important role in Singapore's construction, whether as civil servants or convict labor, and this home from home is colourful evidence of their deeply rooted Hindu traditions.

Week's itinerary

Day 1 Explore the colonial district, visit the **Peranakan Place Museum**, and dine in Nyonya style at Bibi's.

Day 2 Start at the **Botanic Gardens**, explore **Arab Street** and **Little India**, then dine in **Bugis Street**.

Day 3 Breakfast at **Jurong Bird Park**, stop to visit Tang Dynasty City, and finish at **Chinatown**.

Day 4 Visit **Changi**, then take a boat to **Pulau Ubin**.

Day 5 Spend the morning at the zoo, visit the **Mandai Orchid Gardens** then take a harbor cruise. Cross to **Sentosa** and return by cable car.

Day 6 Climb **Bukit Timah** and lunch at Goodwoods. Explore River Valley district, then dine at **Clarke Quay**.

Day 7 Do any last-minute shopping: try Katong ditrict along East Coast Road or Holland Village.

ARAB STREET AND LITTLE INDIA

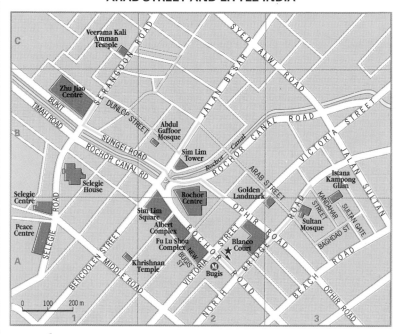

Walk **Mosques, shophouses, and spice stalls**

Take in the sights, smells, and sounds of the Middle East and India by exploring Arab Street, before plunging into the delights of Little India.

From Bugis MRT station walk up North Bridge Road to **Arab Street,** the labyrinthine heart of Singapore's Muslim community where names, sounds, smells, and colors whirl you through the Islamic world. From Baghdad Street, make a short detour past the ironsmiths of **Sultan Gate** to see the delapidated **Istana Kampong Glam,** a 19th-century sultan's residence. The restored shophouses of **Kandahar Street** lead past the imposing **Sultan Mosque,** where the local faithful gather. This colorful souk atmosphere continues along Arab Street, slowing toward Rochor Canal but picking up again in Little India.

In Dunlop Street enter the peaceful courtyard of the arabesque-style **Abdul Gaffoor Mosque,** rebuilt in 1910. The surrounding streets are packed with spices, saris, jasmine garlands, brass statues, and jewelry. In Serangoon Road stop at a modest Hindu temple dedicated to Kali, before heading back along Sungei Road to Bugis MRT via **New Bugis Street.**

Rayon and polyester are fast replacing traditional Asian silks

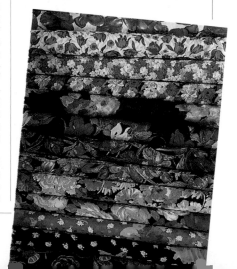

▶ **Nagore Durgha Shrine** 53B2

Telok Ayer Street
MRT: Raffles Place

This small turreted mosque lost in Chinatown is a strange blend of traditional Mogul roof design, neoclassical columns and molded arches. It was built by the southern Indian Muslim community, the Chulias, from 1828 to 1830.

Merlion Park

Created to symbolize the nation of Singapore in the 1960s, the sculpted mythical beast—half lion, half fish—of the water-spouting Merlion stands on a tiny green patch at the mouth of the Singapore river. Now also the symbol of the Singapore Tourist Promotion Board, it is spectacularly illuminated at night.

Petrified museum-goers immortalized in front of the National Museum

▶▶▶ **National Museum** 46C3

Stamford Road
MRT: City Hall, Dhoby Ghaut

One of Singapore's finest examples of colonial architecture, the National Museum was designed by Major McNair for Queen Victoria's Golden Jubilee in 1887 and opened under the name of the Raffles Museum. Leading off the superb domed atrium on the ground floor are galleries displaying documents, maps, and artifacts which trace Singapore's early history, including relics found on Fort Canning Hill. A tedious series of lifeless tableaux illustrates the highlights of Singapore's political and social development, but another more compelling gallery displays the rich culture of the Straits Chinese community. Intricately embroidered slippers and costumes, inlaid blackwood furniture, ornate betel-leaf containers, elaborate silverwork, and the inevitable high-class opium bed all demonstrate the sophistication of Peranakan Straits Chinese taste. Much of the Anglo-Chinese parlor was donated by a certain Mrs Lee Choon Guan (1877–1978), a fast-living Nyonya who

NATIONAL MUSEUM
SINGAPORE
$1
ADMIT ONE
TAX EXEMPTED
VALID FOR DATE STAMPED
NOT REFUNDABLE
ADULT A № 69580

danced until she was 90, was decorated by the British, and was the first Singaporean woman to drive a car.

Upstairs are displays of Indonesian and Malay pottery, ceramics from China, Thailand, and Vietnam, and finally, in the Jade Gallery, the **Haw Par Collection,** a fabulous display of jade carvings. Ch'ing Dynasty sculptures (mid-17th century to 1912) in a wide variety of minerals, including jasper, aventurine, agate, crystal, and rose quartz, reflect a radical development in style. Immediately behind the National Museum stands the **National Art Gallery,** which is used for temporary exhibitions of local art.

▶▶▶ Padang 47C4

MRT: City Hall
Between St. Andrew's Road and Connaught Drive lies the grassy Padang, once the heart of Singapore's colonial life where white-flanneled cricketers mopped their brows, white-skinned ladies promenaded in the evening and the government emitted its edicts from the surrounding stately institutions. At one end stands the **Singapore Cricket Club,** still a members-only enclave but once British-only, and at the opposite end is the **Singapore Recreation Club,** where Eurasians were graciously permitted to gather.

Less carefree are the wartime memories of the Padang: it was here that the Europeans were herded together by the Japanese before being marched off to Changi Prison. Today, the Padang is used for sports and open-air entertainment, and is the focus for the National Day Parade on 9 August.

▶ Parliament House 53C3

MRT: City Hall
Singapore's oldest building, erected in 1827 as a private mansion, assumed numerous functions before becoming the Assembly House of British government in 1954, and finally in 1965 the Parliament seat for the newly independent Singapore. It was designed in typical Palladian style by George Coleman, the colonial architect *par excellence.* In front stands a sturdy bronze elephant presented to Singapore in 1871 by a visiting Siamese king. It is possible to watch a parliamentary session from the Strangers' Gallery by reservation (tel: 336 8811).

▶▶▶ Peranakan Place Museum 46D2

Emerald Hill
MRT: Somerset
This reconstructed Peranakan terraced home nestling at the base of Emerald Hill gives a fascinating insight into the distinctive traditions of the Straits Chinese community (see page 139). Also known as Peranakans or Babas and Nyonyas, the powerful ethnic group grew out of the intermarriage of Chinese traders with Malay women (*peranakan* means born here) and developed its own customs and sophisticated decorative taste.

Guided tours of the small museum (tel: 732 6966 for times) show off nyonyaware porcelain, furniture, and wedding rituals, as well as European objects that were later assimilated into Peranakan style. Adjoining the museum are restaurants and a coffee shop serving Peranakan specialities.

Did Singapore see snow?
One of Singapore's more recent legends dates from World War II, when European prisoners of war at Changi were apparently told by their captors that Singapore would never be free unless snow covered the Padang. This seemingly impossible phenomenon is said to have occurred that very evening when a freak hailstorm blanketed the Padang with white ice.

63

Once home to colonial cricketers, the Padang's activities are now more eclectic

■ **Legendary in his historic stature, Sir Stamford Raffles could not have suspected what dragons he was to unleash when he set foot on the island of Temasek (Singapore) in 1819. Astutely foreseeing the strategic importance of breaking the Dutch stranglehold on trade in the area, he set about laying the foundations of what was to become one of the world's wealthiest and most dynamic cities .....■**

Singapore Sling
Concocted along with the lesser known Million Dollar Cocktail in 1915 by barman Ngiam Tong Boon, the Singapore Sling is the Raffles' alcoholic emblem. To fully savor its delights, non-hotel guests can go to the restored Bar and Billiard Room or the adjoining veranda. The Palm Court, a sundowner favorite, is now out of bounds to all but the happy few staying at the hotel.

Mix your own Singapore Sling with the following ingredients:
½ part of gin
¼ part of Dom liqueur
¼ part of Maraschino cordial
¼ part of lemon soda
A few drops of cherry brandy
A few drops of Angostura Bitters
Ice

Two men shaped the fortunes of Singapore's flourishing balance of payments: Lee Kuan Yew and Stamford Raffles. Thirty or so years of the former and barely four years of the latter have left their indelible marks, but however much Lee Kuan Yew's policies remain in effect, it is the shadow of Raffles that lurks behind Singapore's urban structure, its status as the busiest port in the world and its early colonial buildings—not least the grandiose Raffles Hotel.

Declared a national monument in 1987, Raffles Hotel underwent a major renovation in 1989–1991

Raffles—the man "It is impossible to conceive a place combining more advantages..." wrote Raffles, adding that Singapore possessed "one of the most safe and extensive harbours in these seas." These far-seeing thoughts came from a man born in 1784 of a solid English seafaring family who worked his way up from the modest post of clerk in the British East India Company to become Lieutenant-Governor of Java from 1811 to 1816. Although recalled to England because of catastrophic financial losses, his enthusiasm and scholarly approach to the East (he was a fluent Malay-speaker) took him back in 1817 to oversee the company's trading interests in Bencoolen, Sumatra. From there it was but a short step across the Selat Melaka to Singapore, which Raffles accomplished in 1819.

A firm believer in the British Empire's right to rule the waves, he soon signed a treaty with Sultan Hussein Shah of Johor and the local ruler, the *temenggong*, which grant-

RAFFLES HOTEL

ed the British exclusive rights to Singapore's trade in exchange for annual stipends. Raffles reappeared in 1822, and it was then that he settled down to lay the enduring foundations of the future city. He left again in 1823, soon after to die of a brain tumor at the age of 42.

Raffles—the plan Raffles' urban planning laid out clearly defined areas for each ethnic community and for functional purposes. The commercial district was moved south of the river to its present site, a hill was leveled to create Raffles Place and government offices were erected around Fort Canning Hill. Chinatown was planned to accommodate the different regional Chinese groups, and Kampong Glam was designated for Malays and Bugis, Arab Street for Arabs, Serangoon Road for Indians, and the East Beach for European traders.

Raffles' firm belief that racial harmony was best achieved by segregation would not be popular today, but it has left Singapore with a patchwork of easily definable communities.

Raffles—the hotel One of the world's greatest palace-hotels was founded in 1887 by the enterprising Armenian brothers, the Sarkies. Its original ten rooms soon attracted literati such as Joseph Conrad and Rudyard Kipling, and the hotel rapidly expanded—in 1894 the Palm Court wing was completed and in 1899 the generous doors of the main building were flung open to extravagant fanfares. Thus began the hotel's golden era: writers, prosperous traders, lords, and duchesses flocked to enjoy its electric lights and fans and the gourmet delights of the French chef in a spacious, neo-Renaissance setting.

By the time the Bras Basah wing opened in 1904, Raffles was swinging; tigers were shot under billiard tables, a post office served the guests' exclusive needs, the "finest ballrooom in the East" appeared in 1920 and roller-skating dinners vied with billiard competitions.

Local scandal and gossip offered fruitful inspiration to Somerset Maugham, who penned *The Casuarina Tree* while seated under the frangipani trees of the Palm Court, and over the years Charlie Chaplin, Jean Harlow, Douglas Fairbanks, Maurice Chevalier, Noel Coward, and Edward, Prince of Wales, sallied forth from their luxury suites. Today, after extension and total renovation, the sprawling hotel includes luxury shops, a playhouse and a small museum—but where are the eccentric guests?

Sir Stamford Raffles, architect of the 1819 treaty with Johor's Sultan Hussein Shah, which gave Britain exclusive trading rights

Beware the trishaw drivers
Trishaws, that inimitable form of Asian transport, are virtually past memories in today's Singapore. However, some still do gather in Waterloo Street at the bottom of Orchard Road, lying in wait for the next gullible tourist. If you are really intent on experiencing one, make sure you agree on a price in advance: most of these trishaw drivers charge an exorbitant amount for a 25-minute circuit. If you are lucky you may come across a regular trishaw in Little India or Chinatown, in which case you should only pay a few dollars for a fairly short trip.

▶   **St. Andrew's Cathedral**   47C4

St. Andrew's Road
MRT: City Hall
Although an earlier 1837 construction was twice hit by lightning, the present restored cathedral seems to be holding its own and presents a blinding, virginal-white exterior to the world. Built by Indian convicts in 1862, it has a generous, typically Victorian interior, which harbors incongruous elements such as ceiling fans and superb cane and mahogany pews.

▶▶▶   **Sakya Muni Temple (Temple of a Thousand Lights)**   47E4

366 Race Course Road
Bus: 23, 64, 65
Until his death in the early 1980s an aging Thai Buddhist monk, Vutthisasara, continued to expound his own philosophy and conduct worship in this temple which he founded in 1927. Similar in style and simplicity to a Thai *wat*, although embellished by Chinese technicolor, the focal point is a 50-ft.-high Buddha illuminated by myriads of colored lights. The 330-ton statue was made by the monk himself, as was the giant ebony and mother-of-pearl replica of Buddha's footprint. Around the base of the statue is a sculpted frieze of events from Buddha's life.

The crisp, white interior and mahogany pews of St. Andrew's Cathedral

▶▶▶   **Sri Mariamman Temple**   53B2

244 South Bridge Road
Bus: 124, 174
Even if you don't visit this temple during the fire-walking festival of Thimithi, the building is still a startling sight. Its present form dates from 1862 when it replaced an earlier 1827 Hindu temple, making it Singapore's oldest. Standing in contrast to surrounding Chinatown, the towering *gopuram*, alive with a profusion of realist and imaginary human and animal forms, leads the way to the central shrine. Although this area is reserved for Hindu worshippers, the elaborately frescoed, vaulted ceiling is easily visible, as are the smaller shrines in the outer courtyard. There brahmins and sari-clad women make their offerings to a the sound of taped Indian music.

■ **First cultivated in Singapore at the beginning of the century, the island's exotic national flower actually belongs to one of the largest plant families in the world. Around 20,000 species and 80,000 hybrids exist, ranging from the tiny pinpricks of color seen on forest trails to the luxuriant patterned sprays that are nurtured in orchid gardens all over Southeast Asia .....■**

Flowers of great beauty with a seemingly infinite variety of patterns, orchids are understandably popular yet increasingly vulnerable. Nimble fingers are plucking the exotic blooms of rare species from the depths of the jungles and, as orchid flowers last on average four weeks, the thieves are able to cash in on their traffic. The Convention of International Trade in Endangered Species of Fauna and Flora (CITES) is now considering banning trade in tropical slipper orchids, including many genera unique to Malaysia.

Make-up and varieties Despite their varied appearance, all orchids are defined by the basic structure of the flower. Common to all are the three sepals and three petals, one of which is shaped totally unlike the others and which is called the "lip." In all orchids the male and female parts are on one column, forming part of the flower that may measure less than half an inch. Striped, spotted, stained, or monochrome, the patterns, colors, and shapes of orchids have developed to attract the insects that pollinate them. Although some grow on the ground, most Malaysian orchids are epiphytes—parasites growing on the trunks and branches of trees.

In Peninsular Malaysia wild orchids are abundant in forests from the coastal lowlands up into the mountains. Hardier species colonize roadsides and older trees planted in towns. Sabah alone is estimated to be home to more than 2,000 species, more than half of which occur in and around Gunung Kinabalu. These include the much-sought-after *Paphiopedilum dimorphorcosis*, which displays two different-shaped flowers on one stem.

Orchid gardens Singapore may have little room for wild orchids, but the cultivated version can be seen in over 100 varieties at the beautifully landscaped **Mandai Orchid Gardens** (established in the 1950s) and in renowned luxuriance at the **Botanic Gardens**. Although Singapore pioneered orchid hybridization, its orchid exports have now been exceeded by those of Thailand.

In Malaysia, domesticated varieties flourish in Kuala Lumpur's **Lake Gardens**, in the **Cameron Highlands** and at **Tenom** in Sabah. But ultimately nothing can beat the sight of a brilliantly patterned wild spray suspended in the gloom of the rain forest.

The everlasting version
No room in your luggage for a packaged orchid spray? As usual, Singapore comes up with the solution in the form of more portable and less ephemeral versions. *Risis* orchids are the selected flowers of 300 varieties, electroplated in gold and made into jewelry, and can be puchased in most souvenir shops.

"Vanda Miss Joaquim," a hybrid orchid adopted as Singapore's national flower

Kampong Glam
Although better known to tourists as Arab Street, this historic district was actually named after the glam tree, which grew abundantly in the area and produced a precious medicinal oil. In Raffles' 1819 agreement with Sultan Hussein Shah, Kampong Glam was designated for the Muslim communities of Malays, Arabs, Bugis, and Javanese. Apart from the Sultan Mosque, the sultanate also left its mark at the nearby Istana Kampong Glam, a peeling and faded splendor at the end of Sultan Gate, still in the hands of the sultan's family today.

The Thian Hock Keng Temple was once on the waterfront— before land reclamation began

 Sultan Mosque   47D5

North Bridge Road
MRT: Bugis
The main focal point in the Muslim district around Arab Street is the Sultan Mosque. Designed in 1928 by Denis Santry, a local cartoonist, it replaced an earlier mosque built for the Muslim traders in 1825 with financial aid from Raffles. Two gold onion domes and four minarets rise to the skies, from high up the muezzin call the faithful to prayer five times a day—the most interesting moments to visit the immense prayer hall if you are respectably attired. An adjoining building in the same style functions as the *medressa,* or Islamic school.

▶▶▶ **Thian Hock Keng Temple**   46B3

Telok Ayer Street
MRT: Tanjong Pagar, Raffles Place
Erected by grateful seamen in 1840 on a site that was once the waterfront, this temple was naturally enough dedicated to the goddess of the sea and protector of sailors, Ma Chu Po. Her statue, imported from China, can be found in the main hall and is backed by numerous other shrines including one to Guan Yin. Fine quality materials such as those used in the hardwood ceiling and the granite columns carved with entwined dragons all came from China, but Scottish ironwork and Delft and English tiles were also incorporated into this colorful, animated complex.

▶ **Wak Hai Cheng Bio Temple**   46B3

Phillip Street
MRT: Raffles Place
The most interesting feature of this modest 1850s Taoist temple, cowering in the shade of Singapore's business district, is its roof, alive with sculpted scenes of a miniature Chinese village. The courtyard is a major venue for Chinese opera during festivals.

■ **Monkey's-head soup? Dried deer's penis? Snow frog's glands?** For centuries the Chinese attitude to health has been inextricably tied to food, Eastern doctors claiming long before their Western counterparts that "a man is what he eats." Soups and desserts are prepared with medicinal herbs to preserve the essential *yin* and *yang* balance, but a closer look reveals bizarre ingredients that are not so appealing .....■

In Singapore's Chinatown, **Trengganu Street** and **Sago Street** form the epicenter of traditional *sinseh* physicians, often working in the depths of dimly lit medicine halls that hardly inspire confidence. Yet their array of countless herbs and multiple drawers of ingredients form the basis of more than a hundred specific remedies, each geared to a particular ailment and believed in implicitly by a resilient and industrious Chinese community.

Sinsehs will usually mix the potion while you wait and serve it with tea to help balance the complementary forces of *yin* (the passive female principle) and *yang* (the active male principle) in the body, stimulating the vital *qi* (energy). An alternative is to mix a pungent oil, which is rubbed into the skin to relieve aches and pains. Some remedies are straightforward—try the stem of a leopard flower for respiratory problems—but others are highly complex blends that promise cure-all qualities.

An herb a day For greater enjoyment of medicinal cures, many Chinese head straight for an herbal restaurant where soups and desserts are chosen according to their curative, fortifying or aphrodisiac qualities. Turtle soup, believed to strengthen the body and in particular the heart, is found all over Singapore, but more refined and prized dishes such as bird's-nest soup (considered excellent for respiratory problems and the lungs) are only served in more exclusive establishments.

Choose your remedy Delicious herbal soups will revive flagging energy, giving sustenance if not the curative properties they claim. Turtle and chicken herbal soup is said to be a general *yin* tonic; boiled flying fox cures asthma; *gui fei* tonic soup aims to preserve ladies' youthful complexion; monkey's-head mushroom soup with milk vetch root is multifunctional, improving complexions, enhancing memory, and containing a sedative which prevents stomach cancer; chicken soup with Chinese wolfberry and *tian qi* promotes good blood circulation; stewed shin beef with *Polygonum multiflorum* soup increases longevity and prevents premature greying; and for toning up ligaments, deer tendon and *Rhizoma typhonii* soup cannot be beaten.

Aphrodisiacs are legion, whether the *shuang bian* soup or the famous *lu bian* whip soup, while to recover from excesses a simple walnut cream will nourish the brain and promote sleep.

Ginseng
Centuries ago, Chinese emperors relied on this substance for much desired longevity and sexual potency. The magical powers of these twisted roots have yet to be proven by Western medicine, although their digestive properties are recognized. Singapore, like any other country with a large Chinese population, is rife with ginseng in every form—from tablets to powders, teas and extracts. In Borneo it is known as *pasak bumi*, and is a favorite remedy for malaria.

69

Ginseng production is a highly profitable industry

Excursions

Some of the more benevolent characters at the overhauled Haw Par Villa, formally known as the Tiger Balm Gardens

Feathered champs
Bird-singing competitions are serious business in Singapore as champions are worth up to S$5,000 and hours are spent training them. The main bird café is at the junction of Tiong Bahru and Seng Poh roads (MRT: Outram Park). Contests are at 8:A.M. on Sundays, but training sessions are held on other mornings.

Tired of the inner-city sidewalks? Then head out of town to investigate the numerous excursion sights listed alphabetically over the next three pages.

Thrills with no spills are what's in store at Singapore's recreation park built on reclaimed land—**Big Splash►** (East Coast Parkway; Bus: 14). Strong emotions are guaranteed on a vertiginous toboggan ride into a swimming-pool.

More sober thoughts are inspired by **Changi Prison Chapel and Museum►►** (Bus: 14), at the easternmost point of Singapore in Changi district. Originally built to accommodate 600, Changi Prison housed 12,000 prisoners of war in 1944. Tragic records of their appalling living conditions as well as of their spirited and inspiring response are displayed in a museum standing within today's prison walls. An adjacent replica of the simple *attap* chapel built by the prisoners displays simple memorial cards from the families of those who died.

A few miles west of the city lies **Haw Par Villa Dragon World►** (262 Pasir Panjang Road; Bus: 10, 30, 51, 143). Built by the Aw brothers, inheritors of the Tiger Balm fortune, the park first opened in 1937 to illustrate Chinese myths and legends. Recently completely overhauled, it includes a new ride and five multimedia theaters, although only half the original gaudy plaster statues which created its fame remain. It is a bizarre theme park, the popular "Tales of China Boat Ride" through the dragon's jaws being more like a descent into a Dantesque hell of gruesome punishments adapted to every misdemeanor.

More appealing, perhaps, is the **Jurong Bird Park►►** (Jurong Hill; MRT: Boon Lay Station then Bus 251, 253 or 255). Offering a field day for bird lovers, this 50-acre park is home to over 5,000 birds from some 450 species. Propelled by typical Singaporean efficiency, you may wish to take a ten-minute monorail trip (whose commentary includes musical extracts from "Swan Lake" as it glides past actual swans) for an overview of the park. You can

then continue on foot—a good opportunity to see hummingbirds, parrots, and macaws living in relative freedom.

The park's latest feat is the Southeast Asian walk-in aviary where the doubtful authenticity of a simulated tropical rain forest is heightened by a midday cannon blast announcing a punctual rain storm. Meanwhile, the reversed biorhythms of nocturnal birds are catered for by the "World of Darkness," where twinkling stars and taped jungle sounds create an almost familiar environment for puzzled-looking owls, kiwis, and frogmouths. Other highlights are the Penguin Pool and the toucan and hornbill aviaries. Restaurants, "photo opportunities," and an amphitheater for bird shows ("a big hand to our emus Ernie and Ernest") complete the entertainment venues.

Set in a peaceful park to the north of Singapore is the **Kranji War Memorial▶** (Woodlands Road, junction with Mandai Road; Bus: 181, 182), its design symbolizing the three branches of the armed services. It stands in the center of a cemetery and lists the names of the thousands of Allied troops who died defending the island during World War II.

Rows and rows of multicolored orchid beds cover the gentle slopes of the **Mandai Orchid Gardens▶** (Mandai Lake Road; Bus: 171), located just a few minutes from the zoo. Almost a hundred varieties are cultivated for export alongside other ornamental and foliage plants.

Another of Singapore's ubiquitous simulations, the **Ming Village▶** (32 Pandan Road; Bus: 198 to Boon Lay interchange, then 245) nevertheless features genuine craftsmen at work reproducing the techniques of Ming (1368–1644) and Qing (1644–1911) dynasty porcelain. All their products are for sale.

Designed to introduce children to science and technology in hands-on style, the attractions of the **Singapore Science Center▶▶** (Science Center Road, Jurong; MRT: Jurong East, then Bus 336 or walk) are arranged in seven thematic galleries. Flashing neon, lasers, computers, push-buttons, and lurid sci-fi creatures all aim to nurture the next generation's technological genius. Juvenile thrills reach a crescendo in front of the giant omni-theater screen where spectacular three-dimensional images are projected in seven daily sessions. A recent addition is the Ecogarden, with medicinal plants and a small hydroponic farm.

Ming porcelain
Famous for its blue and white wares, the Ming Dynasty (1368–1644) aimed to equal the Tang Dynasty (A.D.618–907) both in power and splendor. The first Ming emperor founded a ceramics factory which developed rapidly, benefiting from good economic conditions, which in turn increased demand. Although a number of private kilns were established, all production was officially controlled. The early 15th century saw the finest examples of blue and white ware, but the extraordinarily creative Ming potters were equally successful with other monochromatic and polychromatic styles.

A blue and yellow macaw at the Jurong Bird Park

EXCURSIONS

The original Xian
At the time of the Tang Dynasty (A.D.618–907) Xian (or Chang'an) was one of the world's most sophisticated cities, on a par with Baghdad. Located at the eastern end of the Silk Road, it rapidly became a booming cosmopolitan metropolis and soon had a population of more than 1 million. The Tang Dynasty represented the zenith of Chinese culture and prosperity, and in Xian trade flourished, financing carriageways, gilded palaces, theaters, man-made lakes, and a labyrinth of canals. However, a rebellion signaled the end of Xian's heyday and the town was soon deserted. The recent discovery of an underground army of individually sculpted terracotta warriors has refocused attention on this town and has made it one of China's greatest tourist attractions.

One of Singapore's largest temples, the Buddhist **Siong Lim Temple**►► (184 E Jalan Toa Payoh; Bus: 64, 65, 92, 106 to Dhoby Ghaut interchange, then 146) was built in 1908 but continues to expand. An arched bridge leads through an ornate gateway to the central courtyard peopled by numerous carved Thai statues commemorating Buddha's birth and death. Some Chinese deities have also slipped in and a rock garden completes the oriental serenity.

In the northwestern corner of the island stretch 760 blissful acres of mangroves, mudflats, abandoned prawn ponds, freshwater swamp, and coconut groves, which form the **Sungei Buloh Bird Sanctuary**►► (Lim Chu Kang). A last reminder of Singapore's former rural life, it is home to more than 120 bird species, in particular sandpipers, plovers, herons, and egrets.

Back to man-made sites, what better way for a Hong Kong tycoon to fritter away S$100 million than by re-creating the Tang Dynasty capital of Xian? The **Tang Dynasty City**► (2 Yuan Ching Road; MRT: Lakeside, then shuttle service 240), completed in 1993, re-creates in meticulous detail the 7th-century Chinese cultural metropolis. Although its nostalgic street performances are not always convincing, the scale and variety of attractions (including an underground palace housing 1,139 terracotta warriors, a "Great Wall," a five-story pagoda, tearooms, shops, and geisha houses) is impressive within a theme-park perspective. The restaurant is best avoided.

Singapore's pride and joy (and justifiably so), the **Zoological Gardens**►►► (80 Mandai Lake Road; MRT: Yishun, then Bus 171) consist of a remarkable landscaped area on the Seletar Reservoir where animals live in open moated areas surrounded by lush, mature vegetation. Even if you don't have breakfast or tea with the blasé orangutans, you can watch their activities alongside other Southeast Asian species such as the komodo dragons and pygmy hippos, or see more members of the primate kingdom—including mandrills sporting technicolor posteriors. Elephants, tigers, penguins, panthers, polar bears, and reptiles are all housed in exemplary conditions.

Crocs
Three crocodile farms in Singapore have been transformed into tourist attractions: the Jurong Crocodile Paradise (opposite the Bird Park), the Crocodilarium on East Coast Parkway and the Crocodile Farm in Upper Serangoon Road. The latter is the oldest and concentrates on breeding for skins, while feeding times and croc-wrestling are the main attractions of the other two places. All have shops stocking...yes, you've guessed it!

Hippos at Singapore's excellent Zoological Gardens

Islands

Between the oil refineries and the resorts, there is still room on the outlying islands to get away from Singapore's high-rises and traffic. Snorkeling, scuba diving, bird watching, or pony riding are the obvious activities. Ferries or chartered boats leave from the brand new airport-style wharf, the World Trade Center, Clifford Pier or (for the northern islands) Changi Point. Some charter operators rent out snorkeling gear. Check tide times before leaving, as the sea abandons many of the beaches at low tide. If bound for the less developed islands, make sure you take food and drink with you.

The nearest of the southern islands, **Pulau Tembakul (Kusu)▶▶** is a popular weekend destination for its swimming lagoons and good facilities. Legend has it that Kusu was once a turtle that transformed itself into a tiny island to save two shipwrecked sailors; a Chinese temple and a hilltop Malay shrine commemorate this, drawing crowds of pilgrims in the ninth lunar month.

Another of the southern islands, **Pulau Sakijang Pelepah (Lazarus)▶** is less structured but offers good swimming. There is no ferry service.

Coral reefs surround the small island of **Pulau Hantu▶▶** ("ghost island"). It lies in the same group as Pulau Seking and Pulau Subar Laut, and provides excellent snorkeling and diving. It is necessary to charter a boat to get there.

Singapore's last Malay fishing *kampung* is still intact in traditional stilt-house style on **Pulau Seking▶▶**, although only a few families and goats remain. The picturesque island makes a tranquil escape, but is accessible only by chartered boat.

One of the more accessible southern islands, Kusu can be deserted during the week

Harbor and river cruises
Even if you don't have time to experience the islands, you should slip a river or harbor cruise into your schedule. Singapore overtook Rotterdam in 1991 as the busiest port in the world: a vessel arrives or leaves every 11 minutes and Keppel Dock is an impressive sight. The longer harbor cruises, some in colorful restored junks, leave from Clifford Pier and the World Trade Center. Their itineraries are very similar, circling the harbor and taking in the nearest southern islands, and usually last two to three hours (lunch or dinner included). Commentaries in English often have a strong edge of propaganda.

The most interesting of Singapore's offshore destinations is **Pulau Ubin**►►► (meaning "stone island"). Accessible by regular boat service from Changi Point, it offers a rural getaway of beaches, rubber and coconut plantations, traditional Malay and Chinese villages, and, for once, a developing jungle. It is an important nature reserve (see pages 58–59) as the mangrove swamps and secondary forest attract wildlife that has disappeared elsewhere in Singapore. The main Chinese village has several temples and seafood restaurants, and at the nearby Nature House you can rent bicycles or canoes. Rudimentary accommodations are also available. Watch for the traditional *kelongs*, large V-shaped fences erected to trap fish along the coast. The word is out, however, that the traps will also be "cleaned up."

Ferries to Pulau Tembakul continue a few miles on to **Pulau Sakijang Bendera (St. John's Island)**►, a large hilly island with sandy beaches, swimming lagoons, and walking trails laid out across the interior. The bird watching and snorkeling potential may sound idyllic but accommodation facilities have made it a favorite for ebullient local school parties, so you will not be alone.

Surrounded by a coral reef, **Pulau Subar Laut (Sisters' Island)**►► is popular with divers, and its safe beaches and shaded grassy areas make it another day-trip favorite. There is no regular ferry service.

Fast becoming Singapore's favorite playground, **Sentosa**► is accessible by cable car, ferry, or road across the brand new bridge. Countless attractions and three luxury resort hotels have recently been developed to turn it into one big display case. Its southern coast has even become a palm-lined beach thanks to sand imported by the ton from Indonesia!

Heavily geared toward children, the efficient transport system (monorail or double-decker bus) whisks visitors from the spotless ferry terminal past the Fountain Gardens (where evening shows link computer-controlled

Harbor cruises can be taken aboard restored junks

75

jets of water with music and light), Orchid Gardens designed for wedding parties, two golf courses, a roller-skating rink, the Dragon's Trail, the Butterfly Park (worth visiting), the Ruined City (fake Aztec), the Coralarium, the Rare Stone Museum, and, the latest and greatest, the **Asean Cultural Village**. This US$22 million project houses a series of replica villages from the neighboring countries of the ASEAN group, showing off the crafts, entertainment, and food of each culture. Yet another mega-project is a water theme park that simulates volcanic eruptions and whitewater rafting, offers submarine trips to "Atlantis" and shows underwater movies.

Three destinations will appeal to intelligent adults. In the **Pioneers of Singapore and Surrender Chambers** life-size tableaux with taped commentaries trace Singapore's history, but a more effective section is devoted to the Japanese invasion and occupation. Photos, videos, news-papers, and even tape-recorded accounts by eye-witnesses bring this dramatic period alive. Nearby is the spectacular **Underwater World** which opened in 1991. More than 2,000 specimens of marine life—sharks, sting-rays, puffers, and brilliantly colored tropical fish—glide around you as you are transported along an 260-ft. moving walk-way through a transparent tunnel. Finally, **Fort Siloso** is Sentosa's only authentic site: the 19th-century military base contains tunnels, bunkers, and the notorious cannons that pointed the wrong way when the Japanese arrived.

Despite its down side, Sentosa is considered relatively rural by some, and hiring a bike here makes a pleasant enough escape from the metropolis.

Sentosa's attractions include the Dragon's Trail, a nature trail crossing the last suviving vegetation

Cable-car
A bird's-eye view of Singapore harbor and Sentosa can be enjoyed from the cable-car which starts from Mount Faber, a small hill accessible by taxi from the city center.The cable-car stops at the World Trade Center before continuing to the Sentosa terminal, located next to the Pioneers of Singapore and Surrender Chambers. From high above the water, the view is spectacular at sunset. The system operates 10–9 on weekdays and 9–9 at weekends and during public holidays.

Accommodations

For well-heeled visitors, Singapore's choice of international hotels is a delight. Most are geared to the needs of businessmen and in the upper echelons no service is lacking. However, for the budget traveler the situation is more difficult, as many atmospheric oldies are disappearing in the wake of Singapore's cleaning-up process. Those that survive are often upgraded or full, so don't count on turning up unannounced. Occupancy rates are high, although they have dropped in recent recession years from about 80 to 65 percent; peak months are July, August, and December. The best rates are obtainable with a combined flight and accommodations package or a stop-over deal through your airline. As a last resort, use the hotel-reservations desk at the airport on arrival: it will usually meet middle-range requirements.

Singapore's numerous stylish hotels continue to innovate in an eternal battle of the biggest and best

River Valley district stroll
An undeveloped area to explore and perhaps stay in slopes uphill from River Valley Road to the south and Oxley Rise to the north. Many of the roads have Irish names (for example, Dublin, Killiney and Lloyd), thanks to a certain Dr Oxley from Ireland who once owned an estate there. Lloyd Road has some beautiful old houses, while Killiney Road is lined with dilapidated old shophouses. On River Valley Road itself there are some enticing old shops and eating houses, including the renowned Nyonya and Baba Restaurant.

Deluxe Top luxury hotels are mostly clustered around the Orchard and Scotts Road intersection, the heart of shoppers' paradise. There you can go from a jacuzzi at the **Hilton International** to a revolving restaurant at the Mandarin Singapore or a string quartet playing at the **Goodwood Park Hotel**. The latter, a turn-of-the-century architectural curiosity set in luxuriant gardens on Scotts Road, rivals Raffles as a historic hotel and, together with a new complex at the waterfront Marina Square, is one of Singapore's five most expensive.

More lush greenery is found at the luxury **Shangri-La**, situated in isolated splendor out on Orange Grove Road. Back in Scotts Road the superbly designed **Sheraton Towers** (much favored by businessmen) offers personal butlers as part of its impeccable service. All deluxe hotels compete in the personalized-service stakes, and high-tech health clubs, swimming pools, squash courts, and business centers are common currency. For more intimate, old-fashioned luxury, **The Duxton** in Chinatown's Tanjong Pagar renovation district makes a refreshing change, and, of course, nobody can ignore the grand old **Raffles**, now completely renovated and enlarged (see pages 64–65), which dominates the colonial district.

Mid-range Singapore's rather characterless mid-range hotels are usually air-conditioned modern constructions that offer standard facilities such as room service, TV, mini-bar, direct-dial phone, coffee-houses, and/or restaurants, some also having pools.

For exploring Arab Street and nearby Little India the **Golden Landmark Hotel** (good for families) is ideally situated, while closer to the center down Victoria Street is the more upscale **Allson Hotel** and, on parallel Bencoolen Street, the **Bayview Inn**. The slightly run-down **Metropole Hotel**, right next to Raffles, is very reasonably priced. Still in the colonial district the two adjoining blocks of the **Singapore Peninsula** and the **Excelsior** both provide equivalent facilities at the top of this range. Chinatown addicts have the choice of the massive **Amara** and **Harbour View Dai-Ichi** hotels, both towering over the business district, or to the west on Havelock Road an enclave of well-appointed hotels: the **Apollo**, **Kings**, and **River View** (which it really has).

Bottom rung Budget hotels offer a choice of fan or air-conditioning, and private or shared bathrooms. They rarely charge extra service or tax, but accept cash only.

Budget travelers can choose between reasonable hotels around Bencoolen Street (**South-East Asia**, **Strand**), Beach Road (**New 7th Storey**, the cheap **Ah Chew**), and Chinatown where you can't beat the quiet, old-time **Majestic**. The River Valley district houses some idiosyncracies such as **Mario-Ville**, **Lloyd's Inn**, and the crumbling **Mitre Hotel**. Equally convenient for Orchard Road is the comfortable Tudor-style **Sloane Court Hotel**, while the **Mayfair City Hotel** monopolizes the colonial district. Nearby in Orchard Road is the **YMCA**, so popular that it needs advance booking. Lastly, it is worth considering lively Katong (accessible by bus) for the suitably named **Grand Hotel** and the modern **Malacca Hotel**.

77

The deluxe Goodwood Park Hotel is a rival to the more famous Raffles

Food and drink

Teeming with a vast array of restaurants and food stalls, Singapore will convert even formerly unadventurous diners. This is the gourmet capital of Southeast Asia, where you can snack your way through many a Chinese province, India, Malaysia, Indonesia, Thailand, Japan, and Vietnam, as well as sample local Straits Chinese (or Nyonya) specialities. Nor are such epicurean delights necessarily expensive. Singapore's gastronomic haunts range from the simple hawkers' center, where you can pile up dishes for a handful of dollars, to top hotel restaurants where the bill is best forgotten and paid for with a credit card.

Food centers, once relegated to dilapidated parking lots, are now part of every shopping center

Nyonya food
If there is one cuisine that could be defined as truly Singaporean, it is Nyonya. This strongly flavored food combines Malay and Chinese ingredients and methods, creating a rich blend of spices, nuts, and meats (even pork). Reputedly the best and providing a relaxed setting is the reasonably priced Nyonya and Baba Restaurant near the Chettiar Temple. Otherwise, head for Katong, a Straits Chinese district, where bakeries sell Nyonya *pâtisseries* and the temptations at the Peranakan Inn await you.

Chinese Cantonese *dim sum* (*dian xin* in Mandarin), savory steamed dumplings, is a breakfast and lunchtime favorite and can be relished in splendor at the Goodwood's **Garden Seafood** or more atmospherically at **Tai Tong Hoi Kee** in Chinatown. Sophisticated *nouvelle* Cantonese cuisine is served at **Li Bai**, the Sheraton Towers' excellent restaurant, while the terrace of the **House of Four Seasons** in Empress Place throws in spectacular river views with its paper-wrapped shrimp and mango. But for 360-degree revolving views accompanied by succulent Peking duck, go to **Prima Tower Revolving Restaurant** overlooking the harbor.

The steaming methods of Teochew cooking are increasingly popular with the health-conscious: steamed crayfish is a specialty of the established **Ban Seng Restaurant** in Chinatown, and the nearby **Liang Heng** Teochew eating-house also attracts locals for its *muay*, a rice porridge accompanied by numerous side-dishes. The Chinese obsession with health can best be observed at the **Imperial Herbal Restaurant** where jars of medicinal herbs line one wall: dishes are ordered and herbs prepared according to the diner's current ailment. *Yin* and *yang* rule!

Indian The obvious Mecca is Little India where a string of banana-leaf restaurants line Race Course Road. Try **Banana Leaf Apollo** where you pick what you want at the display counter (fish-head curry is a house specialty). Another epicenter can be found around Serangoon Road and Upper Dickson Road: go to the ever-popular **Komala Vilas** or round the corner to **Madras New Woodlands Café** where vegetarian *thalis* stream out of the kitchens. Modest Indian Muslim food (*biryani*, *murtabak*, *roti*, and so on) is concentrated around the Sultan Mosque in North Bridge Road. Head for the long-established **Zam Zam** or any of the neighboring establishments: many date from the 1900s. The richer, less chilified northern Indian curries and tandooris are at their aromatic best in some of the upscale central hotels: try the pioneering **Rang Mahal** at the Imperial.

Malaysian and Indonesian A tempting variety of *satay* smokes away every evening at the open-air Satay Club, a collection of stalls opposite the Padang. Other fish and meat (no pork) specialties can best be sampled at hawker centers and coffee shops, but for more comfort go to the rather touristy **Aziza's** in Emerald Hill. Indonesian *sambal udang* (prawns in chili sauce) or *sayur lodeh* (vegetables cooked in coconut milk) are crowd-pullers at the popular **Sanur Indonesian Restaurant** in Centrepoint on Orchard Road.

Hawker centers
No longer located in parking lots or on building sites, today's hawker centers have moved to custom-designed centers or shopping complexes where they are labeled food centers. However, the best atmosphere is found in the outdoor centers where *satay* sizzles over charcoal burners, noodles are tossed in woks, *roti pratha* dough flies through the air, and pork bones simmer for hours in giant soup tureens. Choose your table, then order from whatever stalls tempt you, giving them your table number. Once the dishes are brought to you, pay immediately. Try the Maxwell Food Center in Chinatown, the Satay Club on Connaught Drive, Newton Circus on Scotts Road, Taman Serasi next to the Botanical Gardens, or the lively Bugis Square Center off Lavender Street.

79

A selection of Chinese dishes at a more upscale restaurant

Shopping

Shopping is Singapore's *raison d'être* and an activity that few visitors can resist, however determined they may be.

Beware Prices are only fixed in department stores and shops with a "fixed price" sign. Otherwise, sales staff, though generally more amenable than their Hong Kong counterparts, are experts at psychological warfare: don't relent if you are unsure of the price or quality of the item and always bargain hard. Prices come down as your purchases multiply, so work out in advance exactly what you need, shop around, and then try to concentrate on one outlet. For certain items better deals can be found in the suburbs where overheads are lower: try Holland Village (MRT: Buona Vista), good for porcelain and antiques; Katong (Bus: 14 and 16) for clothes, toys, and household goods; or Ang Mo Kio (MRT: Ang Mo Kio) for electrical and electronic items.

The Singapore dollar is a strong currency, so watch exchange rates; don't assume prices are necessarily lower here than at home and bear in mind the duty you may have to pay. Beware of counterfeit items, whether watches or "designer" handbags, and only pay what their basic fabrication is worth. One-year guarantees for all electronic goods and cameras should be valid worldwide, so ensure that the card is completed correctly by the retailer. Although widely accepted in department stores and most large shops, credit cards do not help bargaining power, so when possible pay in cash. Insist on an itemized receipt for duty and insurance purposes. Goods made from endangered species should be avoided.

Ethnic goods This is the area where you can test your bargaining prowess without too much risk—so enjoy it! If the response is sour, move on. **Arab Street**, although not what it used to be, offers tempting crafts from Indonesia, Malaysia, and India. Batik in sarong lengths, whether machine printed or the more expensive hand-printed variety, is concentrated in the textile shops of Arab Street itself. On the corner of **Beach Road**, basketware of all shapes in cane, rattan or pandan leaf spills on to the side-

The Arab Street area and Chinatown offer a glittering choice of Asian disguises

Claims and complaints
Singapore is intent on controlling unethical retail practices and the tourist office produces a list of members of the Good Retailers' Scheme, also designated by a red Merlion sticker. If you really feel you have been victimized, contact the Small Claims Tribunal (tel: 530 9896) which can push through tourists' cases for a nominal fee within three days. Complaints about excessively rude service or an unresolved transaction can be made to the Consumer Association (tel: 270 5433) or to the Singapore Tourist Promotion Board (tel: 339 6622).

If you are hard-pushed for luggage space, a bamboo scroll could be the answer

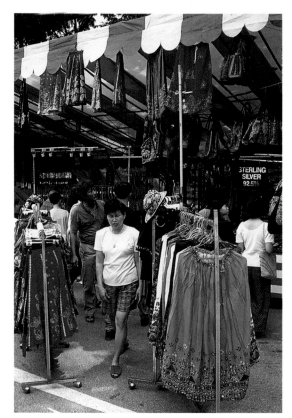

Street markets sell anything, from pungent durians to cassettes and clothes

walk, while **Baghdad Street** offers cheap Indonesian and Indian handbags of tough camel skin or cowhide. The Arab Street textile shops are also good for raw silk by the meter: remember that "Japanese silk" is in fact synthetic. On **North Bridge Road** opposite the mosque there are several perfumers whose glass-stoppered bottles contain perfume essences, and in between are stocks of the necessary apparel for the trip to Mecca.

Between Little India and Arab Street you can build up a very respectable jewelry arsenal. Choose from the sets of artificial gold worn by Malay brides, the filigree-work of the Indian goldsmiths (a specialist shop is at **16 Buffalo Road**), cheap bangles or semi-precious stones. Little India, particularly Dunlop Street and the nearby **Govindasamy** store in Serangoon Road, offers brilliantly colored woven silks in sari lengths (18 ft.), the exquisite Benares brocades having the most intricate designs—and matching prices. The second-floor stalls of the **Zhujiao Center** stock everything from cheap clothes to electronic goods, but search out the brassware shops where you can find old opium weights, snuff bottles, and other tempting bric-a-brac. Leather goods, luggage, spices, and Indian cottons are also good buys in this area.

Chinatown's shopping centers—**Chinatown Point, People's Park Complex and Center,** and the **Chinatown Center**—are a paradise for shoppers of any leaning or budget. Southeast Asian textiles, Chinese embroidered

Sun hats for coolie wannabes?

SHOPPING

silk, the latest electronics and computerware, jewelry, sportswear, cheap luggage, handicrafts, tea, and T-shirts all overflow from these temples of commerce. Pagoda Street, Trengganu Street, Temple Street, and Smith Street are lined with shops geared to tourists, and overflow with ethnic goods. Those hunting for gold jewelry can have a field day in South Bridge Road, and especially at the **Pidemco Center**, which offers mainly 22- and 24-carat gold. It is sold by weight at the market rate, although workmanship and design are calculated and provide the basis for bargaining. Jade is another specialty here, sold in a wide range of colors and forms, but ensure you can distinguish between real and imitation before you buy. The **Tanjong Pagar** area is lined with upscale shops where you can pick up fine tea or stunning lacquered objects at the **Zhen Lacquer Gallery** in Duxton Road.

Cameras, electronics, and computers Prices for electronic goods in Singapore are extremely competitive but, as always, bargaining is all-important. Head for **Sim Lim Square** in Rochor Canal Road where four levels of shops deal in stereo systems, VCRs, cameras, computers, and much more. The **Funan Center** up on North Bridge Road is entirely devoted to computers, while the more centrally located **Plaza Singapura** and **Lucky Plaza**, both on Orchard Road, have a good choice of audio and video equipment.

Fashion and accessories The world's big names are all concentrated in the overwhelming plazas of Orchard

Tailors and dressmakers
When you finally emerge from the sari shop laden with bolts of silk you might want to have some of it made up. Numerous efficient tailors are on hand either in shopping centers (Mode O Day at Tanglin's, Couples at the Far East Plaza) or smaller back-street shops where you see the sewing machine at work. Most textile stores also provide a make-up service or will recommend one. You can have existing designs copied or choose from a pattern but insist on at least one fitting. For this reason the job cannot be done quickly—allow two to three days minimum.

82

Sharpen your bargaining skills at Lucky Plaza

Road: from Issey Miyake to Dior, and from Cartier to Ralph Lauren, luxury labels are as thick on the ground as the marble-lined indoor fountains that help to sell them. Many designers have outlets in several of these strongholds of style. Department stores such as **Tangs** (quality goods), **Robinsons** in Centrepoint, or the fast-spreading Japanese variety, **Daimaru**, **Sogo**, and **Isetan**, allow you to browse in unpressurized bliss. Don't miss the superb new complex of **Raffles City**, where you can stock up on embroidered linens, *cloisonné* or casual, well-designed clothing.

Orchard Road's consumer Mecca comes into its own during the two-month Christmas rush

Antiques The antique shops of the **Tanglin Shopping Center** offer few real bargains, but they do ease the task of searching out good quality Chinese porcelain, embroideries, bronze Buddhas, wood carvings from Borneo, or carved jade. The **Bras Basah Center** also has a good concentration of bookshops and art specialists. For high quality antique Chinese ceramics and porcelain go to the gallery at the **Empress Place Museum**. In **Cuppage Road**, just beyond Centrepoint, several antique shops special-ize in Nyonya ornaments and beadwork. For furniture head north beyond Macpherson Road to **Upper Paya Lebar Road,** where some shops stock battered colonial and Peranakan fur-niture and others restore or make reproductions. On River Valley Road near the junction with Tank Road you can dig around a number of antique and junk-shops to uncover ancient Underwood typewrit-ers, incense-burners or teapots. And don't forget the suburban **Holland Village Shopping Center** which has numerous Asian arts and crafts shops, some of which specialize in collectables such as blue and white porcelain or carved altar tables and screens.

Nightlife

Although lacking the hard edge of Asia's sin cities of Bangkok and Manila, Singapore's nightlife is abundant. Singaporeans love to dance, and discos provide astonishing high-tech effects to add spice to the mainly Western sounds. There are plenty of lively pubs and bars, as well as quieter lounges with live music, many of which are found in the top hotels. Seek out the happy hours (usually between 6:30 and 8) as drinks and/or cover charges can mount up dramatically later in the evening, and even more so on Fridays and Saturdays. Karaoke (jukeboxes providing only the backing music of hit songs) are a popular way of indulging in some mild exhibitionism.

Cultural and cabaret shows
The Lido Palace in Chinatown features top Chinese cabaret, live bands, and disco with Cantonese banquets. Even more dazzling cabaret routines are staged at the Neptune Theater Restaurant on Collyer Quay, again with excellent Cantonese food. More touristy but still fun are the shows at the international hotels: the Cockpit offers lion dancers and a buffet dinner; more pricey is the Hyatt Regency's Malam Singapura which combines Indian, Malay and Chinese performances at a poolside show; and the Mandarin Hotel brings music and dance from the six ASEAN countries to a poolside barbecue dinner.

Discos Status is important, so dress reasonably well; you will be turned away from a number of doors if you roll up in jeans and a T-shirt. Action generally starts warming up after 10 P.M. and most remain open until 3 A.M.

The largest and the most popular with the under-25s is the **Warehouse**, converted from two riverside godowns into a spacious dance floor, backed by a giant video screen. Equally popular is **Top Ten** in the Orchard Towers, characterized by a Manhattan skyline décor. There strobelights compete with top Asian performers on weekends to pull in the crowds. Down at Raffles City, the Westin Plaza disco, **Scandals**, boasts a state-of-the-art sound system and attracts a sophisticated clientele. Similarly upscale are **Xanadu** at the Shangri-La Hotel, where videos and lasers punctuate the art deco style décor, and the **Chinoiserie** at the Hyatt.

For a complete packaged evening out go to **Ridleys**, located in the ANA Hotel where pub, bistro and disco combine under one roof. You can do the same thing at **Thank God It's Friday** (TGIF) in the Far East Plaza: open from midday, it has a relaxed restaurant and bar, and a

Wayang (Chinese opera) is performed above all during the Festival of the Hungry Ghost

small dance floor with video screens. On a grander scale, **Zouk** has eight entertainment spots under one roof and, like the Warehouse, is a riverside godown conversion. For exotic surroundings, join a sophisticated crowd at the Mandarin Hotel's **Kasbah**, not surprisingly designed in Arabian Nights style, or **Caesar's** in the Orchard Towers (below the Top Ten) where toga-clad waitresses glide between the tables.

Pubs and bars Usually open from noon until the small hours, these establishments make congenial meeting-places and often feature live bands playing jazz or Filipino rock. **Brannigans** at the Hyatt Regency remains one of the city's hot spots and is generally packed by 8 P.M. A favorite with expats is the **Casablanca Wine Bar** in Emerald Hill, while opposite, upstairs in Peranakan Place, **Bibi's Theater Pub** provides food, live music, and a relaxed club atmosphere. Nearby, the tiny and unpretentious **Saxophone Bar** features top jazz and blues musicians. You can eat outside if the decibels are too high. Equally popular for good jazz (particularly on Sunday evenings) is the colonial décor of **Somerset's** at the Westin Stamford.

Rock and roll fans should head for **Anywhere**, where talented bands perform at a relatively inexpensive venue. Fans of the 1960s and 1970s will enjoy **Yesterdays**, where both décor and music hark back to that era. Despite the demise of Bugis Street, some traces of entertaining camp behavior can be tracked down: **Cheers** at the Novotel Orchid Inn has stand-up singing waiters and live music, while the 1950s-style **Boom-Boom Room** in New Bugis Street actually features a cabaret show with performers in drag. Finally, have you ever seen a Singaporean cowboy? Well you will at **Ginivy's** in Orchard Towers, where local country and western fanatics put on all their gear to listen to their favorite house band.

Singaporeans depressurize at the Top Ten in Orchard Towers

Chinese opera
Wayang, or Chinese opera, can only really be seen during major festivals, above all the Festival of the Hungry Ghosts in the seventh lunar month (August or September). During this period ramshackle stages spring up near food centers, markets, and temples, and colorful, wonderfully overacted performances take place twice a day. Even for the non-initiated, the dramatic gestures make clear who is the villain of the piece and who is the hero. Vivid make-up, masks, glittering costumes, and the accompanying Chinese percussion all create an intense, noisy spectacle.

Practical points

Language English-speakers will have no problem in Singapore as English remains one of the four official languages along with Malay, Mandarin, and Tamil. In reality, Malay is the national language and English that of the administration, but it is rare to be confronted with a non-English speaker. Mandarin is now being encouraged as a second language in an attempt to iron out Chinese dialects such as Hokkienese or Cantonese.

Money For rapid service and marginally better rates, change foreign currency or traveler's checks at a licensed money changer. No commission is charged and these small counters can easily be found in shopping complexes or in Arab Street and Little India. All the major credit cards are accepted in upscale restaurants, shops, and hotels, but not in local eating-houses and coffee shops or the shops of Chinatown. ATM machines also accept foreign credit cards, although they charge an extra percentage.

Transportation Getting around Singapore is extremely easy. The MRT system, which will expand by 1996 to link the two northern terminals, is extremely economical, efficient, and easy to use. If you are staying for several days buy a stored-value card from any MRT station: this deducts the fare of each trip and can be cashed in with the deposit returned when you leave. Alternatively, you can buy individual tickets for each trip at coin-operated machines. Buses are equally inexpensive and serve some tourist destinations which are far from any MRT station. It is worth investing in a Singapore Explorer ticket which gives unlimited use for one or three days. Taxis are very reasonable but not always available during a sudden downpour or at peak rush hours. Radio-taxi

Not surprisingly, Singapore's Mass Rapid Transit (MRT) is efficient, clean, and ultra-modern

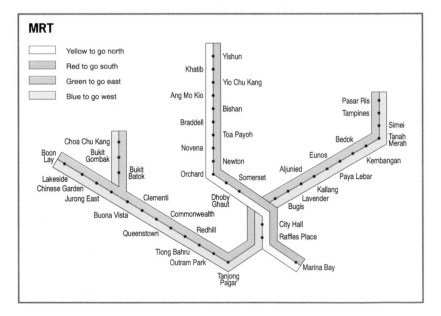

companies are listed on pages 268–281, otherwise it is (surprisingly) perfectly legal to flag one down in the street.

Religious buildings Despite the fact that many temples and mosques figure high on the tourist list, they are essentially places of worship, so respect the local believers. Mosques always demand modest clothing: sleeveless blouses, shorts, or short skirts will generally keep you out of central prayer-halls, though you will be allowed to walk around the ablutions areas. Chinese and Indians are very tolerant of outsiders, but don't walk in front of anyone at the altars or interrupt their worship. Shoes must be removed at mosques and Hindu temples.

Bargaining techniques By the end of your visit you may have refined your souk techniques, but to begin with always take your time. Sales staff are masters at pressurizing, often using guilt as a psychological weapon. Have a good idea of fixed prices, know what you want to spend and only make a counter offer if you are prepared to go through with the deal. It is not good face to back out of a transaction if the vendor has come down to meet your tentative offer. Offer less than you are prepared to pay, leaving room to move up to meet the salesperson halfway. Good humor is an essential element—bargaining should be fun, so don't hesitate to walk away if it's not! Touts outside stores are not a good sign and are usually the most aggressive in terms of sales techniques. As a general rule you can always count on knocking off at least 25 percent.

Security A relaxing aspect of Singapore is its relative safety. The laws and their punishments are legion (see page 55) and, as a result, most citizens are law-abiding. Nighttime strolls are not hazardous, mugging is practically unheard of, and pickpockets are uncommon. This said, be vigilant as you would in any foreign country where your street-wisdom is not at its sharpest.

Trishaws are mainly for the tourists these days, although a few authentic versions still ply the streets of Little India

Motorized tours for tourists!

KUALA LUMPUR

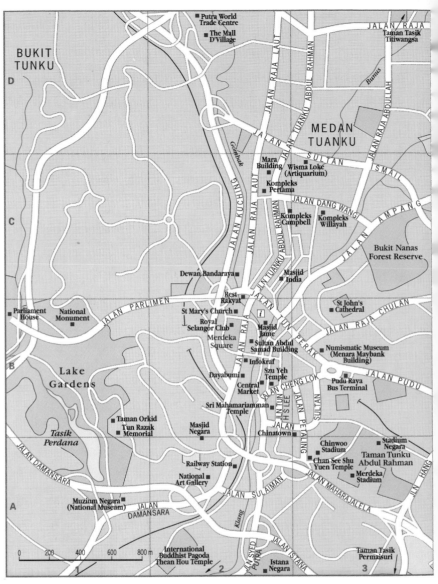

BUKIT TUNKU

Putra World Trade Centre

The Mall D'Village

JALAN RAJA

Taman Tasik Titiwangsa

Bunus

MEDAN TUANKU

Mara Building

Wisma Loke (Artiquarium)

Kompleks Pertama

JALAN DANG WANGI

Kompleks Campbell

Kompleks Willayah

Bukit Nanas Forest Reserve

Dewan Bandaraya

Masjid India

Rest Rakyat

St John's Cathedral

Parliament House

National Monument

JALAN PARLIMEN

St Mary's Church

Royal Selangor Club

Merdeka Square

Masjid Jame

Sultan Abdul Samad Building

Infokraf

Numismatic Museum (Menara Maybank Building)

Lake Gardens

Dayabumi

Szu Yeh Temple

Central Market

Pudu Raya Bus Terminal

JALAN PUDU

Sri Mahamariamman Temple

Tasik Perdana

Taman Orkid

Tun Razak Memorial

Masjid Negara

Chinatown

Chinwoo Stadium

Chan See Shu Yuen Temple

Stadium Negara

Taman Tunku Abdul Rahman

Merdeka Stadium

JALAN DAMANSARA

Railway Station

National Art Gallery

Muzium Negara (National Museum)

JALAN DAMANSARA

JALAN SULAIMAN

Kliang

0 200 400 600 800 m

International Buddhist Pagoda Thean Hou Temple

Istana Negara

Taman Tasik Permaisuri

The modern face of Malaysia's capital, Kuala Lumpur

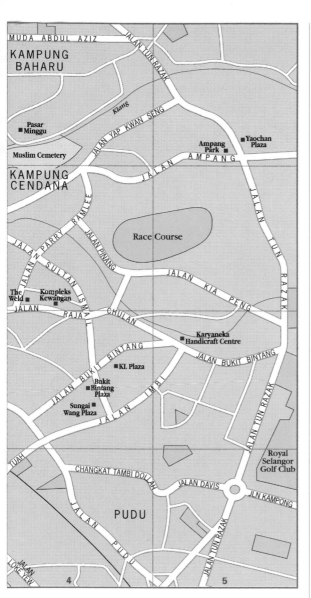

Kuala Lumpur Gateway to Malaysia's jungles and tropical beaches, Kuala Lumpur (or KL as it is commonly known) is a sprawling, chaotic, modern city of freeways and high-rises. Its historical sights are limited, cultural life is virtually nonexistent and it is rarely more than a convenient stopover on visitors' itineraries. Yet within this rather spartan packaging lives a multiracial community whose traditions hold both charm and interest—above all when it comes to food. Despite developing at a phenomenal rate, KL remains pleasantly unsophisticated, and although tourist needs are well met in luxury hotels and shopping plazas, everything else is relatively unstructured and still open to discovery.

KUALA LUMPUR

Weekend itinerary
Day one: visit the Masjid Jame then walk around the Padang. The Masjid Negara and train station are within easy reach. Finish at the National Museum. Have a curry lunch at the Carcosa and recover with a stroll in the Lake Gardens. The rest of the afternoon can be spent at the Central Market and in Chinatown. Dine and haggle in Jalan Petaling.
Day two: Explore the Indian area around Masjid India, cut back into Jalan TAR and stop for a drink at the aging Coliseum. Window-shop along Jalan TAR before visiting the Wisma Loke Artiquarium. Go to the Chow Kit food market, then take a taxi across town to the Karyaneka Handicraft Centre and museum. Do any last-minute shopping in the complexes of Jalan Bukit Bintang and dine at Yazmin's for Malay specialties and a floor show.

Today's high-rises may dwarf their colonial predecessors, but the distant jungle-clad hills remain

Early days Much of Kuala Lumpur's rawness is due to its youth. With today's population standing at 1.3 million it is hard to believe that 150 years ago KL didn't even exist. It was only in 1857 that two enterprising Chinese traders decided to open a trading post at the confluence of the Klang and Gombak rivers (where the Masjid Jame stands today) to supply the nearby tin mines—and thus KL was born.

For years the outpost was rocked by devastating epidemics, fires, and ferocious Chinese gang wars with brothels, opium dens and gambling houses monopolizing the cash flow. Inextricably linked to the tin mines, its predominantly Chinese (80 percent in 1891) population was anarchic, and it took the ruthlessness of the first Chinese headman, Yap Ah Loy (see panel on page 101), to establish some kind of order. Through astute pacts with the Sultan of Selangor and the British Resident, Sir Frank Swettenham, Yap Ah Loy took control of the seedy shanty town, wiping out or taming its lowlife. With close British involvement, an urban structure was imposed and by 1896 KL triumphed as capital of the Federated Malay States. Increasingly cosmopolitan, the big city attracted Malays from surrounding *kampungs*, while Tamils from southern India, brought in to work Malaya's rubber estates, gradually drifted in as well.

Today's cityscape Relics of this boom period at the turn of the century still abound in KL, from the colonial buildings around the **Padang** to the whimsical railway station or Swettenham's residence, now a luxury hotel. Tin-mining fortunes were poured into the elegant mansions of **Jalan Ampang** (or Ambassadors' Row), and ornately stuccoed Chinese shophouses sprang up around Jalan Petaling and Batu Road. Chinese and Indian temples were built and minarets punctuated the skyline.

After Independence in 1957 and above all since 1974, when KL withdrew from the state of Selangor to become a separate administrative entity (Federal Territory), the

city has progressed by leaps and bounds, its suburbs reaching outward, its skyscrapers rising upward and satellite towns such as Petaling Jaya or Shah Alam reinforcing its prestige. And despite an overwhelmingly Muslim spirit reflected in the forms of new buildings such as the Moorish-inspired **Kompleks Dayabumi**, KL hasn't entirely lost the rough-and-ready spirit of its early mining-town days.

Orientation Still compact, the old city center runs along and between the two rivers. Jalan Tuanku Abdul Rahman, or Jalan TAR (formerly Batu Road), Chinatown, the colonial Padang area, the Masjid Negara and the Railway Station all lie on a north–south axis within walking distance of each other. The museum and the Lake Gardens occupy a good part of the west, while in the east KL's Golden Triangle develops apace. Bounded by Jalan Ampang, Jalan Tun Razak and Jalan Sultan Ismail, this area is the city's new commercial center for every self-respecting luxury hotel, shopping complex, office block, or nightclub. Even the old racecourse along Jalan Ampang will disappear in the wake of the futuristic towers of KL's new City Center, a RM3 billion (US$1.2 billion) project looking to the next century.

Yet always visible beyond the pristine shapes of KL's ambitions are distant hills covered in thick jungle where tigers used to roam and latex still flows from the rubber trees—a reminder of the origins of its prosperity.

The 1894 Sultan Abdul Samad Building overlooking the Padang now houses the Supreme and High Courts

Brave new structures around the Central Market echo traditional Moorish forms

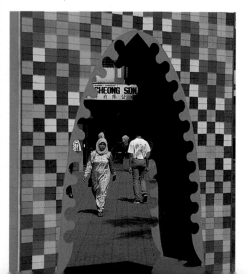

Pasar malam
Literally meaning "night market," the open-air *pasar malam* is a Malaysian institution that can be found all over the country. It combines the social functions of food, household and clothes shopping with entertainment and food consumption, and is one of the best ways to sample odd delicacies. The bright lights, odors, and Malaysian or Chinese rock music are hard to beat, and you are unlikely to escape haggling over a trinket or two before you leave. Jalan Petaling is a favorite for its speedy atmosphere, but you can also head for the more authentic Chow Kit Market on Jalan Haji Hussein. *Pasar minggu*, on the other hand, is the larger weekend market. Although called Sunday market, it actually commences on Saturday night and continues until the next morning. In KL the Sunday market used to be held in Kampung Bahru, northeast of the center, but has now invaded Jalan Tuanku Abdul Rahman and stretches almost to the Padang.

▶▶▶ Central Market   88B2
Jalan Hang Kasturi
What was once KL's meat and fish market is now a buzzing food and shopping center where locals lunch, tourists snap up souvenirs and traditional cultural performances are held. In 1985 a successful conservation project resurrected this airy art deco building, restructuring the interior to create a popular social hub. The alleys running off the skylit nave offer an eclectic mix, ranging from the ubiquitous batik to T-shirts or handicrafts from Borneo. At the northern end is a modern clone, Central Square, which combines cinemas with cafés, galleries, and boutiques. The surrounding area is a favorite venue for street performers, and on Sundays an art market springs into action.

▶▶▶ Chan See Shu Yuen Temple   88A3
Jalan Petaling
This highly ornate ceramic-faced Chinese temple is KL's oldest clan house (1906) and retains all its original features. The intricate wall paintings and sculptures in ceramic, stone, and wood which invade the roof, walls, and windows are the bequest of a determined Chinese tin-miner who vowed to complete the unfinished temple if he became rich—and he did! The open courtyard and symmetrical pavilions are still used by the Chan Clan for ancestral worship. Look out for the beautifully faded photo of the temple's financer near the back.

▶▶▶ Chinatown   88B3
Bordered by Jalan Sultan, Jalan Tun HS Lee and Jalan Petaling, this small commercial area is full of surprises. Stucco-fronted turn-of-the-century shophouses harbor a range of traditional and mordern trades: apothecaries, shoe repairers, sign painters, and casket makers work side by side with opticians and camera dealers. By day, Jalan Petaling's market stalls furnish the kitchens of the

Chan See Shu Yuen Temple: the capital's most elaborate Chinese temple and clanhouse

local community; from 5 P.M. the middle section is closed to traffic and the hawkers spring to life. Food stalls start steaming, rows of cheap watches and racks of clothes materialize from nowhere, Cantonese rock blasts from a cassette stall and the nighttime fun starts. The lively bazaar atmosphere continues until about 10 P.M.

► **Istana Negara (National Palace)**   *88A2*
Jalan Istana
Set on rolling lawns to the south of the city, this official royal residence was originally built for a wealthy Chinese merchant. The gold dome and crown now proclaim its regal status and only the lucky few invited to official receptions and garden parties may enter its gilded gates. An exception is made during festivals such as Hari Raya Puasa when the king holds an open house.

►► **Karyaneka Handicraft Center**   *89B5*
Jalan Raja Chulan
Not far from KL's Golden Triangle of top hotels is this well laid out complex of traditional Malay pavilions displaying the diverse arts and crafts of each Malaysian state. Commerce never being far, the focal point is a gallery-shop, but immediately behind, in a delightful botanical garden crossed by a stream, is a craft museum which exhibits Malaysian cultural artifacts.

►►► **Kuala Lumpur Railway Station**   *88A2*
This Indo-Moorish colonial fantasy, designed by A. B. Hubbock, was completed in 1911. An architectural extravaganza combining gilded cupolas, turrets, towers, and minarets with keyhole arches, the structure, surprisingly enough, served a merely functional purpose. Recently renovated, the air-conditioned interior does not live up to the facade, but you can take in its full whimsical splendor by following Jalan Sulaiman across the tracks.

The inspired façade of the Railway Station was renovated in 1986, but the famous Station Hotel still awaits attention

Station Hotel
Currently and indefinitely "closed for renovation," the fabulous Station Hotel may well rise again from its proverbial ashes. Its air of faded grandeur, vast lobby and restaurant, not to mention the gigantic bedrooms and their Victorian bathroom fittings, make it a rare though dilapidated sight for visitors. Check to see if it has reopened, if only to see the pleasantly archaic décor.

■ Every *kampung* has its modest mosque nestling among palm trees, and every state capital has at least one grandiose onion-domed structure with *muezzin* wailing at regular intervals. Meanwhile, down the side- streets clouds of incense billow out of Chinese temples or a colorful Hindu *gopuram* (gateway) stands out above a row of shophouses. Such are the elaborate prayer-halls of Malaysia's multireligious society. .....■

Mosques The debate continues over the "oldest mosque in Malaysia" label. Is it the superb 18th-century hardwood construction built without nails by Javanese craftsmen, the **Masjid Kampung Laut** located south of Kota Bharu? Or is it the earliest of Melaka's unique Sumatran-style mosques, the **Masjid Kampung Hulu**, whose three-tiered pyramidal roof rose up in 1728?

Onion domes and Mogul-influenced arches may have dominated over the last century, but local characteristics occasionally appear—such as in the village of **Ulu Ceka** near Jerantut, where the mosque exemplifies the early Pahang tradition of wooden towers. Exceptional historic mosques are the monopoly of state and royal capitals: George Town has its **Kapitan Kling Mosque** in imposing Anglo-Indian style (1800); Alor Setar boasts the graceful arches and black domes of the **Masjid Zahir** (1912); Johor Bahru is home to the Italianate and Islamic forms of the **Masjid Abu Bakar** (1892–1900); Kuala Kangsar has the gilded domes and turrets of the **Masjid Ubudiah** (1917); and KL has its elegant **Masjid Jame** (1897).

Pulau Pinang's modern state mosque in George Town

Mosques and temples

Since Independence in 1957 Malaysia has indulged in a spate of mosque building, with many disastrous results. Some traditional mosques, such as Kuala Terengganu's **Masjid Abidin,** were rebuilt in concrete and brick, while others such as Kuantan's **Masjid Sultan Ahmad** brought a new spaceship style to Muslim prayer. KL's magnificent **Masjid Negara** (1965) is sober in comparison, while the gigantic blue dome and minarets of Shah Alam's **Masjid Sultan Salahuddin** (1988) puts it in the running for the title of world's largest.

Chinese temples From the extraordinary to the modest, Chinese temples are strikingly varied in style. Most extravagant and eclectic of all is Pulau Pinang's **Kek Lok Si Temple,** towering over distant George Town in a profusion of Buddhas, Bodhisattvas, pagodas, and prayer-halls. Pinang's oldest is the atmospheric **Guan Yin Temple,** founded by the first Chinese settlers in 1800. Unique to Pinang are the *kongsi* (clan) temples which reflect Anglo-Indian design in the form of porticoes and pillars, a style that peaked exuberantly at the **Khoo Kongsi** and at the **Yap Temple.** However, it is Melaka that boasts the nation's oldest functioning temple: the **Cheng Hoon Teng Temple.** Founded in 1645 but completed in 1704, it is an outstanding showcase of south Chinese carvings, lacquerwork, and porcelain.

Cave-temples are another Malaysian curiosity, concentrated in Perak's limestone formations near Ipoh and also at Panching's **Gua Charas.** Gilded or polychrome laughing Buddhas nestle among stalagmites and stalactites in a flashy display of pure 20th-century Buddhist fantasy.

Indian temples As focal point for the extraordinary Thaipusam procession, the vast **Batu Caves** have been a landmark for Malaysia's Hindu community for a century. Less visited but also the culminating points for the *kavadis* are Pulau Pinang's **Balathandaythanbani Temple** in Waterfall Road and the **Sri Subramaniam Temple** at Gunung Cheroh in Ipoh. Other colourful Hindu structures are concentrated in KL, George Town, Melaka, Muar, Teluk Intan, and Seremban.

Carved detail of the gopuram on Singapore's Sri Mariamman Temple

95

Thai *wats*
Mostly situated in the north of the peninsula where Thai influence was dominant for several centuries, Thai Buddhist temples are another of Malaysia's diverse religious structures. Near the Thai border in Kelantan *wats* are scattered around rural areas and are therefore not easy to reach. Most famous here is the **Wat Pothivihan** with its 130-ft.-long reclining Buddha, but more imaginative is the **Wat Mai Suwankiri**, a recent, brilliantly garish construction in the form of a dragon boat—somewhat surreal in its coconut-palm setting at the tiny village of Kampung Bukit Tanah. Pulau **Pinang's Wat Chayamangkalaram** claims another outsize Buddha (a mere 105 ft. long) and a *stupa* (round dome) dating from 1845. Older still is the *stupa* crowning Pinang's oldest Theravada temple, the Burmese **Dhammi-karama Temple**, built in 1803.

KUALA LUMPUR

When not indulging in makan *(food), KL's inhabitants take off to the Lake Gardens*

The monument's double
The 50-ft.-high bronze National Monument was erected in 1966 in honor of Malay, British, Australian, Fijian, and Maori troops who sweated out the battle wih Communist insurgents in Malaysia's jungle. To some this statue may seem strangely familiar; that is because it was directly inspired by the Iwo Jima Memorial in Washington, D.C., which was spotted by Malaysia's first Prime Minister, Tuanku Abdul Rahman, while he was on a state visit. Sculptor Felix de Weldon was commissioned to produce the Malay version, which now stands in a moat decorated with fountains and pewter water lilies.

▶▶ **Lake Gardens** 88B1

Originally planned in 1888 as a botanic garden by Alfred Venning, a colonial planter, the gardens' 170 acres provide a welcome escape for stressed city dwellers. The large lake, **Tasik Perdana**, offers boating facilities, while young joggers and elderly *tai chi* fanatics stretch their limbs and families picnic in the shade. Tropical flowers are seen at their best both in the **Taman Orkid** (Orchid Garden—more than 800 species) and the recently opened **Hibiscus Garden**. Animal lovers can visit the **Bird Park** and the **Deer Park**. Just over Jalan Parlimen stands the **National Monument**, dedicated to the Malay and Commonwealth forces who died during the Emergency. The monument overlooks the landscaped **Asean Garden** dotted with sculptures by local ASEAN artists.

▶▶▶ **Masjid Jame** 88B2

Jalan Tun Perak

The serene and elegant Jame Mosque occupies the symbolic birthplace of KL at the confluence of the Gombak and Klang rivers. Its pink and white design was adapted in 1897 from an Indian Mogul mosque: three domes and two main minarets soar up, while Muslims gather within a walled courtyard. Visitors should avoid prayer times, be respectably dressed, and remove their shoes.

▶▶ **Masjid Negara (National Mosque)** 88A2

Jalan Sultan Hishamuddin

The 1960s National Mosque is a vast complex housing a Grand Hall for 8,000 worshippers, a library, meeting and ceremonial halls, and a mausoleum for the great in the extensive gardens. The 18-pointed star forming the main dome represents the 13 Malaysian states plus the five pillars of Islam and is surrounded by 48 smaller domes. Marble-clad corridors, pools, fountains, and a 240-ft.-high minaret complete the sense of infinite space.

▶▶▶ Merdeka Square   88B2

Less a square than a triangle, Merdeka Square merges into the **Padang** and remains an important focal point in Kuala Lumpur. Remnants of a colonial past line the edges and cricket matches take place at weekends. The mock-Tudor **Royal Selangor Club** lies along the western side of the Padang; its terrace and bar have not lost their attractions as a society watering hole. Opposite, on the eastern flank, stands another of Kuala Lumpur's eccentric landmarks, the **Sultan Abdul Samad Building** (see page 99). To the north is the modest **St. Mary's Church**, built in 1894.

The square's greatest moment came at midnight on August 31, 1957 when the Union Jack was lowered from the flagpole, the new flag of independent Malaysia was raised and roars of "*Merdeka!*" (freedom) ricocheted off the British landmarks. The square is still the site of national events and the annual National Day parade.

▶▶▶ Muzium Negara (National Museum)   88A1

Jalan Damansara

For visitors arriving in Malaysia, this modern museum gives a wide-ranging introduction to the history, customs, and culture of the Federation and its neighbors. Well-documented sections cover Kuala Lumpur's history, the native Orang Asli peoples, Malaysia's economy and the performing arts—shadow puppets in particular. Wedding and ethnic costumes, jewelry, a reconstructed *kampung* house, a richly furnished Nyonya bridal chamber, and various royal relics (as well as a detailed description of a royal circumcision ceremony) fill the ground floor.

Upstairs are displays of flora and fauna, weapons (including some superb *kris)* and animal snares. A large section of the first floor is devoted to the musical instruments of Asia.

▶   National Art Gallery   88A2

Jalan Sultan Hishamuddin

Housed in the former Hotel Majestic opposite the station is a collection of works by Malaysian artists. Hardly the height of avant garde, the collection is a rather sad reminder of how certain Asian artists feel obliged to paint Parisian rooftops or ape techniques that were long abandoned in the West. There are, however, a few interesting depictions—in social-realist style—of *kampung* life and also some good batik work.

The Spotted Dog
The affectionate nickname for the Selangor Club in its turn-of-the-century heyday, the "Spotted Dog" derived either from the club's emblem—a running leopard—or from a member's pet Dalmatian, often to be found forlornly tied up at the club steps. The truth of the matter was certainly lost in the members' many *stengahs*—a half-shot of Scotch and water—sipped at leisure on the veranda while watching cricket, or more rapidly polished off at the Long Bar inside.

97

Left: Wayang kulit *(shadow plays), a cultural pastime shared by India, China and Southeast Asia, is displayed at the Muzium Negara*

■ The colonial architecture of Malaysia's towns—Melaka and Kuching excepted—is characterized by stylistic borrowing or paternalistic interpretation of Muslim taste. In the late 19th century, British influence and architects moved into west coast states with a vengeance, erecting Victorian masterpieces wherever a Resident or district office was rooted .....■

Pinang's European houses
Known by local Pinangites as *Ang Moh Lau*, a Hokkien term meaning European houses, George Town's Jalan Sultan Ahmad Shah (formerly Northam Road) presents the most extraordinary and eclectic examples of European-influenced domestic architecture in Malaysia. Emulating 18th- and early 19th-century Georgian-style country houses, most mansions were designed by British architects for wealthy Chinese merchants.

Detail from Hubbock's Kuala Lumpur Railway Station

Colonial architecture in Malaysia dates from the 16th century, and ends with the death throes of the British Empire just before World War II. European structures dot every major town of the peninsula's west coast, although the less colonized east coast states are virtually devoid of such relics. Of East Malaysia's main towns, only Kuching's fortress-inspired landmarks escaped the bombs of World War II.

Colonnades and verandas Administrative centers such as Ipoh, Seremban, Taiping, Batu Gajah, and Kuala Kangsar all proved a magnet for colonial architects who churned out ostentatious train stations, district offices, and police stations. These buildings bristled with colonnades, pediments, and verandas, marrying European and Indian styles or surrealistically injecting English stately home style into tropical landscapes.

Melaka is the only west coast town bereft of English structures, as it was already well endowed with solid, heavily timbered, high-gabled Dutch buildings which replaced its Portuguese legacy. Pinang presents colonial architecture at its most varied, with classical facades dating back to the 1790s, as well as unique and extravagant 1900s Anglo-Chinese mansions. In general, the colonial style epitomized neo-Palladianism, stressing symmetry and proportions, and favoring white stucco, pillars and pediments. Verandas and porches, high ceilings for the overhead punkah fans, and louvered windows were all incorporated to help fight off the tropical heat.

Capital city style Declared capital of the Federated Malay States in 1896, Kuala Lumpur was a showcase for the whimsical designs of two architects, A. C. Norman and A. B. Hubbock. Both had arrived by way of Imperial India and excelled in ornate structures reminiscent of Mogul palaces, a style believed would suit the predominantly Muslim Malaya.

Norman's **Sultan Abdul Samad Building**, completed in 1897 as the colonial secretariat, was the first of a string of edifices featuring turrets, spires, Mogul arches, and elaborate stonework. He also designed the mock-Tudor **Selangor Club** (1884) and **St. Mary's Church**.

Hubbock, equally inspired, produced the majestic **Railway Station** and the magical **Masjid Jame** (1897). Not to be outdone, the British Resident Sir Frank Swettenham ensured that his 1904 residency in the Lake Gardens, the **Carcosa**, had an equally imposing presence.

▶ **Numismatic Museum** 88B3

Menara Maybank, Jalan Tun Perak
Located on the first floor of Kuala Lumpur's tallest building (for the moment at least) is a small numismatic museum. Included in the exhibits are copper-based coins from the Straits Settlements era and a collection of solid gold coins donated by Egypt's King Farouk. Collectors can buy sets of Malaysian currency and those really bitten by the monetary bug can continue at the Bank Negara's **Money Museum** on Jalan Dato Onn.

▶▶ **Sri Mahamariamman Temple** 88B2

Jalan Tun HS Lee
Said to be the most elaborate Hindu temple in Malaysia, this is certainly one of the oldest, founded in 1873. Originally located on the site of the present Railway Station, in 1885 it was moved to its present site, where it incongruously towers over one of Chinatown's main streets. The riotously colored, intricately sculpted *gopuram* (gateway) incorporates gold, precious stones, and Spanish and Italian tiles. Outside the gate Tamil women and children sell jasmine garlands. In the tiled courtyard, shrines devoted to Siva and Ganesh are always surrounded by offerings that may range from a packet of sugar to a single hibiscus. The temple is at its most animated during the Thaipusam festival, when pilgrims and penitents start their long trek from here to the Batu Caves.

And the Indians?
Although there is no Little India as such in KL, an approximation exists. Immediately east of Jalan Tuanku Abdul Rahman lie Jalan Melayu and Jalan Masjid India: between and around the two is a network of colorful, animated streets where food-stall owners toss *roti canai* and where shops specialize in saris, bolts of bright cloth, jewelry, and brassware. clustered around the mosque are Indian and Malay traders of in traditional Muslim apparel, Koran inscriptions, Middle Eastern perfumes and more glittering Indian fabrics. In the evenings tables invade the street and spices pervade the night air.

99

▶▶ **Sultan Abdul Samad Building** 88B2

Jalan Raja
This is one of KL's most eccentrically distinctive landmarks, with copper domes, pink brickwork, spiral staircases, ornate arches, and columns following the same Indo-Arab inspiration as the Railway Station. Designed in 1894 by A. C. Norman, also responsible for St. Mary's Church, the elaborate building cost the governor of the time so much money that he was allegedly left in a state of shock. After functioning for years as the State Secretariat, it now houses the Supreme and High Courts. Meanwhile, the "Big Ben" clock tower continues to cast its judicial shadow over the Padang opposite.

The Sri Mahammariamman Temple is the starting point for extraordinary Thaipusam procession to the Batu Caves

CENTRAL KUALA LUMPUR

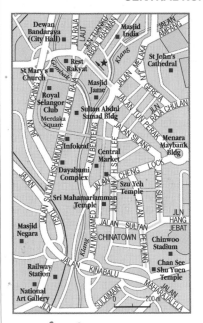

Walk The heart of Kuala Lumpur

Explore the heart of early KL from the colonial Padang to Chinatown, taking in the distractions of Central Market and more spiritual sights of the temples before ending at Jalan Petaling's market and food stalls as dusk falls.

Start by visiting the delightful **Masjid Jame** on Jalan Tun Perak, then continue west, crossing Jalan Tuanku Abdul Rahman to walk around **Merdeka Square**, once the heart of colonial KL. Pass **St. Mary's Church** and the mock-Tudor **Royal Selangor Club,** and admire the extraordinary architecture of the **Sultan Abdul Samad Building** opposite. Cross to Lebuh Pasar Besar to get another view of Masjid Jame.

Turn right into Jalan Hang Kasturi which takes you past the **Central Market**, a good stopover for shopping or refreshment. Crossing a pedestrian area, often crowded with buskers and their audiences, turn left at Jalan Cheng Lock and immediately right down Jalan Tun H S Lee (formerly

Jalan Bandar). This leads you past the colorful **Sri Mahamariamman Temple** and into the heart of **Chinatown**. From Jalan Sultan make a detour to the bottom of Jalan Petaling to the **Chan See Shu Yuen Temple** and clan house. Return to Jalan Sultan, following it around to end at the eateries of **Jalan Hang Lekir**.

Above and below: Mercantile and gastronomic distractions rub shoulders in Chinatown

The Thean Hou Temple symbolizes the ever-burgeoning finances of KL's Chinese community

▶▶ **Szu Yeh Temple**   88B2

Lorong Bandar off Lebuh Pudu

Near the Central Market down a side alley is one of KL's oldest temples. The construction of this tiny 1880s building was much aided by Yap Ah Loy, the Kapitan China (see side panel). Inside the gloomy red and gold hall, the local faithful gather to wave joss sticks or make neat bundles of paper money. Hanging on an altar at the back is a photograph of Yap Ah Loy.

▶ **Taman Tasik Permaisuri (Permaisuri Gardens)**   88A3

Spread over a large site in a satellite town south of the capital, this newly landscaped park (1989) is dedicated to the sixth Queen of Malaysia. A terraced hillside planted as a traditional Malay royal garden abounds with exuberantly colored tropical flowers and also incorporates an aromatic herb garden. The hilltop provides panoramic views across Kuala Lumpur and overlooks a man-made lake.

▶ **Thean Hou Temple**   88A2

Jalan Klang Lama, off Jalan Tun Sambathan

Located on a strategic hilltop site, this modern red-roofed temple is dedicated to the goddess of the heavens. It comes alive during Chinese New Year when opera, lion dances, and souvenir vendors take over.

▶▶ **Wisma Loke Artiquarium**   88C3

Jalan Medan Tuanku

The townhouse setting of this privately owned Asian art and antiques gallery is an extraordinary amalgam of 19th-century architectural styles and details. The gallery contains fine Oriental antiques.

Kapitan China

KL's turbulent past was much influenced by the first Kapitan China (Chinese headman) Yap Ah Loy, an astute Chinese immigrant who left his native country at the age of 17 to seek his fortune in the tin mines of Malaya. With a sharp nose for business, he grew rich and influential, and after artful alliances he was appointed to bring some order into the unruly community. Civil war bubbled as gang wars and murders fueled feuds over mining rights. No saint himself, Yap Ah Loy imposed severe punishments to impose some semblance of order. His wealth multiplied when tin prices doubled in 1879, and so did his activities. Before he died 1885 he was responsible for tax collection, law and order, and social and medical welfare—in compensation for these duties he owned vast tracts of land and monopolized all opium, spirits, gambling, and brothel activities!

Accommodations

La crème de la crème
Set in beautiful tropical gardens overlooking the Lake Gardens is the Carcosa Seri Negara, a sumptuous hotel created from two turn-of-the-century mansions. Opened to the public in 1989 following Queen Elizabeth II's stay there, the hotel is more a cocoon for 13 exclusive suites surrounded by breezy wooden verandas. The first Resident-General of the Malay States, Sir Frank Swettenham, chose the site for his residence, and when he moved in (in 1904) he was already having a "King's House" (Seri Negara) built on an adjacent hillside for his guests. During World War II Carcosa became the Japanese Officers' Mess and then, after Independence and until 1987, the British High Commissioner's residence. Today, if you have a minimum of RM1,000 (US$400), you can taste the delights of colonial comfort. Alternatively, go there on a Sunday for a curry lunch.

As is the case elsewhere in Malaysia, accommodations in the capital city run the gamut from basic Chinese doss-houses to top luxury establishments, most of which are centered in the "Golden Triangle"—KL's real estate hub. There is a good selection between the extremes, but as these are much favored by local businessmen it is essential to book in advance. Top-range hotels slap on a 10 percent service charge and 5 percent tax, cheaper establishments usually content themselves with tax only and bottom-rung places do not charge any extras at all.

Golden Triangle One of Malaysia's great pleasures is that hotel categories which you would not normally even consider suddenly become affordable. For RM350 (US$140) you can scrape into the super-luxury bracket, for RM200 (US$80) you will make the first-class hotels and outside the capital you can knock about a third off these rates. Although only the top few rival the very high standards of Singapore, others are nevertheless moving fast up the ladder. Nearly all the deluxe hotels are clustered along the length of Jalan Sultan Ismail near the shopping-center Mecca. The latest and greatest is the **Hotel Istana**, a glistening white block towering over the crossroads at Jalan Raja Chulan. Intelligently combining Malay decorative traditions and arabesque forms with sleek finishing and facilities, its rooms offer every possible comfort. Equally luxurious and vast is the **KL Hilton**, a favorite with Malaysian royalty, while the even bigger **Shangri-La** (around 700 rooms) keeps carrying off regional hotel awards. **Park Royal**, **Ming Court**, and the **Regent** also fit into this top category. All offer a choice of restaurants, as well as health centers, discos, pools, tennis courts, and business centers.

Middle range Right at the top of this range is the **Holiday Inn City Center**, which represents extremely good value

The award-winning Shangri-La Hotel

103

as its facilities are legion. To experience the heart of Chinatown, go to the **KL Mandarin**, a well-equipped modern hotel in Jalan Sultan, the larger **Hotel Malaya** or the **Hotel Furama** in the Kompleks Selangor. Prices at these three central hotels are all comparable, and amenities in the Mandarin and Malaya are extensive. All rooms have air conditioning and bathrooms.

Further north on Jalan Tuanku Abdul Rahman in the middle of the Chow Kit Market area is the recently upgraded **Asia Hotel**, while halfway between Chinatown and the market lies the ultra-clean **Kowloon Hotel**, where even a dead mosquito would be mopped up within seconds.

Just south of the Golden Triangle, along Jalan Bukit Bintang, is a string of unadventurous but comfortable hotels, all well situated for shopping complexes. Try the **Apollo**, the **Malaysia**, the **Fortuna,** or the gigantic and more expensive **Federal Hotel**, which comes complete with a bowling alley. For more character go to **The Lodge**, a small, friendly place now overshadowed by the Hilton and the Istana.

Budget sleeps Two central districts are havens for travelers counting their ringgits: Chinatown and the Jalan Tuanku Abdul Rahman area. However, beware of blindly marching into a brothel! Also check that the room does not overlook a noisy street, a factor that can make for a very bad night's sleep, especially if there is no air conditioning either.

In the neighborhood of Masjid India (off Jalan TAR) are two reasonably priced, comfortable hotels, the **Chamtan** and the **Champagne**, although you will not be drinking much of the latter as you are surrounded by Indian Muslim restaurants. Slightly farther north in Jalan Medan Tuanku are two adjacent hotels, the **Shiraz** and the **Omar Khayyam**, neither with much character but good value for the air-conditioned rooms with baths.

Chinatown beckons many a backpacker, and several of its establishments have a lot of atmosphere but little comfort. Try the reliable **Starlight**, the modern **Hotel Lok Ann** in Jalan Petaling, or the relatively spacious **Nanyang** in Jalan Sultan. Lastly, the **YWCA** in Jalan Hang Jebat has rooms at reasonable rates for women, couples, and for families, but needs booking in advance.

The Coliseum
Next door to the 1920s Coliseum Cinema in Jalan TAR is the Coliseum Café and Hotel, catapulted straight out of the days of Somerset Maugham (he frequented it, of course) and sporting a suitably gloomy, somewhat crumbling interior. Ceiling fans, dark wood paneling, original art deco furniture, and faded cartoons intensify the air of nostalgia, although the Chinese businessmen who gather there with their mobile phones are very much of the 1990s. The restaurant section maintains a good reputation for Western food—"sizzling steaks" and lamb chops—but the hotel has definitely seen better days.

Food and drink

Food is one of KL's greatest pleasures and sampling it should be included on every visitor's agenda. The multi-ethnic community has left its mark as much on plush air-conditioned establishments as on the hawkers' centers that spring into action at dusk: Malay, Indian and Chinese food can be found on every street, while Japanese and Western dishes are ever-encroaching. Prices, even in more upscale establishments, are not high and become downright cheap as you hit the street stalls. Quality is reliable as Malaysians are hard-nosed customers and competition is high. The only minus in all this is the scarcity and high price of alcohol, ruled out by the Koran and only obtainable in top hotels, Chinese coffee shops, and liquor stores. Beer (Tiger and Anchor brands) is reasonable, but the wisest option is to develop a taste for tea and/or fruit juices, both of these being plentiful throughout Malaysia. Reservations are necessary in KL's finer restaurants on weekends.

Le Coq d'Or
A restaurant with a history, Le Coq d'Or, arguably one of KL's most poular Continental restaurants, was once known as Bok House. Located in the exclusive Jalan Ampang (also known as Ambassadors' Row), this grand old house belonged to a rags-to-riches bicycle-repairman who made good in the tin mines. On Chua Cheng Bok's death his will stipulated that as long as the design, décor, and contents remained intact, his house could become a restaurant. Thus today diners revel in the splendor of porticoed verandas, Italian marble, antique paintings, and furniture.

Malaysian The burgeoning Kia Peng area has two first-rate Malay restaurants. In a decorative traditional bunga-low setting, the **Seri Malaysia** serves regional specialties and has a floor show featuring costumed musicians and dancers. Next door, the better-known **Yazmin Restaurant** offers generous buffet lunches and dinners in the garden, also to the tunes of a cultural performance. For an equally bucolic setting the **Nelayan Floating Restaurant** in the Titiwangsa Lake Gardens is a delight and its daily menu features six different cuisines.

The Bukit Bintang Plaza is home to two excellent Malay restaurants, the **Rasa Utara** and the **Satay Anika**, while the **Bunga Raya Restaurant** in the Putra World Trade Center attracts a similar, well-heeled clientele. For Malaysia's national dish of *satay*, the **Sate Ria** chain is popular and has a central restaurant in Jalan TAR.

Elaborate Chinese specialties won't break the bank

Satay *from a street stand is a treat that must not be missed*

Chinese Good Chinese restaurants are not difficult to come by in KL. Many are found in top hotels such as the Shangri-La (wonderful *dim sum* lunches), the Ming Court (Szechuan cuisine), the Regent Court, the Merlin and the Pan Pacific. Seafood restaurants where you can actually pick your dinner from the tank are rare, but **Dreamland Drink and Food Garden** behind the Equatorial Hotel offers just that. A very popular stretch of restaurants can be found at **The Pines** in Jalan Brickfields, a road running south of the station. Both Malay (barbecued chicken and *satay*) and Cantonese specialties are dished up in a pleasant setting. However, when it comes down to it nothing can beat the atmosphere of dinner in Chinatown—whether at an improvized hawker's stand or in the more entrenched coffee shops and restaurants. In Jalan Petaling, **Seng Kee** claims to be KL's oldest Chinese restaurant, while not far away the modest **Yook Woo Hin** starts churning out breakfast *dim sum* at 6 A.M. Jalan Hang Lekir's eateries aim for the tourists and prices reflect this, but if you nose around back alleys in Jalan Sultan you may be pleasantly surprised.

Indian Famous for its fiery Indian Muslim curries and *murtabak*, the Bilal restaurant chain has three branches in KL, so cannot be missed. An enclave of Indian food lies around Jalan TAR, starting at the rather chic **Bangles**, which specializes in north Indian curries, and continuing at the popular hotel-restaurants of the **Shiraz** and **Omar Khayyam**, both in Jalan Medan Tuanku. Apart from the conglomeration of small eating-houses around the Indian mosque, where the **Moghul Mahal Restaurant** serves particularly aromatic north Indian dishes, Jalan Brickfields has a number of banana-leaf places, notably **Sri Devi**. For outstanding Indian vegetarian cuisine head for Bangsar, where the **Devi Annapurna** continues to attract locals.

105

Hawkers' centers
Leaping into action as daylight fades, these improvised food stands often cook up dishes that you can't find in restaurants. The selection can be bewildering but prices are so low that trial and error becomes common practice. Service is always friendly and the cooks are only too happy to explain the ingredients. One of the liveliest in KL is in Jalan Haji Hussein the red light district of Chow Kit. Matching the hours of the district, it stays open until 2 A.M.

For Indian, Chinese, and Malay specialties head for the animated Munshi Abdullah Food Stalls behind the Indian mosque or the riverbank stalls that set up in Jalan Melayu. And if you are resolutely implanted in the Golden Triangle, the Hilton Drive-In behind the KL Hilton will introduce you to street fare.

Shopping

KL's luxury shopping plazas are fast expanding as the city tries to match Hong Kong and Singapore. A good range of bargains is available, although the lack of free-port status means electronic equipment is not within that category—unless it is locally made. However, as overheads and salaries are lower in Malaysia, stores have a certain elasticity and goods such as sports equipment, watches, cassettes, local handicrafts, and jewelry are enticingly priced. Remember that bargaining is *de rigueur* in most stores except department stores, and the relaxed Malay character generally makes this more enjoyable than elsewhere in Asia.

Shopping complexes The main concentrations to head for are within the Golden Triangle where the diversity of goods and prices will keep you occupied for an entire afternoon. In the northeast at the junction of Jalan Ampang and Jalan Tun Razak is the upscale **City Square**, connected by a glass-roofed walkway to the less exclusive **Plaza Yow Chuan**. The **Ampang Park Shopping Complex**, joined to the latter by a footbridge, is known for its bargains in local fabrics and handicrafts.

KL's newest and chicest complex, **The Mall D'Village**, is in the far northwest on Jalan Putra, opposite the Putra World Trade Center. European designer apparel is everywhere, and there are also a number of reasonable restaurants. South of The Mall in Jalan TAR, the **Kompleks Campbell** and the **Kompleks Pertam** are both stuffed with competitively priced goods, the latter even housing a bazaar in its basement. Nearby, the Malay-style building of **Medan Mara** sells exclusively Malay goods.

However, the throbbing heart of KL shopping lies along and off Jalan Bukit Bintang by the junction with Jalan Sultan Ismail. There avid shoppers are sucked into the maze of **Sungei Wang Plaza** where tailors and travel agents vie with the **Parkson Grand** department store for business. Astutely joined to this hub is the **Bukit Bintang Plaza**, with countless shops and the popular **Metrojaya**

106

The consumer attractions of The Mall, one of the city's up-market shopping complexes, include a re-created turn-of-the-century hawkers' emporium

department store. Opposite Sungei Wang Plaza on Jalan Sultan Ismail stands the exclusive **Lot 10**, a designer-label haven and also home to the Isetan department store. If you are hunting for bargains, head back on to Jalan Bukit Bintang for the **KL Plaza**, a five-floor department store aimed at more budget-conscious shoppers. And for electronics *aficionados*, the modestly scaled **Imbi Plaza**, just behind Sungei Wang on Jalan Imbi, may come up with the goods.

Handicrafts and ethnic goods Apart from the obvious outlets such as Central Market and the government-run Karyaneka Handicraft Center (see page 93), it is worth

The capital's house-wives are firmly attached to the prices and goods of Chow Kit Market

107

investigating Jalan TAR, which has an overwhelming selection of ethnic goods from all over Asia, particularly concentrated along the arcade known as **Aked Ibu Kota**. The famous **Selangor Pewter** company (see side panel) has outlets all over the country, but its central showroom is located here. Just east of Jalan TAR along Jalan Melayu and Jalan Masjid India is a treasure trove of Indian and Indonesian goods—silks, saris, jewelry and prayer rugs spill on to the bustling pavements.

The real bargains Watches can be found on every KL street corner, but Chinatown's night market remains the classic place for picking up a fake Rolex. Haggle fiercely there. Cassettes are incredibly cheap in KL and discerning music lovers should head for the **Love Music Center** in Ampang Park. Sportswear and running shoes are also very reasonably priced and can be found in every shopping complex. Lastly, for the near- and far-sighted, eyeglasses! These can be made up in a couple of hours at opticians all over the city for half the Western price—but don't lose sight of your bargaining techniques.

Selangor Pewter
This family-owned business harks back to 1885 when its founder, Yong Koon, arrived in Malaya penniless but, like most Chinese immigrants, ready to seek his fortune. And this he did with a vengeance as today Selangor Pewter is the world's largest manufacturer of quality pewter. Visitors can tour the factory on the northeastern outskirts of KL at 4 Jalan Usahawan Enam, Setapak Jaya to watch craftsmen at work or, if time is limited, go to the central showroom at 231 Jalan TAR.

Nightlife

In keeping with its developing profile, KL's nightlife is the liveliest in Malaysia although it does not offer the high-life/lowlife variety of Bangkok, Manila, or Jakarta. In the past, luxury hotels have led the way with imaginative discos, but KL's recent economic boom has led a new generation of yuppies to look for their own brand of nightlife. This is increasingly concentrated in Jalan Kia Peng, near the racecourse, where old colonial bungalows have been converted into some of the hottest places in town. Meanwhile, an older generation takes it easy in piano bars or Japanese-style lounges where hostesses will keep the spirits level and the bill high. Pubs often feature live music and, of course, no one can go far without tripping into a karaoke lounge.

Ever changing in popularity, KL's nightclubs are increasingly sophisticated

Cultural nightlife
This category is rather thin on the ground in Malaysia, and KL's choice is limited. Films can be in Malay, Indonesian, Hindi, Cantonese, or English and are more often than not violently action-packed. Check local newspapers for English-language films: movie theaters open at 1 P.M. with last showings around 9; tickets are cheap. Although some of the luxury hotels have recently embarked on "dinner theaters," usually featuring Western plays, there are no regular daily schedules, and again the newspaper is the only likely source of information.

Discos Head for the upbeat Kia Peng district and start at the biggest, **Legends**, where you may be one of 2,000 night owls. Up the road **The Turf** (10 Kia Peng) is a pioneer in the same genre, and its wine bar and disco are firm favorites with KL yuppies. In nearby Jalan Pinang, **Betelnuts** (no cover charge) pulls in KL's youth and also has an outdoor terrace. Next door, **The Sixties Pub** is designed in the op-art black and white for nostalgics of that era with videos and rock 'n' roll sounds thrown in. On Jalan Ampang **Faces**, **Phase II** and the gigantic rooftop **Hippodrome** at the Ampang Park Shopping Center are all high in the popularity stakes. **Sapphire** in Yow Chuan Plaza has its own live band and is fraught with lasers. For a return to hotel luxury and the city's hip crowd, try the Shangri-La's recently refurbished **Club Oz** or the KL Hilton's **Tin Mine**. Meanwhile, around the corner from the Shangri-La, laser technology nears the miraculous at the latest spot in town and the coolest place to be seen—**Fire** (8 Lorong Ramlee).

Pubs and lounges Favorites with business people are spots such as the **Shangri-La** in the Puduraya Building, and the **Pertama Cabaret Niteclub** and **Traffic Lights** in Jalan Sultan Ismail. In addition, all the top hotels have comfortable cocktail lounges with live music.

Practical points

City transport Taxis in KL are both cheap and readily available. A ten-minute trip in the center will never cost more than a handful of ringgits and, as most sights lie within an easy radius, it is the obvious way to travel. From midnight to 6 A.M. there is a 50 percent surcharge. Make sure that the meter is switched on and the taxi driver understands your destination—this is not always the case. For longer trips to the outskirts negotiate the price in advance. Also avoid rush hours (midday and late afternoon) when traffic grinds to a standstill, and Saturday nights when your feet will have to take over.

Two bus systems operate within KL: regular city buses and mini buses. Fares are paid on board the bus, mini buses charging a flat fare whatever the distance. Klang Bus Station serves Klang, Shah Alam, and the airport, and the Bangkok Bank Bus stand serves the Batu Caves. A word of warning for those budget travelers intent on taking the bus to or from the airport (No 47): it only leaves hourly and then takes least another hour to reach its destination. The equivalent trip in a taxi only takes half an hour, and a coupon system exists at the airport for taxis into town, thus preventing rip-offs.

Money Another of Malaysia's bonuses is that tipping is not expected. Major hotels and restaurants include a 10 percent service charge in your bill and nothing more is expected. Staff in smaller places do not look for tips but taxi drivers do—about 10 percent is the norm.

Licensed moneychangers give better exchange rates than banks for traveler's checks and cash; service is rapid and their opening hours are long. However, shop around for the best rates. Credit cards are accepted by all leading stores, hotels, restaurants, and car-rental agencies but never at more modest establishments.

Tourist offices
The Malaysia Tourist Information Complex in Jalan Ampang is housed in an elegant 1936 mansion that was built for a wealthy Malaysian planter. Aiming to be as much a tourist sight in itself as a source of information, its facilities include slide shows on every Malaysian state, a Malaysian Airlines (MAS) counter, Telekom office, Taman Negara reservation counter, a moneychanger, a gift-shop and two restaurants. Cultural shows are held daily and include a dance performance at 3:30 P.M.

Minibuses can provide hair-raising rides

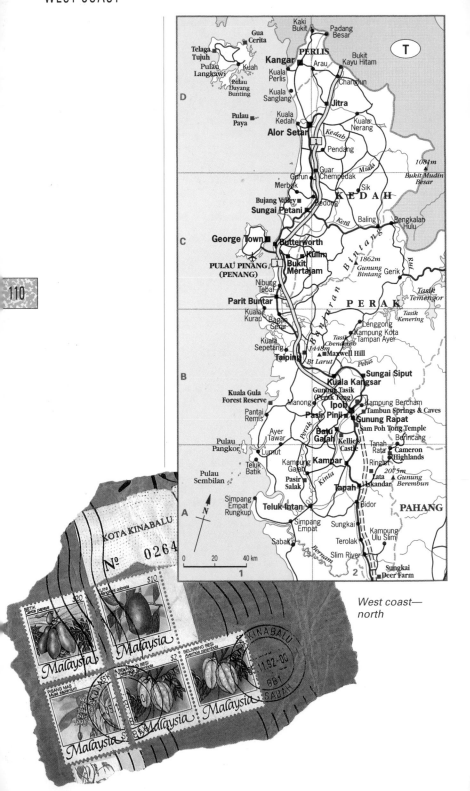

West coast—
north

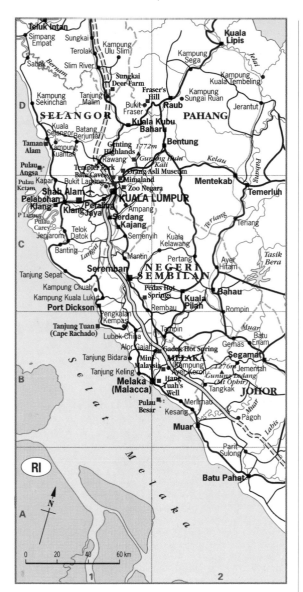

West coast—south

WEST COAST

The west coast A kaleidoscope of cultures, Peninsular Malaysia's west coast encapsulates every aspect of the nation's history and multiethnicity in a brilliant sweep from the Thai border south to Singapore. This is where the main population and power of the nation have always been concentrated, and where industrialization inevitably rears its ugly head. Yet a visitor can still go from a sleepy fishing village to a rural *kampung*, and on through endless rubber plantations or paddy fields to a nature reserve refreshed by waterfalls. Life may be hectic in the many "Chinatowns" bordering the Selat Melaka and in the

*Statues at Pinang's
Kek Lok Si Temple*

Monsoon winds

Malaysia's multiracial population can be put down to the directions of the monsoon winds. More than 2,000 years ago Chinese and Indian traders shuttled back and forth between their great land masses, their fate entirely in the hands of the northeast and southwest monsoons. The west coast of Malaysia, where the two winds meet and where the Indian Ocean and the South China Sea channel into the Selat Melaka, made a convenient stopover. There, sheltered by Sumatra, boats anchored and waited patiently for the winds to change. The southwest monsoon that affects the west coast blows mainly between May and October, although heavy tropical downpours can occur throughout the year, mainly in the afternoon—something to bear in mind when preparing an itinerary.

traffic jams that build up around large towns, but the general rhythm retains a relaxed Malay tempo. Rife with relics of its checkered past, from Dutch forts to British courthouses and Chinese tin magnates' mansions, the west coast also offers a bewildering range of distinctive Hindu, Buddhist, and Muslim temples. And, as the sun sinks behind distant Sumatra, many an idyllic offshore island will beckon today's camera-armed invaders.

North–south diversity Eight of Malaysia's 13 states border the west coast. From the northern rice bowls of Perlis and Kedah, through funky Pinang and mineral-rich Perak and around KL's industrial playground of Selangor, the great north–south diversity extends to the rural hills of Negeri Sembilan before encountering the ghosts of Melaka's many legends and historic intrigues, finally ending at the increasingly built-up Johor and its causeway to Singapore. A recent bonus is the long-awaited completion of the north–south highway which, in a virtually continuous stretch, links the Thai border with Johor Bahru, at last alleviating the congested lines of trucks that plagued the west coast. Parallel to the highway, the west coast railway runs between the central mountainous spine and the coast, taking in most of this area's main towns.

Every state has its river, and every river tells a story. As the centuries rolled by, power and influence moved from one state to the next, dependent on the monsoon winds, the products of the soil, or the vagaries of foreign rulers. In every case attention was focused on a sea outlet, the inland jungle being unassailable even to trusty elephants, although major inland towns such as Ipoh and Taiping managed to grow out of the 19th-century tin-mining boom. Between these outposts of civilization, lonely roads wind through inland jungle or plantations, past rocky outcrops and nature reserves, and, without fail, cross small *kampungs* dominated by the all-important mosque.

From rice bowls to pigtails Long under Dutch, Thai, and subsequently British domination, the northern states of Perlis and Kedah were once one and the same. They still share a serene landscape of luminous paddy fields against a backdrop of undulating hills and limestone bluffs. Between them the states supply over half the country's rice. Fishing is, of course, a major coastal activity, and low-key industry is developing around Alor Setar and Sungai Petani, the latter being virtually a satellite of Butterworth's choked-up radius. However, the jewels in this duo's crown are the spectacular **Langkawi islands** which stud the turquoise depths of the Andaman Sea, and the historically significant **Bujang Valley**.

Off Kedah's coast and biting a chunk out of the mainland is the state of **Pinang**. Like an unruly child, it has lived out its own history, its strategic maritime position governing its fortunes since the 18th century. Pinang's predominantly Chinese population doesn't let time stand still—sometimes to its loss—and today the "Pearl of the Orient" is an intriguing mixture of the rural and the developed, with plenty of historic sights thrown in.

Perak, land of plenty Next is the "silver state," whose riches originated underground in the form of tin-ore and attracted many a rapacious foreigner—the Achinese, the Dutch, the Bugis, the Thais, and the British. Chinese commercial influence has permeated every town ever since fortune-seekers flocked to the mines in the mid-19th century. Although tin has lost its standing in the world economy, the Kinta Valley still churns it out and active or abandoned tin mines dot the plains around Ipoh.

Few visitors linger on inland Perak, but the historic triangle of **Taiping**, **Ipoh** and **Kuala Kangsar** creates a stimulating circuit, taking in astonishing cave-temples,

One of Pulau Langkawi's 105 islands, off the west coast near the Thai border

113

Hindu temple detail, Melaka

Imported foreign words
Many foreign terms are integrated into Bahasa and it is interesting to discern national priorities reflected in the linguistic legacies of invaders. From 16th-century Portuguese come the words *beranda* (veranda), *biola* (violin), *gereja* (church), *kereta* (cart), *mentega* (butter), *minggu* (week), *sekolah* (school), and *palsu* (false); from 17th-century Dutch the Malays retained *balak* (log), *engsel* (hinges), *meleset* (depression, slump), *ongkos* (expenses), and *setolop* (wall lamp). English has supplied practical terms such as *klinik*, *polis*, *bas*, *teksi*, *hotel*, *restoran*, *kadfon* (phonecard!), and the obscure *gustan* (meaning to back up and deriving from "go astern"). Many Hokkien and Cantonese words have also been absorbed, but the most famous of these must be *sah teh*. Meaning "three pieces of meat," it has become Malaysia's unavoidable national dish of *satay*.

Kuala Kangsar's idyllic riverside site and palatial monuments, as well as Taiping's delightful hill station, Maxwell Hill (Bukit Larut). Stone-age caves at Kampung Kota Tampan Ayer, the ruins of a Scotsman's fantasy castle at Batu Gajah, the lush, unspoilt Perak river valley, and the tropical island bliss of Pulau Pangkor all add to the attractions of this underestimated state.

KL's back door At the halfway mark along the west coast is the bustling state of Selangor, marked indelibly by its proximity to KL. On entering it the visitor senses a perceptible buildup in energy; Selangor, the richest and most developed state in Malaysia, divides its economy between rubber, palm oil, tin, and manufacturing. But within this state lie the majestic **Batu Caves** and the futuristic urban experiment of **Shah Alam**, and beyond these are isolated pockets of rural life. Towns such as Kuala Selangor contain vestiges of history, while others, such as the islands off Pelabohan Klang, are reverting to preindustrial days. This said, unless your time is really limited and your base restricted to KL, Selangor is the least inviting of the west coast states.

From buffalo horns to golden Melaka Like Perak, the modest state of Negeri Sembilan is often overlooked as visitors make a beeline for historic Melaka to the south. Only 30 miles of the mountainous state are coastal, the rest being fertile valleys of rubber and oil-palm estates dotted with quiet Malay villages and forest recreation parks. It too has its idiosyncracies, as the Minangkabau settlers drawn to Melaka's 15th-century "Golden Age" also moved inland, bringing their buffalo-horn roofs and sociopolitical organization to the nine states (the literal meaning of Negeri Sembilan), with a common capital in **Seremban**. Pagan stones are another peculiarity of the landscape, and **Pengakalan Kempas** boasts three enigmatic examples. Despite its limited coastline, seaside activities abound from Port Dickson to the forested headland of Cape Rachado overlooking the state of Melaka.

Beyond the historic sights of its 600-year seaport capital, **Melaka** offers picturesque lowlands of rice fields and coconut groves, punctuated by traditional Malay *kampungs* and mud-wallowing buffaloes. Fishing villages enliven the coastline from Pantai Kundor to the pleasant resort beach of Tanjung Bidara, while the small island of Pulau Besar draws snorkelers. A large belt of land around **Ayer Keroh** has been reserved for nature-lovers but, finally, all roads lead to Melaka, the high point of Peninsular Malaysia's history. Dutch churches and Portuguese forts vie with a Chinatown, the latter ruled by the wealth of the Straits Chinese and emblazoned with Malaysia's oldest temples and mosques. Past its glory but conscious of its rich heritage, Melaka is a relaxed showcase for the west coast's treasures.

End of the line Occupying the southern tip of the Malay Peninsula, Johor is a thriving state, part industrial and part agricultural. Its rural economy includes rubber, palm oil, pineapple, pepper, and timber, but tourists are more likely to notice its developing golf clubs, racetracks and sports centers. Proximity to Singapore imparts a different and more upbeat tone, but coastal towns such as Muar, Batu Pahat, and the seafood haven of Kukup all have character, while Gunung Ledang (Mount Ophir) claims the famous legend of its fierce guardian princess.

Islam on the west coast
Although Islam has spread to every village here, the west coast is nowhere near as conservative as the east coast states of Kelantan and Terengganu. However, the states of Johor, Perlis, and Kedah (including Langkawi) observe the tradition of Friday as a day of rest and prayer, and in these states banks, post offices and administrative offices close on Thursday afternoons and all day on Fridays.

115

Trishaws are still common in Melaka and George Town

When Wednesday comes daily

Alor Setar's main idiosyncracy is its market. Called Pekan Rabu, which means Wednesday market, it used to be held once a week, but now functions daily from early morning to midnight. Stalls stock the usual colorful range of household paraphernalia and local farm produce, with some interesting handicrafts also slipped in. It's a great place to try a traditional Kedah speciality, the *dodol durian*, a cake made of sticky rice, coconut, sugar, and durian fruit.

Alor Setar's Balai Nobat houses the instruments of Malaysia's oldest royal orchestra

► ▬▬▬ **Alor Setar** *110D1*

Kedah's capital is an expanding commercial center on the Kedah river with, at its heart, a number of interesting historical buildings grouped around the Padang.

Dominating the Padang are the black domes of the **Masjid Zahir**, one of Malaysia's most striking and harmonious mosques, built in 1912. Its ornately carved columns, arches, turrets and balustrades are of pure Moorish inspiration. Facing the mosque through the spray of a less successful modern fountain stands another masterpiece, the **Balai Besar** (Great Hall). Incorporating elements of Thai architecture, this delicately carved wooden edifice was built in 1898 as an audience hall for the sultans of Kedah and their subjects. Today its function is of a more ceremonial nature, a backdrop for the sultan's appearances on his birthday and during major festivals.

The yellow and white pagoda-like structure topped by an onion dome which stands opposite is a unique Kedah curiosity. The octagonal **Balai Nobat** (Royal Orchestra Hall) exists only to house the instruments of the royal orchestra (precisely three drums, a gong and a flute), whose musicians can only inherit their positions. Three other states have such exclusive orchestras but Kedah's is said to be the oldest.

North of the center on the airport road is the **Muzium DiRaja** (State Museum), very similar in style to the Balai Besar although built much later, in 1936. Its collection includes early Chinese porcelain and Indian artifacts from the fascinating Bujang Valley (see page 119). Near by stands the Royal Boathouse, which contains an unusual collection of well-preserved royal vessels.

► ▬▬▬ **Arau** *110D2*

The gracious **Royal Palace** and uninspired modern forms of the **Royal Mosque** (which seats up to 7,000 people; where do they all come from?) are the only sights in Arau (5 miles east of the state capital of Kangar), but it is a pleasantly rural spot.

► ▬▬▬ **Batang Berjuntai** *111D1*

This small village is situated 25 miles northwest of KL along a picturesque road that winds through hilly jungle and oil-palm plantations, before running as straight as an arrow to the coast and Kuala Selangor. Just outside the village, no different from any other rural *kampung*, is a large bungalow hidden in the foliage. This once belonged to the French oil-palm planter Henri Fauconnier, author of *Malaisie* (1930), one of the most sensitive and penetrating accounts of the Malay spirit by a foreigner. Today the house belongs to SOCFIN, the company that pioneered oil-palm cultivation in Malaysia. From the village it is also possible to take "firefly tours" along the Selangor river to Kampung Kuantan (see panel on page 117).

The end of the line:
the last Hindu shrine
in the depths of the
Batu Caves

▶▶▶ Batu Caves   *111C1*

When an American naturalist accidentally stumbled upon this network of limestone caves back in 1878, he could not have imagined what scenes they would later witness. Soon firmly adopted by the Hindu community to house a shrine to Lord Muruga (Subramaniam), the caves still come alive during the annual Thaipusam festival (see panel overleaf), which climaxes here in a startling and vivid display. The trance-induced state of the penitents, spiked with spears and hooks, has been banned in India and this electrifying sight is unique to Malaysia and Singapore.

The massive limestone outcrop (8 miles north of KL; take Len Omnibus 69 or Minibus 11) is shrouded in vegetation and stands in a semi-industrialized landscape, its peacock-gate entrance concealed by the inevitable traffic jams. Persevere beyond a string of Indian souvenir shops and eating places to where a steep flight of 272 steps rises to the soaring interior of the vast **Cathedral Cave**. Hidden in its shadowy depths are statues of Indian deities, including Lord Muruga, Lord Rama and Sita, Hanuman (the monkey god), and Iduman. Penetrating shafts of light pick out stalactites and weird, ghoulish rock

Tracking fireflies
Kelip kelip is the common Malay term for fireflies, and the best place to witness their nocturnal display is at Kampung Kuantan along the Selangor river. This phenomenon is only to be seen in Southeast Asia and is worth making a small effort to witness. Festooning the trees that overhang the brackish riverbanks, they put on their Christmas-tree lights performance between about 7 and 10 P.M., flashing at the rate of three blinks per second for the males and every three seconds for the females. Point a flashlight at them and they will adjust their rhythm to synchronize with yours, still keeping their impeccable timing. Evening river trips can be arranged from Batang Berjuntai or from Kampung Kuantan where you should contact Encik Jalaluddin at the corner shop (tel. 03 8892403).

The Batu Caves are as popular with botanists as pilgrims: several types of rare flora have been discovered within the vast 120-million-year-old network

Thaipusam thrills
Every year at the end of January or early in February, about 100,000 Hindu pilgrims and penitents converge on the Batu Caves in a brilliantly colorful spectacle. Accompanied by the sounds of pipes and drums, the penitents come all the way from central KL on foot. Struggling under the load of *kavadi*—ornate wheel-like structures that are fixed to their bodies, with steel spokes (the *vel*) piercing their tongues and cheeks—they trudge onward and upward to the caves in a complete trance. No blood flows from the skewered flesh. Once they have splashed their chosen deity with milk, the ordeal is over and they can assume that their penance has been accepted.

formations, while errant cocks crow, pigeons flutter, and unruly monkeys scamper after scraps. At the back more steps (these are much more manageable) lead through to an opening, where another shrine stands.

Two other caves are still accessible to the public from the base of the steps, though these are less inspiring: the **Art Gallery** features a rather garish display of Indian statues (including the nine reincarnations of Lord Mahavismu), and the **Poet's Cave** presents a collection of tablets inscribed with ancient sonnets. Limestone quarrying has made the dozens of other caves out of bounds to visitors, but botanists occasionally make forays to discover specimens of uniquely preserved flora.

▶ **Batu Gajah**   *110B2*

About 10 miles south of Ipoh lies the small town of Batu Gajah, once the administrative centre for the Kinta Valley tin-mining region before Ipoh took over. Stately colonial edifices still reign over a hilltop overlooking the town, while down below commerce goes about its usual business. Outside the center to the east is a popular amusement park, **Taman Tasik SM Noor**, and a few miles farther on you will come to the melancholic ruins of Kellie's Castle (see page 128).

▶ **Batu Pahat**   *110A2*

Halfway between Melaka and Johor Bahru lies the estuary town of Batu Pahat. It is famous for a bizarre combination of heavy floods at high tide and superlative Chinese food, as well as being a growing conference center and a sinful escape for frustrated Singaporeans. At the end of a pretty stretch of coast from Muar, dotted with *kampungs*, coconut palms, and rubber plantations, Batu Pahat marks the beginning of the industrial south. However, its old center still has charm and you may spot a Sumatran sailing boat at the Customs Wharf. Right next door is **Gluttons' Square**, an appropriately named open-air night market where the oyster omelets are delicious.

▶▶▶ Bujang Valley (Lembah Bujang)   110C1

On the southern flanks of Kedah's towering peak, Gunung Jerai, lie the remains of an ancient Hindu civilization which has become Malaysia's richest archaeological site. Excavations carried out since 1968 have uncovered 50 *candis* (temples), as well as stone caskets, statues, *lingams*, gold jewelry, and ceramics. Some of these important finds are exhibited in the on-site museum at Merbok, while others are displayed at Alor Setar and in KL's National Museum.

Although the original civilization grew from the mouth of the Bujang river and spread north across the valley to the foothills of Gunung Jerai, the center of interest today is just outside Merbok, where eight *candis* have been reconstructed around a small archaeological museum (*open*: 9–4 daily, closed Friday 12:15–2:45) that explains the progress of excavations and exhibits certain artifacts. The geometrical stepped brick and stone temples, in particular the 7th-century **Candi Bukit Batu Pahat**, lie in a lush, beautifully landscaped park sloping up from a waterfall which has become an unofficial pilgrimage site for Malaysian Hindus.

Advanced culture
The finds at Bujang Valley prove that between the 7th and 13th centuries India brought a sophisticated civilization to the Malay Peninsula. The site was not only settled by merchants, but also by scholars and Buddhist and Hindu missionaries. The impact of their political, religious, and cultural philosophies was far-reaching, and is evident today in royal protocol and names (for example, rajahs), and in the tales of the *Ramayana* and *Mahabarata* enacted in shadow plays.

▶ Bukit Lagong   111C1

Situated 20 minutes away to the southwest at Kepong, the 1,000-ft. hill of Bukit Lagong is within easy reach of KL. The hill area has been developed into an extensive forest reserve with picnic areas, a waterfall and an arboretum. A clearly defined trail leads up to the peak, and guides can be arranged through the Forest Institute at Kepong.

119

The first archaeological study of the Bujang Valley temples was carried out in 1968

■ **Joseph Conrad, Somerset Maugham, Henri Fauconnier**—these are the classic authors whose lyrical descriptions long fashioned Western visions of Malaysia. However, a look at the works of contemporary writers such as Anthony Burgess and Paul Theroux will create a much clearer picture. Tropical land of *amok*, of jungle spirits and ghosts, and of dark passions seething beneath a surface calm, Malaysia is anything but paradise. .....■

Above: Somerset Maugham

● "You do not know the Malay character. The Malays are very sensitive to injury and ridicule. They are passionate and revengeful."
– Somerset Maugham

● "The life of the Malays is spent trying not to tread on the invisible toes of some ticklish divinity."
– Henri Fauconnier

● "They had an independent bearing, resolute eyes, a restrained manner...boasting with composure, joking quietly; sometimes in well-bred murmurs extolling their own valor..."
– Joseph Conrad

Romantic dreams of the Malay archipelago shattered by harsh realities and the oppressiveness of the jungle; existential doubts heightened by living in isolated outposts; steamy love affairs with Malay women; stuffy colonial clubs offering billiards and tennis. These are the recurring themes of western fiction set in Malaysia. But above all it is the presence of evil spirits and the consequent phenomenon of *amok* that predominates.

Joseph Conrad

Natives amok Endless references are made to this specifically Malay fit, which propels a normally peaceful character into a homicidal rage, so that he swings his *kris* indiscriminately in a wild search for blood. Foreign to the ordered world of colonial clubs, where planters drowned their sorrows in alcohol, the *amok* instilled not only horror in Western writers but also exerted a curious fascination.

Little else besides the rhythmical pattering of monsoon rains, endless plantations, humid jungle, and swamps made an impression on the Europeans who lived in early 20th-century Malaya. Adroitly inverting the *amok* concept, Stefan Zweig (in *Amok*, 1922) transferred this state of mental excess from the Malays on to the personality of a European doctor living in a "stifling greenhouse" and reduced to "a veritable slug...forgotten and unknown like a mussel in the ocean."

Fauconnier presents more classic version of *amok* in *Malaisie* (1930). Here a hypersensitive houseboy imagines he has been humiliated and sets off to seek revenge with a *kris*. As a grand finale to Fauconnier's sensitive and penetrating description of a French rubber planter's life and spiritual dilemmas, it is the ambiguous force of the Malay spirit that triumphs.

Colonial scandal and local spirits If they didn't run amok themselves, Europeans drank (in Maugham's *Before the Party* alcohol inspires an English wife to stab her husband to death—very *amok*), smoked opium, or

consoled themselves with Malay mistresses. These affairs went smoothly enough, unless the woman was abandoned, whereupon she might cast a spiteful spell. In Maugham's *The Casuarina Tree* (1926) a departing planter thus dies of spirit-induced spasms.

Spirits also raise their ghostly heads in Theroux's *The Consul's File* (1977), set in contemporary Ayer Hitam. A Malay medicine-man transforms himself into a deadly tiger, an *orang minyak* (oily man) demon rapes an American woman, and the ghosts of Chinese women tortured by the Japanese haunt a young man with dengue fever. Theroux's work plunges from expatriate banter and politics to a dark Malay underworld of inexplicable phenomena.

Witty, erudite, and incisive but often supercilious, Anthony Burgess, who taught in Kuala Kangsar and Kota Bharu immediately before Independence, describes realistic aspects of life, but he too allows himself to be drawn into the world of demonic spells. In his trilogy *The Long Day Wanes* (1956–1959) the semiautobiographical hero, Crabbe, ends his days mysteriously: was it a malevolent spell or suicide?

Conrad's Malaysia All Western literary routes crisscrossing Malaysia finally lead to Joseph Conrad, the forerunner of them all. Based on his seafaring experiences in the Malay archipelago, *Almayer's Folly* (1895), followed by *Outcast of the Islands* (1896) and *Lord Jim* (1900), trace compelling and finely etched portraits of European traders, adventurers and Bugis chiefs against moody, evocative island and coastal settings.

Making adventure introspective and heroism ambiguous, whether fictionalizing the story of Rajah James Brooke in *Lord Jim*, or capturing the essence of Karain, a Bugis warrior obsessed by a persecuting spirit, Conrad penetrates as no else has the mysteries of the tropical psyche and the humiliating, overpowering beauty of the land. Exoticism is reduced to survival—or tragedy.

● "Is it possible to put down roots here? I don't think so. The Chinese won't, the Tamils can't, the Malays pretend they have them already, but they don't. Countries like this are possessed on the one hand by their own strangling foliage, and on the other by outside interests..."
– Paul Theroux

● "We had hoped to find among the Malayans properties like ancient Oriental wisdom and a lack of the racial snobbery which made the *orang puteh* or white man so detestable. But we found that the Chinese, Malays, and Indians were no wiser and just as much given to racial prejudice."
– Anthony Burgess

Somerset Maugham

121

Bukit Larut records an average annual rainfall of over 1,270in.

St. Anne's Feast
The climax of a nine-day celebration in honor of St. Anne, the mother of Mary, comes on July 26 when 250,000 pilgrims follow a spectacular candelight procession from the graceful old church to the functional new one. St. Anne's symbolic role of matriarch not only attracts Catholics but also Hindus and non-Christian Chinese who don't want to miss a chance to pray—with traditional Buddhist gestures—for the well-being and prosperity of their families and businesses. A hillside path behind the old church represents the Stations of the Cross, and mothers saddled with newborn babies carry out a laborious penitence up this route, which terminates at a well.

▶▶▶ **Bukit Larut (Maxwell Hill)** 110B2

Malaysia's oldest hill station remains blissfully undeveloped. It was originally named after Sir William Maxwell, an Assistant Resident who first cleared the hilltop in the 1880s. Fifty years ago visitors were transported by sedan chair; soon after, ponies replaced the struggling coolies and finally a rugged jeep track appeared. Essentially a rural retreat for the inhabitants of Taiping who walk or jog on its steep road and jungle paths, it is accessible from the northern end of the Lake Gardens only by government Landrovers. This is not surprising, as the 72 hairpin bends twist perilously up the 3,346-ft. ascent and provide some hair-raising sensations. Near the summit are a number of rest-houses, the carefully tended gardens and jungle attracting nature lovers and those yearning for temperatures below 70°F, as well as those intent on hiking to the summit. Rain worshippers can also gravitate there, as it is the country's wettest spot, and clouds often obscure views that otherwise stretch across rolling countryside to the Straits of Melaka. Daily Landrover service starts at 8 and ends at 6, the drive taking about half an hour.

▶ **Bukit Mertajam** 110C1

In the mass of roads radiating from industrialized Butterworth and 6 miles east of the spectacular Pinang Bridge lies the developing commercial town of Bukit Mertajam. The focal point for Catholic worship at the two **churches of St. Anne**, the town bounces into the limelight every July when St. Anne's Festival draws 250,000 worshippers from all over Malaysia. The old church, built in 1888 to replace two 1860s hilltop chapels, was founded by French missionaries, and priests have always been either French or Chinese. During the postwar Emergency period the hill (and its church) was suspected of harboring communist terrorists and declared out of bounds. Thus a new church sprang up in 1957, just 2 miles away. A recreational park has been developed on Bukit Bertajam, with trails over the hilly terrain.

► **Gadek Hot Spring** 111B2

You can cure your dermatological ills in the sulfur waters of Gadek, located about 15 miles north of Melaka on the road to Tampin. A popular local spot, it has generated handicraft and souvenir shops, food stalls and children's playgrounds.

It's the sulfur that makes the difference

►► **Gombak** 111C1

Numbering about 70,000 today, the aborigines of Peninsular Malaysia are known as Orang Asli (meaning "original people"). At Gombak (14 miles northeast of KL) a small museum houses an exemplary display, with accompanying explanations of Orang Asli lifestyle, customs, and crafts. Although you are unlikely to encounter a bark-clothed, blowpipe-carrying native on your jungle explorations, many of the Orang Asli still pursue a semi-nomadic existence; 60 percent are jungle dwellers, others have settled in coastal communities in Johor, Selangor, and Pahang, or are sea gypsies or island dwellers. Three main groups, the Senoi, the Negrito, and the Proto-Malay, are further classified into 18 tribes.

The **Orang Asli Museum** (closed Fridays), located up a side road off the main road a few miles beyond Mimaland, displays Orang Asli weapons, farming tools, costumes and ornaments, musical instruments, sculptures, and craftwork. Their traditional subsistence farming was, and still is, supplemented by hunting, and fascinating examples of blowpipes, bows and arrows, booby traps, and fish traps are also exhibited. Ornaments are restricted to simple forms and materials—carved combs, hairpins, monkey teeth, and bead and shell necklaces—although women will nonchalantly stick porcupine quills through their noses or pierce their ears with bunches of leaves or flowers. The clothes exhibited are those traditionally made of tree bark, although Orang Asli women today are more likely to be dressed in a sarong and T-shirt and men in jeans. Complex basketwork and mat-weaving are on display, along with the wooden sculptures of the Mah Meri tribe, primitive idols of a religion that combines animist and Hindu beliefs. Music is an essential element in Orang Asli lives, and instruments are made from jungle materials—bamboo, wood, and animal skins for drums, flutes and fiddles—although they also use brass gongs.

Blowpipes
Generally made of a double layer of bamboo, the inner tube having a diameter of about ½ inch, these lethal instruments are intricately carved with geometrical patterns, as are the quivers used for carrying the darts. Effective for a range of up to 130 ft., the darts have an immediate and radical impact. Made from the bertam palm, they are dipped in poison from the resin of the Ipoh tree, then inserted into the blowpipe barrel. After a quick puff, the lightweight dart flies toward its target, where the poison attacks the central nervous system of the prey. Monkeys and squirrels are dead within seconds—human beings hold out only a little longer.

123

It took 40 years to mold the limestone caves of Gunung Tasik into a Buddhist temple

Princess of the mountain
Ruling over Gunung Ledang is a mythical, multiform sorceress said to live in a cave at its summit with her pet tiger. As with other Malay legends, the line between history and legend is pleasantly blurred; the most famous story about the princess concerns a real 15th-century Sultan of Johor, Mansur Shah, who apparently tried to woo her. Although the Sultan sent emissaries clad in tiger skins, the unintimidated princess laid down some tough conditions: in exchange for accepting his offer of marriage she demanded that he build a golden bridge, linking her mountain with Melaka Hill, that he collect 10,000 mosquito hearts and 10,000 mites' hearts, and that he send a cup of his blood and also a cup of his son's. Able to meet every condition but the last, which meant inflicting pain on his son, the frustrated Sultan had to renounce his suit.

▶▶ **Gunung Ledang (Mount Ophir)** 111B2

Towering 4,186 ft. over the borders of the states of Johor, Negeri Sembilan and Melaka, Gunung Ledang is as swathed in legends as it is in clouds. The rain forest of this "magic mountain" is not the most welcoming and locals say that you can walk up, but not necessarily down—its thick vegetation and mythical princess (see side panel) confounding all but the most intrepid. Access is from Tangkak, where signs to the waterfall (Ayer Terjun) lead from Sagil to a cluster of hawker stalls at the base of the mountain. A trail follows a stream to the top of the waterfall and offers some superb views. For the more determined, three-day mountain camping trips can be arranged from the Ayer Keroh Country Resort, located in the recreational forest.

▶▶ **Gunung Tasik** 110B2

Typical of the Kinta Valley landscape, this limestone outcrop (about 4 miles north of Ipoh) shoots out of a plain scarred with old tin mines. Less obvious to passing trucks, however, is the **Perak Tong Temple,** which lies within. Founded in 1926 by a Buddhist priest, the cave temple houses a startling array of wall paintings and more than 40 statues of Buddha, including a 43-ft. gilded giant and an immense pot-bellied laughing version. Far from the serenity of a meditative retreat, many of these images reflect a more kitsch nirvana. Steep steps lead past the stalactites of the upper cave to an exterior statue of the goddess of mercy, Guan Yin, overlooking the surrounding countryside. Although the founding priest died in 1980, development of the temple continues and plans are afoot to create an exhibition center for antiques.

► Hang Tuah's Well   111B2

At Kampung Duyong (2½ miles east of Melaka town) a sacred well is said to contain the soul of the 15th-century legendary warrior, Hang Tuah. Its water is believed to have medicinal value, but you are unlikely to spot the soul, apparently reincarnated as a white crocodile and visible only to holy people. **Hang Tuah's Mausoleum** is situated at Tanjung Keling (9 miles west of Melaka).

►► Ipoh   110B2

Ipoh's well-planned center and population (now approaching half a million) grew from the wealth of the tin mines, but it was only in 1937 that it replaced Taiping as Perak's state capital. To the west of the Kinta river a solid colonial past is still very evident in the domes and colonnades of its spectacular railroad station and the stately government buildings, many of which surround the Padang. Immediately across the river a grid of streets makes up Chinatown, a bustling commercial area lined with old shophouses that carry on trades ranging from charcoal-making to striptease.

The **railroad station►►►** is known locally as the "Taj Mahal" and is hard to miss as it reigns proudly over the gardens on the main road to Kuala Kangsar. A 600-ft.-long veranda was, until recently, part of the magnificent Station Hotel but, as in KL, this nostalgic delight is currently closed. Opposite stand the equally dignified neoclassical **Town Hall** and **High Court**, as well as the modern domes of the flamboyant **State Mosque**. Around the nearby Padang several colonial relics include the **Royal Ipoh Club** and **St Michael's School**, while in Jalan Dato Sagor, opposite the State Mosque, stands the **Birch Memorial clock tower**.

For more bucolic pleasures head for the **Japanese Garden** near the Perak Turf Club or the **D R Seenivasagam Park** where the Ipoh tree, after which the city was named, can be seen.

Much of Ipoh's interest lies in the nearby cave temples. Apart from the **Perak Tong Temple** (see Gunung Tasik opposite), other worthwhile Buddhist temples are located at Gunung Rapat►►► (**Sam Poh Tong Temple** and **Kek Lok Tong Temple**) 4 miles south of town. Local Hindus celebrate Diwali and Thaipusam at the **Gunung Cheroh Temple** (immediately north of the center), while Thai Buddhist worship is catered for by the **Meh Prasit Temple** opposite Perak Tong. For Orang Asli cave paintings head for **Gua Tambun** (a few miles east of the city).

From tea to topi
For "The Original—Imitated but never Equated" herbal tea, you are in the right place in Ipoh. The House of Ho Yan Hor was founded in 1945 at a small tea stall in Jalan Bijih Timah and now has 1,200 retail outlets all over Malaysia. A total of 26 herbs are reduced to an essence which is combined with tea leaves in an elaborate process of repeated boiling and drying to concoct Ipoh's own elixir. For more sustenance try *kuey teow* (a delicious rice-noodle dish) at any of the town's excellent food stalls or at Kedai Kopi Kong Heng in Jalan Leech. If the sun proves overpowering, order a topi from the Nam Sang Factory on Jalan Guntong, one of the last surviving makers of pith-helmets in Asia. However, as the basic material is a corklike wood only found in swampland trees accessible by wading through high water, the factory's days may be numbered.

125

An unmistakable sight along Perak's roadsides are pomelos as big as small pumpkins

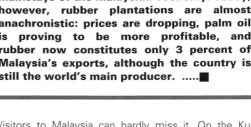

■ **Only 20 years ago rubber and tin were the mainstays of the Malaysian economy. Today, however, rubber plantations are almost anachronistic: prices are dropping, palm oil is proving to be more profitable, and rubber now constitutes only 3 percent of Malaysia's exports, although the country is still the world's main producer.** .....■

Liquid latex: the substance of early Malay fortunes

Seeds of change
Catastrophic for Brazil's Amazon region, yet highly profitable for Malaya, the *Hevea* seed radically transformed both nations. Wild rubber trees in the Amazon region were tapped in a desultory fashion throughout the 19th century until Goodyear's invention of vulcanization and Dunlop's subsequent development of the tire (1888) propelled this substance on to the world stage. The downfall of Brazil's rubber industry began when an Englishman smuggled rubber seeds out of the country and cultivated them at London's Kew Gardens. They were then transported to Singapore, where the botanist Henry Ridley (dubbed "Mad Ridley" for his obsessiveness) campaigned for the plant's adoption by plantation owners.

Visitors to Malaysia can hardly miss it. On the Kuala Lumpur airport road large billboards announce that drivers are crossing a rubber estate. No state on the peninsula is without the rather unspectacular though economically significant rubber trees. Spindly, unobtrusive, and similar to beech trees, rubber trees are instantly recognizable by the small black cup that is attached to the trunk below the lacerated bark from which the latex flows. Slopes and the proximity of rivers are the main requirements for these hardy trees; seven years after planting they start producing latex, which flows for another 25 years or so before gradually drying up.

Tapping and smoking Rubber tappers are traditionally Tamils, brought by the British from the tea estates of Ceylon to man the rapidly expanding rubber plantations of late 19th-century Malaysia. Tapping is carried out before dawn as the latex stops flowing once the heat of the day sets in. Usually allotted an area containing 350 trees, the tapper completes his task in 2½ hours, after which the buckets of latex are transferred to a factory.

At the factory, the liquid is filtered, mixed with formic acid, and then poured into separate sheets, these being left to set overnight. The final stages involve feeding the spongy white sheets through mangles, and then suspending them in a "smokehouse" where they are dried for over a week before being graded and packed.

Tappers often work together in family groups

► ### Kaki Bukit   110D2

In the far north of the tiny state of Perlis, close to the Thai border, lies the small town of Kaki Bukit (meaning "foot of the hill"). Its chief attraction is the 1,214-ft.-long limestone cave, **Gua Kelam**, which contains a tin mine open to the public and a hanging footbridge leading through to the Wan Tangga Valley on the other side. A stream running below the bridge and the illuminated formations of the cavern create a cool, unusual route, much favored by local motorcyclists.

Symbol of Malayan dissent: Birch's monument in Kampung Gajah

►► ### Kampung Gajah   110A1

Peacefully sited beside the lazy Perak river about 30 miles south of Ipoh, Kampung Gajah is no different from any other pretty Malay *kampung* of the valley. Across the river at **Kampung Pasir Salak**, however, is a historical complex displaying some fine examples of traditional houses in the *kutai* style, with their intricately carved eaves, verandas, and steeply sloping roofs. Kampung Pasir Salak is also famous as the site of the assassination in 1874 of Perak's first British Resident, James Birch, and an obelisk commemorates the spot where this happened (a bathhouse by the river). Unpopular for his tax and slave policies, Birch was also tactless in his dealings with the Sultan of Perak, but his murder created such outrage among the British that the sultan was chased into exile and the conspirators executed.

Valley of the kings
The road running north from Kampung Gajah to Parit along the Perak river takes you through an exceptionally beautiful rural valley dotted with the graves of Perak's past rulers. These have become shrines (*keramat*) and are well marked from the road. The area is also rich in traditional Perak country houses and in the unmistakable durian trees.

► ### Kampung Kuala Lukut   111C1

Just outside the town of Lukut (4 miles north of Port Dickson) stand the hilltop ruins of a Malay fort, scene of fierce fighting between Bugis and Minangkabau warriors in the mid-19th century. Built by Rajah Jumaat in 1847, it was later enlarged by his son, Rajah Bot, who also brought in Arab mercenaries. However, in 1874 the fort was abandoned during state boundary disputes and today its moated stone fortifications merge picturesquely into the surrounding vegetation.

Pelabohan Klang is an important port for west coast products

► **Kangar** *110D1*

The state capital of Perlis has a rather ramshackle modern center that holds nothing of interest for visitors, with little to indicate its past under Thai domination. The recreational park of **Sungai Batu Pahat** (6 miles east of Kangar) boasts a bird park and animal farm.

►►► **Kellie's Castle** *110B2*

Situated just south of Ipoh, this Scottish planter's unfinished dream is a wonderfully melancholic site, its ruins emerging majestically from creepers, banyan trees, and fig trees amid fields of crops and buffaloes. Intended as the social hub for wealthy colonial planters and administrators, its four-story tower looms over two floors of Moorish arches, carved balustrades, and columns. Work started in 1915 with laborers, brick, and marble brought in from Madras, but was brought to a halt when some of the builders died from a mysterious illness. Thus William Kellie-Smith focused his attention on building a Hindu temple near by (where a frieze immortalizes him attired in shorts and topi) to appease the deities. Construction of the castle resumed, but soon Kellie-Smith was forced to return to Europe and in 1826, age 56, he died in Lisbon of pneumonia. Today, visitors can wander at will through the often deserted ruins.

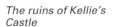

The ruins of Kellie's Castle

► **Klang** *111C1*

Klang and Pelabohan Klang (the latter being KL's maritime outlet, once known as Port Swettenham) still possess great strategic importance, but their historical significance is lost in a maze of modern developments. Klang itself has a 19th-century fort built by Rajah Mahdi on a hill overlooking the town and a riverside warehouse, now converted into a local museum. At Pelabohan Klang (5 miles from Klang) boats leave for the islands of Pulau Ketam and Pulau Carey.

▶▶▶ Kuala Gula Forest Reserve 110B1

Stretching along the coast for 32 miles from Kampung Pekan Matang (just west of Taiping) in the north to Pangkor in the south, the Kuala Gula Forest Reserve is probably Malaysia's best mangrove swamp for bird watching. In the peak season (August to December) thousands of birds flock to the mudflats on their way from Siberia to Australia. More than 120 species have been spotted, from tiny flowerpeckers and brilliant kingfishers to storks, herons, and eagles. Nor are mammals absent; there are smooth otters, dusky leaf monkeys, and long-tailed macaques, as well as the ridge-back dolphin which may also be sighted from fishing boats hired in Kuala Gula. For more information contact the Wildlife and National Parks Office in Ipoh (tel. 05 532411).

▶▶▶ Kuala Kangsar 110B2

Kuala Kangsar, Perak's royal town, lies northwest of Ipoh in an idyllic spot on the Perak river against a background of jungle-clad hills. Most of the action is down by the riverbank, where a sampan will ferry you across the water to

The Istana Kenangan (Palace of Memories), a showcase for traditional building techniques, also houses the Royal Museum

129

reach the village of Sayong, famous for its black pottery.

However, Kuala Kangsar's real *raison d'être* is situated on the hill of Bukit Chandan. There an enormous gilded onion dome announces the superb **Ubudiah Mosque**, bristling with towers and minarets. In contrast to the exterior exuberance, its octagonal prayer-hall is very simple. Beside the mosque, the **Royal Mausoleum** houses the tombs of the sultans of Perak.

At the far end of this hill stand two palaces of opposing style and character: the very showy **Istana Iskandariah**, built in 1933, and, immediately opposite, the graceful **Istana Kenangan** (Palace of Memories). The latter was built in 1926 as a temporary royal residence while the main palace was under construction. It now houses the Perak State Museum (Muzium DiRaja, see page 116), and is a fine example of traditional Perak architecture.

Back in the main town are two more worthy sights: one a prestigious old school and the other a rubber tree, said to be one of the originals transplanted from Singapore's Botanic Gardens. The tree stands in the grounds of the District Office. Nearby, in Jalan Station, is the **Malay College** which once taught spelling to Malaya's royalty. The English novelist Anthony Burgess struggled as a teacher there in the 1950s while penning his first book.

The royal bedroom in Kuala Kangsar's Istana Kenangan

▶▶ **Kuala Kedah** 110D1

This small fishing village (7 miles due west of Alor Setar) is one of the jumping-off points for the islands of Langkawi. If the wait for a ferry is long, try the deliciously fresh seafood—two restaurants are actually set on the sea. Kuala Kedah also claims one of Malaysia's best preserved and oldest forts, accessible by sampan across the river. Aimed at fending off attacks from Siam, it was built in the late 18th century by expert stone masons brought from India. This was not enough to stop the Siamese, who captured the fort and village in 1821 and directly ruled Kedah for 20 years.

► Kuala Perlis   *110D1*

Unless you are embarking for Langkawi or southern Thailand, this haphazardly laid out fishing port is of limited interest. Stilt houses built over mangrove swamps stand on one side of the estuary, while fishing and dock activities are concentrated on the other. If waiting for a boat, indulge in a specialty of Kuala Perlis, *laksa*, a deliciously spicy fish soup with noodles.

The summit of Bukit Malawati is shared by Dutch cannons, the graves of Selangor's sultans, and silver leaf monkeys

►► Kuala Selangor   *111D1*

Surprisingly untrafficked and low-key in atmosphere, Kuala Selangor is only an hour's drive northwest of KL. Rich in history, it became home to the Selangor Sultanate in 1756 when it was chosen because of its two strategically located hills that overlook the mouth of the Selangor river. The larger of the two, **Bukit Malawati**, is dominated by the ruins of a fort (named Fort Altingberg when captured by the Dutch in 1784). Malay and Dutch cannons still point out to sea from the fragmented ramparts, and outside its walls a royal mausoleum was erected in 1977 to enclose the graves of Selangor's first three Bugis sultans. Other hilltop sights are Kuala Selangor's seven wells (which served all the villagers' needs before taps arrived on the scene), a 1907 lighthouse, and several bungalows—including a rest-house. Views from the top are superb, with panoramas of the nature park forests and the sea.

The smaller hill, **Bukit Tanjung Keramat**, was also topped by a fort (renamed Fort Utrecht by the Dutch) although little remains today. A third idyllic hill, **Bukit Keramat Anak Dara** (about half a mile from the center on the river), boasts the grave of a legendary virgin (see side panel).

The legend of Anak Dara
Local legend has it that a beautiful Malay woman called Rubiah was forced by her parents into a betrothal with a man she didn't love. When the wedding day dawned she was nowhere to be found, but nevertheless managed to send a telepathic message to her parents: they dreamed that she forbade them to look for her as she had found a peaceful island retreat near by called Bukit Keramat. The following day the search party arrived on the hill to find her clothes hanging from a tree. And so a tomb was built in her honor and the hill was named.

►►► Kuala Selangor Nature Park   *111D1*

See Taman Alam-Kuala Selangor Nature Park, page 165.

■ **Young Chinese girls in tight miniskirts flaunting their liberty at Malay women enveloped in headscarves and full-length outfits: these are the extremes of the two faces of urban Malaysia. Among the Malays, batik-clad *kampung* women in sarongs contrast with their more monochrome urban sisters, but it is at their weddings that traditional costume breaks out in its most spectacular form .....■**

Divorce laws
A husband could once easily obtain a divorce in Islamic law; he had to pronounce the word *talak* ("I divorce thee") three times before his wife and a witness. Today, however, mutual agreement to a divorce is more common.

132

A Bajau pony rider at Kota Belud, Sabah

Malay costume, like every aspect of the culture, is a hybrid affair with influences from India, China, Java, and Sumatra. Islam has also lent a strong flavor to all Malay costume, giving the men the *songkok* (velvet hat) and the women the ubiquitous *telekung* (scarf head-dress), as well as a varying degree of cover-up.

Every region has its style, depending upon the religious orthodoxy of its inhabitants and the extent of foreign influence. Both Pinang's and Melaka's Nyonyas continue to differentiate themselves with a unique style of dress, while in Negeri Sembilan Minangkabau costume (which originated in West Sumatra) is still worn at weddings.

It's a man's world If not dressed in suits or jeans, sneakers, and a T-shirt, Malay men favor the sarong, a relaxed, breezy, and eminently adaptable garment that suits trishaw-cyclists as much as it does fishermen, the latter often dashingly topped with a headband or turban. One notch up the social ladder, the sarong is worn with a long shirt and finished off with a neat *songkok*. Checked or batik-patterned, the sarong is believed to have originated with the Indian Muslims. *Baju melayu*—a matching shirt and loose trousers with a *kain sampin* (wide sash) sarong—is reserved for formal occasions, while for wedding ceremonies or religious festivals the *kain sampin* is replaced by the superb *kain songket* brocade.

Now you see them, now you don't Lurking behind their headdresses, Malay women at first seem to be unapproachable, forever cloistered in the shadows of Islam. Yet this is Malaysia, not Saudi Arabia, and the easygoing, sometimes hedonistic character of the Malays transcends even the most forbidding attire. However, in Kelantan where the march of fundamentalism is at its strongest, women have changed radically since the 1950s, as described by Anthony Burgess: "The women of the faith scorned purdah and considered themselves superior to the menfolk. The wife would always walk proudly ahead and the husband trail behind."

Today many have adopted the layered *baju kurung*, while in more rural areas the *baju kebaya* dominates, this being a fitted batik blouse worn with a matching or contrasting sarong.

Weddings These costly, long-drawn-out affairs give Malay brides and grooms a chance to slip into regal attire for a day. After the religious ceremony, out-of-town relatives and friends materialize to help with the endless preparations, taking glasses and crockery out of storage and spreading mats over the floor to accommodate the guests, often numbering in their hundreds.

When the setup is perfected, the bride and groom arrive to mount the bridal dais and start the *bersanding*, a remnant of Hindu court ritual. Dressed in *songket* costumes, the groom wearing a diamond-studded crown and the bride resplendent in an ornate gold headdress, the couple survey their friends and traditional gifts at their feet. Guests come forward to shower them with rice and flower petals, henna is smeared over their palms and blessings pour forth.

Once this ceremony is completed, the real fun—games, music, dancing and elaborate feasting—begins. As in India, propitious dates are calculated and dowries are a must—although in Malaysia the latter comes from the groom and usually consists of a small amount sufficient to pay for the bride's clothes and accessories.

In the old days of arranged marriages, festivities accompanied every stage in a protracted process—from fixing the wedding date to the betrothal ceremony, cleansing of the bride's house, henna finger-staining, feast preparation and the climax, the *akad nikah* or the taking of the wedding oath. Games, dances, and complex rituals were carried out by medicine men at each stage, the whole process sometimes stretching over several months.

Malay headdresses
Until relatively recently, Malay men wore their hair long and kept it in place with a turban. This often consisted of a piece of batik cloth, but each wearer used his imagination to fold it in individual ways, devising some jaunty styles which differed from state to state. The royal headdresses or *tengkolok* were given poetic names, the most famous of these now being the official headdress of the king. Called "unending longing," its name originates in the Hindu epic, the *Ramayana*, and refers to the head cloth woven for Rama by his mother.

133

Traditional dance costumes

Deceptive appearances
Superficially a simple fishing village, Kukup has been quietly cashing in over the last decade. When the first fish farm was built in the mid-1980s its success was so immediate that others instantly sprouted up alongside. The farms demand a relatively high initial investment in numerous species of fresh- and saltwater fish, but after that the product takes care of itself, breeding and thriving in a sheltered, natural environment with high oxygen content. Look out for the antecedent of these farms: a Chinese fishing-net is still lowered by a wooden crank into the depths to snare lobsters, crabs, fish, and eels all in one fell swoop.

Ferries and fishing boats cross frequently from Lumut to the marine attractions of Pulau Pangkor

► ▬▬ **Kukup**　　　　　　　　　*187A1*

Chilli crabs are everyone's choice in this thriving fishing village, encircled by fish-farms and with spectacular sunset views over the island opposite. The gastronomic distractions of Kukup (45 miles by road from Johor Bahru) are also favorites with its neighbors, the Singaporeans, and inevitably prices are high. The town's strategic location once made it an ideal smugglers' hideout, but today the inhabitants of the fishing village are more concerned with drying shrimps and anchovies or lifting chubby snappers, garupas, and bass from the nets of the fish farms. In the nearby island water-village (accessible by boat), immaculate bougainvillea-clad homes perched on precarious stilts and connected by rudimentary plank-walks are incongruously pierced by television antennae. Earmarked for development as a marine mangrove park, the hotels will no doubt move in fast.

► ▬▬ **Lumut**　　　　　　　　　*110A1*

Malaysia's main naval base provides this small fishing village (53 miles southwest of Ipoh) with a drifting population of 25,000 sailors. Although well known for its shell and coral handicrafts, Lumut's main interest is as a point of departure for the island of Pangkor, quietly lying beyond in the turquoise waters of the Selat Melaka. If, for some reason, Pangkor exceeds your itinerary, there is a popular stretch of white sandy beach 4 miles from town at Teluk Batik.

▶▶▶ **Melaka**   *111B2*

Evocative of spices, silks, and scented woods, Melaka (once spelt Malacca) has the richest history of any town in Malaysia. Shadows of opulent Sumatran princes and ferocious Bugis pirates, wealthy Indian and Arab traders, pigtailed Chinese merchants, swashbuckling Portuguese and dour Dutch hover at every street corner. Before Singapore and Pinang had even been dreamed of, Melaka was the throbbing pulse of Asia, drawing traders from every corner of the globe to exchange gold, tea, opium, tobacco, porcelain, carpets, exotic woods, and textiles in its flourishing port. Temples, mosques, churches, and forts symbolize this eclectic past, providing a magnet for thousands of tourists. Despite this influx, Melaka maintains a sleepy, low-key profile, injected with an acceptable dose of commercialism.

History Once a humble fishing village, Melaka moved under the spotlight in the early 1400s when the fugitive Sumatran Prince Parameswara, chose it for his new abode. It took barely a century for the village to blossom into the foremost trading port of the Malay archipelago. Melaka reached a zenith during the turbulent reign of Sultan Mansur Shah (1459–1477) when gilded palaces, slave girls and musketeers added even more exoticism to the thriving community. This period also marked the spread of Islam to the rest of the peninsula, most of which fell under Melaka's control. However, the port's easy riches—and above all the spice trade—tempted other nations, and by 1511 it had fallen to the Portuguese, who monopolized this trade for a century from their hilltop A Famosa fortress. In their turn, however, they bowed out to the Dutch in 1641 after a devastating seven-month siege. Between 1795 and 1824 Dutch rule alternated with the British until a treaty finally left the port in British

Ox-drawn carts roam the Padang looking for tourists

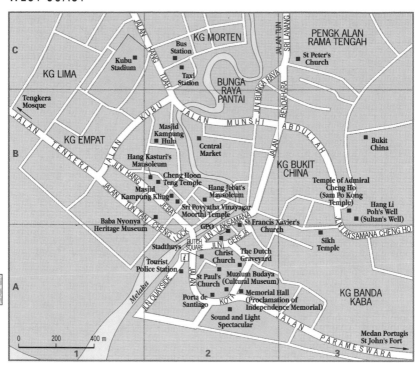

Map labels:

C

KG MORTEN
Bus Station
JALAN HANG TUAH
Kubu Stadium
Taxi Station
KG LIMA
BUNGA RAYA PANTAI
JALAN TUN SRI LANANG
PENGK ALAN RAMA TENGAH
St Peter's Church
JLN BUNGA RAYA

Tengkera Mosque
JALAN TENKERA
KG EMPAT
JALAN HANG
KUBU
JALAN MUNSHI
JLN BENDAHARA
JALAN ABDULLAH
Bukit China

B
Masjid Kampung Hulu
Central Market
Hang Kasturi's Mausoleum
Cheng Hoon Teng Temple
Masjid Kampung Kling
Hang Jebat's Mausoleum
Sri Poyyatha Vinayagar Moorthi Temple
JALAN TUN TAN CHENG LOCK
JLN HANG JEBAT
KG BUKIT CHINA
Temple of Admiral Cheng Ho (Sam Po Kong Temple)
Hang Li Poh's Well (Sultan's Well)
JLN LAKSAMANA CHENG HO

Baba Nyonya Heritage Museum
GPO
JLN LAKSAMANA
St Francis Xavier's Church
Sikh Temple
DUTCH SQUARE
Stadthuys
JLN GEREJA
Christ Church
The Dutch Graveyard

A
Tourist Police Station
St Paul's Church
Muzium Budaya (Cultural Museum)
JLN QUAYSIDE
Melaka
Porta de Santiago
JLN KOTA
Memorial Hall (Proclamation of Independence Memorial)
KG BANDA KABA
Sound and Light Spectacular
JALAN PARAMESWARA
Medan Portugis
St John's Fort

0   200   400 m

1   2   3

Tourist Office
Conveniently situated between the main square (which is lined with Dutch buildings) and the bridge (which leads across the river to Chinatown), the Tourist Office also marks the spot where Sultan Mahmud lost out to the Portuguese, despite his trusty war elephant. It is open on weekdays (8:45–6) and mornings only on weekends; its staff are helpful and will direct you to destinations out of town or advise on hotels. Next door, a pretty though traffic-noisy garden café is a good place for renting bikes, changing money or booking river trips.

hands. The 19th century saw a change in Melaka's fortunes as the new governors were more interested in consolidating their other Straits settlements, Pinang and Singapore. Under the British the buzzing port was left to decline. Despite this, Melaka stayed in British hands—bar the three-year Japanese occupation—until Independence in 1957.

Orientation Divided by its river, which meanders through the center, Melaka's main sights are all within easy walking or trishaw distance of each other and from the waterfront. North of the river is a maze of bustling lanes which harbor Chinese shophouses and elegant Peranakan mansions, interspersed with some of Malaysia's oldest temples and mosques. This is also the area for tracking down treasures in the antique shops of **Jalan Hang Jebat** (Jonkers Street). To the south lie the solid and impressive remnants of the Dutch era: 17th- and 18th-century public buildings, some of which have been converted into museums, encircle **St. Paul's Hill**. East of this historic concentration lies today's commercial center, with its shopping centers, hotels, and restaurants.

Nature spots are focused around the zoo in **Kampung Ayer Keroh** (7 miles to the northeast), while St. John's Fort and **Portuguese Square** are an easy bus ride south. Superb beaches can be found at **Tanjung Bidara** (12 miles northwest), or slightly nearer at the fishing village of **Pantai Kundor**—but you have to travel a fair distance to avoid the pollution around town. For a real getaway, take a 45-minute boat ride from Umbai Jetty to the sandy island shores of **Pulau Besar** (see page 145).

Sights Melaka's most striking sights can be visited over two days. They are described alphabetically over the following pages.

Family owners of the private Peranakan mansion which houses the **Baba Nyonya Heritage Museum►►►** (48–50 Jalan Tun Tan Cheng Lock) conduct informative tours that take place every 45 minutes and last about the same time (*open*: 10–12:30, 2–4:30). A fascinating mix of European, Chinese, and Malay decorative and architectural features, the mansion makes an exceptional showcase for Peranakan culture. The spacious two-story home, built in 1896 around open courtyards, is crammed with exuberant Chinese baroque elements, and with European objects such as Victorian lamps, clocks, and silverware, and Dutch tiles and pottery. Inlaid blackwood furniture, carved panels highlighted with gold leaf, a magnificent teak staircase, lavish silk embroideries, Nyonyaware ceramics, elaborate costumes, and a colorful bridal chamber all build up an intriguing picture of life in a wealthy Peranakan home (see also page 139).

Northeast of the center stands **Bukit China►►**, a hill that boasted the residence of a Chinese royal entourage in the 15th century. Today over 12,000 forgotten graves dot the grassy slopes, making it the largest Chinese cemetery outside China. Many of these ornate horseshoe-shaped graves, eroded by sea winds and monsoons, date from the Ming Dynasty (1368–1644).

Dedicated to Guan Yin, the goddess of mercy, **Cheng Hoon Teng Temple►►►** (Jalan Tokong) dates from 1646 and is Malaysia's oldest. The sober, dark wood interior, lifted with deep red and, for once, only a touch of gold, has some outstanding lacquerwork surrounding its three altars, which represent the doctrines of Buddhism, Confucianism, and Taoism. Outside, the eaves are alive with mythological figures in ceramic and glass, and behind the main hall numerous smaller, more modest shrines are worth seeing. Try to visit the temple on the weekend—the most popular time for weddings—when you may witness a traditional Nyonya bride standing beside a flouncy westernized version.

Melaka river
River trips leave from the quay behind the Tourist Office and last about 45 minutes. Sailing past fish markets, Chinese mansions, warehouses, and leaning wooden stilt-houses wreathed in vegetation, you will pass fishermen mending their nets, Sumatran proas (outriggers) unloading and bartering at the docks in a centuries-old tradition, and motorized sampans ferrying goods upriver. This "behind-the-scenes" view of Melaka is a good reminder of what once created the town's wealth as well as its present-day development.

Cheng Hoon Teng (meaning "Green Clouds Temple") is the oldest functioning Chinese temple in Malaysia

Princess Hang Li Poh
The Chinese emporer's daughter, Princess Hang Li Poh, came to Melaka in 1459 as the bride of Sultan Mansur Shah. Accompanied by no fewer than 500 ladies-in-waiting, reputedly all of great beauty, she was offered Bukit China as her residence and was promised that it would never be taken away. The princess's ladies-in-waiting gradually intermarried with the Malays, adopting certain Malay customs, and became the ancestors of today's Baba Chinese. Hang Li Poh's Well (also called Sultan's Well) is said to have been in existence when the princess arrived. It is said that the famous Muslim eunuch Admiral Cheng Ho drank from the well, thus giving it its legendary purity.

Built to commemorate a century of Dutch rule over Melaka, Christ Church took 12 years to complete

Dominating the main square is one of Melaka's landmarks, **Christ Church▶▶**, a fine example of Dutch architecture that was completed in 1753. Its pinky-red bricks were shipped from Holland and the huge 50-ft.-rafters in the nave were each carved from a single tree trunk. Dutch and Armenian tombstones are embedded in the floor, and the original pews are still in use. Look for the ceramic frieze of *The Last Supper* over the altar.

At the base of Bukit China is **Hang Li Poh's Well▶▶** (also called Sultan's Well), named after the 15th-century Chinese princess who resided there and who used the well daily (see side panel). The waters of the well were successively poisoned by warring Malays, Dutch, and Achinese, and despite long drought it has never dried up. Legend has it that whoever drinks from it will return to Melaka again. Today it is covered by a metal grid, but the site remains a popular pilgrimage spot for Malay Chinese.

Crowned by a tiled green tiered roof, Malaysia's oldest mosque, **Masjid Kampung Hulu▶** (Jalan Kampung Hulu), was built in 1728 and its unique architectural style extends to a minaret that resembles a lighthouse. The simple raftered interior is out of bounds to non-Muslims.

Another architectural feat, **Masjid Kampung Kling▶▶▶** (Jalan Tokong) was completed in 1748 and has a pyramidal roof design similar to that of Masjid Kampung Hulu. Sumatran and Hindu influences in the main structure combine with a five-tiered pagoda-like minaret, English and Portuguese tiles, Corinthian columns, an elaborately carved pulpit and a gigantic Victorian chandelier to create a complete stylistic medley.

Antiques and Jalan Hang Jebat
Formerly called Jonkers Street, this Chinatown street is the focal point for antique and souvenir shops, as well as an idiosyncratic range of traditional Chinese trades. Drop into the minuscule shop of "Wah Aik Shoes Maker" (no. 92). This venerable old gentleman still makes tiny silk slippers to measure for the remaining handful of Chinese ladies with bound feet—yes, they do still exist!

Continued on page 140.

The Straits Chinese

■ **Pinang, Melaka, and Singapore produced a unique and rich culture, that of the Straits-born Chinese, the Peranakans, who created their own distinct environments and traditions through 400 years of inter-marriage with Malays. Ornate relics of this dynamic social group are displayed in many of the larger state museums, but to enter their living world Melaka is the place to visit .....■**

Diversely referred to as Nyonyas (women), Babas (men), Peranakans (meaning "intermarriage") or Straits Chinese, this minority group flourished in the 19th century, when Chinese fled the Manchu regime to better their fortunes in the burgeoning trade of the Straits Settlements. Refined, cultivated, and eclectic in their blending of Chinese business acumen with more relaxed Malay habits such as eating with hands or wearing sarongs, the Straits Chinese still cling to much of their unique heritage. Bound feet have virtually disappeared, but in Melaka's **Cheng Hoon Teng Temple** Nyonya brides frequently appear in exquisitely embroidered traditional costumes, while the mansions of **Jalan Tun Tan Cheng Lock** may house several generations Chinese-style under one roof.

Peranakan anglophilia Thriving under British free-port status, 19th-century Peranakans adopted the English lifestyle as easily as they had the Malay. Grandfather clocks and Victorian tableware soon invaded their Chinese baroque homes.

In Pinang, the newly rich Chinese traders described themselves as "the Queen's Chinese" and an early 20th-century account clearly describes their habits: "They have social clubs of their own to which they will admit no native of China. At these clubs they play at billiards, bowls and other European games and drink brandy and soda ad libitum: yet they adhere strictly to Chinese costume—the queue (pigtail), thick-soled shoes, mandarin dresses and conical hats on state occasions..."

Baba greats
Although fast losing their unique Malay-Chinese nature due to interracial marriage laws (Muslim Malays can only marry fellow or converted Muslims), the Straits Chinese have nevertheless produced their own remarkable personalities. The Tan family of Melaka in particular has left its mark, transforming what was once Heeren Street (former residences of senior Dutch officials) into Jalan Tun Tan Cheng Lock, a street still lined with beautifully maintained Peranakan homes.

Singapore's Peranakan Place exemplifies Straits Chinese style

Made of local hard-woods and using traditional dove-tailing techniques instead of nails, the impressive Muzium Budaya was completed in 1986

The Portuguese legacy
Alone among colonizing nations, the Portuguese actually encouraged inter-marriage and their descen-dants still cling to Portuguese traditions and a language that is the pure 16th-century dialect *Crístão*. Names like Da Souza and Da Silva, songs, dances, Mediterranean-influenced cuisine and a Latin habit of chatting the evening away while seated in the street are the rest of the legacy. Christian festi-vals—Easter, Christmas and, above all, the Festa de San Pedro (the patron saint of fishermen) on June 29—are the best times to wit-ness the Portuguese descendents' colorful and unique traditions.

Continued from page 138.

Outside the center on the Port Dickson road stands Melaka's third historical mosque, **Masjid Tengkera▶▶** (take Bus 18). Dating from the 18th century, its Sumatran-influenced main structure resembles the Kampung Hulu and Kampung Kling mosques, but is less sophisticated and appropriate to the more rural setting. Buried in the graveyard is Sultan Hussein of Johor, who signed over Singapore to Raffles in 1819.

South of Melaka's center is a seaside suburb (take Bus 17) where the Portuguese-Eurasian community, today numbering about 500, were grouped in the 1930s. Although the settlement itself is nothing special, the cen-tral square, **Medan Portugis▶** (meaning Portuguese Square), a walled courtyard of restaurants and bars, bursts into life every Saturday night when Portuguese songs and dances are performed.

Known as the Malacca Club when it was built in 1912 for planters and officials, the pristine white **Memorial Hall▶** (also called the Proclamation of Independence Memorial) is the only British colonial legacy in Melaka. Today it dis-plays documents, photographs, paintings, and videos relating Malaysia's road to independence. It was from the balcony of this building overlooking the Padang that Tunku Abdul Rahman victoriously announced his suc-cessful independence negotiations in 1957.

The multiple winged eaves, breezy verandas, and carved wooden balustrades of the imposing wooden **Muzium Budaya▶▶▶** (Cultural Museum) at the foot of St. Paul's Hill are an exact replica of Sultan Mansur Shah's legendary palace, reconstructed from a historical descrip-tion. Exhibits range from the Sultan's royal bedchamber to regional costumes, musical instruments, *krises*, docu-mentation on Malaysia's mosques and the **Terengganu Stone**. The stone dates from 1303 and its Arabic inscrip-tion in the Malay language is the first evidence of Islamic culture in the peninsula.

All that remains of the formidable Portuguese fort of A Famosa built by Alfonso d'Albuquerque in 1511 is the stone gateway, **Porta de Santiago▶▶▶**. Standing at the foot of St. Paul's Hill, it symbolizes the might of the Portuguese, whose settlement once occupied the entire hill. The gateway bears the crest of Dutch East India Company as well as the date of their restoration of the fort (1670). When the British demolished the A Famosa fort in 1808, Raffles' last-minute intervention saved this one historic remnant.

Just behind Christ Church stands the twin-towered neo-Gothic **St Francis Xavier's Church▶**, built in 1849 to replace a Portuguese church. It is dedicated to the "Apostle of the East," St. Francis Xavier, whose name crops up all over Southeast Asia in the trail of his 16th-century preaching of Catholicism.

Dominating a hill to the south of the town is the late 18th-century Dutch **St. John's Fort▶▶** (take Bus 17), built on the site of a Portuguese chapel. This white-washed fort remains surprisingly intact—it was spared by the British—and the orientation of its gun embrasures reveals that attacks from inland were as much feared as those from the sea. The hilltop offers panoramic views of Melaka, although an adjacent modern high-rise somewhat mars the time-warp effect.

Together with the Porta de Santiago and the Stadthuys, **St. Paul's Church▶▶▶** is one of Melaka's oldest and most moving sights. Decrepit walls dating from 1521 are today open to the sky, but in 1545 St. Francis Xavier spread the word to the masses here. An empty tomb inside the church marks the spot where his body lay before being transferred to Goa in India, and a marble statue of him stands outside. The Dutch held their Protestant services at Christ Church but used St. Paul's as a burial ground; the walls are still lined with engraved tombstones which emerge from flowering bushes.

Sound and light show
A dramatic reenactment of Melaka's history is shown every evening on the Padang below St. Paul's Hill. Set against the silent relics of Melaka's past, it starts with the founder, Prince Parameswara, and through dialogue, music, the slapping of waves, booming of cannons, and spectacular projections, events and characters from the seaport's turbulent history are brought to life. Tracing the successive occupations by the Portuguese, Dutch, British, and Japanese the show culminates with the reedy voice of Malaysia's first Prime Minster, Tunku Abdul Rahman, triumphantly crying "*Merdeka!*" (freedom) to his nation on August 31, 1957. English-language shows start at 9:30 P.M. daily and last one hour.

141

It was from Melaka's Memorial Hall that Tunku Abdul Rahman declared Independence in 1957

Dating from 1710, **St. Peter's Church▶▶**, the oldest functioning Catholic church in Malaysia, is situated on Jalan Tun Sri Lanang just north of the modern town. Its typical Portuguese forms also incorporate Moorish features such as a keyhole niche, and it contains a life-size alabaster statue of Jesus which is carried around the church grounds in a candlelit procession at Easter. One of its bells was cast in Goa in 1608 and today they ring out to the Portuguese-Eurasian community.

Right next to the Sultan's Well at the foot of Bukit China stands **Sam Po Kong Temple▶**, dedicated to the Chinese admiral, Cheng Ho, who first sailed to Melaka in 1403. The temple's name derives from a fish, the *sam po*, which allegedly saved the admiral's ship from sinking by deftly inserting itself into a hole in the keel.

Located on the same "Street of Harmony" (Jalan Tokong) as the Masjid Kampung Kling and the Cheng Hoon Teng Temple, the **Sri Poyyatha Moorthi Vinayagar Temple▶▶** is one of the earliest Hindu temples in Malaysia, having been built in 1781. Brilliantly colored with a deep Mediterranean-blue interior and a mint-green facade, its simple vaulted construction is devoted to the god Vinayagar (better known as Ganesh).

Fitting testimony to over 150 years of Dutch presence, the unmistakable **Stadthuys▶▶▶** is a red-bricked masterpiece of masonry and woodwork that dates from the 1650s, when it housed the Dutch governors. Today it houses a rich enthnographic and history museum, the most interesting exhibits being on the ground floor. Wander along the airy verandas, through rooms filled with sturdy Dutch-style (but made in Melaka) furniture, beneath an original floral ceiling and over polished parquet floors, taking in the displays of Chinese, Japanese, and Nyonya porcelain, weapons, wedding ceremonies, jewelry, costumes, and agricultural tools. Upstairs look out for a superb bronze head of a Siamese Buddha found on St. John's Hill—yet another relic from Melaka's past.

Ayer Keroh nature belt
North of the airport and 7 miles from town is a huge area set aside for back-to-nature activities. The recreational forest offers 160 acres of jungle, complete with trails, labeled trees, picnic spots, cabins, and campsites. Nearby Melaka Zoo is highly rated for its open and natural setting, while Ayer Keroh Lake provides all sorts of boating activities. Those itching for a swing of the golf club should head for the superbly sited 18-hole golf course at the Ayer Keroh Country Club, while others may prefer to spot the flashes of brilliant color in the giant Butterfly Park and Museum.

The Stadhuys once housed Melaka's Dutch governors

►► **Merlimau** *111B2*

This small town (15 miles south of Melaka on the coastal road to Muar) boasts two historic sights. The first, situated just beyond the town, is the **Merlimau Penghulu's House**, a brilliantly colorful and ornate example of a chieftain's house. It was built in 1894 and still belongs to the village headman. Vividly patterned tiles face the steps leading to the veranda where wooden eaves and balustrades are intricately carved and pillars clad in more glazed tiles. The veranda has alcoves containing blue and white couches overlooked by antler-horn hat racks.

Back in town you can visit **Tun Teja's Mausoleum**, yet another reminder of Melaka's turbulent past. Escorted by the famous warrior Hang Tuah to Melaka in order to marry Sultan Mahmud Shah, Tun Teja arrived too late. By then the Portuguese were besieging the town and she died at Merlimau while retreating with the sultan.

A fascinating example of local decorative traditions in the Merlimau Penghulu's House

143

► **Mimaland** *111C1*

Said to possess the largest swimming-pool in Southeast Asia, Mimaland (11 miles north of KL) is a favorite playground for the capital's juvenile population. Located in a jungle setting, its facilities center on outdoor activities from boating to fishing, swimming, and pony riding. The children's amusement center has a small zoo, model dinosaurs and a miniature rubber plantation. Chalet and stilt-house accommodations on the lake are available, but avoid weekends when you will not be alone on those lush jungle trails.

►► **Mini-Malaysia** *111B2*

This complex of architectural styles from the 13 Malaysian states represents an increasingly popular concept in Southeast Asia. Each traditionally crafted house gives an insight into the customs of a different state, whether they be wedding ceremonies, typical games, or religious festivities. Life-size mannequins display regional costumes and various cultural shows are staged in the open air. You can choose to stay overnight in a hotel or chalets in the grounds if you enjoy this kind of artificial environment.

The Melakan home
The small state of Melaka is rich in examples of traditional Malay stilt houses, set against idyllic rural scenes of coconut groves and rice paddies. The Melakan style makes use of decorative steps and multiple pillars—which can number up to 16—holding the house about 6 ft. above the ground. The purpose of the stilts was for ventilation and also to keep wild beasts at bay, and the space below was often used to shelter domestic animals such as goats and chickens. The carved timbers creating the open veranda, long shutters, and eaves are generally taken from tropical trees such as cengal, merati, or damar laut. Chinese influence is evident in the floral motifs of the tiled steps. The Melaka–Muar road is particularly good for spotting these traditional homes.

Hero's tomb

The shrine to Sheikh Ahmad Majnun in Pengkalan Kempas is permanently open and accessible through a gate next to the Chinese cemetery. A sandstone pillar is inscribed with his exploits (not all commendable; one of his deeds was traitorous) and below is a mysterious circular hole. Legend has it that the hole will tighten around the arm of any liar who dares test it.

Boats to the island of Pulau Besar leave from Melaka's Umbai Jetty

 Muar *111B2*

Johor's second largest town lies 26 miles south of Melaka on an estuary, and is a sleepy, laid-back place with few tourists. Its outskirts are steeped in Malay culture and here you can experience the haunting rhythms of *ghazal* music, *silat* (the Malay martial art), or the *Kuda Kepang*, a hobbyhorse trance dance which originated locally. Decorative model horses are *the* Muar souvenir, along with the excellent local coffee. The center is a familiar combination of Chinese shophouses and some grand Victorian buildings; it also has the Masjid Jamek, an ornate mosque built by Sultan Ibrahim.

▶ **Pedas Hot Springs** *111C1*

These thermal springs are situated 10 miles south of Seremban on the road to Tampin. Changing rooms are available for prospective bathers and a restaurant serves local Negeri Sembilan specialties.

▶ **Pelabohan Klang** *111C1*

See Klang, page 128.

▶▶ **Pengkalan Kempas** *111B1*

A group of carved stone monuments collectively known as Kermamat Sungai Udang (Shrine on Prawn River) is located 22 miles southeast of Port Dickson just outside the village of Pengkalan Kempas. Negeri Sembilan boasts many more of these monoliths, often used as shrines (*keramat*) by villagers who believe they have the power to grow. Usually grouped in pairs, they probably mark the graves of ancient warriors or chiefs. The three granite stones at Pengkalan Kempas are known as the Sword, the Spoon, and the Rudder because of their respective shapes. They stand about 6ft. high and are inscribed with Arabic script. Although they are presumed to date from a pre-Islamic pagan culture, they stand guard over the tomb of Sheikh Ahmad Majnun, a Muslim hero who died in 1467 saving the life of a princess (see side panel).

▶ Port Dickson 111C1

A popular seaside destination for KL weekenders and day-trippers, Port Dickson (59 miles south of the capital) was developed as a port in the late 19th century. Since then an Esso oil refinery has sprung up, but the port remains a small, relaxed place, although a little worn at the edges. There are 11 miles of sandy white beach stretching from there to Tanjung Tuan (see page 165), and numerous hotels, boat clubs, and windsurfing and water-skiing centers line the shore, particularly concentrated at Blue Lagoon Beach. Rent a boat from any large hotel and make for the offshore islands where the water is likely to be cleaner, or go just beyond Tanjung Tuan to **Pasir Panjang**, a bird-watching forest reserve.

Port Dickson is popular with locals seeking sun and sand

▶ Pulau Angsa 111D1

Not easily accessible and therefore not an obvious tourist destination, Pulau Angsa lies off the coast of Kuala Selangor, 42 miles from KL. This peaceful little island has one rest-house for those who really want to get away from it all. No ferry services exist, but fishing boats can easily be chartered from the charming fishing village at Kuala Selangor.

▶▶▶ Pulau Besar 111B2

A mere 2 miles off the coast of Melaka lies the captivating island of Pulau Besar (meaning "Large Island" and not to be confused with two others of the same name off the east coast). The 400 acres of unspoilt natural beauty highlighted by history and legends make it a great escape from the mainland. Once an anchorage point for ships sailing from China or the Middle East, Pulau Besar was one of five islets identified as landmarks by Chinese navigators of the Ming Dynasty. A number of *keramat* (sacred graves) are found there, but true hedonists will concentrate on the swimming, fishing, and snorkeling possibilities. More than RM17.5 million (US$7 million) has recently been poured into developing a large beach resort; its effect on the island remains to be seen. For details on access to the island, see side panel.

Boats to Pulau Besar
A 45-minute boat ride by regular service from Umbai Jetty (5 miles south of Melaka) takes you to the island. Alternatively, take the new catamaran service direct from Melaka.

■ Rife with demons, superstitions and *semangat*, or spirits, which inhabit every valley and river, Malaysia has a rich tradition of legends that capture the dreamy soul of the Malays. Naive and imaginative blends of fiction and reality imbue islands, mountains, and lakes with complex tales, enriching the landscape with mythical characters, creatures and events .....■

146

Coconut days
The enormous coconuts found in the Indian Ocean are regarded by Malays as bringing good luck. They are believed to come from fairyland or Pau Jinggeh (the Navel of the Sea), where they grow on a tree guarded by two dragons. The dragons feed on the fruit, but when they overdo it and have fits of indigestion the fruit finds its way across the ocean to the Malay archipelago.

Coconuts—fruit of legends

The rich oral tradition of the Malays grew out of long evenings spent in isolation from other villages without the modern diversions of television, video parlors, and karaoke lounges. Even today you may find your taxi driver happily recounting the dark past of the countryside through which he is driving.

Island tales The myriad and spectacularly beautiful islands of Malaysia are fertile breeding grounds for legends. **Pulau Tioman** is said to be the embodiment of a Chinese princess who, flying through the skies to Singapore, stopped at this spot and loved it so much that she promptly transformed herself into the island so that she could remain there forever.

More tragic is the legend of **Pulau Pangkor**. A Sumatran warrior fell desperately in love with a beautiful princess and sailed off to battle to win her heart. After long months he had still not returned and the princess set off in search of him, eventually reaching Pangkor where she learned that he had died in battle and was buried on the island. On being taken to the grave, she reacted with true heroic passion and threw herself from a cliff on to the rocks below. **Pantai Puteri Dewi** (Beach of the Lovely Princess) is today one of Pangkor's most popular beaches.

Pulau Langkawi and neighboring **Pulau Dayang Bunting** also have tragic princesses. The glowing white sands of the beaches are said to have been created by the innocent white blood of Mahsuri, a princess wrongfully executed for alleged adultery. As she was dying she laid a curse on the island, predicting that it would not prosper for seven generations. Her tomb, a much visited shrine in the center of the island, gives the date of her death as 1819, thus the desolate period of the curse is now over.

Langkawi's other princess is associated with the magnificent freshwater lake, Tasik Dayang Bunting (Lake of the Pregnant Maiden) on Pulau Dayang Bunting. Refused permission to marry her warrior-lover, a Kedah princess retreated to the lake where she became pregnant after drinking its water. On discovering this, the Sultan of Kedah banished her permanently to the lake,

where in deep depression she drowned herself. She was then transformed into a rock while the child she had borne became a white crocodile. Today the lake is said to possess magical qualities for any barren woman who drinks from it.

More credible is the legend of the **Padang Matsirat** (Field of Burnt Rice) which, not long after Mahsuri's death, was set fire to by villagers in the face of invading Siamese. Today, locals claim that blackened rice can still be seen in the sand, especially after heavy rains.

Mountain legends The demanding qualities of the guardian princess of **Gunung Ledang** are well known (see side panel on page 124), but less familiar is the moving tale of **Gunung Santubong** in Sarawak. On its summit lived the daughter of the moon, who for years observed the pure and peerless life of a certain Haji Hassan living in the valley. Her friendship with him developed into love and marriage, but Hassan soon tired of their blissful mountaintop existence, yearning instead for the fun and lights of Kuching.

With his wife's consent he set off for a month's visit, but the spell of the big city proved so strong that he forgot his wife longing for him on the mountain. When he did remember and reascended the summit it was too late: she had disappeared. Desolate, he searched every other mountain year after year until he died of a broken heart. When the peak is bathed in moonlight today, villagers imagine that the daughter of the moon is revisiting her old home.

Malay demons
"What Malays fear from the dead are their thoughts, their passions, their accomplishments which have finally been liberated and exist in themselves, everything a destiny bequeaths to fate.—But what is frightening about all that?—Perhaps it's intuition, at the base of every religion, of the implication of all these things: every desire is non-wisdom; every thought, lack of consciousness; every action, absence of rest." From: *Malaisie*, by Henri Fauconnier (1930).

147

Pulau Tioman is reputed to be a princess in disguise

Boat to Langkawi's Gua Cerita (Cave of Tales)

Pulau Dayang Bunting

Pulau Dayang Bunting sits immediately south of Kuah and is a favorite destination for its Tasik Dayang Bunting, or Lake of the Pregnant Maiden (see pages 146–147). This exquisite freshwater lake is surrounded by towering limestone cliffs and dense jungle. To the north of the lake is Gua Langsir (the Cave of the Banshee). Its reputation for being haunted probably derives from the squeaking of thousands of bats which flit around its gloomy depths.

Getting around Langkawi

The best way to explore the main island is by renting a four-wheel drive or motorbike from agencies in Kuah or at the main beach resorts. There is also an island bus service and taxis are plentiful (at a price). Snorkeling and diving trips to outlying islands are easily arranged from Pantai Cenang and Pantai Tengah.

▶ ▬▬ **Pulau Carey**   *111C1*

Owned by a private company, Carey Island is in fact one big rubber and oil-palm plantation. It is also home to the Mah Meri tribe, famous for their wood carvings of spirits and idols which are sold to visitors at their settlement. Access to the island is either by boat from Pelabohan Klang or across a bridge reached from the Klang–Banting road. Permits to visit the island must be obtained prior to crossing.

▶▶ ▬▬ **Pulau Ketam**   *111C1*

Rickety wooden stilt houses shrouded by palm-trees line the shores of Pulau Ketam (meaning Crab Island), the northernmost of a cluster lying off Selangor's coast at Pelabohan Klang. Picturesque and mainly inhabited by fishermen, Pulau Ketam attracts day-trippers for its abundant seafood restaurants—fresh crabs being an obvious specialty. The sampan crossing takes about one hour.

▶▶▶ **Pulau Langkawi**   *110D1*

Not one but 104 islands make up the archipelago known as Langkawi, and only three of these are inhabited. Floating in the emerald waters of the Andaman Sea and virtually drifting into Thai waters, Langkawi is by accessible air and by boat services from Phuket (Thailand) and Pinang.

The main town of **Kuah** holds little interest; it consists of one rather tacky street full of duty-free shops and is best avoided. Instead, find a seafront food stand and enjoy the bewitching views over the southern islands before setting off to explore (see panel).

Inland sights A wealth of legends and extraordinary tales (see pages 146–147) give Langkawi's main sights an aura of mystery that only enhances their natural beauty. **Makam Mahsuri** is the main pilgrimage spot and lies in the shadow of the island's central limestone peak, Gunung Raya, surrounded by luminous-green paddy fields. Cradled by hibiscus bushes, a white marble tomb pays homage to Princess Mahsuri, a legendary damsel whose blood flowed white when she was stabbed for a crime she didn't commit, leaving the island with its pale powdery sands but also with a curse. Behind the tomb is a reconstructed traditional Kedah house where musicians hold modest performances.

Although celebrated in local legends, the **Padang Matsirat** (Field of Burnt Rice; see pages 146–147) is just another paddy field and hardly worth making a detour to see, but its location spirits you along the main road joining the northern beaches with the west coast resorts. Northwest of Pantai Kok, **Telaga Tujuh** (Seven Wells) cascades 300 ft. down a rock face which rises dramatically out of surrounding forest at the end of a rough track. The steep walk to the top is a hot one, but views are spectacular and the water is refreshingly cool—much appreciated by local teenagers. Hotter water bubbles out of the ground at **Telaga Ayer Hangat** in the northeast, but these

Pulau Singa Besar
Bored with all those turquoise waters and polychromatic fish? Then head for Pulau Singa Besar, a small island just south of Pantai Tengah which has been transformed into a wildlife sanctuary. Monkeys, mouse deer, iguanas, peacocks, and other birds have taken over there, and a visit to the park bird blinds and observation tower combines pleasantly with...more snorkeling! Pulau Singa Besar has some of the best underwater life of the Langkawi islands and the surrounding sea has been declared a marine reserve.

Pulau Langkawi

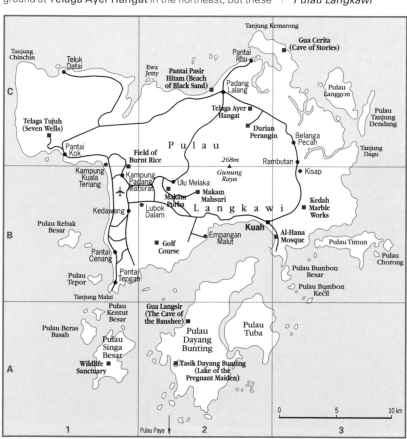

KUALA PERLIS-LANGKAWI FERRY SERVICE SDN. BHD.
加 央 港 口 渡 舞 交 怡 客 船 運輸有限公司
4, Dindong Kuah, 07000 Pulau Langkawi, Kedah. Tel: 04-788272 & 04-788316. Fax: 04-789190
Booking Office: 04-788950, 04-789618, 04-789688 (L'kawi); 04-754494 (K/Perlis);
04-788950, 04-789688 (L'kawi); 04- (Penang)
04-725201 (K/Kedah); 04-

PULAU LANGKAWI ▶ PULAU PINANG

SELESA EKSPRES

DEWASA/ADULT **$35.00** (Ekonomi)

N° 10015   Seat No.: 52   Tempat Duduk:

Date

150

What else in Langkawi?
Round-island boat trips make a good introduction to the main sights of Langkawi Island and island-hopping trips usually take in the main four outlying islands to the south. Pulau Bumbon Besar (10 minutes from Kuah hetty) offers only limited accommodations but has some good beaches.

Jungle-trekking can be organized up the forested slopes of Gunung Raya (2,887 ft.) and golf is available at the 18-hole Langkawi Golf Club, about 3 miles west of Kuah.

Snorkeling is the obvious way to spend the day

hot springs are hardly an essential destination. A cultural theme park, the Ayer Hangat Village, has recently opened there, incorporating a park, pavilions, a bazaar, a theater restaurant, a village spa, and cultural performances.

Beaches The main concentration of budget and luxury hotels, all of which have good beach facilities, is along **Pantai Cenang** and **Pantai Tengah** on the southwestern tip of the main island. However, the sea there can be murky; for a clearer water's edge try the pretty shores of **Pantai Kok** (northwest of the airport), which abounds in beach chalets and one resort. On the north coast the first sight of the beautiful cove of **Pantai Rhu** is marred by a monstrous modern hotel. However, a cluster of towering stone outcrops on the horizon and seafood stands in the shade of casuarina trees on the beach more than compensate for this, while the coral reefs should keep most people's attention firmly under water. **Pantai Pasir Hitam,** midway along the north coast, is famed for its streaked black sand, while a few small beaches dot the lonely coastal road which ends at the beautifully landscaped Datai Bay Golf Club. By 1994 guests at the resort will actually be able to sleep over the water, as an ambitious 150-room floating hotel will be anchored off Langkawi's coast.

▶▶ **Pulau Lumut**   *111C1*
Although not for determined swimmers or divers, this small island offers a relaxed vision of typical Malay *kampung* life in an unspoiled setting. Regular ferries from Pelabohan Klang take one hour.

▶▶▶ **Pulau Pangkor**   *110B1*
On weekends and during public holidays half Perak's inhabitants make a beeline for Pangkor, only 30 minutes

by ferry from Lumut (53 miles southwest of Ipoh). But if you go there on a weekday you may have a beach all to yourself. The island's generous 18 sq miles include lush mountainous jungle peopled by monkeys and mouse deer. Charming Malay *kampungs* arc sheltered by coconut palms, and there is an active fishing port and a tantalizing choice of white beaches. For a taste of history you can visit the ruins of a Dutch fort at **Teluk Gedong** in the southeast corner. The fort was constructed in 1670 to fend off pirates and local Malays.

One main road encircles the island's east, north, and west coasts, while another cuts across the center from the ferry pier in Pangkor village to the main west coast beach, the crescent-shaped **Pasir Bogak**. Most of the accommodations—from simple beach huts to comfortable small hotels—are situated at Pasir Bogak, Pangkor's main west coast beach. The island's best beaches and coves run north of there, ending at **Teluk Belanga** (Golden Sands Beach), the site of a large resort. Rent a bicycle or motorbike and head for **Coral Bay** (its emerald-green waters are the clearest of the island), or make a midnight outing to **Teluk Ketapang** and wait for the turtles to come ashore and lay their eggs (this happens from May to July, but sightings are becoming increasingly rare). Opposite Pasir Bogak lies the private island of **Pulau Pangkor Laut**.

►► Pulau Paya   110D1

About one hour by boat from Kuala Kedah, the spectacular marine park of Pulau Paya's four islands awaits underwater enthusiasts. Reputed to have the largest number of coral species in Malaysia, the stunningly beautiful soft coral garden also harbors a wealth of tropical fish. There are no accommodations on the islands but picnic and bathroom facilities have been set up for day-trippers, many of whom make a three-hour boat trip from Langkawi.

Pangkor's main village – a change from the superb seascapes

Pangkor history
The name of Pangkor is engraved in every Malaysian schoolchild's memory as it was there that the famous Treaty of Pangkor was signed in 1874, giving the British entry into the Malay Peninsula for the first time. This was during the first tin boom and the British, firmly established in their Straits Settlements, were afraid that Perak's profits could fall into another nation's hands. As a result, a new governor, Andrew Clarke, was sent to use a bit of gentle persuasion. In January 1874, while anchored off Pangkor Island, he signed a treaty with local Malay chiefs which settled the dispute over the Perak throne and at the same time set up a British Resident. The state of Selangor soon followed this example and British influence gradually spread through the peninsula.

▶ ▶ ▶   **Pulau Pinang** 110C1

The "Island of the Betel Nut" is, with Melaka, one of Malaysia's great historical destinations. However, Pinang (once spelt Penang) can also offer the visitor good beaches, fascinating traces of an ever-burgeoning Chinese population and an unspoiled rolling interior of jungles and friendly villages where you can really escape from the packaged crowds. Despite decades of promotion as a tourist resort, Pinang continues to stimulate, intrigue, and relax visitors.

History With a population of 1 million—composed of Chinese, Malays, Indians, Eurasians, and Arabs, as well as a smattering of Western expatriates—Pinang owes its historical interest to George Town, where the honorable Sir Francis Light first stepped ashore in 1786 on behalf of the East India Company. By 1808, a few years after his death, British law had been imposed, but in the 1830s the rapid rise of Singapore's status put the brakes on Pinang's thriving port supremacy. Tin and rubber exports came to the rescue and numerous palatial residences scattered over the island are evidence of the tremendous wealth the Chinese magnates enjoyed at the turn of the century. Today, this community is still very much in financial control, and enterprise continues to flourish throughout the island.

Orientation Along the north coast to the west of George Town stretches Pinang's main concentration of hotels and hideous condominiums. These eyesores line the road past the main tourist beach, Batu Feringgi, merging into the rapidly developing Teluk Bahang. South of there, along and inland from the west coast, is an unspoiled rural area rising to the jungly Mount Elvira, which dominates the center of the island.

The south is relatively untouched and barely even punctuated by villages, but hit the east coast beyond the airport and you enter a semi-industrial landscape massed around the entrance to Pinang's stupendous 8½ mile bridge and sprawling back to George Town. It is possible to zip around the island on a motorbike in a day, although this leaves

Members of Pinang's Chinese community prepare for another festival

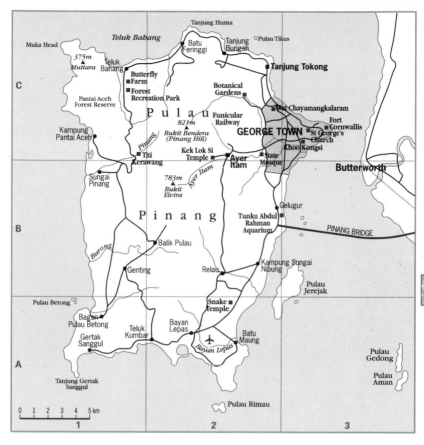

Pulau Pinang

little time for sightseeing and certainly none for sun-worshipping. Pinang is also the cheapest place in Malaysia to rent a car—so make good use of it.

Sights in George Town Lively, compact and by no means a museum town, George Town offers a central grid of picturesque streets lined with faded yet ornately crafted Chinese shophouses, atmospheric old hotels, coffee shops, antique shops, markets, landmark temples, a "Little India," and plenty of street life with an occasional opium den thrown in. To the north, around the Padang, stand monuments to the colonial era, and to the east the town ends abruptly at Pengkalan Weld (Weld Quay) where the stilt-houses and jetties of the Clan Piers topple over the waterfront. On the way to Tanjung Bungah and Batu Feringgi to the northwest, the road follows the coast past "Millionaires' Row"—a once genteel district of palatial Chinese and colonial mansions—while to the south the unmistakable modern KOMTAR (Kompleks Tun Abdul Razak) tower announces the limits of downtown George Town. Easily explored by trishaw or on foot—the ubiquitous "five-foot way" arcades provide shelter from sun or rain—Pinang's capital offers a fascinating synthesis of Malay-Chinese lifestyle which merits at least a couple of days' sightseeing.

This venerable monument in Lebuh Farquhar is Pinang's "Raffles," built in 1885 by the same enterprising Armenian brothers, the Sarkies. Its guests have included Somerset Maugham, Rudyard Kipling, Noel Coward, and Douglas Fairbanks, and the gloomy, wood-paneled bar conjures up this star-studded past. The adjoining ballroom has seen better days, but renovation has spruced up the domed entrance and may spread further.

Descriptions of essential Pinang sights follow alphabetically over the next six pages.

Surrounded by the laundry and plants of a discreet residential square, the **Acheen Street Mosque**▶ (Lebuh Acheh) is George Town's main Malay mosque. It was built in 1808 from funds donated by a local Achinese tycoon of Arab descent.

Pinang's first Catholic mass was held at the **Cathedral of the Assumption**▶ (Lebuh Farquhar) in 1861. Its twin spires end the stretch of 19th-century buildings which dominate George Town's northeast corner.

Saved *in extremis* from the bulldozers, the superb **Cheong Fatt Tze Mansion**▶▶ (Lebuh Leith) is one of only three buildings of this style existing outside China. Built in the 1880s by a Hakka millionaire, it blends traditional Chinese features with western elements such as stained-glass windows. It was recently restored and currently houses an antique collection but may become a hotel—check with the tourist office to see if it is still open.

A magnificent example of 19th-century colonial architecture, the imposing white colonnaded **City Hall**▶▶ dominates the western end of the Padang.

Presented to Pinang by a wealthy Chinese merchant in 1897 in honor of Queen Victoria's Diamond Jubilee, the

elegant **Clock Tower▶** (Lebuh Light) measures 60 ft. high, 1 ft. for every year of her reign. For reasons of diplomacy, it also sports Moorish arches.

Not much remains today of the former British Army headquarters at **Fort Cornwallis▶**, except the ramparts with a few cannons pointing diligently out to sea. Built with convict labor in 1810, it was named after a Governor-General of India.

Pinang's oldest mosque, **Kapitan Kling Mosque▶▶** (Lebuh Pitt), was originally built in the late 18th century for the Indian Muslim settlers, but today's construction is a fairly sober 1916 replacement in Anglo-Indian style.

One of the finest clan houses in Southeast Asia, **Khoo Kongsi▶▶▶** (Cannon Square, off Lebuh Cannon) is tucked away in a courtyard at the bottom of Lebuh Pitt. Standing opposite is a Chinese opera stage and to one side is the clan house adminstrative headquarters where passes are issued to visitors. Intricate carvings made by master craftsmen from China cover every surface and the interior ceiling is richly gilded. Red and gold dominates the central shrine, which is dedicated to the Khoo clan's patron saint, while huge brass incense burners, inlaid ebony furniture and wall-paintings rising into the gloom all add to the sumptuous display.

Clans and triads
Although the Khoo clan house is the best known in Pinang, several other less ornate clan houses exist; along Jalan Burma alone stand the Khaw Kongsi, the modern Lee Kongsi and the combined Chuah, Sin, and Quah clan house. Ancestral worship was accepted by Confucius as its system ensured not only welfare assistance but also the all-important respectable funeral—an obstacle-free path to heaven. Distinct from secret societies and triads, clan membership is restricted to those bearing the same surname—the eternal race—and the clan houses themselves were built as combined temples and meeting places for clan members. However, in the 19th-century Pinang clans and triads became intermingled when one of the Khoo Kongsi's founders established himself as a powerful Hokkien leader. In 1867 rivalries between the Hokkien and Cantonese finally erupted into a vicious gang war over the control of opium and revenue farming, seriously challenging British power. Triad activities were subsequently quashed, and in 1890 secret societies were abolished.

155

Exuberance and refinement at the Khoo Kongsi clan house

Millionaires' Row
The astonishing Northam Road (now Jalan Sultan Ahmad Shah) is Malaysia's longest surviving residential suburb, a forerunner to KL's Jalan Ampang. Many of the luxurious seaside villas changed from European to Chinese hands at the turn of the century. Blending Georgian neo-Palladian styles with features of Indian bungalows and Malay houses, the villas have a style of their own—the "George Town Garden House." European decorative details include pediments, columns, porches, French louvered windows, elaborate fan-lights, stuccowork, and Carrara marble. The houses made a fittingly luxurious setting for the Chinese merchant million-aires—at least until the 1930s Depression brought a crashing end to their fortunes. Sadly, some have already disappeared in the wake of developments and many of the remaining villas are now festooned with commercial signs—one miniature *palazzo* is even a used-car lot.

The **Kuan Yin Teng Temple►►►** (Lebuh Pitt), dedicated to the goddess of mercy, was built around 1800 by the Hokkien and Cantonese communities and is Pinang's oldest. The winged, tiled roof is dominated by two guardian dragons and the facade is intricately carved. Try to visit it on the auspicious 19th day of the second, sixth, or ninth moons when incense thickens the air, and oil, flower and food offerings are placed on the altar.

Originally the Penang Free School, the gracious 1821 building housing the small **Penang Museum and Art Gallery►►►** (Lebuh Farquhar) is devoted to the colorful history of Pinang and is well worth seeing. The refrigerated History Room displays old engravings, paintings, and documents explaining the background of many of Pinang's monuments, some of which have sadly disappeared. Old street signs, school desks, water boilers, and music boxes fill a corridor leading to the

A towering pagoda dominates the vast complex of the Kek Lok Si Temple in Ayer Hitam

extravagant Chinese Hall. Here are displays of superb embroideries, inlaid furniture, calligraphy, porcelain, a Nyonya bridal chamber and the striking paraphernalia of Chinese festivals. The upstairs is used as an art gallery for temporary exhibitions.

Next door is the elegant Anglican **St. George's Church►►** (Lebuh Farquhar), which dates from 1818—making it the oldest such church in Southeast Asia. Shaded by the original graceful angsana trees, the neoclassical forms are perfectly proportioned—a tribute to the skill of the convict laborers who erected the church.

The modestly scaled Hindu **Sri Mariamman Temple►** (Lebuh Queen) was built in 1883 and an elaborate *gopuram* (pyramidal gateway) marks its entrance. Its main focal point is a statue of the god Lord Muruga (Subramaniam), studded with precious stones and surrounded by offerings. Time your visit for the morning or early evening as it may be closed at other times.

Reclining in colorful majesty northwest of the center is a 105-ft. Buddha (dubiously claimed to be the third tallest in the world), housed in the gigantic meditation hall of **Wat Chayamangkalaram►►** (Lorong Burmah), part of a Thai Buddhist monastery. Massive mythical Naga serpents twist up the balustrades at the entrance to the hall, supposedly linking heaven and hell. Monks in saffron robes pad around the hall and numerous other Buddha statues populate the interior. Across the road looms a Burmese Buddhist temple guarded by stone elephants.

Beyond George Town About 6 miles west of George Town beyond the spaceship-style State Mosque is the builtup area of **Ayer Itam** (take Bus MPPP 1). Access to Pinang Hill is from here, but its focal point is the **Kek Lok Si Temple►►►**, an extraordinary Buddhist temple complex ascending the forested slopes between housing blocks. Overlooked by a giant statue of Guan Yin (the goddess of mercy), Pinang's answer to Rio's Corcovado, the temple pagoda is a bizarre amalgam of Chinese, Thai, and Burmese styles. It crowns a labyrinthine network of colorful halls, shrines, gardens, and courtyards, as well as the main monastery which was founded by an immigrant Chinese Buddhist in 1890. The main entrance is through a shadowy, winding arcade lined with souvenir stands that peddle Chinese and Malay trinkets. Looming over the **Ayer Itam Dam** (2 miles from here) is Pinang's largest Hindu site, the **Nattukotai Chettiar Temple** (Waterfall Road), which comes alive during the festival of Thaipusam.

Continued on page 159.

157

Buddhist statue at Wat Chayamangkalaram

■ **In a country that is on the verge of joining the other economic "tigers" of Asia, the feudal sultans are an anachronism, yet they still possess an important degree of sovereignty in their respective states. However, times are changing and many find their thrones wobbling under them after decades of abusing privileges and misappropriating government funds. How long will they last? .....■**

Riches galore
Recent public revelations show that Malaysia's sultans own four times as many polo ponies as Malaysia Airlines owns airplanes (64 aircraft in 1992). Pahang's sultan, one of the wealthiest, owns more than a dozen palaces, a Boeing 727 and 200 polo ponies kept in air-conditioned stables. He has also been granted 36,222 acres of prime timber concessions over five years worth M$260 million (US$103 million).

Pomp and ceremony Nine states of Malaysia have hereditary sultans, some with family trees going back several centuries and still much revered by their Malay subjects. Perlis, Kedah, Perak, Kelantan, Terengganu, Pahang, Selangor, Negeri Sembilan, and Johor relish in the pomp and ceremony, cavalcades of Rolls-Royces (or Lamborghinis and Porsches), polo ponies, palaces, private jets, and sporting exploits of their hero-monarchs who are also titular heads of Islam.

Arrogance and rebellion Historically, Malay sultans were a rebellious lot, invading and plotting against each other inside and outside the palaces. The British attempted to limit their powers after World War II, but local opposition was so great that when Independence came in 1957 a rotating system was devised to elect one of the nine sultans every five years as a constitutional monarch—the Yang di-Pertuan Agung.

The king's consent is necessary for any religious act or parliamentary bill that affects the honor of the sultan. For 35 years the federal government complied with this, even increasing royal influence by granting massive land and logging rights and showering the sultans with hand-outs. However, many Malays feel that enough is enough, and as the nation moves toward its new industrialized status the sultans appear to be losing much ground.

Selangor's sultan and his retinue, 1901

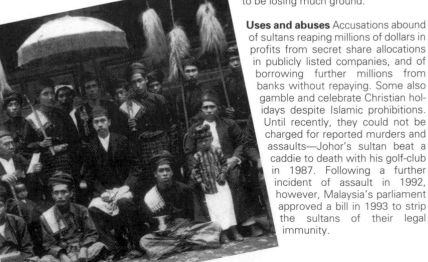

Uses and abuses Accusations abound of sultans reaping millions of dollars in profits from secret share allocations in publicly listed companies, and of borrowing further millions from banks without repaying. Some also gamble and celebrate Christian holidays despite Islamic prohibitions. Until recently, they could not be charged for reported murders and assaults—Johor's sultan beat a caddie to death with his golf-club in 1987. Following a further incident of assault in 1992, however, Malaysia's parliament approved a bill in 1993 to strip the sultans of their legal immunity.

Continued from page 157.

Standing at the crossroads of the southwestern corner of the island, the small town of **Balik Pulau**►► (meaning "back of the island") is a charming blend of peeling Chinese shophouses and outlying Malay *kampung* houses wreathed in bougainvillea. Known as Pinang's durian capital, its daily market is also worth a visit for a bowl of delicious local *laksa* (rice-noodle soup).

Pinang's main tourist resort of **Batu Feringgi**►► (8 miles west of George Town) is hard to avoid. Although the beach-front is now built up with large hotels ranging from the luxury Rasa Sayang to the somewhat older (and evocatively named) Lone Pine Hotel, the strip remains a pleasant, anarchistic jumble of small restaurants, tailors, souvenir shops, moneychangers, and car- and bike-rental agencies, all backed by hilly jungle. Sophistication is to be found inside the luxury hotels—try the Rasa Sayang's superbly landscaped garden restaurant or the Borsalino nightclub at the Park Royal. Water sports run rampant the length of the beach, trips can be made to offshore islands, and a favorite evening promenade takes in hawkers and souvenir stands.

The 74 acres of the tranquil and lush **Botanical Gardens**►► (take Bus MPPP 7) lie a mere 5 miles northwest of George Town, and present a tropical barrage against a confusing network of roads. Cascading down from Pinang Hill is a fabulous waterfall, which has become a popular spot for local children, and which also gives the gardens its alternative name of Waterfall Gardens. Footpaths, bridges, pavilions, and carefully labeled tropical trees are reminders of the British obsession with nature, immaculately tended here since 1844 when Charles Curtis laid out the gardens. Unforgettable are the troops of common leaf monkeys, which rip around the trees and which descend to persecute anyone who has a bag of peanuts.

Impeccable **kampung** *houses dot southern Pinang*

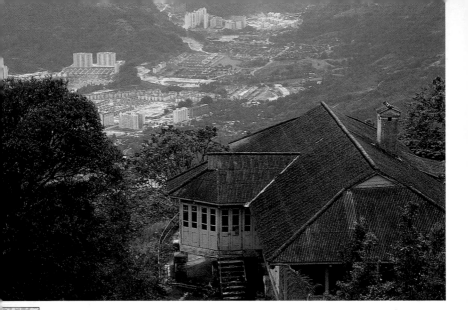

Views from the top of Pinang Hill (Bukit Bendera) take in badly regulated island development

Off the tourist trail

The Protestant cemetery where Sir Francis Light is buried is located at the western end of Lebuh Farquhar. Mildewed gravestones of European settlers draped in vegetation and shaded by fragrant frangipani trees make this one of Pinang's more evocative sights.

Beyond Lebuh Pantai (Beach Road) are the Clan Piers. Boatmen and fishermen, grouped together by clan, have been living in these thatched wooden stilt houses since the 1880s.

For a fabulous panorama of the island from **Pinang Hill▶▶▶** (Bus MPPP 1 to Kek Lok Si Temple, then Bus MPPP 8), take the 30-minute ride on the Swiss-style funicular which grinds up 2,720 ft. through dense jungle and bamboo groves to the summit. Within a few years of his arrival, Light had built a trail to the top to grow strawberries, but visitors had to arrive by sedan-chair or horseback before the miraculous funicular railway was completed in 1923. Sights include graceful colonial buildings and an aviary garden, which is home to a number of regional birds. Visit the summit just before sunset to see George Town coming alight, but avoid weekends and holidays. Trains run from 6:30 A.M. until 9:30 P.M., or the energetic can follow a path from the Botanical Gardens.

On the industrialized airport road 9 miles south of George Town stands the overrated **Snake Temple▶** (take the yellow Bus 66). Also called the Temple of Azure Cloud, it is dedicated to Chor Soo Kong, a Taoist deity whose black statue sits in the main shrine. However, this is not the main object of today's temple, as holy (and live) serpentine manifestations of the deity have multiplied since its construction in 1850. Allegedly appearing mysteriously, the snakes (Wagler's pit vipers) now curl lazily around altars, shrines, and candlesticks, pleasantly drugged by the thick clouds of incense. Photographers are on hand if you want a snake-draped portrait of yourself.

The north coast road reaches the less developed beaches of **Teluk Bahang▶▶** (take Bus 93 to Tanjung Bungah, then Bus 94), culminating in a pretty fishing village fronted by a restaurant appropriately named "End of the World." Boat trips or hill treks can be arranged here to the less accessible northwestern beaches. Inland, on the road leading south, are four major tourist stops: a batik factory, orchid gardens, a butterfly farm, and a forest recreation park.

▶▶ **Seremban** *111C1*

The capital of Negeri Sembilan lies 41 miles south of KL. It is also the capital of Minangkabau architecture, a sweeping buffalo-horn roof style that originated in Sumatra and spread via Melaka to the fertile valleys beyond. Seremban itself has few major sights but its attractive commercial center is a typical century-old mixture of colorful two-story Chinese shophouses and relaxed Malaysian lifestyle. There are also some excellent restaurants.

Colonial relics are few, but the magnificence of the 1912 **State Library** makes up for this. Its neoclassical grandeur resembles an English stately home and it occupies a prominent spot above the **Taman Tasek** (Lake Gardens), to the east of the center. Near by is the unmistakably modern **State Mosque** whose nine pillars symbolize Negeri Sembilan's nine states. Opposite the library stands the **Istana Hinggap** (State Palace), and from there the lush, manicured slopes of the gardens descend to two lakes. On weekends cultural shows are performed on a stage over one of the lakes and a small bird park draws bird lovers, but otherwise this bucolic enclave attracts the usual range of joggers, picnickers, and *tai chi* enthusiasts.

Seremban's main attraction is the **Taman Seni Budaya**▶▶ (Cultural Complex; closed on Thursday afternoons and Friday), which is situated about a mile from town at the junction with the KL highway. The steep winged roofs and elevated latticed wooden walls of the main museum building are a modern remake of the Minangkabau style. The garden contains two outstanding examples of Malay nailless architecture which were dismantled and moved to this site: the **Rumah Contoh Minangkabau** and the **Istana Ampang Tinggi**. The former was built for a Malay prince in 1898 and features a wooden shingled roof and intricately carved pillars, while the latter (dating from 1861) has an *attap* roof and interior carved wooden friezes. Displays include weapons, silver objects, and brassware, all guarded by the British and Malay cannons that loom outside.

Minangkabau inheritance
Apart from their distinctive architecture, echoed in many modern buildings in this area, the Minangkabau settlers also brought with them a matrilineal system in which inheritance passes through the female rather than male line. Negeri Sembilan is unique in Malaysia in its adherence to this system. To see more typical buffalo-horn architecture head east towards Kuala Pilah and Sri Menanti (see page 181); the roadside is dotted with old and new houses reflecting this style. This is also a beautifully undulating scenic route (see Drive on page 167).

161

The former State Secretariat now functions as the elegant State Library

Symbol of Malaysia's fast-developing status, Shah Alam's mosque spikes the skyline of the future

A great escape
Nature lovers from KL also head to Shah Alam for the Taman Pertanian Agricultural Park at Bukit Cahaya north of the town. The 3,180-acre area is still under development but a jungle canopy walk is already in place, as are name-tagged trees and extensive demonstrations of local agriculture.

► Shah Alam 111C1

City of the future, Shah Alam (about 15 miles west of KL) is the new state capital of Selangor. Crisscrossed by highways, spaciously laid out around man-made lakes, and encircled by industrial zones, it is a strangely under-populated place boasting lavish modern landmarks but no life. The number one monument is the unbelievable **State Mosque** (also known as the Sultan Salahuddin Abdul Shah Mosque), a spectacular mirage of a soaring blue and white dome and minarets which rise out of formal gardens. Completed in 1988, the mosque claims to be Southeast Asia's largest and can accommodate 20,000 worshippers. Visitors have to be properly attired, but non-Muslims cannot enter on Fridays and weekend hours are restricted to 5 P.M.–6:30 P.M.

The few locals you will encounter in this concrete wasteland probably come from the bustling campus of the Institut Teknologi MARA, but the museum, cultural center and library (all located near the mosque) are starting to attract visitors from farther afield.

► Sungkai Deer Farm 111D1

This 250-acre park (about 50 miles south of Ipoh) lies almost at the Perak–Selangor border, and is devoted to the breeding and conservation of deer. Situated in Menderang, Sungkai, the project was established in 1978 and today accommodates over 100 deer, which wander freely through natural surroundings. A small sanctuary for exotic birds completes the rural attractions. For more information call the Department of Wildlife at Sungkai (tel: 05 486368).

■ **Whether a neat little mound in the center of your plate or the fluorescent-green expanses of maturing paddy stretching across much of Peninsular Malaysia's northern states, rice is as common in Malaysia as it is throughout the rest of Asia. Kedah and Perlis lead the way in terms of production, but the hills of Negeri Sembilan, Sabah, and, to a lesser extent, Sarawak, all have extensive areas under rice cultivation .....■**

Every marketplace displays a vast selection of grains, ranging in hue from shiny white polished rice through grays, pinks, oranges, and browns to black wild rice from the dry rice fields of the hills. Ironically, tastes are turning to long-grain white rice, a specialty not only of the peninsula but also of Thailand and China, and in Sabah this now has to be imported to cope with demand.

Dry rice cultivation The first rice plants introduced into Malaysia were probably the so-called "dry rice" varieties—hill rice grown on dry land but not necessarily on slopes. Six months of hard labor, from the felling and burning of the forest to the pounding and winnowing of rice grains after harvest, will supply a family with enough rice for a year.

Dry rice cultivation is, however, accompanied by three problems: small birds called munias relish the grains and can wipe out an entire crop; with repeated planting the soil loses its fertility and new areas have to be opened up; and as weeds grow easily in the tropical climate, cultivation becomes progressively more difficult.

The latter two problems have been solved by shifting cultivation to new areas, clearing patches of secondary forest, burning the wood, and, after harvesting three months or so later, abandoning the field. However, this practice of shifting cultivation leaves a patchwork of regrowth on the slopes, and it can take up to 80 years before the land eventually regains its mature forest species.

Wet rice cultivation This variety is grown in water-filled fields beside rivers wherever the soil is fertile and the ground reasonably flat. This solves the weed problem associated with dry rice, although it introduces the risk of flooding.

The extensive coastal flatlands of Kedah and Perlis have formed Malaysia's rice bowl ever since wet rice was introduced to the Bujang Valley by Hindu Indians as early as the 7th century. Fertile hill areas are also cultivated in the high valleys around Tambunan, Ranau, and Bareo in Sabah, after being terraced and irrigated by diverting streams.

Pros and cons
Often used as a counter-argument by local officials fighting a rearguard action against ecology groups, the slash and burn technique used by Borneo's Dayaks for rice cultivation need not in fact weaken the soil. If specific factors are taken into consideration (choice of soil, type of rice, how much to slash, and when to burn), the land cleared for rice crops can be left fallow for two years before being cultivated again. In some parts of Borneo such methods have been practiced for over a century, with no apparent negative consequences.

The rice harvest is still celebrated throughout Malaysia

Taiping's avenue of rain trees echoes its status as the wettest city in the country

Taiping firsts
In contrast to its present low-key profile, Taiping proudly claims a string of Malaysian "firsts." Apart from the first museum and first prison, Malaysia's first railroad station (now closed) was built here in 1885 to transport the precious tin ore to Port Weld (today named Kuala Sepetang). The first English school opened in Taiping in 1878 and the first English newspaper in the Malay states, the *Perak Pioneer*, began publication here in 1894.

▶▶▶ **Taiping**   *110B1*

Another major relic of Perak's tin-mining boom, Taiping was once a tumultuous shanty town rife with secret society feuds. The city was renamed by the British in 1874 to calm triad members' hot tempers and thus became the town of "everlasting peace." In 1935 it lost its status of state capital to Ipoh, 30 miles or so southeast. Still a predominantly Chinese town, the city boasts the justifiably renowned Lake Gardens, Malaysia's oldest hill resort on Bukit Larut (see page 122), the oldest museum, and a town center combining colonial buildings with Chinese shophouses and recent concrete apparitions. ▶

Pride of place goes to the extensive **Lake Gardens**▶▶, which embrace the site of an old tin mine northeast of the town. They were landscaped in the 1890s and now accommodate a zoo, a nine-hole golf course, numerous islands connected by colorful bridges, a superb avenue canopy of rain trees and countless joggers. Despite constant attention, the lake was recently found to contain three estuarine crocodiles—a sign that Malaysia's wilds are never far away. The stately town hall and government offices occupy one corner of the gardens, while on a hillock looms the curious-looking government rest house, a bizarre amalgam of 1960s concrete and the Doric columns of a demolished British Resident's home. An Allied war cemetery adjoins the gardens and Malaysia's oldest prison lies a little farther north.

Immediately to the west of the golf course stands the impressive **Perak Museum**. Popular with children for its natural history section, the museum also concentrates on the history of tin mining and has some interesting displays of weapons, ornaments and Orang Asli implements. The whimsical architecture of the building dates from 1883 and the entrance statue of a colonial hero is another reminder of the early days. The town center has a number of temples and mosques, including Perak's oldest Chinese temple, the Ling Nam, and a colorful Hindu temple in Station Street.

▶▶▶ Taman Alam-Kuala Selangor Nature Park
111D1

Immediately south of Kuala Selangor town, a turn off the main road leads to the entrance of this 720-acre coastal nature reserve, home to more than 130 species of birds as well as armies of silver leaf monkeys. Six nature trails have been laid out through the park (walks last from half an hour to 2½ hours), some taking in a rope bridge and others leading to bird blinds, watchtowers, or a plank-walk through the mangrove forest. Accommodations in simple chalets are available near the visitors' center, which also provides information—and rents binoculars!

▶▶ Tambun Springs and Caves
110B2

Less than 6 miles northeast of Ipoh at the base of a craggy limestone outcrop are the hot springs of Tambun (*open*: 3 P.M.–midnight) where saunas and resting-rooms have been set up. The Tambun Caves, of great historical significance, are located a few miles back toward Ipoh just outside Tambun itself. At the end of a dirt track lies a cave that displays rock-paintings that are thought to be neolithic. Discovered by accident in 1959, these pictograms are rare evidence of the early inhabitants of the Malay peninsula, and are comparable to others in India and northern Australia.

▶▶ Tanjung Bidara
111B1

Some of the best swimming on the Selat Melaka and certainly the most convenient clean beach for Melaka town lie 22 miles to the north. There are plenty of Malay food stalls and a beach resort offers numerous water-sports facilities as well as reasonably priced accommodations.

▶▶▶ Tanjung Tuan (Cape Rachado)
111B1

Overlooking the border between the states of Negeri Sembilan and Melaka, the lighthouse crowning the promontory of Cape Rachado has beamed out across the strait to Sumatra since 1860. It marks the end of an 11-mile stretch of beach running south from Port Dickson, and much of the cape is now a forest reserve.

More Perak springs and cave paintings

Those wanting to experience more natural hot springs can have a field day in Perak: try Sungkai, Pengkalan Hulu, Kampung Ulu Slim, Slim River, Kampung Air Panas in Gerik, or Manong in Kuala Kangsar.

The Lenggong Valley (north of Kuala Kangsar) is turning out to be something of an epicenter for more Orang Asli cave drawings. Kampung Kota Tampan Ayer has revealed evidence of civilization more than 30,000 years ago, while in the limestone caves of Gua Badak, recently resurfaced charcoal cave drawings point to the artistic leanings of the Negrito tribe. Matchstick men, tree-climbing monkeys, hunting parties, tigers, and monitor lizards are among the images that the Negritos sketched perhaps only 150 years ago, although the tribe dates back to the Stone Age.

165

Tambun Hot Springs are a favorite with day-trippers from Ipoh

WEST COAST

Malay animal superstitions
Despite 2,000 years of exposure to Hindu and Muslim ideas, the Malays still attribute vital forces to nature. These animist beliefs are disappearing today, but animals still figure strongly in complex superstitions and omens upheld by village medicine men. Evil forces are believed to emanate from bodies, not only of murdered men but also of slain deer, wild pigs, dogs, certain reptiles, and unusually colored cockerels. The arrival of certain animals in a garden forbodes calamity—thus rhinoceroses, dogs, and deer are treated with due respect. Butterflies, bees, hawks, or woodpeckers alighting on a roof, frogs, monkeys, snakes, and geckos invading a house, a tortoise under a floor, fungus in a kitchen, or two coconuts on a stem all awake fears of poverty, divorce, disease, or death. But the recital of a specific verse from the Koran will, of course, transform these curses into riches, health, and happiness!

Teluk Intan,
Malaysia's Pisa

▶ **Teluk Batik** *110A1*

Teluk Batik (4 miles south of Lumut) is the launch pad for Pulau Pangkor and is the next best thing for those who don't make it across the water. The pleasant palm-fringed shore is popular with campers, picnickers, and, above all, with Malaysian Navy employees from Lumut.

▶ **Teluk Intan** *110A1*

This charming old town, something of a backwater hugging the winding estuary of the lazy Perak river, lies between KL and Ipoh. Once a major outlet for tin from the Kinta Valley, its pride and joy is the leaning tower, a pagoda-like watertower that was built in 1885 by a wealthy Chinese tin magnate who knew nothing of Pisa.

▶ **Templer Park** *111C1*

Just off the Ipoh road and 13 miles from the center of KL is a vast area of partly controlled jungle reserve initiated by and named after Sir Gerald Templer, the last British High Commissioner. About 3,000 acres of land are crossed by paths which wind past waterfalls and streams with natural swimming lagoons. Fishing, picnic areas, and a handful of food stalls are overlooked by two limestone outcrops which rise to 1,000 ft. and contain an explorable network of caves. The surrounding jungle forms a habitat for monkeys and a wide variety of butterflies.

The only place you will see a giraffe is at the zoo

▶ **Zoo Negara**

The national zoo (8 miles east of KL toward Ulu Kelang) covers a generous 150 acres, encompassing ponds and streams in a natural forest setting. Fenced enclosures are home to a good cross-section of Malaysia's wildlife, including tigers, honey-bears, tapirs, wild buffaloes, crocodiles, and mouse deer, and there are two interesting sections devoted to primates and snakes. Children can enjoy rides on camels, elephants, and donkeys or, more conventionally, the zoo train. There are also shows featuring parrots, orangutans, elephants, and sea lions. (*Open:* daily 9 A.M.–5 P.M.)

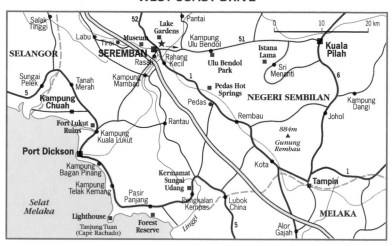

WEST COAST DRIVE

𝒟𝓇𝒾𝓋𝑒 Through Minangkabau country and along the coast

This full day's drive takes you across rolling hills through the heart of rural Minangkabau country, past a royal town and then back to the coast where not only beaches but also pagan stones, a historic lighthouse, and fort lie in wait.

From Seremban, take the Kuala Pilah road (No 51), which winds upward rapidly into spectacular forested hills. Stop at **Ulu Bendol Park** (11 miles east), thick with rivers, waterfalls, and jungle trails. Continue east through this rural region of Minangkabau-style architecture, then turn right along a plunging road toward the pretty royal town of **Sri Menanti**, set peacefully in a verdant valley. Visit the palace museum before continuing to the small town of **Kuala Pilah**, lined with picturesque old shophouses.

Double back slightly but continue to Johol through more mountainous twists to reach Kota and then Lubok China. Just outside the village of Pengkalan Kempas look at a group of carved pagan stones, Kermamat Sungai Udang— typical examples of the region's monoliths.

Continue to the coast past the mud-flats of **Pasir Panjang**, a haven for bird watchers. A short distance on is **Tanjung Tuan** (Cape Rachado) and its old lighthouse, the start of a 10-mile stretch of beach with views across the Selat Melaka to Sumatra. The resort town of **Port Dickson** marks the northern point where a direct road leads back to **Seremban**, providing as a last distraction a turnoff to the atmospheric ruins of **Fort Lukut**.

Sri Menanti's old royal palace now houses the Royal Museum

Jitra
Kuala Nerang
Alor Setar
KEDAH
Bukit Mudin Besar 1081m
Pendang
Guar Chempedak
Gurun
Pengkalan Hulu
Gunung Hulu Titi Basah 1533m
Kampung Pengkalan Kubor
Wat Phothivihan
Tumpat
Pantai Cinta Berahi
Pasir Mas
Kota Bharu
Kampung Laut
Pulau Perhentian Kecil
Pulau Perhentian Besar
Rantau Panjang
Tanah Merah
Kampung Pangkat Kalong
Pantai Dalam Rhu
Kuala Besut
Jertih
Pulau Redang
Sedong
Bujang Valley
Sungai Ketil
Petani
Baling
Jeli
Kampung Nibong
Dabong
Pasir Puteh
Kampung Setiu Lama
Kampung Kuala
Kampung Penarik
Butterworth
Kulim
Bukit Mertajam
Gerik
Kuala Krai
Kampung Merang
Kampung Sungai Air Deras
Nibung Tebal
Gunung Bintang 1862m
Tasik Temengor
Gunung Lawit 1519m
Parit Buntar
PERAK
KELANTAN
TERENGGANU
Kuala Kurau
Lenggong
Kampung Kota Tampan Ayer
Nenggiri
Tasik Kenering
Tasik Kenyir
Kuala Berang
Sekayu Waterfalls
Taiping
Maxwell Hill 1448m
Bt Larut
Sungai Siput
Gunung Tasik (Perak Tong)
Ipoh
Tambun Springs & Caves
Gua Musang
898m
Gunung Ayam
Kuala Kangsar
Kuala Gula Forest Reserve
Pasir Pinji
Gunung Rapat
Sam Poh Tong Temple
Berincang
Taman Negara
2187m
(National Park)
Pantai Remis
Ayer Tawar
Batu Gajah
Kellie's Castle
Tanah Rata
Ringlet
Cameron Highlands
Gunung Tahan
Kuala Tahan
Kampar
Lata Iskandar
2075m
Kenong Rimba Park
Pulau Pangkor
Lumut
Gunung Berembun
Tapah
Bidor
Pulau Sembilan
Pasir Salak
Kampung Ulu Slim
Kuala Lipis
Kampung Tembeling
Gunung Tapis Nature Park
1512m
Teluk Intan
Sungkai
Terolak
Slim River
Kampung Sega
Kampung Sega
PAHANG
Sungai Lembing
Sabak
Simpang Empat Rungkup
Simpang Empat
Fraser's Hill
Kampung Sungai Ruan
Jerantut
Kampung Sekinchan
Tanjung Malim
Bukit Fraser
Raub
SELANGOR
Batang Berjuntai
Genting Highlands
Gunung Ulu Kali 1772m
Kuala Kubu Baharu
Bentung
Mentekab
Temerluh
Kelau
641m
Tasik Cini
Maran
Kuala Selangor
Rawang
Orang Asli Museum
Taman Alam
Templer Park
Mimaland
Zoo Negara
Kapar
Batu Caves
KUALA LUMPUR
Teriang
Tasik Bera
Pulau Angsa
Ampang
Pulau Ketam
Shah Alam
Petaling Jaya
Serdang
Pelabohan Klang
Klang
Kajang
Semenyih
Pertang
Ayer Hitam
Rompin
Selat Melaka
Jenjarom
Pulau Carey
Banting
Montin
Seremban
Kuala Pilah
Bahau
Rompin
Muar
Tanjung Sepat
Pedas Hot Springs
Sri Menanti
NEGERI
Kerinan
Kampung Chuah
Port Dickson
Rembau
SEMBILAN
Gemas
Segamat

0 20 40 60 km

The central region Cutting down the length of Peninsular Malaysia's mountainous backbone, the central region takes in northern Perak, southern Kelantan, a good chunk of Pahang and a slice of northern Negeri Sembilan. This sparsely populated region of dense rain forest shades into hill and montane forest at higher altitudes; at each stage it presents a rich and undisturbed diversity of tropical flora and fauna. No visitor to the Malay Peninsula should miss seeing this often monotonous but always beautiful landscape, a far cry from the historical urban developments of the west coast or the placid coastal *kampungs* and islands of the east. Whether starting from the structured jungle resort of the Taman Negara, the colonial comforts of the hill stations or a primitive lakeside treehouse, trekking is the sole means of entering such a forbidding environment and getting a closeup on its incredible biodiversity. And while you trek along rivers or through thick jungle you will doubtless encounter semi-nomadic Orang Asli tribespeople, the last of Malaysia's aborigines, who have inhabited this region for 8,000 years and who have imbued mountain, river, and lake with fascinating legends.

Rain forest Older than the Amazonian and central African rain forests, the Malaysian rain forest somehow managed to escape both great droughts and the Ice Age. And thus its plant and animal life had a reasonable stretch of eternity in which to develop a complex symbiotic web of relationships. Unique flora and fauna are found here, and nowhere else in the world is there such a diverse concentration. For this reason ecotourism is taking off in a big way, offering specalized guides and activities radiating from well-structured bases.

Primary rain forest proper is found between sea level and 2,700 ft. As one ascends, it evolves from humid dipterocarp to hill forest, and accommodates hundreds of bird and animal species, thousands of plant species and tens of thousands of insect species.

The Malay Peninsula's mountainous backbone peaks at just over 7,000 ft.

CENTRAL REGION

Founded in the 1930s, developed in the 1960s but only blossoming in the 1990s, the **Taman Negara** is the largest of Malaysia's national parks and until recently all tourism was concentrated at the official park headquarters in Kuala Tahan, a three-hour boat ride from Tembeling. However, independent operators are creeping into this vast tract of land and more reasonably priced adventure treks can be organized from smaller camps near Kuala Tahan, from Kuala Lipis, or from Merapoh. Otherwise, you can experience a taste of the jungle on a day-trip to one of the numerous forest recreation parks that dot the center. If you are intent on east coast sun and sea, you can get an unforgettable glimpse of this vast 130-million-year-old forest from the jungle railway, which runs up the spine of the peninsula.

Hill stations Mostly relics of the British colonial era, the hill stations were once essential retreats for perspiring white-skinned officials and planters worn out by coastal humidity, heat, and alcohol. **Pinang Hill** and **Bukit Larut** are classified in the west coast section (see pages 160 and 122), but intrepid explorers of the central region can take high-altitude breaks at the **Cameron Highlands** and at **Bukit Fraser** for trekking, golf, or bird watching, or can indulge in a quick round of baccarat at the gambling Mecca of the **Genting Highlands**.

Surrounding these comfortable bases is the sparser, more scenic vegetation of montane forest that cloaks the hills in oaks, chestnuts, conifers, and a bewildering variety of tree ferns, pitcher plants, and epiphytes. Bird watchers have a field day as eagles, hawks, and brightly colored mountain birds are far more active at this 5,000 ft. level that at lower altitudes. Old colonial bungalows still offer accommodations more appropriate to an English country inn (in "Ye Olde Smokehouse" style), while large modern blocks and more atmospheric Chinese hotels inevitably crop up as well.

Monkey trouble
These highly active creatures are often completely fearless and can easily be observed. The early-morning howls of the white-handed gibbon are common throughout the rain forest, and it is hard to mistake its long-armed, immaculate black and white form heaving through the tree tops. The long-tailed macaque is ubiquitous throughout Malaysia, recognizable by its long curling tail, inquisitive look, and quick twitching movements. In the rain forest, however, you are more likely to see pigtailed macaques scampering across a trail.

170

Ye Olde Smokehouse at Tanah Rata in the Cameron Highlands

Lakeside retreats Riddled with rivers, waterfalls, and lakes, the central region is as much a water lover's paradise as the coastal beaches. Locals from every town have their favorite bucolic picnicking spot at the base of torrential cascades, but less well known and less accessible are the small resorts growing up around some of the lakes. These wide, peaceful expanses make excellent bases for trekking, swimming, canoeing, or fishing expeditions through the surrounding jungle. The sparsely populated area around **Tasik Bera** lies in a remote part of the south. The lake itself has become virtually choked by a wild plant and can only be crossed in a canoe via an intricate maze of passageways.

Better known due to its own legendary version of the Loch Ness monster, **Tasik Cini** is more geared up to visitors—although for the moment it remains pleasantly low-key. The lake boasting most facilities is Tasik Kenyir (covered in the east coast section, see page 216), but little can beat the dramatic sites of **Tasik Temengor** and **Tasik Chenderoh** in the desolate north.

The wild north The few visitors who venture into this sparsely inhabited region may never pass another car for many miles, let alone a *kampung*. Logging and hydro-electric power from the three enormous reservoir lakes are the only source of income, albeit sizable. The newly built **east–west highway**, which cuts across the mountains from Gerik to Kota Bharu on the east coast indicates just how important these power plants are to the local economy. For certain stretches this remarkable feat of engineering offers a lofty vantage point over the rain-forest canopy, affording a view of otherwise invisible treetop orchids and perhaps a glimpse of the tracks of a herd of elephants.

Orang Asli encampments and clearings abound in the area around Gerik. These semi-nomadic tribespeople, mainly Negritos, are considered to be the oldest of Malaysia's aborigines. They are the least integrated and least numerous of the peninsula's three Orang Asli races. You may spot a cigarette-smoking hunter wearing sneakers and carrying a blowpipe along the road—last symbol of this people's limbo status.

Taman Negara provides excellent opportunities for viewing Malaysia's wildlife

Spirits of the forest
The original animist beliefs of Malaysia still linger on, and every tree, plant, animal, and insect of the jungle embodies a superstition or taboo. All classes of objects (from boats to humans) possess external visible souls, mostly living beings that are heard or seen in the jungle. Thus the soul of rattan is embodied in stick-insects, that of the camphor tree in a cicada, that of rice in a grasshopper, that of a large boat in a snake, that of the coconut palm in a bird, and that of man in a firefly.

CENTRAL REGION

The mysterious Mr Fraser
The name Fraser's Hill comes from a certain Louis James Fraser, a solitary English adventurer who was the only person to inhabit this lonely region in the late 19th century. The hill station itself, however, came into being when two English clergymen staggered up a steep path from the Gap in 1917 to arrive at the beautiful yet uninhabited spot. Quick to recognize its potential as a highland resort, they recommended its development and in 1919 work started on the road from the Gap.

▶▶▶ **Bukit Fraser**   168B2

Not easily accessible, the hill station of Bukit Fraser (Fraser's Hill) lies 63 miles northeast of KL in a series of seven hills rising to 5,000 ft. A twice-daily bus service (8 A.M. and noon) runs from Kuala Kubu Bahru, but the last 5 miles of steep winding road are only open on a one-way basis, operating for uphill traffic every "odd" hour and for downhill traffic every "even" hour until sunset, when it is open both ways. The control gate is situated at the Gap near the wonderfully aging government rest-house. Bukit Fraser itself is a typical small township dating back to the 1920s, surrounded by gray-stone bungalows, lawns, and neat gardens. It has a **Ye Olde Smokehouse** hotel, a golf course (nine holes), jungle with prolific ferns and a waterfall (the **Jeriau Waterfall**), flower nurseries, cream teas, bird watching, and pony rides, all in a more compact and generally more tranquil setting than the Cameron Highlands. Drivers beware: there is no gas station at Bukit Fraser.

▶▶▶ **Cameron Highlands**   168C2

Strawberries? Cream teas? Mock-Tudor bungalows? Rose gardens? Average daily temperatures of 70°F? Can this really be equatorial Malaysia? As you drive up 35 miles of severely tortuous road from the west coast highway you enter the hilly backbone of the peninsula. Only wildlife and Orang Asli lived here when a certain William Cameron stumbled upon the place in 1885. In his words he had found a landscape "with gentle slopes and *pamah* [plateau] land with rounded hills shut in all round by loftier ranges." However, it was not until 1925 that development started on a colonial hill resort, tea plantations, and a golf course.

Three main centers are scattered alo this serpentine route, which hovers about 5,000 ft. above sea level: Ringlet, Tanah Rata and Berincang. Then the road terminates abruptly at a succession of peaks rising to over 6,500 ft. Berincang is earmarked to become a highlands crossroad when new roads are built connecting the area to Kelantan and the west coast highway, but for the moment sole access is via Tapah. Those who arrive by public transportation from Tapah can get around the highlands by bus, taxi, or on foot, and long-distance buses from Tanah Rata travel direct to west and east coast destinations.

First stop Misty mornings, clouds drifting over the valley toward a muddy lake, flower nurseries, and strawberry and orange farms are the main features of the town of **Ringlet**, which starts at the 28 mile mark. If you are not staying at the superb Lakehouse, a mock-Tudor hotel overlooking the reservoir a few kilometers out of Ringlet, keep going another 8 miles to Tanah Rata.

Local pottery in the Cameron Highlands

Resort destination The main tourist center of the Cameron Highlands, Tanah Rata▶▶, strongly resembles an out-of-season ski-resort. Strung along the main road are numerous cheap Chinese hotels, tea shops, and Indian restaurants, while a series of more upscale hotels and holiday apartments lines the flanks of an 18-hole golf course at the northern end. The most famous of these is **Ye Olde Smokehouse**, a large mock-Tudor house nestling in an English rose garden and fronted by a bright red British telephone box. As befits the changed times, the owner is now Malaysian-Chinese and the manager is Indian, but this hardly affects the anachronistic English country-home atmosphere with its log fire, ships' lanterns, porcelain, and gently ticking grandfather clock.

End of the line More wild bends lead onward and upward to the last township, Berincang▶, home to a predominantly Chinese community of vegetable farmers. The huge **Sam Poh Temple** on the outskirts is the primary place of worship. Terraced over the high valley, Berincang's main focus is the central square; there even the food stalls boast *trompe l'oeil* Tudor beams. A plethora of small hotels and cheap Chinese restaurants as well as the inevitable karaoke lounge provide the town's distractions.

Continued on page 175.

Walks
Tanah Rata is well organized as a trekking center, and jungle walks and mountain climbs from here can last from half an hour to three or more hours. Sketch maps with numbered trails are available at the information center and at most hotels, but watch out for slippery rocks and unclear trails, and don't be tempted to make detours as the jungle is deceptively dense. Both the Parit Falls and Robinson Falls are an easy one hour's walk from Tanah Rata, and sights here include clouds of fabulous butterflies.

173

Tea pickers' houses are scattered over the plantations

Tea plantations

■ **The Cameron Highlands, the only place in Malaysia to grow tea, offer undulating slopes densely planted with tea bushes. A refreshing change from the jungle, the carefully tended plantations represent the British colonials' obsession with a good cup of tea—a tradition that has been firmly adopted by the Malaysians. .....■**

Tea classifications
Of the two main categories of tea, highland and lowland, the latter recognized as having a higher quality. Different processing produces three types of tea within this category: black tea, green tea, and oolong tea. The first is a fully fermented tea (commonly known as English tea), while green tea is unfermented and undergoes steaming and firing after plucking. All Japanese teas fall into this latter category. The third type, oolong, is a semi-fermented tea, withered in the sun, lightly rolled, and then fired. Most Chinese teas are of this type.

Descendants of the original Indian tea pickers

Tea arrived in the Cameron Highlands in 1929 when John Archibald Russell and his business associate, a tea planter from Ceylon, founded Malaysia's first hill country estate, the Boh Tea Estate. Today supplies are no longer carried up the slopes on the heads of coolies, but the estates of the highlands still provide a spectacular expanse of this labor-intensive product. Rolling green hills cut with graphic rows of tea plants create graded ridges against the horizon and swarm with tea pickers. Bushes are planted every week (they can live for up to 100 years) and Indian tea pickers, bent under the weight of giant baskets, whip through the rows to pluck up to 450 pounds a day.

Processing After transportation to the factory, the green leaf is spread in perforated troughs powerfully ventilated by hot air to reduce the moisture content by 50 percent. The withered leaf is then transferred to rolling machines, which twist and break the leaf to expose its juices for fermentation. This process takes place when the broken leaf is spread on to trays or conveyor belts so that the enzymes are oxidized. Finally, the leaf is fed into machines and dried at high 250°F temperatures, reducing the moisture content to a mere 3 percent. The tea leaf then assumes its familiar crisp, black form. Sorting and grading are carried out by vibrating sieves before the tea is left to mature for three months. Packing is the final task and is still carried out manually.

Varieties More than 3,000 teas exist in the world, usually named after their district of origin, but the specialty of the Cameron Highlands is Assam, a fully fermented black tea from northern India. The largest estate, Boh, produces 8.2 million pounds a year—roughly equivalent to 5 million cups of tea a day—and has three plantations, the main one being accessible from Habu, just north of Ringlet. Both the Blue Valley Tea Estate and Sungei Palas lie along turnoffs from the Gunung Berincang road.

Continued from page 173.

To the summit About 6 miles farther north, past the region's main vegetable market, is a superb **Butterfly Garden** where more than 300 colorful species flutter around a large net enclosure; watch for the brilliant green and black wings of the Rajah Brooke, the king of highland butterflies and a species that normally favors waterfalls. Stick insects, giant spiders, and scorpions also creep around there. You can recover from any visual shocks in the basement of the souvenir shop, a well-designed traditional Chinese tea house. Six more miles of increasingly narrow, steep road take you past a rose garden and more tea estates to the 6,651-ft. peak of **Gunung Berincang►►►**. Spectacular views are guaranteed, even when they are filtered by drifting cloud (rain falls throughout the year, but the rainy season climaxes from April to May and from September to November).

Vividly patterned butterflies add splashes of color to the unrelentingly green landscape

► **Genting Highlands** *168B2*

Definitely reserved for gambling addicts, Genting (Chinese for "on top of the clouds") is a massive development lying within easy reach of KL off the Kuantan highway. As the road winds through gently undulating jungle, the resort rises abruptly from the horizon like a concrete apparition. Malaysia's only casino flashes its neon lights invitingly at the capital and draws many a busload of Singaporeans eager to unload (or preferably multiply) their gains.

Developed in the 1970s, the casino resort has become wildly popular and attracts 2 million visitors annually—despite signs reminding true *Bumiputras* ("sons of the soil") that gambling is forbidden by Islam. Modern hotels, an artificial boating lake, a children's miniature railway, a cable car, a Chinese temple, and a golf course all cater for families, and in 1994 the gigantic SamaWorld theme park will open its doors. However, the star attractions remain the spinning roulette wheels and traditional Chinese games of chance like *keno* or *tai sai*, all attracting gamblers right through the night on weekends and until 4 A.M. during the week.

Highland vegetables
Apart from orchids, tea, and roses, the relatively cool climate of the Cameron Highlands makes it a fertile vegetable growing area. If heading for the Butterfly Garden or Gunung Berincang, stop off at the vegetable market near Kea Farm Village which displays an amazing variety of cabbages, *bok choy* (Chinese white cabbages), capsicums, sweet peas, spinach, carrots, cauliflowers, radishes, runner beans, celery, and broccoli.

The Orang Asli Negritos are thought to have been the original nomadic inhabitants of West Malaysia; most now live in settlements

Jungle railway
An experience not to be missed is the 12-hour jungle railway trip, which cuts up the spine of the peninsula from Singapore to Tumpat on the Thai border. A first-class ticket provides the distinctly surreal experience of sitting in refrigerated comfort and watching the inescapable high-volume video, while on either side endless tropical jungle, red-ocher earth, rivers, and *kampungs* flow by. Services provided on this jungle railway include "conveyance of documents, motorcycles, flowers, vegetables and chicks" (*sic*), a rather limited buffet service and...delays. The Timuran Express runs on Tuesday, Thursday, and Saturday from Singapore and on Wednesday, Friday, and Sunday from Tumpat.

▶ **Gerik** *168D1*

At the start of the impressive east–west highway, which cuts through spectacular scenery parallel to the Thai border before hitting the east coast, Gerik has grown from a modest logging town to a thriving halfway stage. There is nothing of interest in town but it makes a good stopover while exploring this wild, often remote region. Orang Asli settlements pepper the surroundings, and to the east lies the huge Tasik Temengor reservoir (see page 184) with an island containing the Banding fishing resort and rest-house. The building of the east–west highway was hindered as much by the harsh jungle terrain and monsoons as by attacks from the communist guerrillas who hid out here, and an army presence is still very noticeable in the area.

▶ **Gua Musang** *168C2*

Lying on the edge of the great Taman Negara about 115 miles south of Kota Bharu, Gua Musang is another big logging center. Towered over by a limestone outcrop, the small town makes a good center for exploring caves, trekking (including a climb of the 2,939-ft. Gunung Ayam, once home to a legendary Kelantan queen) or making a riverboat safari.

▶ **Jerantut** *168B3*

Jerantut, situated halfway between Kuala Lumpur and Kuantan (each roughly three hours by road) offers little aside from a change of transport on the way to the Taman Negara. It is also on the main jungle railway line. Most life there centers on the bus station and market, where a number of cheap hotels and restaurants are clustered. Buses leave for Kampung Kuala Tembeling to connect with the boats going upriver to Kuala Tahan, the Taman Negara headquarters; the latter leave at 9 A.M. and 2 P.M., and buses leave 45 minutes earlier. If you have time to kill, visit the nearby limestone caves of **Kota Gelanggi** which echo with the squeaking sounds bats, or the immense **Bird Cave** a little further on at Jungkat. Both will require taxis.

▶ **Kampung Kota Tampan Ayer** *168C1*

This small town in the Lenggong Valley on the edge of the beautiful Tasik Chenderoh (about 22 miles north of Kuala Kangsar) is turning into an archaeological focal point. Before recent discoveries were made there, it was believed that prehistoric Malaysian man originated in the Niah Caves area in Sarawak. The center of interest in Kampung Kota Tampan Ayer is a stone workshop believed to be more than 30,000 years old and containing thousands of pieces of stone equipment. A skeleton uncovered in nearby Lenggong in 1991 is believed to be more than 10,000 years old.

▶▶ **Kampung Ulu Bendol** *168A2*

Covering the forested slopes of the modest 2,700-ft. Gunung Angsi, the Ulu Bendol Forest Recreation Park (11 miles east of Seremban) is a popular destination for local weekend picnickers. Jungle trails pass below a canopy of lush vegetation and some lead along a fast-flowing river to a waterfall. The pool at its base attracts crowds of splashing children and families, but if you trek upward and onward humanity is replaced by monitor lizards, forest birds, and monkeys. Although far from the wilds of other central peninsula forest reserves, it makes a good introduction to the rich rain-forest flora and fauna. A large campsite is situated beside the rushing stream; avoid weekends and school holidays.

▶▶ **Kuala Lipis** *168B2*

Once a seat of government for the whole of Pahang, Kuala Lipis is a charming little town with some fine neo-classical colonial architecture on a hilltop overlooking the center. Characteristic old shophouses line its main street. Another pretty area lies along the river where houses on stilts are built out into the water; the lake is particularly fruitful for fishing enthusiasts. For swimming and rock climbing through unspoilt nature, head for the nearby **Kenung Rimba Park** (see side panel).

Kenung Rimba Park
Numerous jungle treks through the park are organized from Kuala Lipis by local guides; some will bring you into contact with Orang Asli. No trip will be easy going as the terrain is tricky, so be prepared. Quickest access is by sampan from Sungai Jelai jetty (next to the railroad station), a 20-minute ride to Tanjung Kiara. Otherwise, a scenic river trip takes two or three hours. Tours of the caves in the park and jungle trekking can be arranged by Tuah Travel (tel: 09 313277), but make sure you check the validity of guides with other travelers as conflicting reports abound.

The mosque at Kuala Lipis, one of the entry points to the Taman Negara

■ Once the domain of tigers and seladang, wild buffaloes that would trample incautious hunters to death, the dense central rain forest of Peninsular Malaysia remains intact above all in the National Park—Taman Negara. This overwhelmingly stimulating natural world peopled by chattering monkeys, strident insects, and more melodious birds is one of the peninsula's highlights, and as tourist facilities are booming even less intrepid nature addicts have little excuse not to visit. .....■

Above: Serious trekkers set off for the jungle wilderness

The dense rain forest that cloaks the central peninsula is 130 million years old and is considered to be the oldest in the world, beating even that of the Amazon. The Taman Negara (National Park) covers an astonishing 1,670 sq miles (over six times the size of Singapore) and offers numerous possibilities for exploring its wilds. Don't believe, however, that you are immediately plunging into unexplored and untouched jungle; the headquarters setup at Kuala Tahan has become increasingly sophisticated and popular, serving every possible need. If you really want to get the flavor of virgin rain forest, you should therefore allow at least five days so that you can camp out in the jungle.

The jewel in this green crown is **Gunung Tahan**, a 7,158-ft.-high mountain, which requires a tough 66-mile trek lasting nine days from the park headquarters to the summit and back. Guides are obligatory for this kind of adventure but there are countless other opportunities closer to base for the less adventurous. Clearly marked trails lead from the park headquarters to the salt licks, blinds, lookout points, fishing lodges, water-

falls, and caves that are situated anywhere from a 1½-hour walk to a full day's walk or more away. Bird watching, swimming, fishing, canoeing, whitewater rafting, and shooting the rapids create further diversions, and when your energy flags you can simply collapse on the veranda of your chalet and listen to the omnipresent jungle symphony.

Practicalities On any jungle trek, even the shortest, you will be plagued by the leeches that proliferate in the constant 90 percent humidity. The best clothes to take to limit the damage are long-sleeved cotton shirts and long pants (jeans and T-shirts become very clammy), ankle-high walking boots, and a pullover or light jacket for early-morning river trips.

Previously closed for the rainy season (November to January), the park headquarters is now gunning to stay open all year round, but may still close between mid-December and mid-January. Advance booking is essential during July, August, and November, but otherwise it is possible to turn up at Kuala Tahan and take pot luck. Reservations can be made from KL (tel: 03 2610393) and this office also arranges transport to the Tembeling Jetty, where permits are issued for the park. The motorized boat ride (departures at 9 A.M. and 2 P.M.) takes between two and three hours along the muddy but picturesque River Tembeling, passing Orang Asli villages, numerous fish traps, flashing kingfishers, and crashing monkeys.

Park headquarters Apart from its booming chalet facilities, park headquarters also serves as a rain-forest information center, and a small reference library offers a good selection of books on local flora and fauna. A rather dated slide show is projected every evening, but this is certainly not essential viewing. To get a real insight into the forest and its incredible biodiversity, hire one of the professional guides who live at the headquarters; their cost is not excessive if shared between a small group and they can be enlightening companions.

Accommodations range from hostel dormitories and campsites (tents can be rented) to comfortable and well-designed wooden chalets (air-conditioned or otherwise), and a supplies shop, cafeteria, and upscale restaurant cater for culinary needs.

Budget camp
If you want to avoid the somewhat touristy park headquarters, head for a recently developed local camp situated outside the limits of the Taman Negara. Nusa Camp (15 minutes by boat from Kuala Tahan—shooting three rapids is part of the experience of arriving) offers a similar range of activities from its simple base. Accommodations in the hostel or chalets are less luxurious, as are prices. Arrangements can be made at their information hut on arrival at the Tembeling Jetty or through their Jerantut office (tel. 09 262369).

Great egrets are just some of the birds that can be seen

179

Taman Negara wildlife

■ Damp, decaying vegetation, bizarre fungi, tangled lianas, parasitic ferns and orchids, majestic buttress trunks, and arrow-straight meranti trees all make up an oppressive but nurturing environment for the National Park's thousands of bird and insect species, monkeys, and more elusive wilder beasts. .....■

Rain forest or dipterocarp?
The two terms are used interchangeably but in fact dipterocarp refers specifically to the tropical rainforest vegetation that is found at altitudes of up to 2,700 ft. Malaysian dipterocarp includes lowland and hill forest and is characterized by its tall, straight hardwood trees. It is these precious tropical timbers that have attracted the commercial loggers.

Below: Jungle flora

Thousands of species crowd the dense dipterocarp forest and riverine vegetation that dominate the lowlands of the Taman Negara, while at higher altitudes oaks, laurels, and palm flora make up the characteristic montane forest, which gives way to the sparser upper montane forest at the summit of Gunung Tahan. A common yet spectacular tree in the lowlands is the meranti, a tall, straight hardwood with a webbed trunk. It can grow to heights of 280 ft.

Birds Avian life is abundant and there are 350 existing species. Mornings are the best time to catch a glimpse of crested fireback pheasants, Malayan pied hornbills, broadbills, bronzed drongos, or blue-throated bee-eaters. Fishing eagles and kingfishers are often seen along the rivers, and the Sungai Tahan attracts many a masked finfoot. However, on the whole, rain-forest birds do not move about much; each occupies its own corner and for this reason bird watching here is a veritable detective operation.

Animals The mammals of the Taman Negara are not easy to spot due to the density of the vegetation and their shyness, even though they are more diverse and numerous there than in the lowlands. Only if you spend a night in a jungle blind are you likely to see tapirs, wild boars, bears, wild ox, or deer lapping at the salt lick. Elephants (many of which were transferred to the park after inadvertent separation from their herds), tigers, rhinoceroses, and leopards are also all present in the rain forest, but again are rarely sighted. Primates are, however, abundant—long-tailed macaques bound along the river banks, and leaf monkeys and white-handed gibbons crash through the tree tops.

Also easy to spot are bats, happily suspended in their daytime cave habitats. Visit any of the dark, dank guano-infested caves in the Taman Negara and you will encounter thousands of bats, each of which uses echolocation to home in on its personal parking spot among thousands of brethren.

Right: A blue-tailed banded pitta

► **Kuala Pilah** 168A3

The small town of Kuala Pilah (23 miles east of Seremban) is essentially a Chinese community that dates from the beginning of this century. Fine old shophouses line the main grid of streets and the Sim Tong Buddhist temple near the bus station houses some fabulous Chinese carvings and porcelain dragons. Another highlight is an ornate corner-house opposite the taxi stand; its decorative glazed tiles, bas-reliefs, stuccowork, and wood carvings stand in bizarre contrast to the old British pillar box outside.

► **Lata Iskandar** 168C2

About 12 miles up the precipitous road from Tapah to the Cameron Highlands is Lata Iskandar waterfall. The surrounding jungle is home to an exotic variety of insect and plant life, as well as Orang Asli settlements.

►►► **Sri Menanti** 168A2

This idyllic valley (20 miles east of Seremban) has been home to the royal family of Negeri Sembilan since 1773, and most of the scattered but elegant buildings play a royal role. Next to the royal golf club stands the **Istana Lama**, former palace of the Yang di-Pertuan Besar (state ruler) and now the royal museum. The palace dates from 1908 and is a stunning example of traditional Minangkabau architecture. The collection shows royal costumes in rich brocades and sturdy but decoratively carved furniture, as well as what must be one of the few royal bathrooms on display in Malaysia.

By contrast, the palm trees and blue-tiled roofs of the white **Istana Besar**, home to Negeri Sembilan's royal family since the 1930s, have a restrained harmony in keeping with the adjacent Royal Mausoleum and Mosque.

►►► **Taman Negara** 168C3

See pages 178–80.

Palace stories
Replacing an earlier palace which was burned down by the British in 1875, the raised, two-story hardwood Istana Lama in Sri Menanti is crowned by a two-floor tower which once housed the royal treasury and served as the private domain of the ruler. Unglazed shuttered windows, fretwork, and pillars and verandas intricately carved with leaf motifs complete the sober beauty of this construction. It was built in 1908 by master craftsmen without any nails or screws, using only wooden bolts, and remained occupied by the royal family until 1931, when they moved to the new palace. The old palace overlooks a turfed square where sporting events were held to entertain the ruler.

181

Halfway to the Cameron Highlands, the cascading Lata Iskandar provides cool relief

■ **Confusion sets in as travelers desperately search for a major downtown street, a hill station long memorized, or a legendary mountain. Have they been erased from the map or razed to the ground? Not so. In Malaysia time marches on and names change in step with sociopolitical transformations. As the nation moves toward the fortieth anniversary of its Independence, few names are left over from the colonial period. .....■**

Above: Kuching, Sarawak; its name derives from the Malay word for cat, kucing

Rest-houses
As you circle in semantic bewilderment, you may decide to recover in a government rest-house. This typically colonial institution, created to give administrators well-sited weekend retreats, still functions today although many of the rest-houses could do with thorough renovation. But don't be fooled: no sign will read "rest-house." Look instead for Rumah Rehat, the Bahasa translation.

Jalan *is Malay for road, and* poskod *derives from the British term "post code"*

As incongruous as their glistening white neoclassical buildings, British placenames imposed by Residents and advisers of the 19th century plastered every street and acceptable settlement, the only exception being Sarawak, where the white rajahs respected the original Malay names. Today, however, Bahasa Malaysia has taken over, transforming names throughout the country in line with its new maturity.

From colonial heroes to Malaysian statesmen The systematic renaming of places and streets creates confusion for local inhabitants and visitors alike. Alien English street names make way for homages to modern Malay statesmen—in particular, Independent Malaysia's first Prime Minister, Tunku (or Tuanku) Abdul Rahman. Colonial figures such as Swettenham, Wellesley, Maxwell, Weld, and Anson step aside from ports, hill stations and towns for local geographical features, historical and mythical characters or often poetic Malay references.

Kota Bharu simply means "new fort" while Tanjung Bunga means "flower point," but what about Bayan Lepas (meaning "the liberated parakeet"), Alor Gajah ("elephant's path") or Janda Baik, referring to "the good widow?"

Other languages creep into Malaysian placenames, with an abundance of Chinese names—from Taiping ("everlasting peace") to Genting ("on top of the clouds")—while Langkawi originates from a Tamil word.

A few Portuguese names remain in the state of Melaka —Cape Rachado (now rechristened Tanjung Tuan) and Tranquerah, for example—but the once-famous Dutch-inspired Jonkers Street now honors one of the Melaka sultanate's great warriors, Hang Jebat. Pinang, too, is in the throes of transformation, with Pinang Hill officially named Bukit Bendera ("flag hill") and Beach Road directly translated as Lebuh Pantai. Still hanging in there, yet prefixed with a local *lebuh* (street) or *jalan* (road), are Carnarvon, Pitt, Bishop, Farquhar, and Light, but for how long? The other problem stems from official changes in spelling, but that's another story...

JALAN RAJA

POSKOD 50050 KUALA LUMPUR

▶▶▶ Tasik Bera   168A3

Once, but no longer the largest lake in Malaysia, Tasik Bera lies in southern Pahang (about 20 miles from Bahau). It is estimated that 96 percent of this still, glassy lake has been eaten up by rasau, a wild plant that grows so profusely that only narrow channels of water wide enough for a canoe remain. Orang Asli settlements lie around its banks, and local anglers are discovering the delights of its abundant tapah, which can weigh up to 22 pounds. Virgin (and leech-free!) jungle skirts the lake and a small local vacation development has started to offer accommodations in primitive treehouses, a far cry from the comforts of the Taman Negara. Terrang provides bumpy access to the lake by car or chartered taxi, and there is a government rest-house at Pos Iskandar. Permits necessary to visit the Orang Asli villages are obtainable from the police station in Temerluh.

▶▶ Tasik Chenderoh   168C1

Another of Malaysia's picturesque lakes, Tasik Chenderoh is formed by the Chenderoh Dam, which interrupts the Perak river as it snakes down from its mountain source to Kuala Kangsar. Parts of the lake are blanketed in water lilies and jungle-clad hills flank both sides. Important archaeological finds are centered on Kampung Kota Tampan Ayer (see page 177), while the Gua Badak caves near Lenggong display some more recent but equally interesting charcoal drawings by the Lanah Negrito tribe.

▶▶▶ Tasik Cini   168B3

Tasik Cini is situated along the Sungai Pahang just south of the KL–Kuantan highway. Despite its apparent proximity to civilization, elephants and tigers have been spotted in the forest reserve surrounding the lake. The most interesting access is via a highway turnoff at Maran, which

Well off the tourist circuit, Tasik Bera offers jungle-trekking and boating to more intrepid visitors

Cini monsters
The local Jakun tribe insist that a horned and red-eyed dragon inhabits the Cini waters. One of their oral legends describes the origins of the lake in typically vivid style: a group of Jakun tribespeople clearing land was confronted by an ancient woman who claimed the land was hers and who pounded her stick into the ground before promptly vanishing. A barking dog drew the Jakun to a nearby spot where a huge log was decomposing; plunging their spears into it they were amazed to see blood spurt from the holes; and then all hell broke loose—thunder, lightning, and gales, and finally the uprooting of the old woman's stick. It was from out of this hole that Lake Cini poured forth.

leads through rubber plantations to the neat village of Kampung Belembing. From there motorized sampans follow a narrow tributary overhung by a canopy of riotous jungle vegetation. The vista opens up 3 miles on past mangroves, over a carpet of giant pink lotus flowers (the best time to see these is between June and September) and towards distant hills. Chalet, dormitory, and camping accommodations are provided in a pleasantly low-key resort, which organizes numerous jungle and lake activities.

►► Tasik Temengor 168D2

The government still fears communist guerrillas springing from the wilds of the hills around Tasik Temengor, a wild area far to the north of the peninsula and just a few miles from the Thai border. The landscape has a powerful and mysterious beauty, which is enhanced by the mists that hover over the lake surface and by the silhouettes of dying trees along its shores. On the island of Banding there is a rest-house (the only comfortable place to stay on the east–west highway) and a developing fishing resort that organizes boat trips; the only other major sight is the massive dam.

► Temerluh 168B3

Situated on the banks of Malaysia's longest river, the Sungai Pahang, Temerluh is a busy industrialized junction town where the KL–Kuantan highway meets the main road from Segamat. It is of limited interest but is a necessary halt for those heading for Tasik Bera, as permits need to be obtained from the police station.

Left and below: Chinese and Malay shopkeepers ply their trades in Temerluh

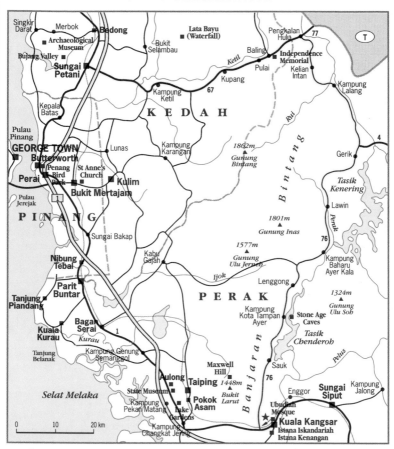

CENTRAL REGION DRIVE

Drive Central mountains and Orang Asli villages

This drive cuts into the remote central mountainous region past lakes, jungle-clad hills, and Orang Asli villages before returning to the more tranquil expanses of Kedah's rice fields.

From Kuala Kangsar, take road No 76 north into upper Perak. Snaking over a causeway across the reservoir of **Tasik Chenderoh** the road enters the **Lenggong Valley**, where evidence of Stone Age man is still being uncovered near **Kampung Kota Tampan Ayer**. Increasingly desolate, the road bypasses Tasik Kenering, winding past Orang Asli villages before reaching the frontier town of **Gerik**.

From Gerik drive north past more spectacular jungle landscapes, waterfalls, Orang Asli settlements, and an abandoned tin mine on the slopes above **Kelian Intan**. There the road runs parallel to the Thai border and at Keroh it passes a customs point. Serene landscapes return as the road (now No 67) descends into the "rice bowl" of the state of Kedah and passes the forest park of Peranginan Bukit Hijau near Baling, before joining the west coast highway near Sungai Petani.

Below: East coast islands offer secluded beaches, coral reefs, and exquisite seascapes

Above: East coast—north

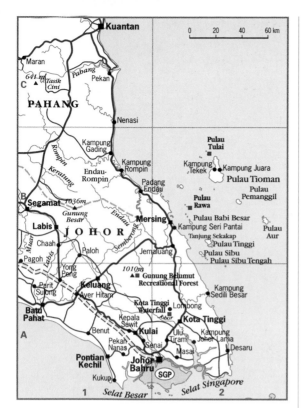

East coast—south

The east coast Endless white sandy beaches, coconut palms, tropical islands, batik fabrics drying in the breeze, colorful fishing boats...these are the picture-postcard clichés of Peninsular Malaysia's east coast. Offshore oil rigs, gigantic modern beach resorts, growing commercialism, fundamentalism, pollution...these are the tourists' fears. The reality lies somewhere in between, but fortunately still veers decidedly in the direction of the clichés.

Luxury resorts do exist, but countless beach communities cater for visitors with limited budgets. Industrialization is also present along a 20-mile stretch north of Kampung Kemaman, but even there it is interspersed with idyllic beaches and pollution is limited to urban debris. Ultimately, however, the tantalizing palette of liquid turquoises and emeralds rolling across the island-studded South China Sea puts everything else in the shade...of coconut palms and casuarinas.

Historical isolation For centuries the east coast was left to its own unhurried agricultural resources while the west coast burgeoned in a frenzy of mining and trading activities. Few Chinese or Indians made their way there—the simple rural life of the *kampung* was a little too close to home and, for similar economic reasons, British Residents arrived much later. Thus it went on in its own mellow way, unadulterated by the outside world and

Pulau Perhentian comprises two islands, both offering accommodations on the beach

Coconuts

A multifunctional tree if ever there was one, the coconut palm is transformed into baskets, bridges, and huts, while its fruit is a familiar sight throughout the tropics. Malaysian cooks excel in using the fresh flesh and milk as a blending ingredient, softening the fire of spices, and making a creamy background to fish dishes. A ripe nut will gurgle when shaken and can produce a quart of juice. This delicious and highly nourishing drink surprisingly is not readily found— Malaysians seem to prefer fizzy canned drinks. When you do find a coconut-seller he will also provide a spoon to scoop out the equally nutritious flesh.

Coconut oil is another valuable spinoff, created by heating the flesh either in the sun or over a low fire. Used as a sunblock, it is also kind to skin that has been submerged for hours in the sea. But watch out for falling nuts—they're heavy!

untouched by colonial influence, though sporadically dominated by overlords from Java, Melaka, and subsequently Johor. The exception was the northern state of Kelantan, which was long subjected to idiosyncratic Siamese rule. At the other geographical extreme, Johor was the last Malay state to bow to British control (in 1914). The massive state of Pahang, the largest on the peninsula, was notable for its strenuous though ultimately unsuccessful efforts to reject British authority during the Pahang War of 1891, and Terengganu and Kelantan only became British protectorates in 1909. The region remained isolated from the rest of the country by the central mountain range and jungle for many years, and even today's main coastal road, although adequate, is hardly a highway.

Cultural cradle Blowing relentlessly every year from November to January, the northeast monsoon regularly leaves fishermen and farmers with weeks of enforced inactivity. High and dry in their stilt houses while their villages and paddy fields are flooded and harbors inaccessible, they have developed a range of crafts and games to while away the time. And the end of every rice harvest, the agricultural highpoint of the year, is an excuse for celebrations that run the full gamut of colorful performances. Kelantan and Terengganu, the kings in this domain, are impregnated with centuries of traditional pastimes including *silat* (a graceful martial art), top spinning, kite flying, drumming, dances, or *wayang kulit* (shadow plays). Although the celebrations are much hyped by the tourist literature, one rarely sees any activity (except kite flying) outside a ceremonial occasion, a competition, or a cultural center.

What every traveler will see without fail, however, is batik and yet more batik. East coast Malay women and men still swathe themselves in batik sarongs, and markets overflow with hundreds of designs. Richer in every respect is *kain songket*, an exquisite silk brocade interwoven with silver and gold threads that is made principally in Terengganu. Pandan-weavings also multiply in this agrarian land, especially in Kelantan. *Pandanus* (screw pine) leaves are fashioned into objects ranging from mats to pouches and boxes. This rich array is topped off with silverwork and wood-carving.

Hardliners Bastions of Islam, the conservative states of Kelantan and Terengganu are polar opposites to Johor Bahru's more liberated attitude to life—at night in particular. Visitors to these states must watch their dress, and women's beachwear should be strictly one-piece. Overt amorous behavior is out of the question, and

Juggling with weekends
Johor, Kelantan, and Terengganu follow the Muslim weekend centered on the Friday day of prayer. Banks, post offices, and government offices close in these states on Thursday afternoons and all day Friday, although museums close on Fridays only. Saturdays and Sundays are treated as normal working days. Pahang is the east coast exception, so depending on how you plan your trip you can either experience four-day weekends or avoid them entirely.

189

A Marang fishing boat

Vietnamese boat-people

Something to remember as you laze beneath a coconut palm is the plight of the thousands of boat-people who fled the strict communist regime of Vietnam in the late 1970s to search for more hospitable climes. Crowded into unstable fishing boats, many did not survive the four-day trip across the Gulf of Siam, and an unknown number drowned at the mercy of pirates or unseaworthy boats. Bodies were washed up on the shores, tragic symbols of unsuccessful quests for freedom. Those who did make it were treated with suspicion by the Malaysian government and herded into refugee camps along the length of the coast. At Kampung Cerating trees were cut down to create a camp and refugees were fenced in on the beach—consigned to bake under a merciless sun only a few feet from the sea.

Roadside stalls with giant jackfruit

pointing or touching someone's head—even that of a child—is regarded as offensive. The wail of the muezzin is at its most strident here and even schoolgirls on the beach are covered from head to toe, while most women wear *telekung* (headdresses). Led by the Sultan of Kelantan, both states have recently called for the establishment of the *charia*, strict Islamic laws that would bring the more easygoing Malay approach a lot closer to Saudi Arabia's more fundamental practices. With a 95 percent Malay (and thus mainly Muslim) population in these states and the whip hand of Terengganu's oil wealth, the future on this front is uncertain.

From fish to lakes From the pineapple and rubber plantations of Johor through the jungle, cocoa, and palm-oil plantations of Pahang to Kelantan's paddy fields, the landscape remains essentially rural; light industry is only visible around the main towns and heavy industry is limited to Johor and Kampung Kemaman. The coast itself is one long stretch of fishing villages, many of which transform the catch into dried fish or crackers—it is common to see ranks of silver fish lying out in the sun to dry. The central markets of **Kota Bharu** and **Kuala Terengganu** will also give an idea of the vast quantities and types of fish available. Even when the monsoons leave the fishing boats portbound, east coasters manage to catch fish from the verandas of their stilt houses or net them along the flooded roads.

Virgin jungle is concentrated in Pahang and Kelantan, although the latter state is logging at such a rate (illegally) that it won't last long. For more intrepid visitors, a trip into the **Endau-Rompin Forest** offers an unadulterated jungle environment rich in rare flora and fauna, as well as Orang Asli settlements. Other protected forest areas can be explored around **Gunung Tapis** and, to a lesser extent,

around the spectacular **Sekayu Waterfalls**. Even more varied is the gigantic **Tasik Kenyir**, high up in the hills of Terengganu; an idyllic retreat from the coastal humidity, it combines cool air, endless boating activities, and treks into the encircling jungle.

Beaches and islands For a dash of luxury, the east coast has the goods. Island resorts are developing rapidly from **Pulau Tioman** in the south to **Pulau Redang** in the north, where a huge development risks contaminating an otherwise paradisiacal spot and its rich underwater life. However, many smaller islands will remain relatively untouched for a long time, as bouncing three-hour boat rides do not suit everyone's tastes or schedule. Backpackers relish negotiating shaky, narrow gangplanks or wading ashore to reach their enclaves of rudimentary beach-living where water may only come from a well and electricity may be nonexistent. There are, however, plenty of accommodations between the extremes, and the southern islands off **Mersing** are particularly well served by a flotilla of craft ranging from bumboats to hydrofoils. Whichever island you choose, the water will be limpid and alive with technicolored tropical fish flitting against a mesmerizing landscape of coral.

Of the coastal beaches, **Rantau Abang** is famous for its turtles, which return every summer to lay their eggs. The neighboring luxury resort at **Tanjung Jara** makes a superb base for viewing this event and for diving around **Pulau Tenggul**. Most developed of all, however, is the coast from **Kuantan** to **Cerating** where a secluded Club Med jostles with numerous beach chalet setups in a lively tourist haven. The tourist facilities extend to **Kampung Baluk** and Teluk Cempedak, Kuantan's main beach. In July and August even the most remote islands can become full, so aim to visit outside this season; you should also avoid the monsoons (November to January).

Fishing keeps east coast inhabitants busy for nine months of the year—until the northeast monsoon breaks

Island essentials
Before embarking for any of the islands, make sure that you have changed enough money on the mainland. Although it is usually possible to change cash on the islands, the rates are never advantageous. Remember, too, the suntan lotions, mosquito repellents, and camera films as these are rarely available. Take as little luggage as possible, as transfers from boats can entail negotiating rocky coastlines or wading to the beach if there is no jetty. If taking a day-trip to an uninhabited island, stock up on plenty of water— always take more than you think you will need. Finally, always check exact destinations and time of arrival.

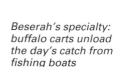

Beserah's specialty: buffalo carts unload the day's catch from fishing boats

▶▶▶ Beserah   186A2

One of the most picturesque fishing villages of this coast, Beserah (6 miles north of Kuantan) still moves in traditional ways although the growing influx of tourists along this stretch is changing the tone. Worth witnessing is the late-morning catch, when mountains of silvery fish are loaded from fishing boats on to buffalo carts before being dragged back to the local anchovy factory. After boiling, the fish are spread out in the sun to dry—in itself a captivating sight. A number of cottage industries in the village include a batik factory, and performances of top spinning and kite flying are held there. Some of the *kampung* houses are still roofed with traditional oiled tiles and their coconut-grove setting makes the waterfront particularly idyllic. Just north of the village is the beach of **Batu Hitam**.

▶ Bukit Keluang   186C1

Just a few miles south of Kuala Besut is an attractive sandy beach backed by a stretch of cliffs which contain a network of caves. A wooden walkway leads from the beach into the caves, making a cool and shady escape from the merciless midday sun.

▶ Desaru   187A2

Way down at the southern end of the east coast lies the coastal resort of Desaru, increasingly touted as a "dream resort" and poised to attract visitors from highly populated Singapore and Johor Bahru. The 12 miles of sandy beach lined with casuarina trees are being gobbled up rapidly by a huge development, which, by 1994, will include no fewer than four 18-hole golf courses, six hotels, 2,500 holiday homes, a campsite, a tennis ranch, and a marina. Essentially a local family vacation destination, Desaru offers plenty of scuba diving, water sports, horse riding, and jungle trekking in an area that was once deserted tropical forest.

A one-man feat: the somnolent Buddha in Gua Charas

▶ **Dungun** 186B2

Halfway between Kuala Terengganu and Kuantan, Dungun is a typical small estuary town with little to hold the traveler back apart from an active waterfront and its proximity to the famous "turtle beaches" to the north. Once an important outlet for iron ore mined 20 miles inland at Bukit Besi, Dungun has now reverted to its traditional fishing activities.

▶▶▶ **Endau-Rompin Forest** 187B1

Straddling the border of the states of Johor and Pahang is a recently designated forest reserve, home to several endangered species and a challenging opportunity for potential trekkers. Boats from the small port of Padang Endau take visitors along the meandering Endau river past mudflats and mangrove swamps before penetrating the remote inner rain forest. This is no lighthearted affair as there are no tourist structures as yet; camping trips have to be well organized, guides and boats hired and supplies bought. Orang Asli settlements abound, and because of this, permits are necessary (obtainable from the State Security Council in Johor Bahru; tel: 07 226922). An alternative means of entry into the forest requires a four-wheel drive: after turning off the Keluang–Mersing road to Ladang Bukit Cantek the route rapidly deteriorates into a rough track.

▶▶ **Gua Charas (Pancing Caves)** 186A2

On the Sungai Lembing road 15 miles inland from Kuantan stands a towering limestone outcrop riddled with caves. This is nothing new, except that reclining in the gloomy inner depths is a 30-ft.-long Buddha. Carved out of rock by a determined Thai Buddhist monk during years of meditation there, the rather awkwardly formed idol represents one man's touching labor of love as all the materials had to be carted up the steep rockface. Visitors who pant up the outer steps are greeted by a bizarre combination of bats, eerie shafts of light, and numerous other statues.

Dungun side-step
A strenuous day can be spent trekking through forest inland from Dungun to reach superb waterfalls. After an hour's drive to Kuala Jengai, hire a boat to reach Kuala Sungai Ceralak (near Kampung Jagung)—this takes about 1½ hours. From here you can set off along a forest trail, fording the Ceralak river to arrive finally at the Ceralak Falls—a verdant, rocky spot echoing with the torrents of the 80-ft.-high Jeram Padang and the lesser Jeram Solo. Then all you need to do is turn around and repeat the process in reverse!

Johor Bahru's Royal Museum
Only recently opened to the public (guided tours only), this museum is an eclectic treasure trove of Victoriana, Chinese, Japanese, Indian and Malay *objets d'art*, hunting trophies, stuffed animals, canopied beds, and glittering French crystal Baccarat chandeliers. Much of the original furniture was ordered in England by Sultan Abu Bakar, and he also personally supervised the landscaping of the botanical gardens. His fervent anglophilia is evident everywhere, not least in a letter from his friend Queen Victoria, although his wily diplomacy managed to keep the state of Johor out of British hands throughout his lifetime. It was only in 1914 while under the rule of his son, Sultan Ibrahim, that Johor finally fell under the sway of a British Resident—the last Malay state to do so.

▶ **Gunung Tapis Nature Park** *186A2*
Accessible only by four-wheel drive, the Gunung Tapis Nature Park (10 miles west of Sungai Lembing) offers fishing, rapids-shooting, and bathing in the abundant hot springs. Gunung Tapis itself rises to 4,949 ft. Trips and overnight camping can be arranged through the Kuantan tourist office (tel: 09 512960).

▶ **Johor Bahru** *187A2*
Hardly the most picturesque of Malaysia's state capitals, industrialized Johor Bahru is mainly geared to visitors from Singapore, its closest neighbor just a half-mile across the causeway. Foreign visitors only arrive to change transportation, although Singaporeans beam in every weekend, treating it as a northern suburb for shopping and sex. The town was founded in 1866 by Sultan Abu Bakar to replace Johor Lama, and today the main historic monument is the **Istana Besar** (off Jalan Tun Dr Ismail), a Victorian-style palace set in superbly landscaped gardens and recently renovated to include the **Royal Museum** (see side panel). Not far away, with a similarly panoramic view over the Strait of Johor, is the intriguingly designed **Sultan Abu Bakar Mosque**, completed in 1900. The lofty tower of the sultan's present palace, **Istana Bukit Serene** (1932), creates a landmark to the west of the center, but otherwise Johor Bahru is a rather messy jumble of cheap modern buildings, high on nightlife but low on aesthetics.

▶▶ **Kampung Baluk** *186A2*
Baluk (9 miles north of Kuantan) is renowned for its excellent windsurfing and is reputed to be one of the ten best locations in the world for this sport. A large modern resort on the beautiful beach offers a variety of water sports, while at nearby Kampung Sungai Karang, the center for local shell crafts, a more rustic resort blends pleasantly into the surrounding palm trees and casuarinas.

▶▶ **Kampung Cenering** *186B2*
Immediately south of Kuala Terengganu at Cenering is a magnificent palm-lined beach culminating in a small fishing village. A favorite with locals from Kuala Terengganu for its fine white sand and long jetty (excellent for fishing), it is also the site of a national deep-sea fishing project.

Johor Bahru's renovated Istana Besar contains a wealth of royal souvenirs

▶▶▶ Kampung Cerating   186A2

A backpackers' delight, the superb large bay of Cerating (as it is usually called) is also home to a luxury Club Med, discreetly situated in exclusive isolation at the northern end of the beach. Cerating has a relaxed, cosmopolitan atmosphere and caters for every possible Western need, but unfortunately leaves little of the Malay in the process. Local fishermen have moved out to make way for hundreds of low-budget sun worshippers, who lie around the lagoon or sip beer at the open-air disco. Cerating's main accommodations are still limited to chalets and beach huts, all of which make an effort to re-create aspects of Malay culture. Biking, horse riding, windsurfing, snorkeling around Snake Island and tours to Tasik Cini (see page 183), Gua Charas (see page 193), or nearby waterfalls can all be arranged from here.

▶ Kampung Johor Lama   187A2

When Melaka fell to the Portuguese in 1511, the Sultan of Johor and his followers fled to Johor Lama (20 miles south of Kota Tinggi) in order to found their new capital. Today the village is a backwater lost in palm-oil plantations and is only accessible by four-wheel drive from the Desaru road. The fort was finally destroyed by the Portuguese, but recent excavations give an idea of its former importance.

▶ Kampung Kemaman   186A2

The southernmost town in the state of Terengganu, Kampung Kemaman merges with Cukai, an adjoining town across the estuary. The boom town of Kertih (20 miles to the north) has been transformed by offshore oil and gas, and this has greatly influenced the fate of Kemaman. However, in between the industrial plants lies a string of dazzling beaches and unspoilt fishing villages; **Kijal** and **Kemasik** both have glorious beaches, the latter sheltered by a palm-lined sandbar.

Kemaman still possesses pockets of tranquillity

Hot-to-trot Johor Bahru
Considered to be the cradle of Malay culture, Johor is also where Bahasa is spoken in its purest form. Yet ironically it has become Malaysia's sin city, catering to thousands of frustrated Singaporeans who flood across the causeway, and to local and foreign workers who are drawn to its booming industrial activities. Invisible to the outsider's eye are the gambling dens, but completely blatant are strip joints, lounges where barely clothed "hostesses" snuggle up to clients before sealing the contract elsewhere. At the notorious "glass houses" clients view potential companions through glass screens before they retire to cubicles for the serious stuff. With this active hot-to-trot industry, Johor Bahru has inevitably been confronted with a major AIDS problem.

FOCUS ON *Tropical fruit*

■ **Vitamin deficiency is hardly a problem in Malaysia as tropical fruits seemingly drop from every tree, whether in the thick of the jungle or on a beach lined with swaying coconut palms. Markets abound with mountains of bizarre fruits, some indigenous, others introduced to Malaysia centuries ago and now part of the landscape .....■**

Fruits of the forest
It has been estimated that fewer than 2 percent of all flowering or fruit-bearing rain-forest trees are in season at any one time, and the "crop" varies considerably from year to year, with occasional vintage years. Most dipterocarp forest fruits are tough and unpleasant tasting, but there are exceptions: the highly prized wild durian, less odiferous than its cultivated versions, has a taste hovering between avocado and hazelnut; wild mangoes, rambutans, and breadfruit are other quite palatable forest fruits.

Rambutan—literally "hairy fruit"

Street stalls are the best place to sample some of these tropical delicacies: refreshing and restoring fruit salads, dextrously prepared for a small sum, can be enjoyed daily.

Bananas Available all year round and coming in all shapes and sizes, Malaysian bananas (*pisang*) have nothing to do with the hard, musty flavored imports found in the West. The smaller they are the sweeter they taste, but they rapidly become overripe.

Chikus Available only during season, the chiku is similar to a kiwi fruit in size and shape. Its soft, sweet, granular flesh is encased in a smooth, brown skin.

Custard-apples Also known as *durian belanda*, soursop or zirzat, the custard-apple has a bumpy green skin and a deliciously creamy (custardy), slightly acidic pulp—best consumed with a spoon to avoid the seeds. Available from June to August, the fruit is ripe when the skin starts to turn black.

Durians Known as the "king of fruits," although the word simply means thorny fruit (referring to its coating of sharp thorns), durians are prohibited in many hotel rooms, so offensive is their sewer-like smell. The distinctive taste of the fruit's creamy, rich flesh is similarly high powered and even appears to be addictive—the high prices reflect this. The fruit can measure up to 10 inches in length.

Guavas A highly potent source of vitamin C, the granular pink flesh of the guava is encased in a thick green pear-shaped skin. Hawkers sell sliced guava with a sour-plum garnish.

Jackfruit The shape of a giant pear with a pimply green skin and measuring up to 16 inches long, the interior of the jackfruit (*nangka*) breaks up into chewy, yellow segments. The seeds can also be

boiled and eaten. Jackfruit are at their best from April to September.

Langsats Small brown-skinned fruits, langsats (*duku*) have a translucent, slightly tart flesh and are in season between May and July.

Mangoes Varieties are plentiful in Malaysia, from the apple mango to the Indian coconut mango, and the thin green- or yellow-skinned fruits encasing sweet orange flesh are grown in nearly every Malaysian *kampung*.

Mangosteens The size of a small orange with a deep purple outer skin, this delicious fruit has juicy white segments with an acidic sweet flavor, but the purple juice stains notoriously. Mangosteens follow the same season as the durian, and the Chinese claim its *yin* balances the durian's *yang*.

Papayas Renowned for their high vitamin A and C content and for their meat-tenderizing properties, sliced papayas are usually eaten with a squeeze of lime juice. The refreshing, orange flesh is a stronger version of melon and is said to aid digestion.

Fruit is sold whole, sliced, or transformed into healthy and refreshing juices

Pineapples Available throughout the year, pineapples are eaten locally with salt and a dash of soy and chili sauce.

Pomelos The size of a soccer ball and the biggest of all citrus fruits, pomelos are almost exclusively cultivated in Perak. Their peak season in August coincides with Chinese festivities, when they are given as offerings and presents.

Rambutans Indigenous to Malaysia, the rambutan (meaning "hairy fruit") has a furry red coat encasing sweet white flesh similar to that of lychees.

Starfruit Also known as carambola, the starfruit's name becomes evident when its segmented casing is sliced across its width to reveal immaculate, star-shaped slices of crisp, refreshing, pale yellow flesh.

Sugarcane
More a bamboo-like stem than a fruit, sugarcane is a rich source of natural sugar. To reap its benefits, cut through a piece of stem, slice it into tubes, peel off the thick white rind until it looks like a stick of white wood, then bite into it, sucking its juice. In town markets sugarcane mangles are a common sight; they consist of a manually worked wheel, which does the hard extraction work for you.

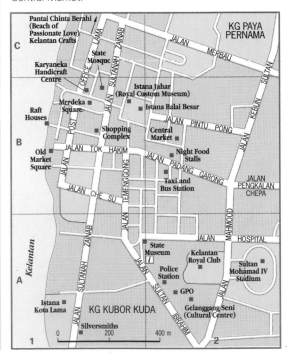

Beach of Passionate Love
With a name like Beach of Passionate Love (Pantai Chinta Berahi, or PCB for short), you might expect to witness wild romantic scenes. Not so. This is conservative Kelantan and women often bathe fully dressed. However, this blissful stretch of white sand and rolling waves is only half an hour's bus ride from Kota Bharu's Central Market along a pretty rural route which follows the river, so it is worth considering as an alternative to staying in town. Food stands selling fresh seafood and a pleasantly limited number of hotels— from small motels to chalet resorts—are all situated right on the beach in the shade of palms and casuarinas. Other bonuses are the proximity of the craft workshops along the road between PCB and Kota Bharu, as well as Kuala Besar, a local favorite for seafood specialities. Bus 10 departs every half-hour from the Central Market terminus.

Kota Bharu

▶▶ **Kampung Merang**   *186B2*

Though often confused with Marang (see page 204), the sleepy fishing village of Merang lies 15 miles to the north of Kuala Terengganu and is actually quite opposite in tone. This village extends along a flat stretch of coast bypassed by the main road, which explains why its secluded charm remains surprisingly free of development. The clear, calm waters are edged by a gentle sweep of beach where limited chalet accommodations are available and boats leave for the island of Pulau Redang (see page 208).

Following the increasingly isolated road north is a string of small *kampungs* that nestle among coconut palms along miles of deserted beach; try **Penarik**, **Kampung Bari Besar,** or **Kampung Kuala Setiu Lama** where, as yet, there are very few accommodations. Although the beaches are superb, the surroundings are somewhat featureless. To enliven otherwise endlessly indolent days, watch for monkeys scampering up the coconut palms, for this is the region where they are trained to climb the tall, swaying palms and pick the fruit.

▶▶▶ **Kota Bharu**   *186C1*

Endlessly promoted as the capital of traditional east coast Malay culture, Kota Bharu in fact has considerably less charm than Kuala Terengganu, the neighboring state capital. Too much effort has been put into packaging Kelantanese culture in a rather ostentatious fashion, but that said, trips out of town can be rewarding. Sights are easily reached on foot or by trishaw, and buses to out-of-town attractions leave from the bus station opposite the Central Market.

Main sights Dominating the Padang area and fronted by a ceremonial arch is the **Istana Balai Besar**, a wooden structure built in 1844 and still used for ceremonial and legislative purposes. It is not open to the public, but the nearby **Royal Museum►►** (closed Friday) is worth a quick visit. This elegant blue 1939 building belongs to the royal family and the collection includes photographs and a family tree going back to 1418. Between this museum and the main palace stands a superb example of intricate Kelantanese craftsmanship, the **Istana Jahar►►**, built in 1889 and now housing the Royal Custom Museum.

Other sights around the Padang are the rather dull State Mosque (1926), the Islamic Museum, which is housed in another beautifully crafted building dating from 1914, and the oldest brick building in Kelantan, now the War Museum and once the Japanese Army headquarters. Along the side road past the Royal Museum is the **Karyaneka Handicraft Centre ►**, an imposing new structure built in traditional style but displaying a limited collection of carvings, silver, brocades, and pandan-weaving.

Of more interest is the **State Museum►►►** situated on the clocktower crossroads, where stuffed tigers, reconstructed neolithic caves, pottery, ceramics, traditional instruments, and shadow puppets present a rounded vision of Kelantanese culture. Just a few steps away, the tourist office is very helpful for arranging *kampung* stays, river trips, and the like. The Gelanggang Seni (Cultural Centre) on Jalan Sultan Ibrahim stages free demonstrations of top spinning, martial arts, drumming, and dance dramas daily at 3:30 P.M. and 9 P.M.

Finally, nobody should leave Kota Bharu without experiencing the bustling atmosphere of the **Central**

Kelantan crafts

Kota Baru is renowned as a center for batik, *songket*, kite making, silverware, wood-carving, and pandan-weaving, with its main cottage industry area clustered in the *kampungs* strung along the beach road. Ideally, a bicycle is best for covering the distance, but those with more elastic budgets can always negotiate a taxi for a couple of hours. At Kampung Penambang, batik, *songket* (go to Minah) and kites are all made, while further on at Kampung Badang there is a silversmith, a coppersmith, and the Esah Batik Workshop. For more silverwork, go to Jalan Sultan Zainab in Kota Bharu where there are a number of craftsmen.

199

A typical multiple-headlight trishaw in Kota Bharu

Kampung Laut
Threatened by floods, Malaysia's oldest mosque (hotly disputed with that in Melaka) had to be transferred from its former riverside site opposite Kota Bharu to the village of Nilam Puri, 6 miles south of the state capital on the Kuala Krai road. Made entirely of the valuable tropical cengal wood, it was built by Javanese craftsmen in the 18th century without nails and following the two-tiered pyramidal roof style. The mosque can easily be reached by Bus 44 or Bus 5, from Kota Bharu's local bus terminal on Jalan Padang Gurong.

Kota Bharu's fresh market was originally a floating market in the 19th century

Market►►► (not to be confused with the old market on Jalan Datok Pati), where women traders tend mountains of unusual fruits, vegetables, fish and grains spilling over two floors. The top floor specializes in household goods, clothes, and batik. Another good destination for inexpensive local goods is the Bazaar Buluh Kubu, which lies between the Central Market and the Padang. And in the evening don't miss the night market which, come rain or shine, springs into action outside the Central Market.

►   **Kota Tinggi**   187A2

About 35 miles northeast of Johor Bahru, the Kota Tinggi waterfalls (also called the Lombong Falls) crash down 118 ft. to create a series of pools that have become favorites with local families. There are rental chalets, food stalls, and campsites; avoid weekends.

►   **Kuala Besut**   186C1

Generally only thought of as a trampoline for backpackers on their way to the Perhentian Islands, the small fishing port of Kuala Besut is a rather ramshackle place. Watching the fishermen unloading the morning and evening catches is the main highlight, and a small resort hotel is located south of the river. To the north, at Semerak, is one of Kelantan's most secluded beaches, poetically named Pantai Bisikan Bayu—the Beach of Whispering Breeze (see Pantai Dalam Rhu, page 205).

►   **Kuala Krai**   186C1

Apart from a small zoo and a handful of dingy hotels, the only reason for passing through Kuara Krai (44 miles south of Kola Bharu) is to take a river trip from here to **Dabong**, two hours to the southwest. The river meanders through dense jungle, and you can take a short walk from Dabong to caves and a waterfall. Dabong is also on the jungle railway (see page 176), so the trip can easily be continued either to the north or south.

■ **Peninsular Malaysia's east coast is the focus for a wealth of distinctive games and pastimes that have evolved over the centuries. These games occupy villagers during the idle months when the monsoon winds and downpours put a stop to any agricultural or fishing activities. .....■**

Of kites and tops Introduced by the Chinese, kites (or *wau*) have been popular ever since the days of the 15th-century Melakan sultanate. Kelantan monopolizes the tradition today, and colorful, elaborate kites drift through the skies over villages after the rice harvest or during special competitions. Made from bamboo frames mounted with intricately stenciled colored paper and sometimes fitted with a bow that produces a humming sound, kites take the shape of the moon, fish, cats, or birds. The *wau* winner is the one that flies highest.

Equally competitive but reserved for muscular adults, top spinning (*gasing uri*) contests are a far cry from the Western toddler's variety. Kelantan and Terengganu lead the way, with large metal tops weighing up to 11 pounds and 8 inches in diameter. The winner is the person whose top spins the longest—they can whirl for up to two hours. Competitors make the tops spin by tightening a long rope around the top, and then launching it on to a dais where it is scooped up on a bat and transferred to a stand to continue its spin.

Defensive dances and drums More graceful than kite flying or top spinning is the Malay art of self-defense, *silat*, once used in battle but today developed into a stylized dance performance often accompanied by drums or gongs. Like many martial arts, *silat* traditionally aimed to instill loyalty, spiritual awareness, and self-discipline through strictly controlled movements. Whether enacted by apprentice adolescents or older masters of the art, a *silat* performance can be captivating.

Buffalo-skin drums made from huge hollowed-out logs also come into their own during Kelantan drum-beating festivals (*rebana*) when drum-beaters try to outdo their opponents in tone and rhythm.

Right: East coast drummers come into their own during festivals

Ball and board games
Others games include *sepak raga* and *sepak takraw*, a ball game developed during the heyday of the Melakan sultanate and now integrated into Asian sports meetings. Any part of the body except the hands is used to keep the rattan ball aloft, as it is propelled between two competing groups. Whichever side has most contact with the ball wins. Less strenuous is *congkak*, an indoor game which, for once, is open to women. The Malay equivalent of backgammon, the game is played on a beautifully carved wooden board containing two rows of five to nine holes and two larger "homes" used for stocking the playing pieces—seeds, seashells, or pebbles.

201

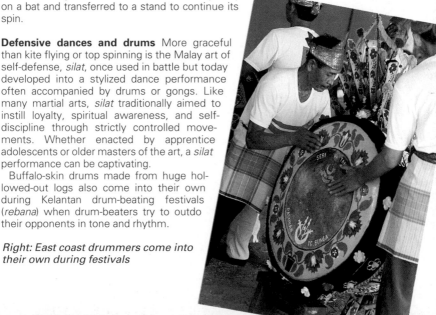

Jalan Bandar is the focal point of the Chinese community

▶▶▶ **Kuala Terengganu** *186B2*

Often bypassed by travelers making a beeline for the east coast beaches or the cultural hype of Kota Bharu, Kuala Terengganu in fact has a down-at-heel appeal which is accentuated by the inhabitants' nonchalance. Trishaw drivers rattle around the backstreets, a labyrinthine market monopolizes part of the waterfront, a street of old Chinese shophouses injects an unexpected Oriental flavor, and activity on the island-studded river never stops. This does not mean that Kuala Terengganu has not succumbed to 20th-century development; indeed, high-rises loom in the main commercial street of Jalan Sultan Ismail and the town's only international hotel is a concrete mass towering over the beach. Evidence of the center's recent oil wealth is symbolized by a new bridge spanning Pulau Duyong and joining the main coastal road.

Central sights Head for Jalan Sultan Zainal Abidin, which curves around the harbor, and you will cover most of the town's sights in an easy wander. Opposite the Central Market are the imposing post office and tourist office, flanking the elegant Istana Maziah▶, the sultan's official residence which was built at the beginning of the century to resemble a minor French château. Set in gardens behind is the Masjid Abidin▶, the concrete and brick State Mosque that replaced the undoubtedly more interesting original wooden building.

Back on the waterfront, the Central Market▶▶▶ and sprawling open-air bazaar (*pasar payang*) are essential sights, presenting a familiar cornucopia of fresh tropical fruit, vegetables, herbs, flowers, fish, and grains. Pick your way past mountains of watermelons and coconuts to the first floor of the modern market building, where hawkers and handicraft stalls offer tempting bargains.

202

Losong and the State Museum

A short bus or taxi ride from the center is a newly created historico-cultural complex set in superbly landscaped gardens overlooking the Terengganu river at Losong. The Istana Tengku Long and the Istana Rumah Tele are two magnificent high-gabled wooden palaces dating from the 1870s that were transferred here from other sites. The *pièce de résistance* is the enormous new State Museum, built in similar traditional style at the entrance to the gardens. The museum, one of the country's best, displays royal relics such as portraits, rich *songket* costumes, and tacky thrones, as well as a fine porcelain collection which includes rare Chinese Islamic ware, mainly from the 17th century. Embroidery, gold, and silverware, intricate jewelry, brass gongs, and a remarkable display of weapons complete the exhibition.

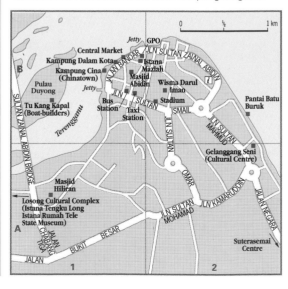

Kuala Terengganu

Preparing the unbiquitous ABC, a colorful dessert of grated ice, beans, jelly, and syrup

Terengganu craft centres
As rich as Kota Bharu in traditional crafts, Kuala Terengganu makes a good base for visiting local workshops. The Sutera-semai Centre (3½ miles south at Kuala Ibai) houses Malaysia's pioneer silk-weaving center, where you can follow every stage of production from the mulberry bush to the finished woven product (13,100 yards are made annually). A few miles along on is the handicraft center of Rhusila, where demonstrations of pandan-weaving, *songket*-weaving, and batik-printing are held. It is also a bastion of Islam, so be properly attired. Scattered along this stretch of road are numerous workshops and retail outlets. However, prices are definitely geared to tourists and you may strike a better bargain at the Central Market.

203

Beyond the market area is **Jalan Bandar►►**, the one-street Chinatown of Kuala Terengganu, where jewelers, tailors, barbers, watch sellers, and coffee shops combine pleasantly in an atmospheric stretch of old shophouses culminating at a Buddhist temple. At the end is a taxi stand and the main jetty where ferries cross the river to **Pulau Duyong►►**, an extraordinary relic of traditional coastal Malaysia. Here, in a picturesque and roadless island dotted with stilt houses, boat builders carry on a craft that is passed down from generation to generation. Tropical hardwoods are molded without the benefit of plans or designs into anything from modern yachts to typical fishing trawlers. Numerous other river trips can be taken to islands and fishing villages near by.

For cultural activities, the **Gelanggang Seni►►** (Cultural Center) is located on the beach road at the other end of town, past the Pantai Primula Hotel. Performances of *silat* (the Malay art of self-defense), traditional dances and games are held here from Thursday to Saturday at 5 P.M. Even if you miss the show, the blissful stretch of beach along Pantai Batu Buruk will give a good idea of local activities.

Kuantan's new mosque

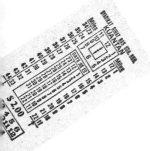

The ubiquitous *kris*
Displayed in countless forms in every state museum of Malaysia, the variously spelled *keris* or *kris* has deep roots in local superstition and spiritual symbolism. This deadly instrument is the traditional Malay weapon *par excellence*, and for more than 600 years has governed the fate of many a warrior or ruler. Although the owner can order any shape he likes, preference usually goes to a wavy blade which, when inserted between the shoulderblades, pierces parts that other daggers cannot reach. Originally imported from Java, according to legend the dagger actually flew, seeking out and killing any worthy enemy. Elaborate craftsmanship produces decorative hilts in carved ivory, finely chiseled gold or silver, or intricately carved wood. At least two kinds of iron are used for the blade, their proportions directly influencing the amount of good or bad luck the *kris* will bring.

▶▶ Kuantan   186A2

Occupying a strategic site halfway up the east coast and within an easy four-hour drive of KL across the peninsula's center, Kuantan is a bustling estuary town and the state capital of Pahang. The most interesting area to investigate lies by the waterfront along Jalan Besar and the parallel Jalan Mahkota. Colorful old shophouses, hotels, the bus station, the taxi stand, and the tourist office are all clustered there, as is an outdoor food center which supplies enormous prawns along with a view of the river. Handicraft shops, some old shophouses, and a lively fish market complete the town's sights.

A few miles to the north is the beach at **Teluk Cempedak**, focus for the luxury hotels. Starting at a rocky headland, a superb expanse of sand sweeps south past souvenir shops, mainly Chinese restaurants, and the gigantic Hyatt Hotel. Plenty of water sports are available, the Balai Karyaneka has a display of local craftwork and, for those wanting an escape from the madding crowd, trails lead from the headland into a forest reserve.

▶▶ Marang   186B2

Much vaunted as an idyllic, unspoilt fishing village, Marang (9 miles south of Kuala Terengganu) is rapidly turning into a backpacker's ghetto, gearing itself solely to their needs and losing its uncommercial east coast character in the process. So far it remains completely undeveloped, and the traditional wooden *kampung* houses lining the waterfront create a picture-postcard vision against the backdrop of a palm-lined lagoon mirroring rows of colorful fishing boats—except when low tide

reveals local rubbish. Marang is a popular stopover for those on their way to Pulau Kapas (see page 207), and offers plenty of cheap accommodations and eating places, all of which unfailingly run snorkeling trips, boat trips to Kapas or along the Marang river, and inland jaunts to the Sekayu Waterfalls (see page 213). Batik is similarly omnipresent and restaurants offer dishes more reminiscent of Bali. However, for those interested in exchanging island tales with other travelers, this is where it's at!

Marang's lagoon is a magnet for backpackers

205

► Mersing 187B2

The largest coastal town in Johor, Mersing (82 miles north-east of Johor Bahru) is a busy fishing port. A "no-sights" town apart from the hilltop mosque, Mersing is really only a stepping stone to the myriad coral islands lying off shore. Of these, Pulau Tioman (see pages 210–211) is the number one destination. However, if boat, bus, or tide timetables leave you there overnight there is a good range of hotels and enough atmosphere around the harbor to keep boredom at bay. The main street leading to the seafront, Jalan Abu Bakar, is lined with Chinese, Indian, and Malay coffee shops and restaurants, cheap hotels, and travel agencies that organize three-day trips to the Endau-Rompin Forest (see page 193). There are some respectable beaches nearby, particularly at Ayer Papan (8 miles north), and at Seri Pantai and Sekakap (a few miles south), the latter marking the end of the road.

►►► Pantai Dalam Rhu 186C1

Also known as Pantai Bisikan Bayu (meaning "Beach of Whispering Breeze"), this typical east coast stretch of white sand, fringed by soft, shady casuarina trees and exuberant tropical greenery, lies 36 miles south of Kota Bharu on the state border. Adjoining the fishing village of Semerak, it is reached by taking the Kuala Besut bus from Pasir Puteh which, in its turn, is accessible from Kota Bharu by SKMK Bus 3. The beach is a ten-minute walk from the road, but it is never busy and the clear waters offer good snorkeling.

Gunung Belumut Recreational Forest
About 40 miles inland from Mersing on the road to Keluang is a lush forest park equipped with jungle trails, campsites, and picnic sites. Ardent climbers can attack Gunung Belumut (meaning "Mossy Mountain") itself, which rises to 3,306 ft. Two rivers flow through the forest and there are innumerable waterfalls on the way to the summit as well as plenty of mossy trunks and stones.

■ **One of Malaysia's most skilled crafts, *kain songket* is the lustrous cloth of sultans and rajahs, a silver- and gold-threaded brocade that is transformed into formal headdresses, jackets, and sarongs. Traditionally employing family looms, the industry is now spreading to state workshops in order to keep this disappearing skill alive. .....■**

Songket designs

The intricate *songket* designs once represented the royal insignia or symbols of the family for which it was woven. Local inspirations include flora such as hibiscus flowers, persimmons, or pumpkin seeds, while bamboo plants are rendered in various stylized forms. Traditional man-made objects from the *kris* to fans and decorative dish covers have also been incorporated by weavers into their complex designs. Geometric border patterns form the finishing touch for each length of cloth.

206

Costing anything from RM200 to RM10,000 (US$80 to US$4,000) for a sarong-length, this highly prized brocade is produced in the east coast states of Kelantan, Terengganu, and, to a lesser extent, Pahang. Once made exclusively for royalty by court artisans, *songket*-weaving is now a flourishing cottage industry dominated by women, each one with a clearly defined role in the demanding process. In these democratic times, *songket* has become the most popular material for both bride and groom's wedding costumes, as well as forming the basis of ceremonial and formal evening wear. Every museum in Malaysia displays early royal versions, sumptuous and subtle designs twisted and pleated into a variety of turbans or exquisite expanses of sarong.

Warp and weft *Songket* is a highly labor-intensive craft, on average requiring three months for a sarong length or six hours to weave 6 inches. Weavers work in a hierarchy, the young apprentices setting simple patterns while the experienced master weavers create new designs and set the warping frames. Two women operate each handloom, interweaving colored silk thread with silver and/or gold threads day after day until the piece is complete. Quality is judged by the evenness and neatness of the weave, by any mistakes that occur in the pattern, and by the subtlety of the gold in comparison to its background color.

Most traditional cloths are deep maroon, blue, or green, with yellow reserved for royalty. However, in Terengganu moves are being made to stimulate the industry by introducing pastel colors and even Indonesian *ikat* and batik designs. Synthetic *songket* can easily be spotted by its brighter colors and infinitely lower prices.

Lustrous kain songket, *a craft unique to the east coast*

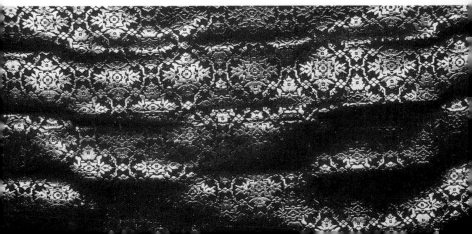

The diminutive but increasingly popular Pulau Kapas

▶▶ Pekan   187C1

Pekan (28 miles south of Kuantan) is the royal capital of the state of Pahang. It governs the estuary of the almighty Pahang river, from which many a war party has set off. Entrance from the north is via a toll bridge, underlining Pekan's exclusive status. The royal family has endowed this town with a stately style, and old shophouses, wide avenues lined with regal street lamps, and colonial-style bungalows or minor palaces set in beautifully manicured lawns all contibute to its unique charm.

Although the wealthy sultan, an avid gambler, possesses ten homes in Kuantan, he chooses to spend most of his time in London. His flamboyant palace, the **Istana Abu Bakar**, flanks the Royal Golf Club and the Royal Polo Club where Pekan high society flocks to an exclusive nightclub converted from an old locomotive. The Pahang sultans (who trace their lineage back to 15th-century Melaka) have left a wealth of memorabilia at the State Museum (closed Monday; see side panel), which is housed in the old British Residency between marble mosques. About 3 miles from there at Pulau Keladi is an interesting silk-weaving center.

▶▶▶ Pulau Kapas   186B2

The small tropical island of Kapas (4 miles off Marang) offers a thickly jungled interior and the obvious delights of blissful powdery white beaches. Simple chalet accommodations are concentrated on one beach, although a resort hotel may soon disturb this peaceful, low-key environment. Boats from Marang cross to the island in 30 minutes, making it highly popular with weekend hordes.

Although the island's less accessible eastern beaches offer some good snorkeling, better underwater views can be found around neighboring Pulau Raja. Transport to Pulau Raja can be arranged either from Marang or from Kapas itself.

Pahang's State Museum
Fronted by a Japanese fighter plane, a reminder of the Occupation, the State Museum in Pekan houses a rich collection of royal and historical memorabilia. Superbly crafted objects, costumes, and accessories include intricately worked silver and gold buckles and belts, betel-containers, bronze teapots and 14th-century jars showing a marked Chinese influence. The Royal Gallery is, of course, air-conditioned, and displays sumptuous costumes and jewelry. On the upper floor the extensive Weapons Gallery exhibits some remarkable *kris* and spears, the Ceramics Gallery covers pea-green Sung Dynasty ware (10th to 13th centuries), later Ch'ing Dynasty porcelain (mid-17th century to 1912) and *cloisonné*, and the Natural History Gallery shows stuffed wildlife specimens. Completing the Pahang picture are the Textiles Gallery and Games Gallery.

Pulau Babi Besar

Tiger, clown, angel, and butterfly fish glide around the turquoise waters surrounding Pulau Babi Besar, a mere 9 miles from Mersing and an hour by boat. Windsurfing, snorkeling, and diving keep the tourists happy—many stay in one of the four resorts on four-day packages from Johor Bahru. Although years ago only a few fishermen went there to gather the marine harvest from their *kelongs*, the island is now a popular hideout and the season peaks sharply during the Malaysian and Singaporean holidays.

▶▶▶ Pulau Perhentian   *186C1*

Another blissful tropical getaway, the two Perhentian Islands lie 12 miles and a two-hour boat ride from Kampung Kuala Besut. Their relative remoteness makes them less prone to day-trippers than Pulau Kapas or Pulau Redang, and for the moment development is limited to one well-disguised beach resort overlooking a fabulous coral reef and a string of beach huts and chalets.

Pulau Kecil, the smaller of the two, boasts the only fishing village, a straggling waterfront of little interest, but as its accommodations are less concentrated than that on the larger island you should head there if you want real tranquility. **Pulau Besar** is uninhabited except for the beach huts lining its west coast; the atmosphere is low-key with all interest firmly focused on the coral reef at the northern end or on negotiating the rock-strewn beach to get there. Walks can also be made into the hilly jungle. Boats leave Kuala Besut daily when full until about 4 P.M.

▶▶ Pulau Rawa   *187B2*

Hardly an hour's boat ride from Mersing, the tiny island of Rawa saw its first and only chalet resort built in the early 1970s, and the resort boat offers the only transport from Mersing. Snorkeling, diving, fishing, and boating to nearby islands are the main activities, but most of the surrounding coral is now dead. As always on the east coast, conditions are totally relaxed and the bungalows and chalets are well designed to blend into the surrounding palm grove.

▶▶▶ Pulau Redang   *186C2*

Surrounded by eight offshore islets, Redang is an underwater paradise with rocky promontories shooting into the sea and magnificent coral reefs teeming with baby reef sharks, seahorses and brilliantly colored tropical fish. Its far-flung isolation—it takes three hours to reach by bumboat from Kampung Merang—has left it wonderfully underdeveloped. At present the string of chalets near Telok Dalam and stilt house fishing village at Telok Siang are the only signs of human life. However, all this will soon change as a massive resort development starts to take shape. By 1994 the first phase will include a golf course, 150 bungalows, and a horse ranch. Ferries will leave from Kuala Terengganu and the island peace will be shattered. Travelers with camping equipment may still be able to escape the hordes on this 10-sq-mile island, but this will entail hiring a boat as the most idyllic beaches have no road access.

Snorkelers in search of coral

▶▶▶ Pulau Sibu   *187B2*

This tiny virgin island lies south of Mersing, between 1½ and 2½ hours away depending on the boat. A lush jungle interior, mangrove swamps, endless beautiful beaches,

rich coral and marine life, anchovy *kelong* (fish traps), a fishing village, canoeing, windsurfing, and accommodations ranging from comfortable chalets to basic beach huts make it a perfect version of paradise in the South China Sea.

Fishing boats shuttle passengers between Pulau Perhentian and Kuala Besut

▶▶▶ Pulau Sibu Tengah   187B2

This island, part of the same cluster as Sibu (the group also includes Pulau Sibu Hujong and Pulau Sibu Kukus), could have been another of *Robinson Crusoe*'s settings. Virtually uninhabited, it offers similar natural splendors to Sibu, with powdery sand, hilly jungle, and fantastic marine life. Two comfortable chalet resorts are the only form of accommodations. Sibu and Sibu Tengah can be reached from Tanjung Sedili, 20 miles from Kota Tinggi.

▶▶ Pulau Tenggul   186B2

Until recently the small, rocky island of Tenggul (11 miles from Dungun) was restricted to day-trippers and campers. However, a 20-room chalet development, the Pulau Tenggul Aqua Resort, has recently opened there, offering scuba diving and water-sports facilities. Steep, jungle-clad slopes slide into a white beach before descending to dramatic sunken cliffs thick with coral. The island is also known for its abundant reptile life. Transport can be arranged from Dungun or the Tanjung Jara resort.

▶▶▶ Pulau Tinggi   187B2

One of the larger islands of the group lying off Mersing, Tinggi was christened "General's Hat Island" by Chinese traders over 600 years ago—an apt description of its conical shape, which rises to about 2,300 ft. in the center. From the peak there are superb views in all directions toward outlying islands. One small fishing village interrupts an otherwise endless stretch of white beaches and coves, and the island's coral reef is a haven for snorkelers and divers. For the moment there are only two traditionally designed resorts, with prices to match the relative luxury they offer.

Snorkelers' and divers' special
Considered one of the best places in the world for diving and snorkeling, the South China Sea has been attracting scuba-divers for a long time. Diving equipment can generally be hired from the larger resorts (Pulau Perhentian, Pulau Besar, and Pulau Tinggi), and basic snorkeling masks are nearly always available for hire at the smaller places. Very often the richest underwater life is found around outlying islets; boat trips to these are easily arranged. The best period for transparent seas unsullied by the monsoon winds and rain is from May to October.

Diving delights

Tioman's waters are classed as a marine park for their wealth of multi-colored *Acropora* (stag-horn) corals, sea fans, translucent soft corals, and flowerlike sea anemones. The sea floor is clear to a depth of 100 ft., so even snorkelers can revel in the flashy cardinal fish, parrot fish, wrasses, damsel fish, and butterfly fish which flit through the coral landscape. All beaches have a wealth of marine life, particularly in the shallow reefs of Salang (off Air Batang) and around Pulau Rengis opposite the resort beach. However, the most spectacular coral reefs are at Pulau Tulai (Coral Island) and Pulau Cebeh, two islets off the northwest point; boat trips to these run from all the beaches and equipment can be rented at numerous diving centers. If, for any reason, you don't like getting wet, glass-bottom boat tours of the coral reefs are also available.

►►► Pulau Tioman   187B2

Paradise? Hollywood certainly thought so in the 1950s when they filmed the musical *South Pacific* on this large, mountainous island flung far out in the crystalline azure of the South China Sea. So did Chinese and Arab traders over 1,500 years ago as they plied along the spice route, using Tioman as a bountiful stopover. And so do hundreds of Singaporeans every weekend of the year when the monsoon is not blowing. Tioman, 30 miles from Mersing, four hours by "slow boat" and 1½ hours by hydrofoil, still captivates every traveler who sets foot there—unless his or her foot lands on one of the many sea-urchins that plague the shores. Mountains, jungle, waterfalls, coral reefs, and perfect palm-fringed beaches all create a setting that even the visitors pouring off the daily flights from KL, Kerteh, Kuantan, and Singapore haven't yet managed to destroy.

Beaches With choices ranging from luxury chalets to basic beach huts, visitors can opt for high, low or intermediary life. The main beaches are on the west coast, although on the east coast **Kampung Juara** offers a superb sandy bay and simple accommodations, all in relative isolation as it is only accessible by a three-hour jungle trek across the island or by a twice-daily sea bus. Other

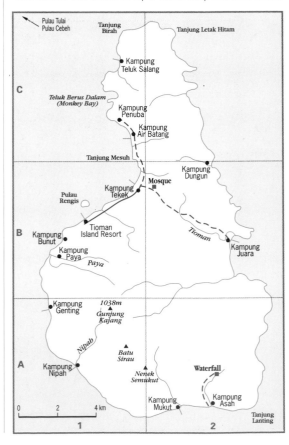

Pulau Tioman

Basic A-frame huts for budget travelers line the island's beaches

Tioman legend
Legend has it that Tioman is the resting place of a dragon princess who, on a journey from China to Singapore, was so enamored of the spot that she terminated her trip there and transformed herself into the island.

secluded spots well away from the main buzz are at the northern end of the west coast road, at **Kampung Teluk Salang**, a beautiful little bay with a good diving center, or, in the deep south and accessible only by boat, at **Kampung Nipah**. Between the two lies the main village, **Kampung Tekek**, where the airport, the main jetty, shops, and a mosque (and sometimes a lot of litter) make it an obvious focal point. The more picturesque side of Tekek lies south of the jetty. About two miles to the north, backpackers arrive in droves at lively **Kampung Air Batang,** where cheap beach huts front the lush vegetation along a partly rocky shore. A short jungle stroll over the headland brings you to **Kampung Penuba**, a more tranquil spot with far fewer hotels.

Whiling the day away Those who tire of sun worship have the underwater world at their doorstep. Round-island trips give a good overview and all stop at the famous "Happy Talk" waterfall, a short walk inland from Kampung Asah in the south. Mountain lovers can gaze at the twin granite peaks (often shrouded in mist) soaring 3,300 ft. out of the jungle, but more realistic is the cross-island trail from Tekek, climbing through dense jungle past a river and waterfall before panning out into an area of rubber plantations. Golf and horse riding are offered at the resort, while windsurfing, canoeing, sailing, and fishing can be experienced by all—sometimes at a price. The latter can rise from July to August and during any local holiday period, but bargains can be found early and late in the season when sporadic downpours add drama to the skies and seas.

Development has yet to spoil Tioman's stunning beaches

211

FOCUS ON *Turtles*

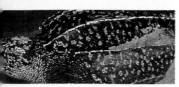

■ **Malaysia's turtles have been sighted as far away as the Atlantic Ocean, but each year they miraculously make their way home to lay their eggs—an opportunity for long nights of turtle-watching from beach shelters or more comfortable chalets .....■**

Labor of love
"When they came, those great, gravid females, it was at midnight, out of mountainous seas, and they labored harder than any woman in birth... It was a most poetic sight, that moment when the huge beast reentered her element."
From: *Turtle Beach* by Blanche d'Alpuget (1981).

The atavistic capacities of turtles are remarkable: year in, year out they return to their own birthplace to lay the eggs of the next generation, which will repeat the same process in an endless cycle—for as long as the species exists. A stretch of coast 90 miles north from Cerating to beyond Rantau Abang, as well as certain islands off Mersing, are prime nesting areas for giant leatherbacks, while in East Malaysia the Turtle Islands Park off Sandakan (see page 250) plays host to green and hawksbill turtles. The nesting season for leatherbacks is from June to September, peaking in August; for green turtles it is from August to October, and for hawksbill turtles it is from February to April.

Laying the eggs Despite increasing concern about their fate, the giant leatherbacks continue to make their nocturnal appearance at Rantau Abang, dragging their 6–10 ft., 1,500-pound hulks up on to the beach where they scout around for the right spot to dig their hole. Then starts the lengthy process of laying 100 or so eggs, apparently so painful that the turtles have been known to cry (in reality, this moisture is used to lubricate the eyes and cleanse them of sand). Once the eggs have been laid, the turtle fills and conceals the pit before lumbering back down the beach, only to return several times during the season to lay more. It's a turtle's life indeed.

Female turtles climb up the beach beyond the high-water mark to build their nests

Protecting the young The Department of Fisheries is now trying to ensure that the eggs, considered a delicacy by locals, are not removed. If left untouched the eggs hatch after about 55 days. Then starts another critical period—the perilous journey of the baby turtles across the sands to the sea, at the mercy of every predator around. Today, inspectors aid nature by making a morning collection of hatched turtles before releasing them into the sea; a beach hatchery also affords completely protected hatching conditions. Officially about 40,000 young have to be returned to the sea each year before any egg-collecting is allowed. The Turtle Islands Park in Sabah was a pioneer in this domain, and was established in 1964 as a protected turtle farm. However, despite these efforts turtles are still diminishing in number and Malaysia's turtle beaches may not be around for too much longer.

The Sekayu
Waterfalls are rated
among Malaysia's
most spectacular and
can be combined
with a visit to nearby
Tasik Kenyir

▶▶ Rantau Abang 186B2

The much-vaunted "Turtle Beach" of Malaysia's east coast lies a few miles north of Dungun. Crowds peak from June to September when giant leatherback turtles waddle up the beach to lay their 100 or so eggs (see opposite page). All the low-key development focuses on this event, and an information center provides extensive background details and film shows.

▶▶▶ Sekayu Waterfalls 186B2

Seven cascades crash down a rocky slope through thick jungle to create large, cool pools of fresh water at this spot (35 miles southwest of Kuala Terengganu). The spectacular sight and setting naturally draw the crowds, but during the week you can get away from it all by trekking or camping in the rain forest surrounding the falls. At the base of the falls a rest-house, a few chalets, a miniature zoo, a bird park, and a wildlife reserve (deer, tapir, and, perhaps, tigers) keep visitors happy.

▶ Sungai Lembing 186A2

Sungai Lembing (27 miles west of Kuantan) is home to Malaysia's only underground tin mine, closed since the 1980s, when tin prices tumbled. This virtual ghost town offers little of interest bar a few crumbling colonial buildings, but real enthusiasts may get permission to visit the mine—apparently the world's second largest—from Pahang Consolidated Ltd. Obtain further details from the Kuantan tourist office (tel: 09 512960).

▶▶▶ Tanjung Jara 186B2

A few miles south of Rantau Abang, the Tanjung Jara Beach Hotel (8 miles north of Dungun) has become a west coast landmark (see side panel). Although strong currents make swimming in the sea dangerous, the undulating palm-lined beach is ideal for endless promenades.

Tanjung Jara Beach Hotel
Beautifully crafted from tropical woods and following the traditional Malay palace style this harmonious, unpretentious, and moderately priced resort is an example for the rest of Malaysia to follow. In fact, its discreet charms were rewarded with the Aga Khan Prize, a triennial architectural award for Islamic countries. Landscaped gardens dotted with carved wooden longhouses surround a natural lagoon, and the soaring, timbered lobby and restaurant are open to the gardens.

■ **Rain forests aside, Malaysia's greatest natural wonder is the wealth of its coral reefs, these surrounding hundreds of outlying islands off both the peninsula and East Malaysia. Many of the reefs have now been declared marine parks in an attempt to preserve their prolific and sensational aquatic life—a contrast to unprotected areas where overfishing has led to the disappearance of many larger fish. .....■**

214

Underwater sights

Snorkelers can easily see algae beds, giant clams, sea slugs, sea anemones, starfish, hard and soft corals, a wealth of luminous spotted and striped tropical fish—butterfly fish, angel fish, parrot fish, lion fish, damsel fish, and cardinal fish—and the adroitly camouflaged stone fish which hides to await its prey. Divers in deeper waters may encounter lobsters, barracudas, common rays, mantas, garupas, whale sharks, and the mysterious flashlight fish. Remember always that apart from being a tourist attraction, the reef forms a delicate environment which also helps to control coastal erosion. When part of the balance is disturbed it sets off a chain reaction that affects the whole reef often with disastrous results.

From the west coast's Pulau Paya to east coast island havens or Sabah's more numerous isolated dots of paradise, the choice of marine parks is vast. Because of the monsoons (whose violent winds and rains churn up even these pristine underworlds) each area has its prime diving time. Between October and March the west coast should be your destination; from January to May the islands west of Sabah come into their own, although Sipadan's unique season continues until December; and from May to October the east coast islands lie in a crystalline state of perfection.

Marine park regulations As the objective of the marine parks is to preserve endangered species and the natural environment, certain activities are prohibited within these zones. Water-skiing, speedboats, spear- and line-fishing, lighting fires on beaches, littering, removing coral, and anchoring boats over coral areas are all strictly prohibited. However tempted you are to collect shells or coral from the seabed, refrain from doing so as this destroys the delicate ecosystem and diminishes the coral's base. Similarly, be aware of certain dangers such as tides and strong currents, as well as poisonous and dangerous organisms—the stinging sea nettle, fire coral, Neptune's cup sponge and spiky sea urchins are among the most common irritants, but others can do much more damage to the unwary snorkeler.

Visitors' centers on most of the marine park islands provide the necessary information about these hazards.

Five-star swims Lost off the west coast between Langkawi and Pinang, **Pulau Paya** and three other islands are blessed with a coral garden reputed to have the largest number of species in Malaysia, and the water they inhabit is clear to a depth of 100 ft. The carefully protected islands offer no accommodations.

The northern marine park of the east coast includes **Pulau Perhentian, Pulau Redang, Pulau Kapas,** and **Pulau Tenggul,** all scattered off the coast from

Butterfly fish feed around the coral reefs

Kampung Kuala Besut to Dungun. All the islands offer accommodations. Close to Redang and Kapas are numerous other uninhabited islets with even richer aquatic life. Tenggul is renowned for its near-vertical sunken cliffs, a haven for numerous rare specimens in the shady depths and caves. The islands of **Sibu**, **Mentinggi**, **Tinggi**, **Besar**, **Tengah**, **Hujung**, and **Rawa** (all off Mersing in the south) offer fantastic underwater sights (although around Rawa much of the coral is dead). However, the prime attraction remains the **Tioman** group, also off Mersing but lying farther north and farther out. Like Paya, Tioman's **Cebeh** and **Tulai** mushroom out of a sea so transparent that the bottom is clear at a depth of 100 ft.

In Sabah the most easily accessible marine park lies off Kota Kinabalu, where four main islands are collectively named the **Tunku Abdul Rahman National Park**. Proximity to civilization combined with exposure to the force of the monsoon winds have

Vast beds of both soft and hard coral await divers

left their mark, and although marine life here is of great beauty, visibility is better off the east coast at Sipadan. About 30 miles southwest of Tunku Abdul Rahman National Park, three islands comprise the **Pulau Tiga Park**, whose emerald depths harbor delicate sea fans, stag-horn corals, and a familiar array of neon fish. You may choose to avoid the waters around Pulau Ular, which are full of poisonous sea snakes! Sabah's **Turtle Islands Park** has an abundant coral garden where you might find yourself paddling along in the company of a green turtle.

Without doubt, however, **Pulau Sipadan** is the icing on Malaysia's diving cake. Lying off Sabah's southeastern coast in the Celebes Sea, it is the country's only oceanic island (in other words, not connected to the continental shelf). A limestone pinnacle offers a 2,300-ft. wall dive just a few yards off the beach. Underwater cliffs, caverns, funnels, and ledges create a dramatic backdrop to turtles and abundant reef fish of every shape, and visibility can reach 230 ft.!

Coral
A living organism, coral is made up of millions of tiny coral polyps, cup-shaped creatures consisting of a ring of tentacles surrounding a mouth. Many corals resemble plants, but they are in fact carnivorous animals related to the sea anemone and jellyfish. They feed on microscopic plankton which float in the sea, catching them with tentacles that are charged with stinging cells.

Ornate Buddhist wats are part of the Thai legacy after centuries of sporadic rule

Kenyir Dam
Tasik Kenyir was created in 1985 by the construction of the massive Kenyir Dam. The dam is open to the public daily 8–6 (closed for lunch) and the visitors' center proselytizes about the merits of hydroelectric power.

▶▶▶ **Tasik Kenyir** *186B1*

This vast inland sea (142 sq miles) dominates a hilly region 33 miles southwest of Kuala Terengganu and spouts rivers in all directions. Several floating chalet hotels have sprung up around its shores, making it a spectacular spot for a few days' fishing, boating, jungle trekking, or waterfall swimming. Access is via Kuala Berang, where there are also limited accommodations.

▶ **Tumpat** *186C1*

Knocking on Thailand's door at the end (or beginning) of Malaysia's east coast is the small town of Tumpat. From there it is just a short hop to Kampung Pengkalan Kubor, the customs point for entry into Thailand. Tumpat (12 miles north of Kota Bharu) lies in a rural district of paddy fields and orchards dotted with *wats*, the distinctive Thai Buddhist temples. The town is the final stop on the jungle railway, hardly a claim to fame, but there isn't even a hotel for those who get off there. The nearest accommodations are at the local beach, Pantai Seri Tujuh, where a rather tacky resort sprawls beside a beautiful natural lagoon. However, if you are driving the region offers some verdant landscapes, unspoiled *kampungs*, *wats* and water buffaloes.

▶ **Wat Phothivihan** *186C1*

Yet another of Southeast Asia's largest Buddhas (or Asia's second largest, depending on the source) is claimed by this modern Buddhist temple (2 miles from Kampung Jambu, between Tumpat and Kota Bharu). You really need to take either a taxi or a car to get there as there is no public transportation.

The polychromatic Buddha reclining in eternal peace measures 130 x 29 x 36 ft., and greets all those intrepid enough to reach the temple. An adjoining guest house is

Drive

Royal palaces and beach resorts

EAST COAST DRIVE

Starting at Kuantan, this drive gives a glimpse of Pahang's regal tastes, a vast troglodyte Buddha, inland and coastal *kampungs*, and beach resorts before finishing at Beserah.

From Kuantan take the KL road (No. 2), turning left at Kampung Batu Enam on to road No. 3. Drive past paddy-fields and wooded areas before crossing Peninsular Malaysia's longest river, Sungai Pahang. A toll road leads you into the elegant royal town of **Pekan**, official home of Pahang's sultan and his extended family. Drive past palaces, the Royal Polo Club and colonial-style bungalows before visiting the State Museum.

  Return via the fishing *kampungs* of the coast road, bypassing **Kuantan** to reach the Sungai Lembing turnoff. Drive 14 miles up this road and then turn right through rubber and oil-palm plantations to the foot of **Gua Charas**. One of the caves in this towering limestone cliff houses a giant Buddha that was carved by a Thai monk.

  Return to the main road (No. 3), soon turning left along road No. 14, which winds inland through mountainous terrain to the west. At Kampung Air Putih turn right to regain the coast at **Kampung Kemaman**.

Follow the palm-lined coast road, stopping at **Kampung Cerating**'s spectacular beach or farther south at **Baluk Beach**, popular with windsurfers. Last port of call is the charming fishing village of **Beserah**, 6 miles north of Kuantan.

217

EAST MALAYSIA

D

C

B

A

0   50   100   150   200 km

Pulau Labuan
Victori

Tanjung
Baram
Lutong
Miri
Limbang
BRU
Lambir Hills
National Park
Beluru
Marudi
2371
Gunun
Mulu
Niah National Park
Batu Niah
**Niah
Caves**
**Gunung Mulu
National Park**
Lon
Serid
Similajau
Long
Lellang
Banjara
Tama
Bintulu
Kemena
Tubau
Tinjar
Baram
Tutoh
Tanjung Sirik
Oya
Mukah
Igan
Oya
Mukah
S A R A W A K
Belaga
Tatau
1280m
Bukit
Kanawang
Sibu
Pelagus
Rapids
Pergunungan Iran
Sarikei
Binatangor
Rajang
Mujong
2012m
Bukit Batu
Balui
Tanjung Datu
**Gunung Gading
National Park**
Pantai Damai
(Kampung Budaya
Sarawak)
**Rumah
Layang**
Song
Kapit
Baleh
Sematan
Lundu
Santubong
Bako National Park
Bako
Kuching
Bau
Semenggoh
Simunjan
Kampung
Padawan
Crocodile Farm
Serian
Batang
Ai
Pergunungan Kapuas Hulu
Banjaran
Gunung Nieuwenhuis
**Bandar Sri Aman
(Simanggang)**

1   2   3

Map labels:

Selat Balabac

Pulau Balambangan · Pulau Banggi

Sikuati · **Kudat**

Mengkabong Water Village · Langkong · Pulau Jambongan

Tandek · Kota Belud · nku Abdul Rahman Nat Park

4101m G Kinabalu · Turtle Islands National Park

Tuaran · **Kinabalu National Park** · Teluk Labuk

Kota Kinabalu · Kampung Poring · Klagan

Penampang · Kg · Hot Springs · Beluran · **Sandakan**

lau · Kundasang · Ranau · Sepilok

rk Kuala Penyu · Papar · Tambunan · Orang-Utan Sanctuary · Gomantong Caves

S A B A H

abfort · Banjaran Crocker · Kampung Tulid · Kampung Kuala Tongod · Tomanggong

ampung mbok · Keningau · Lahad Datu

Sipitang · Tenom · Banjaran Maitland · Pinangah · Danum Valley

awas · Tomani · Sapulut · Banjaran Brassey · Teluk Lahad Datu

ong kang · Maligan · Kampung Batu Punggul · Kunak · Pulau Bohey Dulang

Long Pa Sia · Sigattal · Tawau Hills National Park · Semporna

Long Semado · Kalabakan · **Tawau**

Ba Kelalan · Pulau Sipadan

2438m Gunung Murud

Bareo

Pidas

Labuk

Kinabatangan

Segama

Teluk Labuk

RI

4 · 5

East Malaysia Flying into East Malaysia from the Malay Peninsula takes you one gigantic leap toward Melanesia. Leaving behind the urban patchwork of Malay, Chinese, and Indian cultures, travelers enter the distinctive land of Borneo. Echoes of headhunters, hornbills, white rajahs, pirates, and rampant wildlife reverberate through virgin rain forest. The first aerial view takes in serpentine rivers twisting endlessly through the dense green landscape, raising the specter of infinite mystery. But the 20th century rolls on and other realities soon emerge. Oil boom towns, Kentucky Fried Chicken, Guinness, sophisticaed hotels plugged into CNN, vast tracts of desolate logging areas and modernized longhouses are the flipside of the world's third largest island. Yet anyone with a spirit of adventure can take advantage of a bewildering number of opportunities, whether they choose to be cosseted by local tours or pursue lone treks through the sweetly rotting jungle.

EAST MALAYSIA

Sarawak's Cultural Village lies less than an hour's drive from Kuching

Land of adventure Marketed as "The Land of Adventure," Borneo is occupied by the Indonesian state of Kalimantan in the south, with Malaysia's semi-autonomous states of Sarawak and Sabah slicing out a chunk of the north. Sandwiched in between is the tiny oil-rich sultanate of Brunei. A distinct history, strong ethnic traditions, and a Malay minority give East Malaysia a fragmented identity. The region embraces the remote upper reaches of the interior as well as the capitals of Kuching and Kota Kinabalu, home to high-rises and Chinatowns, and where Dayaks or Kadazans drive Toyotas. Wild, prosperous, impoverished, and bewitching, East Malaysia is like one of its many forest spirits, luring visitors deeper and deeper into the interior and dispensing magic from its mountains to its marine underworlds.

Past powers Sarawak, "The Land of the Hornbills," and Sabah, "The Land Below the Wind" (a poetic reference to its site below the typhoon belt of the Philippines), both threw off the British cloak to join Malaysia in 1963, six years after Peninsular Malaysia had gained independence. Their colonial backgrounds, however, were quite distinct from one another, Sarawak having been ruled by its "white rajahs" from 1841 to 1941, and Sabah by the uninhibited economic interests of the British North Borneo Chartered Company from 1888 to 1941.

Japanese occupation was followed by postwar stirrings for independence, exacerbated by their new status as British Crown Colonies. Sarawak was torn by a bloody anti-cession movement after the last white rajah chickened out of reconstructing his country. Further unrest accompanied Filipino and, more actively, Indonesian claims to North Borneo, resulting in jungle warfare between Commonwealth and Indonesian forces along the Kalimantan border up until 1966.

Children peeping from the window of a water-village stilt house

Today's powers Since joining Malaysia in 1963, Sabah and Sarawak have remained troubled. Both are fully aware of their economic importance, whether in offshore oil and gas fields or in the considerable profits from the increasingly depleted rain forest. Their privileged semi-autonomous political status often creates conflicts with the federal government, both on economic and immigration issues. Sabah's local government has been led since 1985 by an opposition party, Parti Bersatu Sabah, and Prime Minister Mahathir even interpreted recent confrontations as a move toward independence. Japanese and Taiwanese investment in the timber industry is significant, although official logging quotas remain cloudy, and traditional shifting cultivation has also left its destructive mark, albeit negligible when compared to the logging.

Although the cost of living is higher in East Malaysia, luxury goods are cheaper and Peninsular Malaysians flock in to buy cars in Sabah or hi-fis in the duty-free port of Labuan. Sarawak, Malaysia's largest and least densely populated state (1½ million people spread over 47,690 sq miles), is also a hotbed for corrupt officialdom, most of it fired by the allocation of logging licenses. And within this web of intrigue the losers are the native peoples, whose traditional fishing and hunting grounds have been (and still are) seriously affected by the inexorable advance of the chain saws.

Borneo is home to...
- The world's largest flower (the *Rafflesia*).
- The world's largest undivided leaf, 10 ft. long and 6½ ft. wide (the *Alocasia macrorrhiza* plant)—found in Sabah.
- The world's fastest-growing tree, known to reach 36 ft. in 13 months (the *Albizzia falcata*).
- The world's slowest egg-layer, producing only two eggs over a week (the masked booby).
- The world's largest cave chamber at the Gunung Mulu caves in Sarawak.
- The world's oldest and richest rain forest. Any 25-acre plot of Borneo jungle reputedly possesses 800 different trees; 25,000 species of flowering plants exist, compared with Europe's meager 6,000.

A Bajau water village in Sabah

Medicine or otherwise
In more remote areas of Borneo, villagers have no access to modern medicine at all as they are too distant even for the "flying doctor" helicopter service. As a result, they tend to rely on traditional Bornean plant remedies. The nomadic Penans who live far in the interior are acknowledged by other indigenous groups as experts in the use of medicinal plants. For stomachache they grind the pink roots of the *siksok* plant into a paste and apply this to the navel area, or boil bark shavings from the *tulong* tree to make a digestive tea. Lemon-grass oil is used as a mosquito repellent or as a massage oil. Stems and roots of the *galangga* tree are used for skin infections, and the petals of the melastona flower are used to remove scars or treat superficial wounds.

Tropically wild adventures Putting politics aside, the average visitor can indulge in a great escape into vast and magnificent nature reserves of untouched rain forest, record-breaking caves, jagged granite mountains, deserted coastlines, and brilliant underwater coral worlds. The national parks system has successfully saved enormous areas of natural beauty to protect surviving flora and fauna. Of Sarawak's seven national parks, the most justifiably famous are **Gunung Mulu, Niah**, and **Bako**. Adequate and still relatively low-key facilities enable visitors to explore these diverse regions or even trek for several days by river and through jungle. Sabah, which is just over half the size of Sarawak, claims six well-preserved parks and numerous reserves, the most famous being that of **Gunung Kinabalu** which spikes the clouds at the highest point of Southeast Asia.

Sabah's three seas—the South China Sea, the Sulu Sea, and the Celebes Sea—boast 38 islands, including the west coast marine parks of **Pulau Tiga** and **Tunku Abdul Rahman**, the latter only a few minutes from Kota Kinabalu. **Turtle Islands Park** and the diver's paradise of **Pulau Sipadan** lie to the east in seas that are still infested with Filipino and Indonesian pirates—just another taste of excitement to enliven your visit.

Longhouses and ethnic peoples What most people itch to see are the longhouses, a touch of the primitive and a guaranteed time-warp. Increasing exploitation of this unique institution, where families live communally in one long wooden building raised high on stilts, is changing the attitude of the innately hospitable inhabitants—whether they are Sarawak's Dayaks or Sabah's Rungus and Muruts. Gone are the days when disheveled and weary travelers could roll up at a longhouse, dispense a few beads and cigarettes, and instantly be offered a mat for the night by tattooed, feather-sporting natives.

Today's native peoples, although geographically isolated, are very much in touch with the outside world, and with Sarawak's tourism growing at an annual rate of 20 percent, longhouse visits are now firmly established on tour agency itineraries. Yet despite the fact that many longhouses sport corrugated-iron roofs and some even have been targeted for Western "incentive groups" (with the champagne brought in by helicopter), there are thousands more in the remote interior that remain in pristine condition. Hot, humid jungle walks, leeches, mosquitoes, and minimal levels of comfort, plus the obligatory consumption of a potent rice wine (*tapai* in Sabah and *tuak* in Sarawak) are part and parcel of this quest for the wilds.

In Sarawak the upper reaches of the **Rajang river** and, even less accessible, the Kelabit Highlands of **Bareo** offer infinite possibilities for exploring, while in Sabah the promontory of **Kudat** and the southwestern corner around **Long Pa Sia** are the most fertile longhouse areas. Guides are essential for such distant forays, and when boats have to be chartered costs mount up. Those with little time can gain a good though sanitized idea of traditional longhouse customs and architecture at the **Sarawak Cultural Village** (see page 245). And if you want a souvenir of your stay, superlative ethnic crafts are omnipresent in Kuching and at Sabah's colorful *tamus* (markets, literally "meeting place").

Locomotion With overland transport limited mostly to rivers or tracks, East Malaysia's transportation system is an adventure in itself. Sarawak's only sealed roads radiate from Kuching and Miri, but Sabah is gradually improving its coastal network. Four-wheel-drive vehicles are necessary for negotiating rough tracks to certain caves, longhouses, and parks, but river transport really wins the day. Labyrinthine waterways covering the entire region have formed the native people's transport routes for thousands of years, although dugouts have been replaced by fast express launches with air-conditioning and kung fu videos. Those with fatter wallets can use the excellent internal flights (often with bumpy Twin Otters), which extend to obscure up-country airstrips.

Whatever your means, planning is essential as the people of Borneo are a mobile lot and seats are not always available. Weather is another undetermined factor to consider; have you ever flown through the might of a monsoon or negotiated a flooded river?

Pigtailed monkeys at the Sepilok Orang-Utan Sanctuary

Stop-press tourist developments
Two new destinations are being opened up in Sabah. The first, billed as a new Sipadan, involves a mega RM62.5 million (US$25 million) development. Focused on Layang-Layang, a coral atoll in the Spratly Islands about 170 miles northwest of Kota Kinabalu (KK), it can be reached by cruise ship from KK. For the more budget-conscious, a new jungle resort called Batu Penggul is being developed in the southwest of Sabah. Although difficult to get to, it can be reached by heading for Keningau (at the southern end of the Banjaran Crocker), then south to Sapulut. From there a motorized longboat bucks through rapids and travels past jungle for four hours or so before reaching the resort where chalets and a Murut-style longhouse offer food and accommodations.

223

Sarawak's Bako National Park

Bako birds and wildlife
Even if you barely venture from base at Telok Assam you are likely to see long-tailed macaques, silver leaf monkeys, giant monitor lizards, wild boars, shy mouse deer, and proboscis monkeys, the latter unique to Borneo's mangrove swamps. The 150 indigenous bird species include the pied and the black hornbills, kingfishers, sunbirds, and reef egrets, while during the migratory season from September to November plovers, wagtails, pipits, shrikes, warblers, and flycatchers all home in from Siberia. On the beach you can observe fiddler crabs, mud skippers, and shell-dwelling hermit crabs.

▶▶▶   Bako National Park   218A1

Phosphorescent tides, luminous mushrooms and glow-worms, and spectacular sunsets over the South China Sea—these are the nocturnal sights of Bako National Park, Sarawak's oldest and smallest (10 sq mile) national park. However, its unique feature is its geology, as sandstone cliffs and offshore sea stacks have been weathered into extraordinary shapes and textures.

Easily and cheaply accessible by bus and boat from Bako, or directly by boat from Kuching, the park offers fairly simple accommodations (from a campsite to a "deluxe" rest-house) concentrated on the beach at Telok Assam. From there a network of 16 color-coded trails leads through swamp forest, mangroves, rivers, desert-like scrub, and dipterocarp rain forest, culminating in the startling coastal spectacle of sandstone formations.

You can spend a day trekking to the other side of the promontory and arrange to be picked up by boat—but beware of nightfall, which drops suddenly at 6:30 P.M. Permits and reservations can be arranged at the Kuching Tourist Office (tel: 082 410944); avoid the monsoon (November to March) as the park may be inaccessible.

▶▶   Bareo   219B4

On a high plateau near the Indonesian Kalimantan border in the Kelabit Highlands, Bareo is one of Sarawak's best bases for visits to remote longhouses. The local Kelabit people are skilled agriculturalists, cultivating vegetables and hill-rice in their beautiful high valleys where Christian crosses outnumber Islamic crescents. Mountaineers can attack **Gunung Murud**, Sarawak's highest peak at 7,980 ft., but will need to hire a guide for this and any of the strenuous treks to distant longhouses. Daily Twin Otter flights serve the Miri–Marudi–Bareo route.

▶   Belaga   218B3

This is the end of the road for travelers who have survived the perilous river trip from Kapit through the seven Pelagus Rapids, and one rarely obtains permission to go any farther. The market town of Belaga is home to the Kayan and Kenyah tribes, expert boatsmen, craftspeople, and dancers. The town has a few facilities but little else.

■ **Not just a market, more a meeting place and social high point of the week, *tamus* are peculiar to Sabah. They offer the best opportunity of seeing hill-people mingling with Kadazans, Bajaus and Rungus in a frenetic interaction of weird and wonderful jungle produce, buffaloes, handicrafts, parangs, and T-shirts. .....■**

Tamu activities can be tracked down on any day of the week in towns scattered all over Sabah. The market traders start at around 7 A.M. and pack up at noon to cover the long distances back to their villages. Each *tamu* has its own character and specialties, depending on the agricultural fruits of the area and needs of the inhabitants.

From buffalo auctions to betel nuts Kota Belud hosts the largest, most hyped, and most popular *tamu* with locals and visitors alike. There snazzy Bajau horsemen hold buffalo auctions against a backdrop of fading canvas awnings and umbrellas. Wrinkled old women squat behind piles of salted fish, giant clams, rice, traditional medicines, jungle fruits, and worms, while young men hawk racks of cheap clothes, batik, and cassettes, punctuated by mountains of rattan and basketware. Prominent among the more equivocal foodstuffs are piles of cream-colored dough cakes. These Bajau cakes are made of yeast mixed with cooked rice and are left to ferment overnight. For the Kadazans, however, this same yeast is used for their powerful alcoholic drink—*tapai*.

Most colorful of all the products are the gaily striped food covers—easily mistaken for outsized hats or lampshades. Betel nuts are bought, sold, and chewed as if chewing gum had gone out of fashion, and locally woven *dastar* cloth—traditionally worn by Kadazan (Dusun) men—is a common sight, both on and off the body.

Both **Tuaran** and **Tamparuli** (within two hours of Kota Kinabalu) hold interesting and authentic *tamus*, while that of KK itself, held on a Sunday morning, offers a wealth of local handicrafts.

Tamu days and venues
● Monday—Tandek.
● Tuesday—Kiulu and Topokon.
● Wednesday—Tamparuli.
● Thursday—Keningau, Tambunan, Sipitang, Telipok, Manggis, Simpangan, Tenghilan, and Nabalu.
● Friday—Susuron, Weston, and Mesapol.
● Saturday—Penampang, Beaufort, Sindumin, Matunggong, Kinarut, and Babagon.
● Sunday—Toboh, Tambunan, Tenom, Membakut, Kota Belud, Papar, Tuaran, Putatan, and Kota Kinabalu (Jalan Gaya).

225

Below: Goods on sale in Sabah's tamus

Bird's-nest collecting is now strictly regulated

Gading remembered
"During the night I heard the Argus pheasant crying in the woods, in response to distant thunder. These beautiful birds roam about the hill of Gading, which is close by the bungalow and thickly covered with virgin forest. The sound they make is uncanny and sorrowful, like the cry of lost souls wandering in the somber wilderness of innumerable trees, seeking to fathom the secrets of an implacable world. Any sudden loud sound, as of a dead tree falling or the rumble of thunder, however remote, apparently calls forth an echo of terror from these birds."
From: *My Life in Sarawak* by Margaret Brooke, Ranee of Sarawak (1913).

Bintulu   218B2

Drunk on offshore oil wealth, Sarawak's small coastal town of Bintulu is of absolutely no interest unless you find yourself stranded there on the way from Sibu to the Niah Caves or vice versa. Boats leave for the Similajau National Park and express launches zoom up the Kemena river to Tubau, a logging center from where a logging road eventually reaches Belaga.

►►► Gomantong Caves   219C5

The limestone Gomantong Caves (about 20 miles south of Sandakan in the east of Sabah) are another of East Malaysia's bird's-nest sanctuaries. For centuries acrobatic collectors have scaled rattan ropes and bamboo ladders to gather the valuable nests hidden high in these bat-infested caves (see page 251). Recent annual income from this activity nets RM500,000 (US$200,000). The smaller **Simud Hitam Cave**, whose roof nevertheless soars higher than 300 ft., furnishes the more common "black" nests, while the larger and more accessible **Simud Puteh Cave** is home to the highly prized "white" nests made of pure swiftlets' saliva.

Access is easiest by a two-hour boat ride from Sandakan, then by Landrover through secondary and logged forest teeming with butterflies and birds—watch for crested serpent eagles, Asian fairy bluebirds and kingfishers. Permits are necessary and are obtainable from the Sandakan Forest Department through Sabah Park (tel: 089 273453). The region is earmarked for development into a 100,000-acre park, and will then serve as a protected area for proboscis monkeys and elephants.

►► Gunung Gading National Park   218A1

At 2,966 ft., Gunung Gading is the highest peak of a small range of mountains 30 miles west of Kuching. The least developed of Sarawak's national parks (there are no visitors' facilities at present), it nevertheless covers 208 sq miles and its rugged beauty and waterfalls pull in the day-trippers from nearby Lundu, Sematan, and Kuching. Jungle trails lead through the forest and this is also the only place in Sarawak where you have a chance of seeing the foul-smelling but magnificent *Rafflesia* flower, the largest in the world (see side panel on page 231).

Nature is left to its own devices in East Malaysia's national parks

▶▶▶ Gunung Mulu National Park   218B3

Just when access was made easy with direct flights between Miri and Mulu, Sarawak's star attraction became reserved for tour groups only, making it a costly although rewarding trip. Accommodations are growing fast to cope with the increased influx of visitors who are willing to crawl and clamber to see these immense caves.

The 209 sq-mile Gunung Mulu Park has no rival in the world for the sheer size of its caves, including the world's largest cave, the **Sarawak Chamber**, the largest cave passage, the spectacular **Deer Cave**, and the longest cave in Southeast Asia, the gloomy **Clearwater Cave**, as well as lofty limestone peaks and underground waterways. Until recently, complicated though exciting river access limited the crowds and even now only a small part of the gigantic cave network is accessible: 121 miles have been surveyed by international expeditions so far, representing an estimated 38 percent of the total.

Flora and fauna grow richer and richer in diversity as you ascend from lowland peat swamp and heath through dipterocarp and moss forest to the upper montane vegetation at the summit of Gunung Mulu. Trekking to this 7,761-ft. peak takes four days, while a three-day trip to **Gunung Api** takes in the spiky limestone **Pinnacles**. Both are only for the super-fit.

Cave-crawling is no picnic either, and all treks require guides and boat trips from the park headquarters, an aspect that puts the prices of the organized tours into perspective. Shop around before booking as prices differ considerably between agencies. Several days are necessary to really appreciate the natural wonders of this remote region where 5 million years of formation and erosion become almost palpable.

▶ Kapit   218A2

Strategically situated up the Rajang river, Kapit contains little of interest aside from a small fort dating from the days of Rajah Charles Brooke. The fort was built in 1880 to prevent headhunting Ibans from decapitating the more docile Kenyahs and Kayans upriver. The town itself is a familiar juxtaposition of Chinese shops, shabby huts, modern government buildings, karaoke lounges, and cheap hotels, with a fair range of services thrown in—including a flashy new civic center which even houses a small museum. Roads lead nowhere and the only escape route is by river or air, but it makes a good launchpad for visiting longhouses further upriver. Permits for such trips can be obtained from Pejabat Am Office, State Government Complex (tel: 084 796 706). Departures depend on water level, currents, and weather; tourist prices escalate, although you can negotiate rides on the small boats that regularly crawl upriver to Belaga.

Mulu statistics
Sarawak's answer to the Malay peninsula's Taman Negara and Sabah's Kinabalu National Park, Mulu has its own unique range of animal and bird life, the most spectacular of these being the hundreds of thousands of free-tailed bats that flock out of the Deer Cave in an eerie black cloud at sunset. A 45-minute walk along planks from the park headquarters leads to the cave entrance. Otherwise, 262 species of birds (including all eight types of hornbills) have been spotted there, 74 species of frogs, 47 fish species, 281 butterfly species, and 458 species of ants! On a larger scale it has been calculated that the Sarawak Chamber can accommodate 40 Boeing 747s or 16 football fields, and that the Deer Cave can swallow five replicas of London's St. Paul's Cathedral without any problems. Apart from this, the rich wildlife pickings make it a favorite haunt for the local Penans.

227

The Deer Cave boasts the world's largest cave passage, a 460-ft.-high waterfall and thousands of bats

FOCUS ON *Indigenous peoples*

■ **Sabah and Sarawak between them are home to ten main ethnic groups, broken down into 54 subgroups, who inhabited the island long before any Malay or Chinese set foot there. Some are still semi-nomadic, while others have adapted to coastal urban living. The majority, however, still live in upriver longhouses or hill villages, with one foot in an express launch and the other firmly set in a paddy field .....■**

Customs, crafts, costumes, subsistence activities, and physical characteristics differ greatly between Borneo's ten main ethnic groups, and are much dependent on their geographical location and conditions.

Iban existence and identity are still strongly connected to the river

228

Sarawak Around 30 percent of Sarawak's population is Iban, once pirates and known as Sea Dayaks, but today mainly farmers. Every lowland river is dotted with their wooden longhouses, where all communal domestic activity takes place on a long veranda (*ruai*), off which lead individual family rooms. Known as much for their prodigious tattoos as for their subtle dyed-in-the-warp *pua kumbu* weavings, the Ibans were Sarawak's feared head-hunters; many longhouses are still adorned with nets of shrunken heads.

Less adventurous in spirit, the coastal-dwelling **Melanau** represent almost 6 percent of Sarawak's population; great fish- and sago-eaters, they once lived in enormous defensive houses raised nearly 50 ft. above the ground, where they fashioned their "sickness images," intricate carvings used in healing ceremonies.

A further 8 percent of Sarawakans are **Bidayuh** (formerly called Land Dayaks and the Rajah Brooke's first allies), mainly concentrated in the western hills beside the Sarawak and Sadong rivers. Adept at cultivating dry rice and brewing potent rice wine and sugarcane toddy, they are also skilled woodcarvers.

The generic term **Orang Ulu** (meaning "upriver dwellers") encompasses several ethnic groups who live in the middle and upper reaches of Sarawak's longest rivers (the **Penans**, **Kayans**, and **Kenyahs**), or beyond navigable limits in the highlands (**Kelabits** and **Lun Bawangs**). The Kenyah women are outstanding in their appearance: heavily tattooed from an early age, many also have pendulous earlobes, stretched by the weight of brass ornaments to well below their shoulders. Beads are equally symbolic of their social status, and their decorative two-color bead-work covers anything from head bands to war coats and betel-nut holders.

The Orang Ulu are also the most skilled of Sarawak's carvers, famous for their elaborate lute-like instruments called *sape*, as well as for their finely plaited basketware and giant blowpipes.

Sabah Though it contains no fewer than 31 ethnic sub-groups, Sabah is primarily occupied by three main groups—Kadazans, Muruts, and Bajaus. The largest group, the rice-growing **Kadazans** (also called Dusuns), have now spread from their original hills around Gunung Kinabalu to urban areas, abandoning most of the pagan rites, totems, and symbolic stones associated with every stage of the rice crop.

The last Bornean tribe to abandon headhunting, the **Muruts** occupy the hilly region between Sarawak and Sabah, where they hunt with blowpipes and carry out slash-and-burn cultivation. Like the Kadazans, they believe implicitly in the powers of certain animals and often carry bizarre charms.

Most extravagant in appearance are the **Bajaus**, formerly seafarers and now strictly Muslim cowboys and buffalo-breeders who inhabit the coastal areas from Kota Kinabalu around to Tawau. Their ceremonial horseback appearance is electrifying: agile men in white tunics and colorful turbans brandish swords while riding ponies decked out in bells, bright saddles, and bridles.

Other equally fascinating communities include the **Rungus** (a Kadazan subgroup), the **Sulus** (originally from the Philippines), and the odd Cocos Island community around Tawau.

Above: Tattoos often recount major events in a man's life
Right: Pandan-mat weavers

The last of the nomads
The last remaining nomadic group in Borneo, the Penans hunt monkeys, wild pigs and porcupines from the Baram river eastward to the hills of Gunung Mulu. However, since the mid-1980s, massive logging in their lands has depleted natural resources, chasing wildlife away, polluting rivers, and threatening their existence. Embittered by inadequate compensation, they finally issued the following statement:
" … We see with sorrow the logging companies entering our country. In these areas where timber is extracted there is no more life for us nomadic people. Our natural resources like wild-fruit trees, sago-palms, wood-trees for blowpipe, dart-poison and other needs will fall… Please you, our Sarawak government and you Timber-companies, respect our origin rights…"

Mount Kinabalu's extraordinary flora includes giant tree-ferns

Practicalities

Even if you are wary of attacking the summit, a visit to the park headquarters and its forest trails makes a fascinating day-trip from Kota Kinabalu (50 miles away). A wide range of accommodations are available at the headquarters and two restaurants cater for all budgets. Access is possible by a bus or mini-buses, which leave KK at 7.30 A.M. up until noon, but this entails spending the night at the park and returning on the 8 A.M. bus. Alternatively, numerous group tours are arranged from KK or a taxi can be chartered for the day. Those heading for the summit should make advance bookings in KK for guides, porters, and accommodations at the 3,300m (10,800-ft.) level, which is the overnight stop before the final ascent at 3 A.M. Warm clothes, gloves, rainwear, good walking shoes, flashlight and water bottle are the basic essentials—anything else can be bought or rented at the rest-houses.

▶▶▶ **Kinabalu National Park** 219C4

Southeast Asia's highest mountain has risen 13,424 ft. into drifting clouds for nearly a million years. Its jagged granite peaks were carved by gale-force winds and torrential rains before the Ice Age, but meteorological extremes continue to leave their mark today, chipping and molding the gigantic slabs which are still rising at a rate of ⅕ inch a year. An abundant and spectacular range of vegetation ascends through four bands, starting at the montane forest around park headquarters and steadily changing until the edge of the treeline is reached and a weird moonscape of stark granite slabs unfolds to Low's Peak. The two-day climb to the summit is arduous, requiring a good level of fitness, and is timed for arrival at sunrise. The recompense is the extraordinary spectacle of the sun rising below you and dawn spreading over Sabah from the Banjaran Crocker to outlying islands—until the clouds form and the difficult descent begins.

Real and imaginary past For the local Kadazans, Gunung Kinabalu is a grieving widow, a whimsical reference to the lines of white quartz that run down the folds of the granite. Local legend recounts the tale of a Kadazan woman who was in love with a Chinese prince. Tearfully awaiting his return on the mountain, she was struck by lightning and turned to stone.

Back to reality, the peak was first conquered by Sir Hugh Low in 1851, although the true summit was only reached in 1888 by the zoologist John Whitehead, who spent several months there collecting bird and mammal specimens—many of which were named after him. The first woman to make the peak (in 1910) was a British Museum botanist, who also turned up 87 plant species which were completely new to science.

Since the park was mapped in 1964, the 5-mile trail to the summit has been well covered by thousands of plodding feet and even the less plucky can struggle along the 7 miles of well-marked paths that radiate from park headquarters. A mountain garden has been developed there to give a foretaste of the flowering plants that flourish in the forest, and in 1994 a herbarium will be added.

Unique flora An Alice-in-Wonderland universe, the slopes of Gunung Kinabalu abound with thousands of strangely proportioned plant species, from the smallest known pin-head orchid to stems of 6 ft., natural bonsai-like trees and giant moss which grows to a height of 3 ft. Around 450 types of fern have been identified, some reaching 33 ft. in height, as well as nine types of the insectivorous pitcher plant (five of which are only found on Kinabalu). The biggest pitcher plant is *Nepenthes rajah*, one specimen of which was found to contain 2 quarts of water and a drowned rat. Kinabalu's unique interaction of climate and geology means that at heights above 3,000 ft. over half the plant species are endemic, their closest relatives being found in the mountains of New Guinea, Australia, and New Zealand. Most famous is the *Rafflesia* flower (see side panel) whose fleshy red petals can extend to 28 in. in diameter. A more attractive perfume emanates from the flowers of Low's rhododendron.

The montane forest which occupies almost half the park area (a total of 290 sq miles) is rich in epiphytes such as orchids, mosses, and ferns that sprout from the branches of oaks and chestnuts—a far cry from the gnarled, often stunted trunks of the mossy or cloud forest which starts at 6,000 ft. In this dramatic "dwarf forest," tree-ferns thrive in damp gullies, bamboo shoots spike the all-pervading mist, and thorny rattans and shrubs make any detours from the trail impossible. At 9,000 ft. the soil and plants change radically again, forming a world of twisted, peeling silvery-gray trunks bent and sculpted by the winds. This level in turn gives way to tumbled granite boulders and a last gasp of mossy forest which announces the end of the treeline. Few plants survive at this level; those that do nestle in the crevices or the shade of the boulders that are strewn across the breathtaking expanse of the Summit Plateau.

The *Rafflesia*
This parasitic, stemless flower (first recorded by Sir Stamford Raffles in 1816) grows in undisturbed lowland forest. A gestation period of nine to ten months is necessary for the giant flower to bloom from a tiny bud to sizes of 20–28 in., making it the world's largest flower. But life is short even for the *Rafflesia* and the flower only lasts four days, one of the reasons why sightings are so rare. The Poring area of the Kinabalu Park is the most likely place for spotting this voracious plant.

231

At 13,424-ft. Mount Kinabalu is Southeast Asia's highest peek

Tanjung Aru Beach

A few miles southwest of the city center toward the airport lies Tanjung Aru, a beautifully clean beach dotted with palm trees, food stalls, and seafood restaurants, dominated at one end by the Tanjung Aru Beach Resort. Sunsets over the outlying islands of the Tunku Abdul Rahman National Park are the main attraction, but facilities include a marina which organizes boat trips, diving trips, and water sports, helicopter tours and a nine-hole golf course. Beyond the resort the beach stretches emptily and seemingly endlessly toward the airport. The intelligently designed resort (recently expanded) is set in spacious landscaped gardens and makes a perfect though pricey base for exploring the region. Near by is Prince Philip Park, a coastal area earmarked for beach development and the construction of a gigantic hotel.

Kota Kinabalu

▶ **Kota Belud** *219C4*

The hub for Sabah's "cowboys," the striking and brightly costumed Bajaus, Kota Belud (48 miles north of Kota Kinabalu) is chiefly known for its huge Sunday *tamu* (open-air market). The *tamu* draws betel-nut-chewing Kadazan women to buy and sell household goods, fruit, vegetables, handicrafts, herbal remedies, and other exotic jungle products alongside Bajau horsemen who trade buffaloes and ponies. The cowboys' cavalier skills have recently been formalized in a galloping parade, which starts at 10 A.M. The colorful *tamu* also acts as a magnet for minibus convoys of tourists, so don't expect 100 percent "authenticity."

From Sunday afternoon onwards, Kota Belud returns to its normal sleepy self. The town has no sights of historical interest as it was devastated by bombing during World War II, but to the north of the town lies a 29,650-acre bird sanctuary.

▶▶▶ **Kota Kinabalu** *219C4*

Orientation Shortened to the more manageable KK, Sabah's relaxed capital is a sprawl of high-rises situated between the shore and the rugged green silhouette of the Banjaran Crocker range. Gunung Kinabalu is an ever-present distant peak, while out to sea lie the coral islands and reefs of the Tunku Abdul Rahman National Park (see page 252).

Although confusing at first, you will soon discover that KK's interest shrinks to three main roads running parallel to the waterfront along which the main hotels and services are concentrated. Outside this area to the southwest lie the museum, mosque and water-village of **Kampung Ayer**, and to the north is a semi-industrial zone of godowns which culminates at the glittering 72-sided tower of the **Sabah Foundation**.

Formerly known as Jesselton, KK was founded in 1899 by the British North Borneo Chartered Company as the terminus for Sabah's railway. It became the state capital in 1946, replacing the previous capital of Sandakan as the latter suffered heavily from Allied bombing at the end of World War II. With a population approaching the 30,000 mark, KK is changing shape rapidly through land reclamation and the construction of uninspiring high-rises. However, pockets of tradition do remain—although probably not for long—in Kampung Ayer, and at the Central Market and Filipino Market along the waterfront.

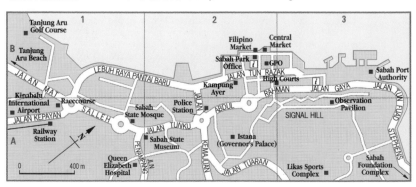

Sunsets from Tanjung Aru beach start punctually at 6:30 P.M.

Tourist essentials
To book accommodations and guides for the Kinabalu National Park (essential, particularly on weekends and during local holidays), go to the Sabah Parks Office (tel: 088 211585/211652) opposite the Filipino Market on the seafront. The tourist office (tel: 088 218620) provides useful information on local points of interest and is housed in the former post office, a rare colonial building on Jalan Gaya at the base of Signal Hill. For more general information on Sabah, cross the road to the Tourist Promotion Board of Malaysia (TPB) office (tel: 088 242064). Both places have very helpful staff who will suggest reliable tour agencies.

Sights The **Central Market** is a hive of early-morning activity when ranks of fresh fish are laid out beside mountains of produce which Kadazan women bring down from Kampung Kundasang near Gunung Kinabalu. The **Filipino Market**, however, is a sad sight as it acts as a focal point for hundreds of refugees who try to eke out a living by selling anything they can. For more local products go to KK's excellent *tamu*, which is held every Sunday morning in Jalan Gaya.

The **State Museum** (closed Fridays) on a hill overlooking the mosque is well worth a visit; an unwieldy, over-ambitious building loosely based on local longhouse style, it nevertheless houses some interesting exhibits. Archival photos of KK and Sandakan retrace British trading interests and urban catastrophes, while the **Ceramics Gallery** displays superb Chinese jars alongside Japanese and Indochinese ceramics and Murut burial jars. The small **Ethnic Gallery** is a mine of information on Sabah's many tribes, their costumes, weapons, basketware, and carvings, but the Natural History Gallery is a far cry from the equivalent display in Kuching's Sarawak Museum (see page 236). Within the museum complex is a **Science Centre**, an **Art Gallery** and **Multivision Theatre**, landscaped gardens, and reconstructed longhouses.

Across Jalan Tunku Abdul Rahman, the **State Mosque** is a far more successful contemporary architectural feat, its gold dome glistening against a backdrop of jungle-clad hills; non-Muslims are admitted except on Fridays.

First vision of the 1920s Istana

"The Astana Palace was a fantastic medley of beauty and bad taste. Outside, its walls were white and it had a gray tower where a sentry stood on guard day and night. Inside, tremendous rooms stretched the whole length of the building. There was nothing wrong with their proportions but the old Rajah had filled them with appalling imitation stuff from every period of English and French history."
From: *Queen of the Headhunters* by Sylvia, Lady Brooke, wife of Charles Vyner Brooke (1970).

► **Kampung Kundasang**   *219C4*

This is Sabah's truck garden, set high in the misty foothills of Gunung Kinabalu where Kadazan farmers cultivate an extraordinary variety of fresh fruit and vegetables, all of which are transported to local *tamus* from Tamparuli to Ranau or KK itself. Only a few miles from the entrance to Kinabalu National Park, several hotels have sprung up along the road. A war memorial commemorating the Sandakan Death March (see side panel on page 245) stands in the abandoned fort.

►►► **Kuching**   *218A1*

Kuching (meaning "cat"), capital of Sarawak and once home to the "white rajah" dynasty, is one of Malaysia's most intriguing towns due to its unique ethnic mix, noteworthy historical relics, and picturesque, undulating riverside site. The notorious Ibans, once Borneo's fearsome headhunters, comprise 30 percent of the population, followed closely by the Chinese community. Malays only represent 20 percent of the population and Bidayuhs and Melanaus another 15 percent. Easygoing but industrious and with a compact center, Kuching makes an economical base for trips to numerous more isolated spots, including national parks, wildlife sanctuaries, beaches, and longhouses—although the latter are likely to be handled solely by package-tour operators.

Pirates and rajahs Long ruled by the Sultanate of Brunei, the rebellious Dayaks of Sarawak were ripe for change

Kuching

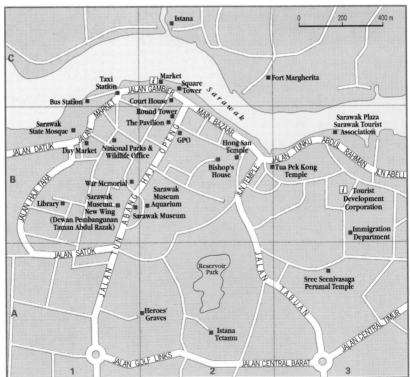

when James Brooke sailed in and helped quell an uprising in 1839. Appointed Rajah of Sarawak, he set about creating social order from his Kuching base and oversaw the building of the Bishop's House, Sarawak's oldest dwelling (dating from 1849). However, most of the town's monuments were constructed during the so-called golden era of his nephew, Charles Brooke (1868–1917). These Victorian edifices paradoxically gave grace, structure, and some security to the trading settlement, previously a favorite target for pirate forays.

Sarawak's less dynamic last "white rajah," Charles Vyner Brooke, ruled until World War II when Japanese forces took over, and in 1946 it became a British Crown Colony before joining Malaysia in 1963.

Mangoes are more often used for pickles than eaten as fruit

Orientation and sights Most of the sights and action are situated on the south bank of the river, but one of Kuching's best panoramas is across the river to Fort Margherita and the Istana commanding the grassy slopes of the north bank. **Fort Margherita** was built in 1879 and named in honor of Charles Brooke's intrepid though later estranged wife, Margaret. Occupied by the Japanese during World War II, it assumed the role of Police Museum in 1971 (closed Fridays), displaying early Sarawak Rangers' weapons and relics of the Japanese Occupation and the Emergency period (1948–1960). The **Istana**, an impressive crenelated construction set on rolling lawns, was built in 1870 by Charles Brooke as a wedding gift for his wife. Today it is the official residence of Sarawak's head of state and is not open to the public. Both the fort and the Istana can easily be reached by boat from the Pangkalan Batu landing stage behind the meat and fish market.

Back in the hub of urban action on the south bank, the 1874 **courthouse** dominates the waterfront between Main Bazaar and Jalan Gambier. The courthouse served as the Rajah Brookes' seat of government—an obelisk

Food
It's hard to go hungry in Kuching as hawker centers and restaurants are thick on the ground. Try the food stalls in the downtown market area or Lebuh India for Malay and Indian restaurants. In Jalan Song Thian Cheok there are some excellent Chinese coffee shops, while the Capital Café in Chinatown is full of atmosphere.

235

Ceramic bas-relief in the Hong San Temple

Kuching shopping

Kuching's tourist shops have tantalizing displays at exorbitant prices. Most are concentrated along Main Bazaar but others are situated beyond the Holiday Inn on Jalan Padungan and up Jalan Tabuan. Browse, check the prices at the museum shop, and then bargain like hell! If you are in Kuching on a Saturday don't miss the enormous "Sunday" market, the *pasar minggu* on Jalan Satok, which is Kuching's Saturday night hot spot. A feast of edible sights from boars' heads to bowls crawling with worms, dried jungle fungi, or century-old eggs are displayed by Dayaks who come down from the hills. You will also find an eclectic cornucopia of hawkers' food, cassettes, clothes, and watches.

outside commemorates Charles Brooke. Shady, colonnaded inner courtyards and carved local motifs create an unusual pathway to the Corinthian columns of the **General Post Office**, a surrealistic structure that was erected in 1931. Opposite stands the **Pavilion**, an elaborate 1907 edifice which adjoins the diminutive Round Tower dating from 1886.

On the waterfront opposite the courthouse is another Kuching curiosity, the **Square Tower**, further evidence of Charles Brooke's almost pathological obsession with fort-like edifices. Used as a prison, a fortress, and even a dance hall, it now adjoins the excellent tourist office. Behind the GPO, Lebuh Carpenter harbors a fascinating mix of goldsmiths, beauty parlors, tailors, and food shops, as well as two decorative Chinese temples thick with incense, lanterns, and embroidered banners. The street culminates on the waterfront at Kuching's oldest temple, the Tua Pek Kong, formally dated 1876 but rumored to have existed since 1843. Unfortunately, it is now overshadowed by the Hilton Hotel.

A famous collection Considered by many to be Southeast Asia's richest museum, the **Sarawak Museum►►►** is certainly an essential Kuching destination and houses some unique ethnological exhibits. Two buildings joined by a footbridge across Jalan Tun Abang display well-documented specimens of local fauna. The exhibits of local birds, many of which were collected by Alfred Russell Wallace, a great naturalist and friend of Charles Brooke, are especially good. There are also displays of tribal and Malay weapons, musical instruments, charms, carvings, complex pandan-weavings, rattan basketry, intricately woven textiles, Chinese ceramics, and furniture. Reconstructed longhouses complete with Iban, Bidayu and Melanau artifacts, shrunken heads,

costumes, and jewelry all reflect the Sarawak people's decorative skills and imagination. Both the 1891 building and its 1983 annex are well filled, so be generous with your time.

►► Kudat   219D4

Although it hardly looks like a former capital of Sabah, Kudat commands a strategic position on the northern tip of Sabah and was an important trading port for Chinese ships *en route* to Europe. Its proximity to the Philippines has imbued it with a distinctive flavor and the population presents as many Filipino faces as those of Kadazans or Rungus (the local subgroup). A handful of basic hotels makes Kudat a good starting point for heading out to some authentic Rungus longhouses. A four-wheel drive is advisable if you wish to explore this remote region 110 miles north of KK. You will also find blissfully deserted beaches north of Bak Bak, the main town beach, or across the promontory at Sikuati.

► Labuan   218C3

Blessed with duty-free status, the island of Labuan is a rambling, uninteresting destination for alcohol-starved Westerners working in Brunei and for Malaysians stocking up on food-processors and hi-fis. Curiously, it once had an equal ranking with Melaka and Pinang as part of the Straits Settlements governed from Singapore. World War II saw Japanese overlords, followed by integration with Sabah until 1984 when it became a Federal Territory. Labuan can be reached in 45 minutes by speedboat from Menumbok or directly from KK or Brunei as well as by air. The port of Victoria is well stocked with overpriced hotels for weary shoppers and employees of its gas and oil fields. Papan, a small offshore island, has some good beaches and is gearing itself up for development into a resort.

Labuan and World War II
Captured by the Japanese, Labuan was renamed Maida and remained under Japanese control until the war ended in 1945, when it was the site of the official surrender of North Borneo and Sarawak to the British government. A Japanese garden and war memorial mark this spot near Layang Layang village on the west coast. The Japanese officers responsible for the barbaric Sandakan Death March (see side panel on page 245) were also tried there. About 2 miles from town is a landscaped cemetery containing the Allied Forces War Memorial and the graves of 3,904 Australian, New Zealand, and British soldiers who lost their lives defending North Borneo.

237

Above: Charles Brooke, controversial shaper of Sarawak
Left: Fort Margherita was originally built to protect Kuching from pirate attacks

The proboscis monkey
The proboscis monkey, found only in Borneo, is distantly related to the silver leaf monkey. Mature male proboscis are enormous, weighing up to 50 lb., but their outstanding feature is an outsized, pendulous cucumber-like nose. Proboscis monkeys only live in coastal or riverine forests and large troops of them can be seen along the lower Kinabatangan river (south of Sandakan) and in Sarawak's Samunsam Sanctuary (west of Kuching but only visitable with special permission).

▶▶ **Lambir Hills National Park**   *218B3*

This 17,178-acre area of rugged sandstone escarpments and rolling dipterocarp forest lies 15 miles south of Miri. The park offers easy access to waterfalls, swimming holes, and jungle trails—but always avoid weekends. Chalet accommodation can be booked through the National Parks and Wildlife Office in Miri (tel. 085 36637).

▶▶▶ **Menkabong**   *219C4*

Although prominent on every KK tour agency's itinerary, Menkabong water-village remains a compelling sight and you can easily visit it on your own by taking a share-taxi from KK or Tuaran. The unruly and colorful Bajau people—once known as Sabah's "sea-gypsies"—live in this precarious network of houses and plankwalks built high above the water (except at low tide). The best way to visit is by sampan. Despite the sporadic tourist influx it is an impoverished place and you should be sensitive to the feelings of the people who live here. Also remember that Bajaus are strict Muslims and may object to having their photos taken.

The Bajaus of Menkabong relish cockfights

▶ **Miri**   *218B3*

The Las Vegas of Sarawak, Miri flashes its neon signs in English and Chinese, oblivious to its Malaysian political identity. Offshore oil fields are its *raison d'être,* and many inhabitants are expatriates from as far afield as Pakistan and the United States. On weekends residents from nearby Brunei flock there looking for a bit of weekend action.

Despite a brash cosmopolitan atmosphere accentuated by numerous modern hotels, restaurants, money-changers, prostitutes, wide roads and Carlsberg and Guinness signs, small-town Miri has an engaging character and you could do a lot worse in a stopover to more remote areas in Sarawak. Tour agencies and inexpensive lodging houses are plentiful, and the National Parks and Wildlife Office is a necessary destination for those who need to arrange bookings to Niah, Lambir or Mulu. For a glimpse of more traditional activities, head down Jalan China to the harbor, where a Chinese temple and a market stand against a backdrop of moored fishing trawlers.

▶▶▶ Niah National Park 218B3

Even the complicated access followed by a sweaty 2½-mile hike along plankwalks through thick jungle cannot prepare visitors for the awesome sight of the first Niah cave, the **Traders' Cave**. But this is soon surpassed by the suitably named **Great Cave**, one of the world's largest. Dank guano odors fill the nostrils, flashlights beam through the shadowy depths, and invisible bats flutter above.

The cave network is surrounded by 7,760 acres of rain forest which was declared a national park in 1975, 20 years after its archaeological importance had been recognized. A 40,000-year-old skull was found together with Stone Age implements and 8th-century Chinese pottery—proof that the Oriental penchant for bird's-nest soup is long standing.

The third cave, the **Painted Cave**, was an ancient burial site for Mesolithic and Neolithic man, housing their "death ships." Its name derives from primitive red haematite wall paintings, estimated to be 1,000 to 2,000 years old. Unfortunately, human traffic and its erosive effects led to the closure of the Painted Cave in 1992; it will remain closed until funds for restoration become available from Unesco. Meanwhile, visitors can scramble up and down wooden steps through the gloom of the Great Cave and, during the season from October to March, watch bird's-nest collectors shinning up 230 ft. of *belian* (ironwood) poles (see page 251). In the Traders' Cave, a 90-year-old wooden structure is still used by guano collectors. The collectors carry heavy sacks of the bat excrement, prized as a fertilizer, along the plankwalk to the river.

Situated 68 miles from Miri and 81 miles from Bintulu, the village of **Batu Niah** can be reached by bus or taxi; it is then a 25-minute boat ride or 15-minute drive to park headquarters. Hostels, chalets, and a campsite in the village are clustered around an information center, and next door a new museum displays artifacts from the caves. The jungle plankwalk (see side panel) starts from across the river behind the main store where the necessary flashlights, water, and other basics can be bought.

Guano-collecting structures in the Traders' Cave

Niah flora and fauna
The sturdy plankwalk from Batu Niah leads through peat swamp and mixed dipterocarp forest, but two slightly more tricky jungle trails take intrepid trekkers into the heart of the undergrowth. Long-tailed macaques, flying lizards, squirrels, Rajah Brooke butterflies, bulbuls, and trogons are among the jungle's most commonly spotted creatures, although more perspicacious visitors may spot a hornbill or the elusive mouse deer. Best of all, however, is to leave the caves around sunset when literally a million or so bats and swiftlets change shifts, the bats heading out for night forays and the swiflets returning to sleep. And on the torchlit walk back to base the path glows with luminous mushrooms—a memorable spectacle.

Shooting the rapids
"With Dana and Inghai (Iban crew) paddling ferociously to keep the dugout from turning sideways to the current, Leon managed to start the engine at the third pull; we swung violently out into the center of the swollen river and began to move with extraordinary speed."
From: *Into the Heart of Borneo*, by Redmond O'Hanlon (1984).

The currents of the Padas river can be experienced on whitewater rafting expeditions

▶▶ **Padas River**   219B4

From its source high in the western mountains of Sabah, the Padas river flows through the Banjaran Crocker and Tenom, then, paralleling East Malaysia's only railway line, it sweeps past Beaufort before hitting the coast. The peaceful little town of Beaufort is flooded regularly by the torrential river, which is at its most spectacular when thundering through the narrow Padas Gorge.

You can experience the river's power at first hand by whitewater rafting through its swirling rapids, when you will be tossed, churned, and thrashed by violent eddies. Recommended for experienced rafters only, trips are arranged from Kota Kinabalu. For others, the Tenom–Beaufort railway gives sufficiently fantastic views over the river as it runs through jungle-clad hills.

▶ **Papar**   219C4

If you want to get wet somewhere other than around the coral reefs of the South China Sea, go to Papar (28 miles south of KK) for some beginner's whitewater rafting along the Kiulu and Papas rivers. The road from KK takes you past stone megaliths to the modern estuary village set in a monochrome tapestry of dazzling paddy fields farmed by local Kadazans. The village is, however, more notable for its potent *tapai* (rice wine), an essential element in longhouse highlife.

Those looking for a quieter time can take a leisurely boat ride through lush valley landscapes toward the source of the river in the Banjaran Crocker. Whitewater rafting expeditions need to be organized through a tour agency in Kota Kinabalu.

▶▶ **Penampang**   219C4

The pretty village of Penampang (8 miles south of KK) marks the start of the main road skirting the Banjaran Crocker. Boasting Sabah's oldest church, **St. Michael's** (1897), Penampang also has exotic Kadazan graveyards in which enormous Chinese burial jars traditionally filled with human bones stand as stark evidence of the rituals associated with death. Even more memorable is the **House of Skulls**, a village house with 42 skulls ghoulishly hanging from its ceiling.

▶▶▶ Poring Hot Springs

219C4

Although the entrance is a visual letdown, Poring Hot Springs offer an incredible overnight experience. During their World War II occupation, the Japanese devised an ingenious method of piping the hot sulfur water into open-air cement tubs. Today these baths are particularly appreciated by climbers recovering from the ascent of Gunung Kinabalu. On emerging from this steamy cloud, the next step is an invigorating plunge into a swimming pool of cool mountain water. Situated in the foothills of Sabah's majestic peak at 1,571 ft., Kampung Poring can be reached from Ranau by chartered or share-taxi, or directly from KK, about three hours away. Avoid weekends and holidays, and book accommodations in advance at the Sabah Parks Office in KK.

Accommodations and facilities Nondescript chalets, a hostel, and a campsite are clustered at the entrance to the springs, but beyond a river suspension bridge lie the outdoor baths. A nocturnal sulfur soak amid the racket of the surrounding jungle and the scent of frangipani bushes is hard to beat. For the moment there is no restaurant, so bring food for overnight stays—a small, pricey store sells the basics and cooking facilities are provided.

Natural splendors The highlight is a canopy-walk network, its rope bridges swaying high in the trees and affording closeups of birds, orchids and other canopy flora and fauna that remain invisible from below. Further drama is created by artificial lighting used at night to illuminate the forest. Back at ground level, the dipterocarp forest is the habitat of the rare *Rafflesia* flower (see side panel on page 231), along with pitcher plants, wild fruit trees, lianas, and spiny *rotan* (rattan) palms. Flying lemurs, red leaf monkeys, and even orangutans have been seen along the undisturbed trails, and the rich birdlife is totally unlike that seen in the montane forest around Kinabalu park headquarters. As with humid rain forest everywhere, however, leeches will also be your trusty companions.

A sulfurous soak in the jungle; a rare relic of the Japanese occupation

Elephants in Sabah
As their traditional habitat shrinks, elephants are becoming an increasingly rare sight in Sabah today, although this state claims a larger number than any-where else in Malaysia. Areas of untouched jungle such as the 300,000-acre Tabin Wildlife Sanctuary in Lahad Datu (eastern Sabah) were estimated until recently to be home to 250 elephants. However, poaching continues and in 1992 it was discovered that a syndicate was killing one elephant a month—thus leaving a short life expectancy for the remaining members of the herd.

Above: Sipadan's waters are rated among the world's best for divers

Right: Chromis fish and Acropora *coral*

Island reserve
Pulau Sipadan was declared a marine reserve in 1981 to protect its spectacular reef. It has also been a bird sanctuary since 1933 as it is a stopoff point for migratory species such as the Nicobar pigeon.

▶▶ **Pulau Bohey Dulang**   *219B5*

Idyllic deserted beaches fringe the shores of countless islands lying off Semporna on the southeastern tip of Sabah, but with no accommodations or regular boat services visitors must hire fishing boats and dodge east coast pirates and sharks—both notorious in these waters. Bohey Dulang was home to a thriving Japanese-owned pearl culture industry but in 1993 was declared a marine park, together with nearby Gaya, Tetagan, Maiga, Sibuan, and Mantabuan. Visitors' facilities should be in place by 1994 and will include chalet accommodations.

▶▶ **Pulau Sipadan**   *219B5*

Mushrooming out of the Celebes Sea, Sipadan Island is considered to be Malaysia's best diving spot—and visitors pay through the nose for the honor. It is the only oceanic island in Malaysia, with a 2,000-ft. sheer dropoff that provides incredible underwater sights. At **Barracuda Point** divers may find themselves in the company of hundreds of these fish. Farther along the eastern coast is the spectral **Turtle Cavern**, inhabited by the skeletal remains of turtles, stalactites, and flashlight fish, while the **Hanging Gardens** is an underwater theater set of

delicate pastel-shaded coral. Lobsters and turtles are regular visitors to the waters, particularly between April and September, and visibility is breathtakingly clear (65–200 ft.) from mid-February to mid-December.

Beach hut accommodations are owned by Borneo Divers (based in KK, tel. 088 222226), recently joined by the more reasonably priced Sipadan Dive Center (KK, tel. 088 240584/218710), both of which arrange all-inclusive trips from KK via Semporna. Boats for day-trippers run from Tawau on Sunday mornings or fishing boats can be hired (at a price) to cross the 20 miles from Semporna.

▶▶▶ Pulau Tiga Park   219C4

Currently under development as a marine research center, Pulau Tiga and its two tiny outlying islets offer technicolor sunsets and distinctive untouched landscapes of bubbling mud volcanoes surrounded by casuarinas, wild fruit trees, mangrove forests, a rich bird and butterfly population and troops of long-tailed macaques. Easily accessible coral reefs fringe the islands and are home to species found nowhere else on Sabah's west coast.

No facilities exist for tourists, but from the park headquarters on the south coast a network of trails radiates over the island. Visitors need to bring camping equipment, food and water (there is no fresh water supply, one of the reasons for its lack of habitation), but they will be rewarded with the experience of dropping off to sleep to the eerie knocking sounds of nightjars against the background hum of the jungle. Access to Pulau Tiga is by 45-minute boat ride from Kuala Penyu (87 miles southwest of KK by road).

▶▶▶ Rajang River   218A2

Sarawak's longest river and Malaysia's busiest and widest, the Rajang is deep enough for oceangoing vessels and thus plays a vital role in Sarawak's economy and society. For the Ibans of its upper reaches it has always been a lifeline to the outside world and the main wharf at Sibu is chockablock with river buses that speed upstream—sometimes hair-raisingly so—to longhouses, settlements, Kapit, and Belaga.

Roads are nonexistent in this densely forested interior, although the logging trade is ever-present. Bulldozed topsoil has turned the once-green lower reaches into a muddy brown, and convoys of barges and log rafts drift downriver laden with timber, often on their way to Japan. Canoes and small boats dot the river highway, while floating Chinese trading launches stop at longhouses and logging camps; these sturdy tongkangs are piled up with drums of gasoline, cases of jeans and T-shirts, Guinness, and parangs (sheath knives). Meanwhile, off-duty Chinese crewmen gamble hard and basket-laden Ibans and Kayans stagger on and off at their villages.

For assaults on the more remote upper reaches of the Rajang and its tributaries (the Mujong, Baleh and Balui) permits need to be obtained at Kapit (see page 227), although this may turn out to be a subtle exercise in diplomacy. Currents and water levels are major factors in determining the practicability of journeying through certain stretches—above all the infamous Pelagus Rapids—so make sure you have good boatmen.

Old-time Kapit to Belaga

"The Rejang River...is a magnificent roadway to commerce in the interior, and once the headhunting propensities of the tribes in its neighbourhood are abolished, it promises to be a great center of activity and trade... The great charm of the undertaking lay in the fact that to get to Belaga innumerable rapids had to be surmounted, and we had to go through an interesting stretch of country lying between Kapit and this distant Fort, for it is essentially the land of Kayan people, and here and there along the banks of those higher reaches of the Rejang are to be seen interesting and wonderful monuments of Kayan industry in the shape of tombs carved by the people containing the remains of their most famous chiefs."
From: *My Life in Sarawak*, by Margaret Brooke (1913).

243

■ **Some 450 species of birds inhabit Malaysia, and more than 150 migrant species wing in annually from more than 3,000 miles away to escape the northern Asian winters. Borneo is home to 26 endemic species, but most famous of all is the hornbill, mimicked by the Iban people in their famous dance and once much sought after for the precious horn of its enormous bill .....■**

Hornbill spinoffs
Called *kenyalang* by the Ibans, the sidestepping rhinocerous hornbill is central to their rituals (Sarawak is often called "The Land of the Hornbill"). The bird's leisurely flight is imitated in the graceful hornbill dance and its long plumed tail feathers are much favored for elaborate male headdresses.

The wreathed hornbill is recognizable by its yelping call and by the loud flapping of its wings

Southeast Asia is home to more than 1,000 species of birds, out of a global total of 8,500 species. Most of the resident birds of East Malaysia are found in lowland rain forest, although the dense vegetation often forms a successful natural camouflage. Many species are only active in the early morning and late afternoon. Identifying bird-calls is an easier task than actually sighting the birds, for many hover high above the forest canopy. Really keen bird-watchers should arm themselves with *The Birds of Borneo*, by Bertram E. Smythies (1960, 1981).

Vantage points One of the best ways of spotting some of the colorful species is to find a large, strangling fig plant in fruit, recognizable by its tangled web of smooth, woody roots. The abundant yellow or reddish fruits are favored by 20 or more species, including hornbills, "chonking" barbets, parrots, and pigeons.

More bird-watching opportunities are provided by secluded valleys in the depths of the dipterocarp forest. Insect-eating birds, the most numerous category, inhabit the mid-story level of the forest. Unique to Borneo is the Bornean blue flycatcher, while particularly spectacular is the paradise flycatcher, with long, silky white tail-feathers that can measure up to 18 in.

Eagles, hawks, and other daytime birds of prey are hard to spot, although you will often hear their piercing calls. Owls are omnipresent, especially in the vicinity of caves such as Niah or Mulu.

Hornbills Flapping heavily across the forest canopy, hornbills are a magnificent sight, unique to tropical Africa and Asia. Eight types of hornbill exist in Borneo, the largest being the rhinoceros hornbill and the helmeted hornbill. Spectacular for its enormous ivory "casque" (head growth), the rhinoceros hornbill was once hunted by Chinese traders who paid a high price for this "yellow jade." The rhinoceros hornbill is now protected.

▶ Sandakan
219C5

Like Kota Kinabalu, Sandakan was wiped out by Allied bombing at the end of World War II, and today an equally characterless sprawl of high-rises hugs a strip of land between mountains and the island-studded Sulu Sea. The area was known for centuries by Chinese and Sulus as a prolific source of pearls, camphor, turtles' eggs, and birds' nests, and was used by Germans and Spanish as a gun-running base, although Sandakan itself (meaning "the place that was pawned") was only founded in 1879 as a center for the British North Borneo's trading interests.

Rich from timber and shipbuilding, the large Chinese community displays its wealth in numerous Buddhist temples, from the oldest, built in the 1880s and dedicated to **Guan Yin** (the goddess of mercy), to the eminently kitsch **Puu Jih Shih Temple**, built in 1987 for a piffling RM5 million (US$2 million). Other denominations are served by the incongruous stone **St. Michael's Church** (1893), and the purist modern **Sandakan Mosque** on the bay next to the immaculate water-village of **Kampung Buli Sim Sim**. The usual colorful crowds pack the **Central Market** and **Fish Market**.

The tragedies of World War II are commemorated by the **Australian Memorial**, erected on the site of the prisoner of war camp which saw the start of the horrifying Sandakan Death March (see side panel); Japanese war victims and young girls brought to work in brothels are buried in the hilltop **Japanese Cemetery**.

An eight-hour journey by road or a short flight from KK, Sandakan is primarily worth a visit for the nearby Turtle Islands Park (see page 250), Gomantong Caves (see page 226) and Sepilok's orangutan sanctuary (see page 248).

▶▶▶ Santubong
218A1

The charming fishing village and fine beaches of Santubong lie 20 miles north of Kuching by road or river boat. Hindu- and Buddhist-inspired rock-carvings, Sung Dynasty (10th to 13th centuries) and Yuan Dynasty (13th to 14th centuries) ceramic fragments, beads, and gold discovered in this region all point to a thriving civilization that was mysteriously abandoned in the 14th century. A superb panoramic corniche road leads from this low-key spot around the base of the legendary Gunung Santubong, a peak inhabited by the "daughter of the moon" and visible from Kuching, where its outline was once said to resemble the profile of James Brooke. The road ends at the new tourist hub of **Damai Beach**, where Sheraton and Holiday Inn guests indulge in water sports—when the tide is not a frothing line on the horizon—or meander around the Kampung Budaya Sarawak (**Sarawak Cultural Village**), a completely artificial but enlightening reconstruction of ethnic longhouses in a beautifully landscaped lagoon site.

Sandakan Death March
The blackest memory of the region concerns 2,400 Australian and British POWs interned in Sandakan during World War II. As conditions deteriorated and supplies dwindled early in 1945, the Japanese decided to transfer the prisoners inland to Ranau, 150 miles away in the foothills of Gunung Kinabalu. Three groups set off through the thick jungle, often shoeless and without rations. Of the few who reached Ranau, just six Australians survived—and that was only because they managed to escape.

245

Sandakan's Puu Jih Shih Temple

■ **Only found in Sumatra and Borneo, the orangutan is another of the world's endangered species. The elusive, often comic red creature is the largest primate and the only great ape naturally occurring outside Central Africa. The older orangutan can resemble a shaggy sumo wrestler, but it conquers everyone with its inimitably human gestures, grimaces, and appeals for food. .....■**

Not what they seem
However endearing orang-utans may seem, their strength cannot be under-estimated. Biruté Galdikas, who set up Indonesian Borneo's only sanctuary in 1971 and who has become a world expert on orang-utans, relates how she has escaped attempts on her life by potential protégés several times. The orang-utans' strength comes into its own when pushing over dead trees aimed at over-curious spectators. But their best ammunition is provided by streams of hard-hitting urine and fast-flying dung—so keep a safe distance and be wary of their apparent charm!

A daily diet of milk and bananas keeps Sepilok's orphans swinging

Man's ancestor? Eternally fascinating to scientists, the orangutan (meaning "man of the forest") has at times been considered a variation on *Homo sapiens*. In the 18th century James Burnett believed they merely had an acci-dental speech impediment and he supported this theory by taking his pet ape dressed in jacket and tie to dinner parties. Late 19th-century science seriously considered Borneo the possible birthplace of mankind, and for Ernst Haeckel the "speechless ape-man" provided the missing link in the evolutionary tree.

Today, Borneo maintains three laudable sanctuaries at **Sepilok** (see page 248), **Semenggoh** (see page 247), and in Indonesian Kalimantan. It is still not known whether the rehabilitated orangutans, which weigh more, mature faster, and give birth earlier than wild-born orangutans, will dominate food resources when they are released back into the forest.

One is company Unlike gorillas and chimpanzees, the orangutan is a solitary creature, spending most of its time alone in the trees swinging gracefully through the jungle canopy. Adult males only seek company to mate, and adult females travel only with young, but otherwise these independent apes are off on their own, rooting around for fruit, leaves, bark, and insects. It is estimated that only 10,000 to 20,000 remain today, their numbers diminish-ing due to the loss of their natural rain-forest habitat.

Lifestyle Average adult males can weigh more than 200 lb. and stand about 3 ft. tall, their long arms covered in a rusty-orange coat, while females are slightly smaller. They live for up to 30 years and start breeding when around seven to ten years old, but females only produce three or four offspring in their lifetime.

Their favored territory is swampland and lowland diptero-carp forest near rivers, where they build tree nests daily from twigs and branches. The young remain dependent on their moth-er for at least five years, but when fruits are depleted they are abandoned—one of the reasons why many of the centers' inmates are helpless young.

▶ Sematan

218A1

It's hard to get farther west than this in Sarawak. Beyond Gunung Gading National Park the road ends abruptly at the white sands of Sematan Beach, bordered by a tiny relaxed village which has limited chalet accommodations among coconut palms, and a handful of Malay and Chinese restaurants. There are plans for development, but it will take some time before the natural beauty of the site is completely spoilt.

▶▶ Semonggoh

218A1

A 45-minute bus ride from Kuching past over-grown Chinese cemeteries, fruit farms, and jungle brings you to the wildlife sanctuary of Semenggoh (20 miles south of Kuching).

The **Wildlife Rehabilitation Center** itself is home to porcupines, honey bears, hornbills, eagles, storks, and gibbons, as well as Borneo's star attractions, the orangutans. Only a few of these endearing creatures are visible, kept strictly within their enclosures. The patriarch, Bullet, is a hairy 24-year-old orange monster so named because he and his mother were shot at during his infancy. Feeding times are at 8:30 A.M. and 2:30 P.M., when the orangutans are at their liveliest.

▶ Semporna

219B5

Lying at the southeastern tip of Sabah, Semporna is the gateway to hundreds of coral islands flung across the Celebes Sea. Some of the islands are inhabited by Bajau Laut, Sabah's renowned "sea-gypsies." Tourist facilities are virtually nonexistent, so any excursion is costly; accommodations in Semporna are limited to an upscale hotel on stilts over the water and some very basic Chinese hotels. The small town has a colorful frontier character, heightened by its lively Bajau and Sulu inhabitants. All activity is centered on a prodigious waterfront market where lobsters, crabs, and prawns abound.

Semporna's harbor has a water-village, a floating market, and a stilt hotel

Sabah's Bajaus form 22 percent of the population and are mainly concentrated in coastal areas

Jong's Crocodile Farm
A favorite stop-off for tourists *en route* to a Skrang river safari, this large crocodile farm is situated in a fruit farm region 18 miles south of Kuching. It is a 15-minute drive from Semenggoh and can also be reached by bus directly from Kuching.

Research on orangutans at Sepilok began in the 1930s

Anti-cessionists
When Vyner Brooke insensitively announced his intention to cede Sarawak to Britain in early 1946, it was badly received and only passed by a narrow majority in the Council Negeri. Many Malays tried to have the decision reversed. The climax came in 1949 when Duncan Stewart, the second British Governor of Sarawak, was assassinated in Sibu by a young Malay teacher who belonged to the anti-cession movement.

▶▶▶ **Sepilok Orang-Utan Sanctuary**   219C5

Sabah's greatest wildlife sight lies 15 miles west of Sandakan in 16 sq miles of rich rain forest. Since 1963 the orangutan has been a protected species and the rehabilitation center was set up in 1964 to help orphaned or captive orangutans recover and readjust before being returned to the wilds. Despite these efforts their numbers are declining: clandestine poaching for food or zoos and the inexorable disappearance of the rain forest have taken their toll, and many are in fact rescued from logging camps.

Feeding time is the high point of the day (9:30 A.M. and 2:30 P.M.): these uninhibited primates swing in from all directions to demolish bananas and milk and have a quick frolic with the wildlife rangers, giving visitors a Bronx cheer at the same time. Some of the orangutans recently stripped an unsuspecting French tourist entirely naked—apparently out of a malicious sense of fun—so be warned! Brightly colored clothes are apparently their predilection. The surrounding rich forest has some good trails and a nature education center provides audiovisual information on this capricious creature.

▶ **Sibu**   218A2

A disordered, uninspiring town whose only landmark is a brightly colored Chinese temple overlooking the bustling wharf, Sibu is only worth stopping at if you have to change boats and/or planes there. The town is the main outlet for the logging industry on the "Rajang highway" (see page 243), and it blatantly lives off the rain forest. Timber mills (often Japanese- or Taiwanese-owned) line the river, and rafts and barges piled high with logs ply its course. Taxi-touts, boat-touts and bus-touts, as well as a constant flux of sailors, give it a rough-and-ready atmosphere, but if you are staying the night there, you will find a wide choice of hotels, eating places, and...karaoke.

▶ **Similajau**   218B2

Sarawak's second largest national park (after Mulu) remains for the moment very underdeveloped and can only be visited on a boat day-trip from Bintulu—in itself not Sarawak's most fascinating place. However, the blissful solitude of the unbroken coastline (whose steep beaches are much favored by egg-laying green turtles) makes this a good spot for bird watching—look for sea eagles and brahminy kites in particular. It is also common to see saltwater crocodiles, wild boars, and macaques along the beach.

▶▶▶ Tambunan
219C4

High in Sabah's backbone of the Banjaran Crocker, the village of Tambunan nestles in a beautiful fertile valley. The 50-mile road from KK winds past lush greenery and clear rivers, reaching heights of 4,255 ft. with views toward Gunung Kinabalu, before penetrating the forest and emerging beside picturesque rice terraces, wallowing water buffaloes, bamboo groves, and the lazy Pegalan river. This is bamboo territory *par excellence*—of both the cultivated and constructed varieties—and the annual high point is the Kadazan Harvest Festival in late May. A recent bamboo addition is the riverside **Tambunan Village Resort**, a lookalike tourist village of longhouses and chalets. Visitors can follow trails to waterfalls, go to the *tamu* on a Thursday or pay homage to the grave of Sabah's greatest hero, Mat Salleh (see side panel).

▶ Tawau
219B5

Sabah's last frontier, looking out at Indonesian Borneo across the bay, is a developing trade center and port for cocoa and palm oil from the interior. Timber is also taking over where Sandakan's devastated forests left off, and Tawau throngs with workers and immigrants.

The town offers nothing of interest bar an impressive mosque, but there are some beautiful spots to the north in the **Tawau Hills National Park**, a rugged volcanic landscape crisscrossed by streams and jungle trails, and punctuated by waterfalls, hot springs, and volcanic peaks. This scenery stands in stark contrast to the flat monotony of the plantations fringing the access road to the west.

▶▶ Tenom
219C4

Tenom, the railhead for Sabah's toy train at the southern end of Banjaran Crocker, occupies a fertile valley of cocoa, corn, and rubber plantations. Blowpipes are still made at the surrounding Murut longhouses (at Kampung Kalibatang), and many inhabitants continue to carry on the practice of shifting cultivation. The small, friendly town is characterized by Chinese shophouses interjected with the usual snooker and video-game halls. There are a few reasonably priced hotels—top of the scale is a 1970s hilltop monster. However, Tenom's main feature is its **Agricultural Research Center** about 9 miles outside town at Lagud Seberang. Research there concentrates on experimental crops and the adjoining area is being developed into a public agricultural park similar to that at Shah Alam (see page 162). The existing **Orchid Center** will eventually be joined by an agro forest.

Another Tenom curiosity is its welcoming role as a winter home for millions of common sparrows, which fly in from Siberia between September and March—the only drawback is that their droppings become a serious hazard!

The Mat Salleh rebellion
On a grassy hillock at Tambunan an old stone marks the grave and last stand of the legendary Sabah hero, Mat Salleh. A painful thorn in the British North Borneo Company's side in the late 19th century, Mat Salleh and his faithful followers were mainly rebelling against the company's rice and poll taxes. He was eventually offered a pardon if he stopped his guerrilla-style rebellion. Strongly suspecting some double-crossing, Mat Salleh set about building a sophisticated underground fort at Tambunan. Undeterred, the British North Borneo Company besieged his installation and cut off the water supply. At noon on January 31, 1900 Mat Salleh and his followers emerged to face the British bullets.

Much of Sabah's forest has been converted to plantations

Danum Valley
This 168-sq.-mile forest conservation area administered by the Sabah Foundation is probably the best place in Sabah for observing wildlife in an unspoiled rain-forest environment. Situated 90 miles north of Tawau and immediately southwest of Lahad Datu, the Danum Valley Field Center is a magnet for visiting scientists and local research project members. Visitors can stay overnight in a hostel or rest-house and explore jungle trails, but permits, bookings, and transport from Lahad Datu need to be arranged in advance, preferably through the Sabah Foundation in KK (tel. 088 422211) or at the foundation's offices in Lahad Datu (tel. 089 81031). Other wild spots untouched by tourism lie to the south of Danum Valley—in particular the Baturong Caves, bordering on Tawau Hills National Park—but guides and four-wheel-drive vehicles are essential.

▶ **Tuaran** 219C4

Tuaran (20 miles north of KK) is renowned for its pottery workshops located along the KK road. It is worth stopping to see the long tunnel-shaped brick kilns, wood-fired and stoked by sweat-drenched Chinese. Some pieces are hand-thrown, others churned out mechanically, and the more outrageous designs include traditional burial jars which measure up to 5 ft. and incorporate arabesque whirls with Chinese form. Tuaran itself has nothing to offer apart from its local beach, **Pantai Dalit**, and its Sunday *tamu* where Kadazans haggle over huge black crabs, tobacco, fish, and rice.

▶▶▶ **Turtle Islands National Park** 219C5

Sabah's turtle reserve (see page 212) actually consists of three islands some 25 miles to the north of Sandakan. This is the first of a chain which stretches across the Sulu Sea to the Philippines and creates channels still haunted by pirates. A hatchery established in 1966 officially became a marine park in 1977 and now offers limited chalet accommodations and a restaurant on **Pulau Selingan**. Fabulous white beaches and coral reefs also add to the lure of these islands.

The green and hawksbill turtles waddle up to nest throughout the year; peak periods are from February to April and from August to October, with certain sightings at the full moon. Much of the original island vegetation has disappeared to make way for coconut palms, so animal and birdlife is not a high point here. Bookings and permits need to be arranged at the Sabah Parks Office in KK (tel. 088 211585/652) or Sandakan (tel. 089 273453), but as there is no regular boat service for the three-hour trip an excursion to the park is a fairly costly undertaking.

Above: Tuaran pottery for sale

Right: Suspension bridge at Tuaran

Bird's-nest collecting

■ For centuries Chinese traders have been homing in on Sabah's limestone caves to harvest precious swiftlets' nests, a great delicacy which are also believed to possess important medicinal qualities. This highly lucrative and specialized trade is now regulated by the Malaysian Wildlife Department. The sight of the collectors at work on their precarious climbing structures helps to explain why 1 pound can fetch over RM2,000 (US$800). ·····■

Scaling the heights From the famous **Niah Caves** or **Gomantong Caves** to the lesser known **Madai Caves**, edible bird's-nest collecting continues apace using the same techniques that Chinese traders perfected over 1,000 years ago. Twice a year licensed collectors scale rattan ladders, clamber over bamboo platforms and shin up *belian* (ironwood) poles with lamps made from old beer bottles to reach the soaring heights of the caves, where swiftlets build their tiny, immaculate nests. The poles or ropes can be 200 ft. high, and the skill and agility of the collectors is clearly evident—although a few casualties are recorded every year. Each group of collectors has the rights to a certain patch of cave, their own "field," and during the off-season guards now camp in the gloomy depths to ward off poachers.

In 1989 a three-year total ban was imposed on bird's-nest collecting at the Niah Caves as swiftlets were decreasing in number. Since 1992 harvesting has been limited to two seasons: from March to April, just after the nests have been built (thereby forcing the swiftlets to build new ones), and then from September to October after the eggs have hatched.

The fate of the nests Even after the collectors have risked their lives acquiring the nests, a great deal of skill must be expended in preparing them. The delicate "black" nests are built with feathers and hardened swiftlets' saliva, and an elaborate operation is required to free the feathers and create cakelike pieces of pure saliva. Soaking the nests, picking out feathers with tweezers, and finally drying the cakes over a ventilator in a mold (once performed by manual fanning) achieves the finished product. When the bird's-nest cakes arrive in Hong Kong, Singapore, and China, they are priced higher than the equivalent Western delicacy of caviar. Even more precious are the "white" nests, which do not require the elaborate preparation process as they are made of pure saliva.

Powerful broth
But what is so great about swiftlets' saliva? According to the Chinese, the substance cures breathing problems and is excellent for the complexion. The nests are made into bird's-nest soup or jelly-like desserts.

251

*Below: The "roofless villages' inside Niah's Traders' Cave—once home to bird's-nest and guano collectors
Bottom: A swiftlet on its nest*

Pulau Manukan and its neighbors were cut off from the mainland as the sea level rose after the last Ice Age

When and how?
The islands of this marine park can be visited all year round, but between May and October storms may materialize in minutes, so some care should be taken with boating arrangements. The heaviest rain falls during the monsoon from November to January and the driest months are from February to May. Fishing boats can be hired from the harbor next to Central Market in KK—it only takes 15 minutes to reach Gaya—or more organized arrangements can be made through the enterprising marina at Tanjung Aru.

▶▶▶ **Tunku Abdul Rahman National Park** *219C4*

Each of the five islands of the park has its own character, but all offer snorkeling or diving in the extraordinarily dramatic depths of the coral reefs.

Big is beautiful The largest and least spoiled island, **Pulau Gaya**, was actually the site of the North Borneo Chartered Company's first settlement in 1882, but was soon after burned to the ground by Mat Salleh. Even earlier, Bajau and Sulu sea-gypsies stopped off at Gaya to water their boats and bury their dead in sandy graves.

Today's less industrious visitors head for Police (Bulijong) Bay on Gaya's north coast, where the water is exceptionally clear and the beach beautifully fringed with casuarina trees. Camping shelters are available here and trails lead through its rocky spine and dense jungle. Outside the park boundary to the north is a small resort and on the south coast facing KK sprawls a huge water-village, complete with a mosque. Most of the village's residents are impoverished Filipino refugees.

Jewels in the crown A mere hiccup off the south-western tip of Gaya, **Pulau Sapi** has good facilities for day-trippers, as well as shady beaches and calm coral-rich waters. A circular inland trail can be covered in an hour but the vegetation is not as lush as on Gaya.

Farther south lies **Pulau Manukan**, the second largest and the most developed, home to park headquarters, jungle trails, chalet accommodations, a restaurant, tennis courts, and, for those who do not want to glide around the coral reefs, a swimming pool. Much favored by local youths, this island should be your last priority.

Closest to the coast is **Pulau Mamutik**, once privately owned and now offering a characterless bungalow for group accommodations, but washed by crystal-clear waters. Finally, rocky **Pulau Sulug** boasts a long sand spit, limited facilities and superlative emerald waters sheltering fantastic marine life. It really does live up to its hype as a desert island getaway.

Arriving
Malaysia

By air Terminal I of KL's Subang Airport serves international flights and Terminal II serves all domestic routes. A rather infrequent shuttle operates between the two, but cheap taxis are always available. The airport is 14 miles from downtown and prepaid taxi vouchers are sold at the taxi stand. Both terminals have duty-free shops, banks, car-rental offices, post offices and telephone services, as well as bars and restaurants.

Visas for three-month stays are not required for British, Irish, Commonwealth, European, or U.S. nationals: one month is automatically given and can be extended. Passports must be valid for at least six months. Hold on to the immigration card stub that is returned to you, as you will need to present it on your departure, when you will also have to pay airport tax.

After any break in a trip of more than 72 hours always reconfirm your ongoing flight with the airlines office. **Malaysian Airlines** (MAS), tel. (03 2610555).

By sea India, Indonesia, and Thailand offer regular sea services to Malaysia. The longest route is Madras–Pinang with the casino-equipped 800-passenger *MV Vignesswara* (Greenseas Shipping Co.). From Indonesia, there are routes from Sumatra to the peninsula (Medan–Pinang, Dumai–Melaka) and a short trip from Kalimantan (Borneo) to Sabah via Nunukan/Tarakan–Tawau. Boats from Thailand operate from Phuket or Satun to Langkawi and Pinang.

By land International Express trains leave Bangkok daily for Butterworth, with connections to KL and Singapore. To reach the east coast or center, trains connect at Hat Yai in southern Thailand for Tumpat and the "Jungle Railway" (see page 176). For more information contact **KTM** (Malaysian railways) in KL, tel. 03 2757263. Express buses from Bangkok to Singapore take the west coast route.

Singapore

By air Duty-free shopping is available to passengers arriving at Changi Airport, although prices are not cheap. European, U.S., and Commonwealth visitors do not need a visa, just a passport valid for at least six months. Only 14 days are allocated. For extensions, contact the **Immigration Office**, South Bridge Centre (tel. 532 2877).

Departure tax can be paid in advance at your downtown hotel or at the airline office. **Singapore Airlines**, tel. 223 8888; **MAS**, tel. 336 6777; **airport flight information**, (tel. 542 2222).

Taxis, hotel shuttle services, or Bus 390 (to Orchard Road area) whisk you the 14 miles to downtown.

By sea Cruise ships and regular services operating between Indonesia and Singapore all dock at the World Trade Centre, within easy reach of the center by bus or taxi. The islands of Batam and Bintan (Tanjung Pinang) are favorite destinations, the latter being farther out (four hours) and more interesting. Contact **Dino Shipping** (tel. 221 4916) or **Yang Passenger Ferry Service** (tel. 223 9902).

By land Trains from Bangkok, Butterworth, KL, and the east coast terminate at Keppel Road Railway Station, adjacent to Chinatown and the business district.

A newly developed luxury train service, the Eastern & Oriental Express, makes weekly return trips between Singapore and Bangkok (with stops at Melaka, Pinang, Phuket, and Hua Hin), taking 41 hours and including two nights on board. Otherwise, daily express trains leave Singapore for KL and Butterworth at 7:45 A.M. and for KL only at 2:45 P.M. (a seven-hour trip).

For more information contact the **Singapore Railway Station** (tel. 222 5165).

Express buses to and from Malaysia leave from the Lavender Street terminus (for Butterworth, Pinang, KL, Kuantan, Melaka, and Mersing) or from the Ban Ban Street terminus (for Johor Bahru).

Camping

Malaysia Although camping in the Malaysian wilds is becoming increasingly popular, few structured campsites exist and there is now a law prohibiting camping wherever you please, although permission can be obtained through local tourist offices (see pages 265–266) or parks offices. Taman Negara, Tasik Cini, Tasik Kenyir in the Peninsula, and Bako and Niah national parks in Sarawak are specifically geared toward camping, but you will need to take everything with you.

Singapore The island of Sentosa offers two campsites with tents to rent and the East Coast Parkway also has a site.

Car breakdown

Malaysia The Automobile Association of Malaysia (AAM) has an extensive list of appointed workshops throughout the country. Contact its head office in KL for 24-hour assistance (tel. 03 2425212), or its branch offices in Pinang (tel. 04 376073) or Ipoh (tel. 05 545846). Car-rental companies always supply the necessary information.

Singapore The Automobile Association of Singapore (AAS) has a 24-hour breakdown service (tel. 748 9911). There is also an alternative service (tel. 737 0831).

Car rental

Malaysia International and local car-rental firms operate from major airports, hotels, and towns. Compare the rates as some come up with special offers; generally speaking local firms are a better bargain than the international firms but drop-offs are more difficult to organize. An international driver's license is obligatory and credit card deposits are accepted. Cars all have air-conditioning and chauffeurs are available.

- **Avis**, KL (tel. 03 2423500).
- **Budget**, KL (tel. 03 2625800).
- **Hertz**, KL (tel. 03 2486433).
- **Mayflower**, KL (tel. 03 2611136).
- **Orix**, KL (tel. 03 2423009).
- **SMAS**, KL (tel. 03 2307788).

In Sabah reliable local firms in Kota Kinabalu are:

- **Adaras** (tel. 088 222137).
- **Borneo Car Rental** (tel. 088 429041).
- **Kinabalu Rent-a-Car** (tel. 088 232602).

Sarawak's limited roads do not invite car rental, but the service still exists! Try:

- **Mahana Rent-a-Car**, Kuching (tel. 082 423435).
- **Saga Servis**, Miri (tel. 085 413622).

Singapore Chauffeur-driven cars are useful for exploring the more rural northern area of Singapore for periods as short as three hours, and they cost little more than a taxi. Reliable firms include:

- **Elpin Tours & Limousines** (tel. 235 3111).
- **Presidential Pacific Limousine** (tel. 223 3668).

If you want to rent a car by the day or week check local firms listed in the Yellow Pages under "Motorcar Renting and Leasing," or try the following:

- **Avis** (tel. 737 1668).
- **Hertz** (tel. 734 4646).

Climate

Singapore's temperatures average a constant 80°F, with rains peaking in November and December when humidity increases. In Malaysia temperatures range from 72°F at night to 90°F during the day, but are almost 20°F lower in the hill stations.

The northeast and southwest monsoons blow alternately, affecting Singapore, the east coast, the center, and East Malaysia from November to February, and the Peninsula's west coast from May to September. During the more destructive northeast monsoon many east coast services stop, and Sabah and Sarawak turn into mud baths.

Crime

This region is one of Asia's safest, with law-abiding Singapore the safest of all. In certain more impoverished regions of Malaysia, care should nevertheless be taken with valuables, but bag-snatchers and pickpockets are only a hazard in KL (Chinatown in particular), Pinang, Sandakan, and Kota Kinabalu. If necessary contact the Tourist Police, identified by checkered bands on their caps.

Customs regulations

Malaysia Customs allow the import of 200 cigarettes or 250g of tobacco, 1 liter of liquor, and perfume not exceeding RM200 in value. Used cameras and cassette players are not subject to government tax but video equipment may require a deposit, refundable on departure (bring the receipt of purchase with you just in case). Weapons, pornography, and walkie-talkies are strictly prohibited, as are drugs, for which there is a death penalty. There are no currency restrictions and no health regulations except for visitors from regions infected with yellow fever.

Singapore Duty-free allowances are 1 liter of spirits, 1 liter of wine, and 1 liter of beer. Duty must be paid on

cigarettes, cigars, and tobacco. Serious medication must be accompanied by a personalized prescription and narcotics are, of course, banned. Be careful with publications considered seditious or pornographic (for example, *Penthouse*), as well as tapes and videocassettes. Toy coins and currency are also prohibited. Passengers from Africa or South America will need a yellow fever vaccination certificate.

Disabled travelers

Malaysia Facilities are not good and Malaysia cannot be recommended for disabled travelers although Malaysians will be helpful. Certain hotels have specific facilities (Mutiara Group, Holiday Inn Group and Park

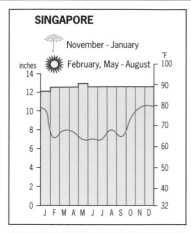

SINGAPORE

November - January

February, May - August

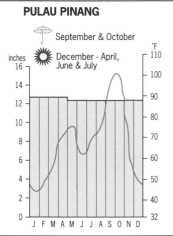

PULAU PINANG

September & October

December - April, June & July

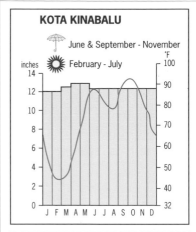

KOTA KINABALU

☂ June & September - November

☀ February - July

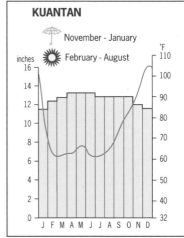

KUANTAN

☂ November - January

☀ February - August

Domestic travel
Malaysia

By air MAS has an extensive network of domestic routes at reasonable prices, although it has yet to come up with a viable form of tourist air pass. Group fares are available for three or more passengers (25–50 percent off), while they offer good deals in off-peak periods and on night flights. Beware of "no-show" penalties, which can cost 25 percent of the fare. Before booking your international ticket at home, check with MAS to see what reductions are offered on domestic routes combined with an international flight.

All domestic flights from KL leave from Subang Airport's Terminal II. Flights to East Malaysia involve higher airport taxes and you will need a passport for immigration control on arrival. Kuching and Kota Kinabalu are the main destinations, with connecting flights to upcountry airstrips on Twin-Otters and Fokkers.

Pelangi Air, a subsidiary of MAS, operates on certain routes such as Tioman, and flights can be booked through MAS.

MAS reservations:
- **Ipoh** (tel. 05 514155).
- **Johor Bahru** (tel. 07 220888).
- **Kota Bharu** (tel. 09 747000).
- **Kota Kinabalu** (tel. 088 213555).
- **Kuala Lumpur** (tel. 03 230 5115). For 24-hour reservations or reconfirmations, tel. 03 7463000.
- **Kuantan** (tel. 09 521218).
- **Kuching** (tel. 082 246622).
- **Melaka** (tel. 06 235722).
- **Pulau Langkawi** (tel. 04 788622).
- **Pulau Pinang** (tel. 04 620011).

Royal in KL), but local and domestic transport as well as sightseeing will prove very difficult. For more information contact: **Malaysian Rehabilitation Council**, 12 Lengkongan Jenjarom, Batu 2.5, Jalan Kelang, KL (tel. 03 2742714), or your local Malaysian TPB office.

Singapore Far more conscious of disabled people's needs than Malaysia, Singapore abounds in specially designed ramps, elevators, toilets, and telephones. Most new hotels are equipped with the necessary facilities. A detailed guide to easily accessible attractions can be obtained from: **Singapore Council of Social Services**, 11 Pinang Lane (tel. 336 1544).

By boat Ferries, hydrofoils, and fishing boats operate between coastal ports and outlying islands. Services are frequent outside the monsoon season and usually run on a fixed-price ticket basis. For more obscure destinations some bargaining may be necessary with local fishermen.

In Sarawak express launches operate from Kuching, Sibu, Miri, Marudi, Limbang, Kapit, and Belaga. There is also a regular Labuan–Kota Kinabalu service. Local tourist offices (see pages 265–266) supply timetables and prices; advance booking is advisable.

By road Intertown and interstate bus services are cheap and excellent, although the multiplicity of private companies complicates matters; contact the local tourist office (see pages 265–266) for more specific information. Long-distance buses are a viable option for budget travelers, but avoid crowded "milk-train" versions that stop at every *kampung* on the way. Drivers are generally safe, but timetables are often approximate.

An alternative and stimulating means of intertown travel is by shared taxi. A very reasonable fixed flat rate is charged for the trip and divided between four passengers. Taxi stands (*teksi*) are located close to bus stations, fares are roughly twice those of buses and rides are often hair-raising.

By train KTM (Keretapi Tanah Melayu), the nationalized railway, operates regular north–south routes although none crosses from east to west. Comfortable, economical trains with first-, second-, and third-class cars are either express (stopping only at main towns) or ordinary (stopping virtually every 15 minutes).

The best bets are the **Ekspres Rakyat**, the **Ekspres Sinaran**, and the **Timuran**. Faster than the regular express service, these trains link Singapore–KL–Butterworth and Singapore–Tumpat. The west coast line from Singapore branches at Gemas to travel northeast to Kota Bharu and join the Thai railways.

"**Visit Malaysia**" rail passes, available at main train stations, entitle foreign tourists to ten or 30 days unlimited rail travel, although sleeping berths are extra.

Singapore

See Public transportation.

Driving tips
About 20,000 miles of roads (some unpaved) and highways crisscross Malaysia, but in East Malaysia driving is only feasible in coastal areas of Sabah as Sarawak's roads are limited. You will need a four-wheel drive for exploring remote rural areas. Driving is unnecessary in Singapore as it possesses an excellent public transportation system.

Malaysia's west coast highway is due to be completed in 1994, but certain stretches may still be under construction. Toll charges are minimal and the uncongested lanes are a joy. The two east–west highways (Butterworth–Kota Bharu and KL–Kuantan) cut through spectacular mountain scenery. Elsewhere, trucks are the main drawback, particularly on winding mountainous routes, although as they avoid minor rural roads these are a breeze.

Cars are driven on the left, priority at traffic circles is to drivers on the right, and speed limits are 50kph (30mph) in towns, rising to 90kph (55mph) on rural routes and 110kph (65mph) on highways. Seat belts are compulsory. International traffic signs are used, supplemented by a few local ones—*Awas* (caution or danger), *Ikut kiri* (keep left), *Kurangkan laju* (slow down), *Jalan sehala* (one way), and *Berhenti* (stop). Distances are given in kilometers but people still talk in miles. Note that some gas stations may be closed on Fridays and others on Sundays (see Opening hours).

Electricity

Voltage is 220–240V throughout Malaysia and Singapore. Upscale hotels supply adaptors and transformers for 110V. Plugs are square three-pronged types.

Embassies and consulates

Malaysia

● **Australian High Commission**, 6 Jalan Yap Kwan Seng, K.L. (tel. 03 2423122).
● **British High Commission**, 185 Jalan Ampang, K.L. (tel. 03 2482122).
● **Canadian High Commission**, Plaza MBF, 7th Floor, 172 Jalan Ampang, K.L. (tel. 03 2612000).
● **New Zealand High Commission**, 193 Jalan Tun Razak, K.L. (tel. 03 2486422/6560/8776).
● **U.S. Embassy**, 376 Jalan Tun Razak, K.L. (tel. 03 2489011).

Singapore

● **Australian Embassy**, 25 Napier Road (tel. 737 9311).
● **British Embassy**, Tanglin Road (tel. 473 9333).
● **Canadian Embassy**, 80 Anson Road #14-00, IBM Towers (tel. 225 6363).
● **Irish Embassy**, 541 Orchard Road #08-02, Liat Towers (tel. 732 3430).
● **New Zealand Embassy**, 13 Nassim Road (tel. 235 9966).
● **U.S. Embassy**, 30 Hill Street (tel. 338 0251).

Emergency telephone numbers

Malaysia Fire, police, and ambulance, tel. 999.

Singapore Police, tel. 999; ambulance and fire, tel. 995.

Credit card losses: **American Express** (tel. 235 5788); **Diners Club** (tel. 294 4222); **MasterCard** (tel. 336 0755); **Visa** (tel. 800 1544).

Health

Malaysia Even the smallest town in Malaysia has a clinic where private consultations cost only a nominal amount, and major towns have helpful government hospitals. Visitors should be vaccinated against typhoid, hepatitis A, polio, and tetanus before arriving, and antimalarial precautions are recommended if traveling into the interior of East Malaysia, where dengue fever is also on the increase. AIDS consciousness is high, but the number of victims continues to rise.

Although the usual rules for tropical survival apply in Malaysia, risks are minor compared with many neighboring countries. Tap water in major towns is drinkable, hotels provide boiled water, and mineral water is available everywhere. The main danger is dehydration and salt-loss, particularly when jungle trekking; those who sweat profusely may need salt tablets. Your first-aid kit should contain the following: a tube of antihistamine cream for stings and insect bites; a kaolin preparation for upset stomachs; aspirin for headaches or fever; a course of general antibiotics for emergencies; and mosquito repellent.

Singapore Medical standards are high in Singapore but, outside emergencies, you are unlikely to need them. The same tropical precautions apply as in Malaysia.

Insurance

Travel insurance should be taken out before leaving home. If you intend to

indulge in an adventure such as whitewater rafting, mountain trekking or scuba diving, check the small print thoroughly to make sure your policy covers these activities.

Language
Visitors to Singapore will have absolutely no difficulty communicating in English, one of the four official languages along with Mandarin, Malay, and Tamil. In Malaysia the official language is Malay (Bahasa Malaysia), but English is also widely spoken. East Malaysians are particularly fluent in English, and someone will always be ready to assist with translations.

Useful phrases
good morning	selamat pagi
good afternoon	selamat petang
good night	selamat malam
goodbye	selamat tinggal, selamat jalan
how are you?	api khabar?
I'm fine	khabar baik
yes	ya
no	tidak
never mind	tidak apa
thank you	terimah kasih
you're welcome	sama sama
OK	baiklah
what's your name?	siapa nama awak?
my name is	nama saya
I am sorry	saya minta maaf
when?	bila?
tomorrow	esok
today	hari ini
yesterday	semalam
how long will it take?	berapa lama?
Monday	senin, isnin
Tuesday	selasa
Wednesday	rabu
Thursday	khamis
Friday	jumaat
Saturday	sabtu
Sunday	ahad
how much?	berapa har ganya?
expensive	mahal
cheap	murah
how far?	berapa jauh?
where?	di mana?
eat	makan
drink	minum
water	air
coffee	kopi
tea	teh
bread	roti

Local customs and courtesies
Although generally easygoing, Malaysians appreciate visitors' politeness. This is particularly true where religion is concerned: always respect worshippers in mosques and temples, and remove your shoes before entering all except Chinese temples. Accept a drink or food if offered, and if eating with hands only use the right hand—the left is considered unclean. Seniority is important and it is polite to offer anything to the oldest person first. Pointing with the finger is considered very rude—use the whole hand if you must. The head of the body is considered the most sacred part, so avoid giving affectionate pats to children. Feet, considered the lowest point of the body, should never be put on a table in front of other people. In restaurants or hotels do not whistle, wave, or snap fingers; raising your hand is sufficient. Avoid criticizing Islam, sultans, or the government—all delicate subjects.

Lost property
Once you have checked the places where you may have left the item

concerned, contact the local police to report the loss for insurance purposes. Lost passports need to be reported to your embassy and traveler's checks to the issuing bank.

Media
Malaysia The country staggers under a plethora of publications: on the peninsula alone there are 16 dailies and periodicals in Bahasa, eight in English, nine in Chinese, and four in Tamil. The main English-language newspaper, the *New Straits Times* (on Sunday it becomes the *New Sunday Times*), is informative, and often lively, although firmly in the government camp. East Malaysia publishes the *Borneo Post*, *Daily Express*, *Sarawak Tribune*, *Sabah Times*, and 15 others in Chinese! Foreign newspapers are available a couple of days after publication in Kuala Lumpur, Pinang, Kuching, and Kota Kinabalu.

RTM (Radio and Television Malaysia) controls 18 national and local radio stations and two national TV channels (IV1 and IV2), joined in the Peninsula by a third private network—TV3. English-language news is broadcast on TV3 at 7 P.M. daily and all the top hotels in the country are linked to CNN.

Singapore Singapore Press Holdings owns and runs all but one of the nation's eight dailies. Leading English-language papers are the *Straits Times* and *Business Times*. The *International Herald Tribune* is printed locally and available the same day, but its contents are rigorously controlled. A wide selection of foreign publications is available in hotel newsstands and central bookstores.

TV channels are as multilingual as everything else in Singapore. Channel 5 and Channel 12 offer news, documentaries, sports, and cultural programs in English, and CNN is available in most hotels. The BBC World Service can be picked up on 88.9Mhz.

Money matters
The same rules apply for Malaysia and Singapore: shop around and when possible stick to licensed

moneychangers who also accept traveler's checks (these often double up as newsdealers). Rates can vary considerably, the worst being offered by hotels. Credit cards are widely accepted in hotels, upscale restaurants, and shopping centers in Singapore and KL, but elsewhere in Malaysia you will have to rely entirely on cash except in the international hotels. Some islands have no money-changing facilities, and when they do the rates are generally unfavorable, so be prepared. Always keep small notes on you for taxis, trishaws, buses, and food stalls.

The Malaysian unit of currency is the ringgit (RM). It is divided into 100 sen and notes range from RM1 upward, to RM1,000. The strong and stable Singapore dollar (S$) uses bills for S$1 to S$10,000 and coins for 1¢ to 100¢. Brunei dollars sometimes crop up—these are completely interchangeable with the Singapore dollar but not with the less valuable Malaysian ringgit.

National holidays
Varying considerably from state to state depending on their respective ethnic balances, Malaysia's public holidays include numerous Muslim, Hindu, Chinese, Dayak, and Kadazan festivals, as well as the birthdays of state sultans. The following are celebrated nationally (those indicated with asterisks are movable). If

possible, avoid visiting sights during the school vacations in June and November.

Singapore celebrates the same holidays, minus Maal Hijrah and the birthdays of Prophet Muhammad and the Yang di-Pertuan Agong. Its National Day is August 9 and Good Friday is an extra public holiday.

- **New Year's Day** January 1 (not every state)
- **Chinese New Year*** January or February
- **Hari Raya Puasa*** dates follow Islamic calendar
- **Labor Day** May 1
- **Wesak Day*** May 17
- **Yang di-Pertuan Agong's birthday** June 6
- **Hari Raya Haji*** one month after Hari Raya Puasa
- **Maal Hijrah*** July 2
- **National Day** August 31
- **Prophet Muhammad's birthday*** September 9
- **Diwali*** October or November (except East Malaysia)
- **Christmas Day** December 25

Opening hours

Malaysia Most of the country follows the Monday to Saturday week but in more orthodox Johor, Kedah, Perlis, Kelantan, and Terengganu, Friday replaces Sunday as the day of rest, so banks, government offices, and many shops close at midday on Thursday, and reopen on Saturday morning. Shops are generally open 9:30–7, and supermarkets and department stores 10–10. Government offices operate 8–12:45 and 2–4:15 (with a longer lunch break on Fridays for prayers) and on Saturday (or Thursday in orthodox states) 8–12:45. Banks open 10–3 and 9:30–11:30 on their half-days.

Museums are open daily 9:30–5 with a long midday prayer break on Fridays. In Kelantan they close on Wednesdays and in Melaka on Friday afternoons. In East Malaysia museums close on Fridays, while in smaller towns in Peninsular Malaysia you may find them closed on Sunday.

Singapore Opening hours in Singapore follow the Monday to Saturday week. Government offices open 8–5 on weekdays and 8–1 on Saturdays. Shops operate from 9:30, most staying open until 10 and some even opening on Sundays. Banking hours are 10–3 on weekdays and 9:30–11:30 on Saturdays, and in the Orchard Road area many open on Sundays too. Museums and attractions generally open daily at 9, closing at any time between 4 (public) and 10 (private).

Pharmacies

Shopping centers nearly all have pharmacies (open until 10) and pharmacists in upscale hotels stock the basics. Qualified pharmacists in every main town are always helpful with advice, sometimes making visits to doctors unnecessary as many medicines are available without prescription. Most common drugs are available, so unless you have specific needs this is not something to worry about unduly (see Health).

Malaysian shops are generally open from 9:30 to 7

Places of worship

Malaysia Although Islam is the official religion, Malaysia is open to all forms of worship. Churches abound in KL (**St. Andrew's Presbyterian Church**, 31 Jalan Weld; **St. John's Roman Catholic Cathedral**, Bukit Nanas; **St. Mary's Anglican Church**, Jalan Raja; **Wesley Methodist Church**, Jalan Wesley; **Baptist Church**, 70 Jalan Hicks) as well as in Pinang, Melaka, Johor Bahru, Kuching, Kota Kinabalu, and many small East Malaysian towns where Christianity is more widespread. There are no synagogues.

Singapore The main place for Protestant worship is at **St. Andrew's Cathedral** in Coleman Street. Other places of worship include:
● **Baptist Church**, 90 Kings Road (tel. 466 4929).
● **Wesley (Methodist) Church**, 5 Fort Canning Road (tel. 336 1433).
● **Cathedral of the Good Shepherd** (Catholic), Queen Street (tel. 337 2036).
● **Jewish Synagogue**, Waterloo Street (tel. 336 0692).

Police

See Crime and Emergency telephone numbers.
   In Singapore dial 999; in Malaysia ask for the Balai Polis or telephone:
● **Johor Bahru** (tel. 07 232222/245522).
● **Kota Bharu** (tel. 09 785522).
● **Kota Kinabalu** (tel. 088 58111).
● **Kuala Lumpur** (tel. 03 2415522/2435522).
● **Kuching** (tel. 082 241133).
● **Melaka** (tel. 06 2222222).
● **Pulau Pinang** (tel. 04 615522).

Post offices

Malaysia Large hotels supply stamps and every town has a central post office—in KL it is Pejabat Pos Besar Kuala Lumpur, 2nd Floor, Dayabumi Complex (tel. 03 2741122). Opening times are Monday to Friday 8–5, Saturday 8–noon, except in Johor, Kedah, Perlis, Kelantan, and Terengganu, where they close on Thursday afternoons and Fridays. Major towns operate poste restante systems (address mail to: Poste Restante, Pejabat Pos Besar, town name, state).

Singapore The Orchard Point Post Office (*open*: 8–8 daily) is the most convenient for visitors. Poste restante and fax facilities are available at the GPO, Fullerton Building, Fullerton Road, and the post office at the Comcenter, 31 Exeter Road, never closes. Other post offices open 9–5 on weekdays and 9–1 on Saturdays.

Public transportation

Malaysia
For domestic air, rail, bus, and boat information see Domestic travel.
   In towns the easiest locomotion is by taxi or trishaw, but negotiate a price in advance, either for a specific destination or an hourly rate. Rates for trishaws are roughly RM2 per km, or RM12–15 per hour depending on the driver and the time of day.
   Taxis cost slightly more, but again negotiate in advance as few use meters outside KL. Major airports have prepaid voucher systems.
   Municipal buses are hardly worth investigating, but for out-of-town sights the local tourist office will advise on routes.

Singapore
Mass Rapid Transit (MRT)
Singapore's exemplary MRT (subway) covers most central sights. Trains operate from 6 A.M. to midnight on two color-coded routes. Coin-operated ticket dispensers are located in each station; tickets need to be kept and fed into the exit gate at the end of your ride.
   More convenient if you are staying for several days is a stored-value pass, which subtracts the fare for each ride until the card is finished. Any remaining value can be cashed in on departure and the small deposit is refunded.

Buses Single- and double-decker buses are useful for destinations that the MRT does not serve. The network is as efficient and inexpensive as the MRT, operating either with individual fares (correct change is essential) or with Singapore Explorer tickets for unlimited travel over one or three days. These tickets can be bought at hotels or travel agents and come with a detailed route map showing tourist attractions.

Taxis Singapore's 10,000 taxis are clean, metered, air-conditioned, and reasonably priced. Surcharges are applied from midnight to 6 A.M. and for trips to or from the central business district during rush-hours. Taxis can be flagged down in the street or ordered by phone:
- **Clementi Taxi Service** (tel. 466 8386).
- **Comfort Taxi Service** (tel. 452 5555).
- **SABS Radio Taxi** (tel. 250 0700).
- **Singapore Radio Taxi** (tel. 468 6188).

Student and youth travel
A superlative destination for young travelers, Malaysia offers cheap accommodations, food, and transportation as well as a good dose of adventure. Visit Malaysia rail passes and air passes can be good investments, although the latter restricts you to travel within the Peninsula, Sabah, or Sarawak without moving between them. MAS offers youth reductions on domestic routes and night rates on specific flights. Student concessions are only available for those studying in Malaysia. Hitching is fairly common and popular with local students and budget travelers.

Telephones
Malaysia The country has an advanced and efficient telecommunications system, although east coast island lines are sometimes bad. Major hotels have IDD (international direct dialing) but add a surcharge. Telekom offices in major towns offer fax services as well as telephones. Coin-operated telephone booths can be found in supermarkets, post offices, public buildings, and in the street. Phone-card booths are increasingly widespread, but annoyingly they function with two incompatible systems: Kadfon and Unicard. Cards are sold at post offices, newsstands, airports, and gas

stations. To make an overseas call, dial 007, the country code (Australia 61; Canada and USA 1; Ireland 353; New Zealand 64; UK 44), followed by the town code and number. For information dial 103, and for the international operator dial 108.

Singapore All major hotels have IDD, but budget-minded visitors should head for a nearby Telecom telephone booth instead, armed with a card bought at a hotel, newsdealer, or post office. Faxes and international calls can also be made at the Fullerton Road GPO and at Comcentre, Exeter Road (24 hours). For calling outside Singapore, dial 055 before the country code (listed above). For local information dial 103, and for the international operator dial 104.

Time
Malaysia and Singapore are 16 hours ahead of Los Angeles, 13 hours ahead of New York, eight hours ahead of GMT (seven hours ahead of British Summer Time), four hours behind Auckland and two hours behind Sydney.

Tipping
Officially discouraged in both countries, tipping is very much discretionary, although staff at international hotels appreciate a modest tip above the 10 percent service charge. Taxi drivers do not expect anything, but won't refuse a handful of change. Tour guides can be tipped 10 percent of the tour cost if you are satisfied.

Toilets
Large hotels, shopping centers, museums, gas stations, restaurants, and tourist spots all have toilets (tandas), in Malaysia marked perempuan (women) or lelaki (men). In Malaysia always carry a supply of toilet paper and in Singapore do not forget to flush toilets or you could be fined.

Tour agencies
Tours range from Singapore or KL highlights to island packages and up-country adventure breaks. Local

tourist offices will recommend suitable agencies for your needs, necessary above all in East Malaysia where some spots are very expensive or impossible to reach independently. Listed below are recommended Malaysian agencies:

● **Api Tours** PO Box 12853, 88831 Kota Kinabalu (tel. 088 221233; fax: 088 221230).

● **Asian Overland** 33 Jalan Dewan Sultan Sulaiman, Kuala Lumpur (tel. 03 2925622; fax: 03 292 5209). Branches all over Malaysia.

● **Borneo Adventure** PO Box 2112, 93742 Kuching (tel. 082 245175/410569; fax: 082 422626).

● **Borneo Overland** PO Box 725, 93714 Kuching (tel. 085 80255; fax: 085 416424).

● **Coral Island Cruises** G19, Wisma Sabah, Kota Kinabalu (tel. 088 223490; fax: 088 223404).

● **Discovery Tours** Wisma Sabah, Kota Kinabalu (tel. 088 57735) and Sandakan (tel. 089 2211244).

● **Tropical Adventure** Lot 228, Jalan Maju, Miri (tel. 085 419337; fax: 085 414503).

Tourist information

Malaysia Every state capital has a tourist office and the showcase central office in KL provides advance information. Opening hours are Monday to Friday 8–4:15 and Saturday 8–12:45, although offices in Johor, Kedah, Perlis, and Kelantan close from Thursday afternoon to Saturday morning.

State tourist offices

● **Alor Setar** State Secretariat, Wisma Negeri (tel. 04 722088).

● **Ipoh** State Economic Planning Unit, Jalan Dato' Sagor (tel. 05 532800).

● **Johor Bahru** Bangunan Sultan Ibrahim (tel. 07 241957).

● **Kota Bharu** Jalan Sultan Ibrahim (tel. 09 783543).

● **Kota Kinabalu** 51 Jalan Gaya (tel. 088 218620).

● **Kuala Lumpur** 109 Jalan Ampang (tel. 03 2434929).

● **Kuala Terengganu** Jalan Sultan Zainal Abidin (tel. 09 621433).

● **Kuantan** Jalan Haji Abdul Aziz (tel. 09 512960).

CONVERSION CHARTS

FROM	TO	MULTIPLY BY
Inches	Centimeters	2.54
Centimeters	Inches	0.3937
Feet	Meters	0.3048
Meters	Feet	3.2810
Yards	Meters	0.9144
Meters	Yards	1.0940
Miles	Kilometers	1.6090
Kilometers	Miles	0.6214
Acres	Hectares	0.4047
Hectares	Acres	2.4710
U.S. Gallons	Liters	3.7854
Liters	U.S. Gallons	0.2642
Ounces	Grams	28.35
Grams	Ounces	0.0353
Pounds	Grams	453.6
Grams	Pounds	0.0022
Pounds	Kilograms	0.4536
Kilograms	Pounds	2.205
U.S. Tons	Tonnes	0.9072
Tonnes	U.S. Tons	1.1023

MEN'S SUITS

U.K.	36	38	40	42	44	46	48
Rest of Europe	46	48	50	52	54	56	58
U.S.	36	38	40	42	44	46	48

DRESS SIZES

U.K.	8	10	12	14	16	18
France	36	38	40	42	44	46
Italy	38	40	42	44	46	48
Rest of Europe	34	36	38	40	42	44
U.S.	6	8	10	12	14	16

MEN'S SHIRTS

U.K.	14	14.5	15	15.5	16	16.5	17
Rest of Europe	36	37	38	39/40	41	42	43
U.S.	14	14.5	15	15.5	16	16.5	17

MEN'S SHOES

U.K.	7	7.5	8.5	9.5	10.5	11
Rest of Europe	41	42	43	44	45	46
U.S.	8	8.5	9.5	10.5	11.5	12

WOMEN'S SHOES

U.K.	4.5	5	5.5	6	6.5	7
Rest of Europe	38	38	39	39	40	41
U.S.	6	6.5	7	7.5	8	8.5

265

The Pinang tourist office will provide information on Batu Feringgi hotels

- **Kuching** Main Bazaar (tel. 082 410944).
- **Melaka** Jalan Kota (tel. 06 236538).
- **Pulau Langkawi** Kompleks Jeti Kuah, Kuah (tel. 04 789789).
- **Pulau Pinang** 10 Jalan Tun Syed Sheikh Barakbah (tel. 04 620066).

Overseas tourist offices (TPB)
- **Australia** 65 York Street, Sydney, NSW 2000 (tel. 02 299 4441/2; fax: 02 262 2026). 56 William Street, Perth, WA 6000 (tel. 09 481 0400; fax: 09 321 1421).
- **Canada** 830 Burrard Street, Vancouver, BC, V6Z 2K4 (tel. 604 689 8899; fax: 604 689 8804).
- **Singapore** 10 Collyer Quay, #01-03, Ocean Building (tel. 02 532 6351/21; fax: 02 535 6650).
- **UK** 57 Trafalgar Square, London WC2N 5DU (tel. 071 930 7932; fax: 071 930 9015).
- **USA** 818 West 7th Street, Los Angeles, CA 90017 (tel. 213 689 9702; fax: 213 689 1530).

Singapore Predictably, Singapore's ultra-efficient Tourist Promotion Board produces an abundance of literature about the island and tours. Individual guides can be hired for specialist needs and free sightseeing tours are available for transit passengers—contact the STPB's tour desk in the Changi transit lounge. Downtown offices are located at:
- Raffles City Tower #01-19, 250 North Bridge Road (tel. 330 0431/2; *open*: daily 8:30–6).
- Scotts Shopping Centre #02-02, Scotts Road (tel. 738 3778/9; *open*: daily 9:30–9:30).

Overseas tourist offices
- **Australia** Suite 1604, Level 16, Westpac Plaza, 60 Margaret Street, Sydney, NSW 2000 (tel. 02 241 3771/2; fax: 02 252 3586); 8th floor, St. George's Court, 16 St. George's Terrace, Perth, WA 6000 (tel. 09 325 8578/8511; fax: 09 221 3864).
- **Canada** 175 Bloor Street East, Suite 1112, North Tower, Toronto, M4W 3R8 (tel. 416 323 9139; fax: 416 323 3514).
- **New Zealand** Dataset House, 143 Nelson Street, Auckland (tel. 09 358 1191; fax: 09 358 1196).
- **UK** Carrington House, 126–30 Regent Street, London W1R 5FE (tel. 071 437 0033; fax: 071 734 2191).
- **USA** 590 Fifth Avenue, 12th Floor, New York 10036 (tel. 212 302 4861; fax: 212 302 4801); 8488 Wilshire Boulevard, Suite 510, Beverly Hills, CA 90211 (tel. 213 852 1901; fax: 213 852 0129).

Women travelers
Singapore and Malaysia are relatively safe destinations for women travelers, the former presenting absolutely no problems as Singapore women tend to be liberated and urbane. Malaysia, being a Muslim country, enforces some rules that restrain public behavior. The east coast states of Kelantan and Terengganu are the strictest: avoid wearing shorts, revealing T-shirts, or bikinis—bring out your one-piece swimsuit and never consider sunbathing topless. At the other end of the scale, cosmopolitan Pinang is the most easygoing, while between the two extremes you may encounter minor hassles—or respectful deference.

HOTELS AND RESTAURANTS

HOTELS AND RESTAURANTS

ACCOMMODATIONS

The following hotels have been divided into three price categories:

- budget ($)
- moderate ($$)
- expensive ($$$)

SINGAPORE

Ah Chew Hotel ($) 496 North Bridge Road (tel: 336 3563). Don't sneeze at this traditional inexpensive Chinese hotel between the colonial district and Arab Street. Basic, cash only.

Allson Hotel ($$) 101 Victoria Street (tel: 336 0811; fax: 339 7019). Stylish modern hotel near Raffles in colonial district. Standard facilities, pool, business center.

Amara Hotel ($$) 165 Tanjong Pagar Road (tel: 224 4488; fax: 224 3910). Sophisticated facilities include jogging track, gym, pool, business center. Large block at south of Chinatown and business district.

Apollo Hotel ($$) 405 Havelock Road (tel: 733 2081; fax: 733 1588). Top of middle range. Modern hotel convenient for Chinatown and business district. Free shuttles to Orchard Road; health center, business center, nightclub.

Bayview Inn ($$) 30 Bencoolen Street (tel: 337 2882; fax: 338 2880). In colonial district, modern block with rooftop pool and reasonable rates.

Broadway Hotel ($) 195 Serangoon Road (tel: 292 4661; fax: 291 6414). Rare modern hotel in Little India; excellent value at top of budget range. Air-conditioned rooms with safe, TV, telephone, and 24-hour room service.

The Duxton ($$$) 83 Duxton Road (tel: 227 7678; fax: 227 1232). Superlatively restored Chinese shophouse in Tanjong Pagar conservation area. Sophisticated style and French restaurant.

Excelsior Hotel ($$) 5 Coleman Street (tel: 338 7733; fax: 339 3847). Right in center, a featureless but comfortable modern hotel with pool, shops, and health center.

Golden Landmark Hotel ($$) 390 Victoria Street (tel: 297 2828; fax: 298 2038). Well located for Arab Street and Little India, the hotel echoes this style in its Aladdin Café. Pool, baby-sitting, business center and free shuttles around town.

Goodwood Park Hotel ($$$) 22 Scotts Road (tel: 737 7411; fax: 732 8558). Beautifully landscaped gardens with two pools surrounding grandiose architecture. Rivals Raffles for old-time atmosphere without going too far.

Grand Hotel ($) 25/26 Still Road South (tel: 345 5261). Delightful old Victorian house in Katong. Quiet location, rooms with TV and telephone at reasonable rates.

Harbour View Dai-Ichi Hotel ($$), 81 Anson Road (tel: 224 1133; fax: 222 0749). At the far southern end of business district. Good business facilities.

Hilton International ($$$) 581 Orchard Road (tel: 737 2233; fax: 732 2917). Jacuzzis in bathrooms, rooftop pool, business center, butlers, nightclub—all standard five-star amenities.

Kings Hotel ($$) 403 Havelock Road (tel: 733 0011; fax: 732 5764). Fairly expensive, convenient for Chinatown and business district. Pool, shops, and karaoke.

Lloyd's Inn ($) 2 Lloyd Road (tel: 737 7309). Small modern hotel convenient for downtown sights. Value, comfort, and tranquillity make it popular so it's often full.

Majestic ($) 31–7 Bukit Pasoh Road (tel: 222 3377). Immaculate rooms with telephone but few with bath in old Chinatown shophouse. Interesting area and good rates; cash only.

Malacca Hotel ($) 97/99 Still Road (tel: 345 7411). When every other budget hotel is full, try this one in Katong.

Basic modern hotel on busy road. Cash only.

Mandarin ($$$) 333 Orchard Road (tel: 737 4411; fax: 732 2361). No fewer than 1,200 rooms fill this mammoth landmark. Characterless but efficient and costly.

Mario-Ville ($) 64 Lloyd Road (tel: 734 5342). Sharing a faded colonial house with a ballet school near Orchard Road, a last surviving atmospheric haunt. Good value, cash only.

Mayfair City Hotel ($) 40–4 Armenian Street (tel: 337 4542). Last budget survivor in colonial district. Reasonable air-conditioned rooms with bath.

Metropole Hotel ($$) 41 Seah Street (tel: 336 3611; fax: 339 3610). Small modern block next door to Raffles. Slightly run down but well-equipped rooms, business facilities, baby-sitting. Good value.

Mitre Hotel ($) 145 Killiney Road (tel: 737 3811). Increasingly decrepit, characteristic old hotel with garden. Basic but cheap.

Nature Traveller House ($) Pulau Ubin (tel: 542 6124). For those looking for a quiet life away from downtown Singapore. Island retreat with dormitories and rooms. Avoid weekends.

New 7th Storey ($) 229 Rochor Road (tel: 337 0251). Close to Arab Street, an amusing 1950s building between old shophouses. Good value and facilities. Cash only.

Raffles Hotel ($$$) 1 Beach Road (tel: 337 1886; fax: 339 7650). Queen of Singapore, historic hotel now extensively renovated. Suites only make it Singapore's most exclusive; it's hard to be disappointed by the colonial-style luxury.

River View Hotel ($$) 382 Havelock Road (tel: 732 9922; fax: 732 1034). Towering over Singapore river, convenient for Chinatown and business district. Good amenities, pool.

San Wah Hotel ($) 36 Bencoolen Street (tel: 336 2428). Tiny old Chinese hotel. Calm, clean, some air-conditioned rooms. Cheap; cash only.

Shangri-La ($$$) 22 Orange Grove Road (tel: 737 3644; fax: 733 7220). Colossal modern block boasting landscaped gardens, pool, outdoor restaurant and exceptional service. Close to Orchard Road.

Sheraton Towers ($$$) 39 Scotts Road (tel: 737 6888; fax: 737 1072). Winner of numerous hotel awards. State-of-the-art modern hotel aimed at flush business travelers. All imaginable amenities, indoor waterfall, and excellent service.

Singapore Peninsula ($$) 3 Coleman Street (tel: 337 2200; fax: 336 3020). Good central location; anonymous hotel geared to budget-minded businessmen. Pool, cabaret, and restaurant.

Sloane Court Hotel ($) 17 Balmoral Road (tel: 235 3311). Plush little Tudor-style hotel with garden near Orchard Road. Good facilities plus an English pub.

South-East Asia Hotel ($) 190 Waterloo Street (tel: 338 2374). Excellent value in quiet but lively location. Air-conditioned rooms with telephone and TV.

Strand Hotel ($) 25 Bencoolen Street (tel: 338 1866; fax: 336 3149). Large modern block near the action. Mid-range facilities for reasonable prices.

YMCA ($) 1 Orchard Road (tel: 337 3444). Advance booking essential for this high-class youth hostel with roof-top pool, gym and modern features. Very popular though not cheap.

YWCA ($) 8 Fort Canning Road (tel: 336 3150). Equally central. Rooms or dormitories for couples and solo women.

KUALA LUMPUR

Apollo Hotel ($$) 106–110, Jalan Bukit Bintang (tel: 03 2428133). Small, very reasonable hotel in shopping center hub.

Asia Hotel ($$) 69 Jalan Haji Hussein (tel: 03 2926077).

Formerly the South-East Asia, now tarted up and with higher prices. In heart of Chow Kit market area.

Carcosa Seri Negara ($$$) Taman Tasik Perdana (tel: 03 2821888; fax: 03 2827888). KL's ultimate in refined luxury. Two elegant, restored colonial mansions in hilltop landscaped gardens. Suites only.

Champagne Hotel ($) 141 Jalan Masjid India (tel: 03 2986593). Pleasant small hotel surrounded by Indian Muslim shops and restaurants. Standard rooms at reasonable rates.

Chamtan Hotel ($) 62 Jalan Masjid India (tel: 03 2930144). Excellent value for air-conditioned rooms with telephone and bath in KL's lively Indian Muslim district. Clean and friendly.

Equatorial Hotel ($$) Jalan Sultan Ismail (tel: 03 2617777). In the hub of KL's Golden Triangle, well-appointed hotel with pool, business facilities, shops, parking lot.

Federal Hotel ($$) 35 Jalan Bukit Bintang (tel: 03 2489166; fax: 03 2438381). Good shopping location. Gigantic, flashy, top of mid-range hotel with extensive amenities, parking lot.

Fortuna Hotel ($$) 87 Jalan Berangan (tel: 03 2419111; fax: 03 2418237). Just off Jalan Bukit Bintang. Modestly scaled with standard facilities.

Holiday Inn on the Park ($$$) Jalan Pinang (tel: 03 2481066). Well located near the action. Uninspired décor but good views and amenities.

Hotel Furama ($$) Kompleks Selangor, Jalan Sultan (tel: 03 2302110/1777). Lively Chinatown location. Modern hotel, reasonable but soulless air-conditioned rooms. Parking lot.

Hotel Istana ($$$) 73 Jalan Raja Chulan (tel: 03 2419988; fax: 03 2440111). Superlative luxury and service in KL's latest exclusive hotel. Imaginative interior, strategic location, every possible amenity including

ballroom, pool, garden, tennis courts, and a business center.

Hotel Lok Ann ($) 118A Jalan Petaling (tel: 03 2389544). Small modern hotel in heart of Chinatown. Clean, characterless rooms, some with air-conditioning. Cheap and popular.

Kowloon Hotel ($$) 142–6 Jalan Tuanku Abdul Rahman (tel: 03 2926455). Super-hygienic rooms with telephone and bath in small modern building. Lively, central location; reasonable rates so often full.

Kuala Lumpur Hilton ($$$) Jalan Sultan Ismail (tel: 03 242222/122; fax: 03 2442157). Golden Triangle location for vast, modern, multi-amenity international hotel. Health center, shops, disco, business center, pool, parking lot.

Kuala Lumpur Mandarin ($$) 2–8 Jalan Sultan (tel: 03 2303000). Good Chinatown location. Well-appointed modern hotel with wide range of room prices.

The Lodge ($$) 2 Jalan Tengah (tel: 03 2420122). Off Jalan Sultan Ismail. Old-fashioned and friendly with small pool and comfortable rooms.

Malaya Hotel ($$) Jalan Hang Lekir (tel: 03 2327722). Reasonably priced rooms with air conditioning and bath; in middle of Chinatown's night market.

Malaysia Hotel ($$) 67–69 Jalan Bukit Bintang (tel: 03 2428033). Centrally located, modestly scaled hotel with standard facilities.

Ming Court Hotel ($$$) Jalan Ampang (tel: 03 2618888; fax: 03 2623428). Huge luxury hotel north of center along Embassy Row.

Nanyang Hotel ($), 83 Jalan Sultan (tel: 03 2387477). On one of Chinatown's main roads so check noise level. Large air-conditioned rooms with bath, slightly run down but good value.

Omar Khayyam Hotel ($) 5 Jalan Medan Tuanku (tel: 03 2988744). Nothing special but well situated. Air-conditioned rooms with bath. Excellent Indian restaurant.

HOTELS AND RESTAURANTS

Park Royal ($$$) Jalan Sultan Ismail (tel: 03 2425588). Well-appointed semi-luxury hotel near shopping complexes.

Pudu Raya ($) 4th floor, Pudu Raya Station, Jalan Pudu (tel: 03 2321000). Atop a bus and taxi station near Chinatown, so good for budget stopovers. Clean, quiet, air-conditioned rooms, pool, parking lot. No beauty spot.

Regent of Kuala Lumpur ($$$) 160 Jalan Bukit Bintang (tel: 03 2418000; fax: 03 2430525). Superb luxury hotel in Golden Triangle. Well-appointed tasteful rooms, all amenities. Parking lot.

Shangri-La ($$$) 11 Jalan Sultan Ismail (tel: 03 2322388; fax: 03 2301514). In heart of business, shopping and entertainment district. Glamorous luxury hotel and winner of numerous awards for service and amenities. Parking lot.

Shiraz Hotel ($) 1 Jalan Medan Tuanku (tel: 03 2920159). Unremarkable but good value for air-conditioned rooms with bath. Lively location off Jalan TAR. Small so often full. Good restaurant.

Starlight Hotel ($) 90–92 Jalan Hang Kasturi (tel: 03 2321744/5). Recommended budget hotel in Chinatown. Air-conditioned rooms with bath available.

Youth Hostels Association ($) 21 Jalan Kampung Attap (tel: 03 2306870/1). Air-conditioned youth hostel near train station.

YMCA ($) 95 Jalan Padang Belia (tel: 03 2741439). Some distance south of center. Cheap dormitories and rooms for both sexes.

YWCA ($) 12 Jalan Hang Jebat (tel: 03 2383225). Good location near Chinatown but often booked. Women, couples, or families only.

WEST COAST
Alor Setar
Hotel Grand Continental ($$) 134 Jalan Sultan Badlishah (tel: 04 735917). Centrally located on Alor Setar's main drag, a new 122-room hotel with standard air-conditioned rooms.

Hotel Samila ($) 27 Jalan Kancut (tel: 04 722344). Across river from Padang. Excellent value, good facilities.

Mahawangsa Hotel ($) 419 Jalan Raja (tel: 04 721433). Convenient for central sights, a small hotel with air-conditioned rooms.

Batu Pahat
Hotel Carnival ($$) 2 Jalan Fatimah (tel: 07 415122). Fairly stylish mid-range place with restaurant and health center.

Rumah Rehat Batu Pahat ($) 870 Jalan Tasik (tel: 07 441181). Air-conditioned doubles for reasonable resthouse rates.

Bukit Larut (Maxwell Hill)
Bukit Larut Hill Resort ($/$$) Taiping (tel: 05 827241). Central bookings office for bungalows and rest-houses at top of Bukit Larut, varying from basic to VIP style.

Ipoh
Excelsior Hotel ($$) 43 Clarke Street (tel: 05 536666). Well situated in old Chinatown. Large modern hotel with all top-range facilities.

Hollywood Hotel ($) 72–6 Jalan C M Yusof (tel: 05 515404/322). Cheap Chinese hotel on main crossroads southeast of center. Nothing special but friendly and good restaurant.

Ritz Garden Hotel ($$$) 79 Jalan C M Yusof (tel: 05 547777). In a cluster of anonymous hotels southeast of center. Glittering standard facilities but high prices.

Royal Casuarina Hotel ($$$) 18 Jalan Gopeng (tel: 05 505555; fax: 05 508177). Good views over hills from large modern hotel outside center with extensive facilities, airport shuttle, pool, disco.

Station Hotel ($$) Jalan Club (tel: 05 512588). Check to see if this magnificent colonial relic has reopened.

Winner Hotel ($) 32–8 Jalan Ali Pitchay (tel: 05 515177). Spotless Chinese hotel in lively central location. Large air-conditioned rooms with bath at reasonable rates.

Kangar
Federal Hotel ($) 104 Jalan Kangar (tel: 04 766884). Small-scale, reasonable hotel with restaurant and parking lot. Fan-cooled or air-conditioned rooms.

Pens Hotel ($) 138 Main Road (tel: 04 760487/491; fax: 04 760472). Superior budget hotel with pool, restaurant, bar, and parking.

Kuala Kangsar
Mei Lai Hotel ($) 7F Jalan Raja Chulan (tel: 05 861729). The top hotel in town! Rooms with bath and air-conditioning or fan. Fairly basic but cheap.

Rumah Rehat Kuala Kangsar ($) (tel: 05 851699/185). A 16-room rest-house with air conditioning.

Kuala Selangor
Rumah Rehat Kuala Selangor ($) Bukit Malawati (tel: 03 8891010). Rest-house in superb hillside location among historic sites. Three rooms, each with fan and bath.

Taman Alam-Kuala Selangor Nature Park ($) Jalan Klinik (tel: 03 8892294). Chalet accommodations in nature reserve; some rooms with shared bathroom, others for four people with attached bath.

Melaka
Accordian Hotel ($$) 114A Jalan Bendahara (tel: 06 221911; fax: 06 221333). Dwarfed by Ramada Hotel, a standard mid-range place in central location. Reasonable rates, clean but characterless.

Ayer Keroh Country Resort ($$) Ayer Keroh (tel: 06 325211; fax: 06 320422). About 8 miles north of Melaka town in a newly developed recreational area. Motel and chalets with tennis, pool, golf course bounded by lakes and jungle. Good family spot.

Choong Hoe Hotel ($) 26 Jalan Tukang Emas (tel: 06 226102). Fantastic location in the "street of harmony" containing Malaysia's oldest temples and mosques. Old Chinese hotel with cheap basic air-conditioned rooms, bath or not. Often full.

City Bayview ($$) Jalan Bendahara (tel: 06 239888; fax: 06 236699). Large modern hotel near Ramada. Standard facilities include car park.

Majestic Hotel ($) 188 Jalan Bungah Raya (tel: 06 222367). Rambling old colonial place with ceiling fans, swing doors, and other nostalgic features. Bar, restaurant, and fading rooms at cheap rates.

Malacca Village Resort ($$$) Ayer Keroh (tel: 06 323600; fax: 06 325955). About 10 miles inland from Melaka town, an imaginatively designed luxury resort with chalets in traditional Malay style. There is horseback riding, a pool, tennis, a health center, and good service.

May Chiang Hotel ($) 52 Jalan Munshi Abdullah (tel: 06 239800). Convenient for bus and taxi stations, and near center. Friendly, clean and fairly basic.

Ramada Renaissance Hotel ($$$) Jalan Bendahara (tel: 06 248888; fax: 03 249269). Melaka's best hotel, towering over commercial district and within easy reach of historic sights. Excellent amenities include rooftop pool, disco, restaurants, squash courts. Great views.

Tanjung Bidara Beach Resort ($$) Tanjung Bidara (tel: 06 542990/5). A pleasantly scaled hotel with chalets on a beautiful bay 22 miles north of Melaka town. Best Straits swimming, water sports, and a beachside pool.

Westernhay Hotel ($) Batu 4, Klebang Besar (tel: 06 239800). You will find this idiosyncratic old Chinese mansion by the sea a few miles out on the Port Dickson road. Friendly, clean and good value.

Muar

Hotel Sri Pelangi ($$) 79 Jalan Sisi (tel: 06 918088). Large hotel with standard amenities and wide range of prices.

Rumah Rehat Muar ($) 2222 Jalan Sultanah (tel: 06 927744). Pleasant location overlooking river. Relatively large rest-house (16 rooms) with restaurant.

Port Dickson

Ming Court Beach Hotel ($$) Batu 7½ Jalan Pantai, Teluk Kemang (tel: 06 405244; fax: 06 405899). Almost in luxury category, an upscale beach resort hotel south of town with numerous facilities.

Sri-Rusa Beach Resort ($$$) Batu 7, Jalan Pantai,Teluk Kemang (tel: 06 405233). Nothing special but good beach location and decent facilities.

Lido Hotel ($) Batu 8, Teluk Kemang (tel: 06 405273). Reasonably priced small hotel set in spacious grounds on beach.

Pulau Besar

Tapa-Nyai Island Resort ($$) (tel: 06 242088; fax: 06 236769). Recently opened upscale resort with chalets in landscaped grounds.

Pulau Langkawi

AB Motel ($) Pantai Cenang (tel: 04 911300). In main concentration of beach hotels but one of the originals. Good value, spacious chalets and restaurant.

Asia Hotel ($) 1A Jalan Persiaran Putra (tel: 04 788216). If you are forced to stay in town near jetty, this is reasonable and clean. Air-conditioned rooms with bath and TV.

Country Beach Motel ($) Pantai Kok (tel: 04 911212). Very laid-back beach hotel with chalets of varying comfort and price. Good restaurant, bike and motor bike rentals, island trips.

Langkawi Holiday Villa ($$$) Pantai Tengah (tel: 04 911701/411 ; fax: 04 911504). In recently developed southwestern corner of island. Standard facilities geared to package groups. Garden, pool, sunsets, and good beach.

Langkawi Island Resort ($$$) Pantai Syed Omar (tel: 04 788209/788252; fax: 04 788414). Stunning location overlooking outlying islands. Excellent service, landscaped pools, but beach not the best for swimming. Wide price range.

Mutiara Beach Resort ($$) Tanjung Rhu (tel: 04 788488). Must be Langkawi's ugliest hotel, monopolizing a superb secluded bay on north coast. Reasonable facilities and prices.

Pelangi Beach Resort ($$$) Pantai Cenang (tel: 04 911001; fax: 04 911122). The latest in luxury, the Pelangi sprawls over landscaped gardens overlooking beach. Traditional Malay-style low-lying architecture incorporates all imaginable facilities with flair.

Semarak Beach Resort ($$) Pantai Cenang (tel: 04 789777/911377). Near Pelangi Beach Resort, comfortable mid-range chalets in garden overlooking beach. Family chalets, good restaurant.

The Last Resort ($) Pantai Kok (tel: 04 740545/911046). The last in a string of beach-hut hotels. A pleasant, well-maintained group of chalets with baths and air conditioning or fan.

Pulau Pangkor

Beach Huts Hotel ($$) Pantai Pasir Bogak (tel: 05 951159). Well sited on beach, wide price range for varying facilities.

Pan Pacific Resort ($$$) Teluk Belanga (tel: 05 951091/399). Mammoth Japanese-owned resort on secluded bay to north of island. Endless luxury facilities and water sports.

Pangkor Anchor ($) Pantai Pasir Bogak (tel: 05 951363). Basic A-frame beach huts, minimal comfort but very clean.

Pangkor Laut Resorts ($$$) Pangkor Laut (tel: 05 951375/973; fax: 05 951320).

HOTELS AND RESTAURANTS

One of Malaysia's most exclusive resorts on a private island off Pangkor's west coast. Coral Bay and Royal Bay now boast upgraded luxury villas, some on stilts. Superlative amenities at bumper all-inclusive prices.

Seaview Hotel ($$) Pasir Bogak (tel: 05 951605). Friendly hotel on beach with spectacular sunsets. Spacious air-conditioned rooms, outdoor restaurant, bar.

Pulau Pinang

Bellevue Hotel ($) Pinang Hill (tel: 04 699500/892256; fax: 04 632242). Beautiful old mansion set in gardens atop the famous hill. Very reasonable for its unique location and tasteful decoration. Small so often booked.

272

Cathay Hotel ($) 15 Lebuh Leith (tel: 04 626271). Wonderful old Chinese mansion with clean, spacious rooms, fan or air conditioning. Front rooms can be noisy.

City Bayview Hotel ($$) 25A Lebuh Farquhar (tel: 04 363161; fax: 04 337282). Towering edifice with revolving restaurant and great views. Disco, parking lot, pool, reasonable rooms.

Eastern and Oriental Hotel ($$) 10 Lebuh Farquhar (tel: 04 630630; fax: 04 634833). Pinang's grande dame, built in 1885 right on the waterfront. Delightful garden and small pool. Partly renovated though also pleasantly old-fashioned.

Holiday Inn ($$) Batu Feringgi Beach (tel: 04 811621/601/833). Well located in thick of beach action. Water sports, tennis, disco, parking at reasonable rates.

Lone Pine Hotel ($$) Batu Feringgi Beach (tel: 04 811511/2; fax: 04 811282). Dating from the early 1950s, this was the first hotel on this once spectacular beach. Pleasantly low-key and modestly scaled, garden restaurant, baby-sitting.

Modern Hotel ($) 179C Lebuh Muntri (tel: 04 635424). Pleasant old hotel with basic comforts, some

rooms with terrace.

Oriental Hotel ($$) 105 Jalan Pinang (tel: 04 634211). Well situated on central crossroads near the action. Good sized air-conditioned rooms, restaurant, shops, bar, parking lot.

Rasa Sayang ($$$) Batu Feringgi Beach (tel: 04 811811; fax: 04 811984). Belongs to excellent Shangri-La Group which also owns next-door Golden Sands and Palm Beach. Pinang's top beach hotel lays on the luxury. Newly opened wing doubles already huge capacity. Landscaped gardens and pool on water's edge with extensive water-sports facilities.

Swiss Hotel ($) 431F Lebuh Chulia (tel: 04 620133). Cheap travelers' favorite set back from lively street.

Seremban

Carlton Hotel ($) off Jalan Dato' Sheik Ahmad (tel: 06 725336). Reasonable range of rooms, some air-conditioned, some fan-cooled.

Tasik Hotel ($$) Jalan Tetamu (tel: 06 730994/5/6). Pleasantly located on hill by Lake Gardens. Well-equipped rooms with TV, bath, air-conditioning, telephone. Pool, business center.

Taiping

Panorama Hotel ($$) 79 Jalan Kota (tel: 05 834189/192). Large modern hotel with standard facilities. Well situated.

Rumah Rehat Baru Taiping ($) Jalan Sultan Shah, Taman Tasik (tel: 05 822571). Rambling concrete rest-house in pretty Lake Gardens setting, fronted by ruined neoclassical columns. Spacious but run-down rooms with fans and bath. Restaurant and parking lot.

Teluk Intan

Angsoka Hotel ($) 24 Jalan Changkat Jong (tel: 05 623755/6). A 40-room hotel with coffee house, pool, and parking lot. Very reasonable rates.

CENTRAL REGION

Bukit Fraser

Fraser's Hill Development Corporation ($) (tel: 09 382044/201/248). Central information and booking office for all government bungalows in Bukit Fraser. Moderate rates, rising during peak season. A little dilapidated but service usually helpful and friendly.

Merlin Inn Resort ($$) Jalan Lady Guinemard (tel: 09 382274/300). Large modern edifice overlooking golf course. Offers extensive sports amenities and comfortable rooms. Restaurant, bar, pool, tennis courts.

Puncak Inn ($) (tel: 09 382055). Central location above small shopping center. Reasonable rooms.

Rumah Rehat Gap ($) Gap (tel: 09 382227). Situated at Gap junction 8km below Bukit Fraser itself. Old-fashioned rest-house in pretty setting. Excellent value with good restaurant.

Cameron Highlands

Bala's Holiday Chalets ($) Tanah Rata (tel: 05 941660). Up sliproad ½ mile north of town. Quiet and bucolic setting with friendly service. Accommodations range from dormitories to comfortable rooms with all facilities. Restaurant. Popular so often full.

Golf Course Inn ($$) Tanah Rata (tel: 05 901411; fax: 05 901462). Somewhat dilapidated modern hotel overlooking golf course. Full room facilities; popular hotel for families.

Kowloon Hotel ($) Lot 34/35, Berincang (tel: 05 941366). Good value modern hotel on main square.

Merlin Inn Resort ($$) Tanah Rata (tel: 05 901211). Large modern hotel overlooking golf course. Full room facilities, restaurant, bar, disco, tennis, parking lot.

Parkland Hotel ($$) Lot 45, Berincang (tel: 05 901803; fax: 05 901803). Very comfortable, pristine modern hotel on main square. Restaurant.

Rumah Rehat ($) Tanah Rata (tel: 05 901254). At uphill

exit of town, one of best deals around but booked up well in advance. Garden, tennis, friendly and comfortable.

The Lakehouse ($$$) Km 48, Ringlet (tel: 05 996152; fax: 05 996213). Superb position overlooking lake, a modestly scaled mock-Tudor house with cottages, all filled with antique furnishings. Good fishing and jungle walks in vicinity. Restaurant, bar, parking lot.

Town House Hotel ($) 41 Main Road, Tanah Rata (tel: 05 902868). Centrally located, good value. Cream teas, tours, long-distance bus tickets.

Ye Olde Smokehouse ($$) Tanah Rata (tel: 05 941214). The classic, much photographed colonial-style hotel set in English rose garden. Wide price range with four-poster beds at top end. Cream teas served in garden.

Genting Highlands
Genting Highlands Hotel ($$$) (tel: 09 2111118). Huge hotel with 700 rooms and Malaysia's only official casino. All luxury amenities, flower nursery, cable car, heliport, golf, shops, revolving disco, etcetera!

Highlands Hotel ($$) (tel: 09 211 2813). Has 244 rooms with full facilities, pool, restaurant, bars, and use of facilities at Genting Highlands Hotel.

Pelangi Hotel ($) (tel: 09 2112812/3). Large modern hotel with moderately priced rooms and a restaurant.

Gerik
Dinamid Hotel ($) 40A Jalan Sultan Iskandar (tel: 05 892388). Modest, basic hotel—top of the town!

Rumah Rehat Gerik ($) (tel: 05 891474). Veteran rest-house but rooms are spacious with attached bath. More expensive than the Dinamid.

Gua Musang
Kesedar Inn ($) (tel: 09 901229/491). Most comfortable hotel available, just

outside town. Reasonable rooms with air conditioning and bath.

Kuala Lipis
Hotel Sri Pahang ($) Tingkat Satu, Bangunan UMNO (tel: 09 312445). Fairly basic hotel with minimal comfort.

Rumah Rehat Kuala Lipis ($) Bukit Resident (tel: 09 312599/600). Well located on hill, a rest-house with 16 rooms and wide price range, depending on comforts.

Taman Negara
Nusa Camp ($) SPKG Tours, 16 LKNP building, New Town, Jerantut (tel: 09 262369; fax: 09 264369). Low-budget jungle resort. Cheap dormitory, A-frame chalet or cottage accommodations. Camp is located just outside Taman Negara boundaries but jungle is equally dense. Small office at Tembeling Jetty (tel: 09 262284).

Taman Negara Resort ($/$$$) Suite 1901, Pernas International, Jalan Sultan Ismail, Kuala Lumpur (tel: 03 2610393 fax: 03 2610615). Central booking agency for Taman Negara accommodations. Also arranges transport from KL to Tembeling Jetty. Complete range from campsite to dormitory, basic chalets, or deluxe versions. Restaurants and shop, plus the jungle.

Tasik Bera
Tourworld ($) Lot 4-2, 1st Floor, Kompleks Udarama (tel: 03 4420050/6609; fax: 03 4422769). Only agency that organizes trips to this remote lake. Sleeping in basic treehouses, washing in lake. Fishing and jungle treks.

Tasik Cini
Lake Chini Resort ($) c/o Malaysian Overland, KL (tel: 03 2433890) or c/o Perbadanan Kemajuan Negeri Pahang, Kompleks Teruntum, Jalan Mahkota, Kuantan (tel: 09 505566; fax: 09 500510). Superbly sited low-key resort on banks of

Tasik Cini, comfortable wooden chalets, dormitory accommodations, and campsite. Restaurant, bar.

Temerluh
Rumah Rehat Temerloh ($) Jalan Dato' Hamzah (tel: 09 51254). Good strategic spot on hill. Ten-room rest-house.

The Centrepoint Hotel ($) C308–311 Jalan Kuantan (tel: 09 292288). Reasonable rooms with air-conditioning, telephone, and bath, almost mid-range.

EAST COAST
Desaru
Desaru Golf Hotel ($$$) Tanjung Penawar (tel: 07 821101). Luxury resort on beach.

Desaru Holiday Resort ($$) Tanjung Penawar (tel: 07 821211). Modestly scaled. Similar location to above with good facilities.

Desaru View Hotel ($$$) Tanjung Penawar (tel: 07 821221). Super-luxury hotel with hefty prices that caters to Singaporeans.

Johor Bahru
Fortuna Hotel ($) 29A Jalan Meldrum (tel: 07 228671). Clean, well-maintained rooms with air-conditioning and bath.

Holiday Inn ($$$) Jalan Dato' Suleiman, Century Garden (tel: 07 323800). Johor Bahru's top hotel about a mile north of center in garden setting. Usual good service and facilities, though unimaginative décor. Facilities include a pool, restaurant, disco, and parking lot.

Straits View Hotel ($) 1-D Jalan Skudai (tel: 07 241400). Mid-range hotel looking out to Singapore. Has 30 well-appointed rooms, parking lot and karaoke!

Top Hotel ($) 12 Jalan Meldrum (tel: 07 244755). Air-conditioned rooms with bath. Reasonable rates.

Tropical Inn ($$) 15 Jalan Gereja (tel: 07 221888/ 247888). Large modern hotel—restaurant, health center, bar, parking lot.

273

HOTELS AND RESTAURANTS

Kampung Baluk and Beserah

Beserah Beach Resthouse ($) JKR110, Kampung Pantai Beserah (tel: 09 587492). The closest accommodations to the village of Beserah. Has ten rooms at reasonable rates.

Coral Beach Resort ($$$) 152 Sungai Karang (tel: 09 587544). All resort facilities plus excellent windsurfing and water sports.

Le Village ($$) Lot 1260, Sungai Karang (tel: 09 587900). Rustic *kampung*-style chalets and rooms. Full recreational facilities, bike rental, pool.

Tanjung Gelang Beach Resort ($) Km 15 (tel: 09 587254). Very reasonable considering location. Aging but comfortable.

Kampung Cerating

Cherating Beach Recreation Centre ($) Kampung Cerating Lama. At northern end of beach, small cluster of beach huts, some with bath, right next to open-air disco/bar.

Cherating Holiday Villa ($$) Lot 1303, Mukim Sungai Karang (tel: 09 508900). Half-way between Kampung Cerating and Kampung Baluk, 86 rooms and apartments, good service and superb setting.

Cherating Inn Beach Resort ($) Kampung Cerating Lama (tel: 09 503343). Comfortable chalets on beach, favorite with Singapore package tours.

Cherating Mini-Motel ($), Kampung Cerating Lama (tel: 09 508900). Has 17 chalets on beach, quite comfortable, some with air-conditioning. Good restaurant.

Club Méditerranée ($$$) Batu 29, Jalan Kuantan (tel: 09 591131/181). Pioneering French resort. Exorbitant prices to play at going back to nature. Secluded spot north of main beach concentration.

Coconut Inn ($) Kampung Cerating Lama (tel: 09 503299). Friendly owners. Well-maintained A-frame huts and chalets with bath.

Palm Grove Beach Resort ($$$) Lot 1290 Mukim Sungai Karang (tel: 09 513399; fax: 03 2622634). Traditional Malay-style room blocks in landscaped gardens. Good water-sports facilities, plush rooms.

Kampung Kuala Besut

Primula Besut Beach Resort ($$) (tel: 09 976311; fax: 09 976322). Secluded beachfront location, uninspiring small modern hotel. Restaurant, pool.

Kampung Merang

Man's Homestay ($) Jalan Penarik. Very basic guesthouse facilities or huts. Friendly owners who arrange fishing trips or camping trips on Pulau Redang across the water.

Merang Beach Resort ($) Pantai Peranginan. Simple A-frame chalets, some with bath and fan, on superb stretch of isolated beach. Not much food around. Own car advisable.

Kota Bharu

Indah Hotel ($) 235 A–B, Jalan Kebun Sultan (tel: 09 785081). Overlooking Padang and royal palace. Air-conditioned rooms, restaurant, parking lot. Good value.

Kencana Inn ($$) 177–81 Jalan Padang Garong (tel: 09 747944). Flashy air-conditioned hotel right near Central Market. Coffee house and bar.

Longhouse Beach Motel ($) Pantai Cinta Berahi (tel: 09 731090). Located right next to food stands, this pleasant low-budget place has reasonable rooms and beach huts.

Murni Hotel ($$) Jalan Dato' Pati (tel: 09 782399). Well situated, good facilities. Popular with local businessmen.

Pantai Cinta Berahi Resort ($$) Pantai Cinta Berahi (tel: 09 732307). Pleasantly landscaped small resort on beach.

Perdana Hotel ($$$) Jalan Mahmud (tel: 09 785000; fax: 09 747621). Good central location, all top facilities.

Pool, tennis, parking lot.

Perdana Resort ($$$) Pantai Cinta Berahi (tel: 09 785222/733000; fax: 09 747621). Out on Kota Bharu's "Beach of Passionate Love." Reasonably priced chalet resort with restaurant, bar, tennis courts, pool, and parking lot.

Suria Hotel ($) Jalan Padang Garong (tel: 09 746477/567). Cheap air-conditioned rooms with bath and free breakfast if you're lucky. Opposite Central Market and bus station.

Temenggong Hotel ($) Jalan Tok Hakim (tel: 09 783844/130). Good value, top of budget category. Fully air-conditioned, restaurant, bar. Popular so often full.

Tourist Office ($) Jalan Sultan Ibrahim (tel: 09 785534/ 783543). Organizes three-night *kampung* stays with Malay families. Local crafts and cooking instruction all thrown in.

Kuala Terengganu

Motel Desa ($$) Bukit Pak Apil (tel: 09 623033). Small hilltop hotel with good views and breezes. Beautiful garden setting. Well-appointed rooms for price, restaurant.

Pantai Primula Hotel ($$$) Jalan Persinggahan (tel: 09 622100; fax: 09 633360). This concrete sore thumb (at the southern end of town on Pantai Batu Buru) is KT's top hotel. Restaurants, rooftop disco, pool with waterfall. The beach is just a few steps away. Reasonable air-conditioned rooms and very friendly service.

Seaview Hotel ($) 18A Jalan Masjid Abidin (tel: 09 621911/623048). Spacious rooms with fan or air-conditioning, central location although palace view replaces sea view!

Seri Hoover Hotel ($) 49 Jalan Sultan Ismail (tel: 09 633823/833). Right on KT's main commercial street. Top of budget range although a little drab. Air-conditioned rooms with TV and telephone. Restaurant, bar.

Sri Terengganu Hotel ($) 120 A/B Jalan Sultan Ismail (tel:

09 634622). Modest, friendly hotel. Clean rooms with air-conditioning or fan, with or without bath.

Kuantan

Hotel Beserah ($) 2 Jalan Beserah (tel: 09 526144/245). Worn at edges but spacious rooms. Carpark.

Hotel Kuantan ($) Telok Cempedak (tel: 09 524755). Modest little establishment with old-fashioned style. Some rooms with air-conditioning and bath. Soon to have its sea view blocked by Hyatt extension.

Hyatt Kuantan ($$$) Telok Cempedak (tel: 09 501234; fax: 09 507577). Fantastic location on gentle sweep of bay north of town center. Extensive range of international facilities, superb pool with swim-up bar, beach at feet. New extension may spoil it though.

Merlin Inn Resort ($$) Telok Cempedak (tel: 09 522300/388; fax: 09 503001). Adjoining Hyatt on beachfront. Far from the luxury of the Hyatt but the rates are slightly lower.

Samudra River View Hotel ($$) Jalan Besar (tel: 09 522707). Best place in town center right on river. Fully air-conditioned, restaurant, pool, parking lot.

Marang

Angullia Beach House ($/$$) Batu 12, Kampung Pantai Rhu Muda (tel: 09 681322). Singaporean-owned resort on beautiful stretch of beach with wide price range depending on comforts. Restaurant not recommended.

Marang Guest House ($) Lot 1367/1368, Kampung Paya Bukit Merah (tel: 09 682277). Cheap guest house; best rooms have mosquito nets. Overlooks lagoon and Pulau Kapas.

Mare Nostrum ($) 313 Jalan Pantai (tel: 09 681433). About a mile south of Marang, fenced-in Swiss-owned resort on beach. Basic A-frame huts or more luxurious chalets. Good restaurant.

Taman Rehat Semarak ($) Km 22, Pantai Kelulut (tel: 09 682288). Isolated resthouse on beach 14 miles south of Marang. Vast family chalets or reasonably priced rooms.

Mersing

Embassy Hotel ($) 2 Jalan Ismail (tel: 07 793545). Central location near main roundabout, excellent value. Clean, comfortable rooms with bath and fan.

Merlin Inn ($$) 2 Jalan Endau (tel: 07 791311/2/3). Situated 1 mile north of town, modestly scaled, fully air-conditioned modern hotel. Pool, disco, restaurant.

Rumah Rehat Mersing ($) 490 Jalan Ismail (tel: 07 792102). Beach location outside town center, 18 air-conditioned rooms with bath and telephone. Often fully booked.

Pekan

Pekan Hotel ($) 60 Jalan Tengku Ariff Bendahara (tel: 09 571378). Rock-bottom prices and matching comfort.

Rumah Rehat Pekan ($) Jalan Sultan Abu Bakar (tel: 09 421240). Five-room resthouse, slightly more comfortable than the above.

Pulau Besar Tengah

Pirate Bay ($$) (tel: 07 241911). Only resort on this blissful island, owned by Malay-Italian couple. Restaurant serves excellent food. Upscale chalets, quite pricey.

Pulau Kapas

Kapas Island Resort ($) Bookings at Marang (tel: 09 632989/682597). Basic A-frame huts and more comfortable chalets in beautiful island setting.

Mak Cik Gemuk Beach Resort ($) Bookings at Marang (tel: 09 681221). Ten reasonably priced chalets.

Primula Kapas Island Resort ($$) Book through Kuala Terengganu Primula Hotel (tel: 09 622100; fax: 09 633360). Has 40 thatched wooden chalets with veran-

das set among coconut palms on beach. Comfortable. Restaurant, pool, water sports.

Zaki Beach Resort ($) Bookings at Marang (tel: 09 620258/628181). Ten beach chalets, some with fan and private shower.

Pulau Perhentian

Coral View ($) Pulau Besar Perhentian. Simple A-frame huts well situated on beach near coral reef. Restaurant.

Perhentian Island Resort ($$) c/o Menara Promet, 25th floor, Jalan Sultan Ismail, Kuala Lumpur (tel: 03 2480811). Best spot on island overlooking coral reef bay. A-frame chalets or comfortable air-conditioned bungalows. Pricey restaurant, bar. Popular with diving groups.

Rumah Rehat Perhentian ($) c/o District Office, Kampung Kuala Besut (tel: 09 972328). Prettiest chalets on island. Book and pay in Kampung Kuala Besut.

Pulau Rawa

Rawa Safaris ($$) c/o The Tourist Centre, Mersing (tel: 07 791204/498). Established resort offering wooden chalets in coconut grove on water's edge. Double rooms with verandas and shower rooms. Superb snorkeling spot.

Pulau Redang

Camping ($) Camping Holiday, Kuala Lumpur (tel: 03 7178935). Organizes camping trips to island.

Dahlan Beach Chalets ($) Pasir Panjang (tel: 09 627050). Chalets or tents on beautiful bay to south of island. Organizes diving trips and transport from Kampung Merang.

Pulau Sibu and Pulau Sibu Tengah

Omar & Helena ($) Kampung Hut, Pulau Sibu (tel: 07 793125). Owned by Anglo-Malay couple. Range of comfort and prices, English breakfast.

Sea Gypsy Village Resort ($) Pulau Sibu (tel: 07 793125). Spacious chalet

accommodations in the north of the island. Friendly service, good restaurant.
Sibu Island Cabanas ($) Pulau Sibu (tel: 07 317216). Upscale beach chalets.
Sibu Island Resort ($$) Pulau Sibu Tengah (tel: 07 818348 or 07 316201 in Johor Bahru). Large, luxury resort. Extensive facilities.

Pulau Tinggi
Koperasi Felda Chalet ($$) (tel: 07 223432). Wide range of prices and facilities.
Smailing Island Resort ($$) c/o 17 Tingkat 2, Kompleks Tun Abdul Razak, Jalan W A Fook, Johor Bahru (tel: 07 246490; fax: 07 246491). A 120-room luxury resort built in traditional Malay style. Air-conditioned chalets with TV, telephone and bath. Sophisticated restaurant. Numerous water sports.

Pulau Tioman
Desa Nipah ($), Kampung Nipah. Most isolated beach on Tioman. Good snorkeling, traditional chalets with bath but no electricity and no telephone. Dormitory, restaurant.
Genting Damai ($) Kampung Genting. At end of road south on untouristy beach. Comfortable chalets and good restaurant. No telephones.
Nazri's Place ($/$$) Kampung Air Batang. Long-established, well-located chalets on best stretch of beach in main backpackers' Mecca. Has 50 chalets, rooms and huts, some very comfortable, plus lively restaurant.
Nora Chalets ($) Kampung Salang. Most northern point of island on superb bay. Huts set back from beach among trees, good beachfront restaurant. Friendly.
Panuba Inn ($) Peaceful location to north of Tekek. Ten beachfront bungalows among rocks and trees, some with good views.
Paya Beach Resort ($$) Kampung Paya (tel: 07 762534). Vast restaurant, often filled with tour groups. Superior accommodations, water-sports facilities.

Samudra Swiss Cottages ($) Kampung Tekek (tel: 07 248728). Situated in largest tourist village of island. Overpriced though comfortable chalets.
Tioman Island Resort ($$$) (tel: 09 445445 or KL 03 2429611; fax: 09 445718 or KL 03 2488249). Well-run luxury resort with 220 air-conditioned traditional chalets in hillside garden overlooking sea. Facilities include golf, tennis, horse riding, and water sports. Good restaurant, bar.

Rantau Abang
Dahimah's Guesthouse ($) Clean rooms with shower and fan right on turtle beach. Restaurant.
Merantau Inn ($$) Kampung Kuala Abang (tel: 09 841131). Situated 2 miles south of turtle beach. Reasonably priced, roomy modern bungalows, bath and fan. Restaurant.
Rantau Abang Visitor Centre ($$) Batu 13, off Jalan Dungun (tel: 09 841533/881/882). Ten traditional timber chalets run by Tanjung Jara Hotel. Organized for turtle-watching. Prime location.

Sekayu
See Tasik Kenyir.

Tanjung Jara
Tanjung Jara Beach Hotel ($$) Batu 8, off Dungun road (tel: 09 841801/2/3; fax: 09 842653). Award-winning beach hotel in beautiful landscaped gardens. Traditional Malay palace-style room blocks and chalets, tasteful decoration, friendly low-key service. Reasonable rates for quality and facilities, particularly out of turtle season.

Tasik Kenyir and Kuala Berang
Hutan Lipur Sekayu ($) Pejabat Perhutanana, Kuala Berang (tel: 09 811259). Reasonably priced and well maintained rest-house chalets and bungalows. Avoid weekends.
Kenyir Lake Resort ($$) Kenyir Dam (tel: 09 950609).

Idyllic lakeside spot offering houseboat accommodations and restaurant that allows you to fish as you eat. Boating, jungle treks. Three-day packages only.
Shafiq House ($) Taman Dato' Rahman Kassim, Kuala Berang (tel: 09 812137). Modest hotel convenient for Sekayu Waterfall or Tasik Kenyir.

EAST MALAYSIA
Bako
Bako National Park ($) c/o Sarawak Tourist Information, Main Bazaar (tel: 082 248088/410944). Fantastic seafront site with superior and standard rest-houses, lodge, hostel, camp-site. Cooking utensils provided. Park canteen.

Beaufort
Beaufort Hotel ($) (tel: 087 211911/2). Fairly cheap air-conditioned rooms with bath and TV. Central location, restaurant.
Mandarin Inn ($) (tel: 087 212800/798). Modern hotel outside center across river. Air-conditioned rooms with bath.

Belaga
Belaga Hotel ($) Belaga Bazaar (tel: 084 461244). Cheap hotel which also arranges riverboat rental.
Huan Kilah Lodging House ($) Belaga Bazaar (tel: 084 461259). Marginally higher standard and rates than the Belaga Hotel.

Bintulu
Plaza Hotel ($$$) 116 Taman Sri Dayang, Jalan Abang Dalau (tel: 086 35111). Flashy, large, modern hotel—top of the boom town. All possible amenities, pool, tennis, health center.
Sunlight Hotel ($) Jalan Abang Dalau (tel: 086 32577). Reasonable air-conditioned rooms with bath.

Damai
See Santubong.

Gunung Mulu
Gunung Mulu National Park ($/$$) c/o Section Forest Office, Miri (tel: 085 36637)

or National Parks Office, Kuching (tel: 082 442180). Large rest-house with suites, hostels, chalets, private guesthouses, and bat observatory! Restaurant facilities. Temporarily restricted to tour operators.

Kampung Kundasang

Hotel Perkasa ($$) Gunung Kinabalu (tel: 088 889511; fax: 088 889101). Unattractive modern hotel in superb location near entrance to Kinabalu National Park.

Kanowit

Rumah Kerehatan Kerajaan ($) Jalan Lukut (tel: 084 752187/92173). Four-room rest-house.

Kapit

Ark Hill Hotel ($) (tel: 804 796168). Pleasant new hotel. Rooms with TV, air-conditioning and bath. Located off Main Square.
Hotel Meligai ($$) 34 Jalan Airport (tel: 084 796611). A 41-room modern hotel. Reasonably appointed rooms. Loud live music in pub nightly.
Rejang Hotel ($) 28 Main Bazaar (tel: 084 796709). A 26-room hotel with a wide range of rooms from the very basic to fan-cooled or air-conditioned with bath.

Kinabalu National Park

c/o Sabah Parks Office, Block K, Sinsuran Kompleks, Jalan Tun Fuad Stephens, Kota Kinabalu (tel: 088 211585/652/881). Hostels, standard or deluxe cabins, chalets, luxury villas. Canteen and restaurant, cooking facilities.

Kota Belud

Government Resthouse ($) c/o District Office (tel: 088 67532). Telephone for possible accommodations.
Hotel Kota Belud ($) 21 Jalan Francis (tel: 088 976576). Small, simple hotel with clean, air-conditioned rooms.

Kota Kinabalu

Asia Hotel ($) 68 Bandaran Berjaya (tel: 088 53533).

Green setting outside main hub near museum. Air-conditioned rooms with bath at reasonable rates.
Diamond Inn ($) Kampung Ayer (tel: 088 225222/5). In night market area. Good value rooms with airconditioning, bath, TV, minibar.
Hotel Kinabalu ($) 21 Jalan Tugu, Kampung Ayer (tel: 088 245599; fax: 088 218937). Fully air-conditioned modern hotel in lively downtown area by night market.
Hyatt Hotel ($$$) Jalan Datuk Salleh Sulong (tel: 088 219888/221234). First-class hotel with full facilities in prime central location. Sweeping views over off-shore islands and city.
Sabah Inn ($$) 25 Jalan Pantai (tel: 088 53322). Well-appointed rooms with all basic facilities. Coffee house, bar, health center.
Shangri-La ($$) Bandaran Berjaya (tel: 088 212800). Good value top-range hotel with all facilities.
Tanjung Aru Beach Hotel ($$$) Locked Bag 174 (tel: 088 58711/225800; fax: 088 217155). Sabah's top luxury hotel, spectacular beach setting a few miles south of town. Tasteful rooms and general design blending into gardens. All possible amenities including marina, pool, health center. Excellent restaurants and Shangri-La Group service. Expensive.

Kuching

Arif Hotel ($) Jalan Haji Taha (tel: 082 241211). Cheap, friendly hotel near mosque and lively market area. Fan-cooled or air-conditioned rooms, with or without bath.
Borneo Hotel ($) 300-F Jalan Tabuan (tel: 088 244121/4). Uphill from center, a well-appointed air-conditioned hotel. Bar, disco.
Green Mountain Lodging House ($) 19 Jalan River (tel: 082 246952/41244). In quiet area set back from central action. Rooms with fan or air conditioning, TV on request.

Holiday Inn ($$$) Jalan Tunku Abdul Rahman (tel: 082 423111; fax: 082 426169). Superb riverside location with views towards fort and Istana. Unimaginative rooms but good service and value. Terrace bar overlooking pool, all amenities.
Longhouse Hotel ($) 101 Jalan Berjaya (tel: 082 419333). Top of budget range. A 50-room hotel with good facilities. Discount rates for rooms are sometimes available.
Metropole Inn ($) 22-3 Jalan Green Hill (tel: 082 412484/494). Glitzy air-conditioned hotel with 22 rooms. Doubles up as booking office for boat rides to Sibu.
Riverside Majestic ($$$) Jalan Tunku Abdul Rahman (tel: 082 247777; fax: 082 425858). Kuching's latest and greatest, towering over Holiday Inn opposite. Top dining and sports facilities at a price.
Telang Usan Hotel ($$) Ban Hock Road, PO Box 1579 (tel: 082 415588; fax: 082 425316). Quiet hotel set back from town center. Dayak artifacts are a plus. Reasonably priced, efficient, and friendly.

Kudat

Government Resthouse ($) c/o District Office (tel: 088 61331/49/04). Seven-room rest-house.
Hotel Sunrise ($) (tel: 088 61517). Best place in town, with air-conditioned rooms plus bath and a good restaurant.

Labuan

Hotel Emas Labuan ($$) 27-30 Jalan Muhibbah (tel: 087 413966). Uninspiring but comfortable mid-range hotel, all room facilities and services. Restaurant.
Labuan Hotel ($$$) Jalan Merdeka (tel: 087 412311/502; fax: 087 415355). Labuan's luxury hotel with 150 rooms, pool, restaurants, bars, shops, and full room facilities.
Victoria Hotel ($) Jalan Tanjung Kubung (tel: 087

412411). Air-conditioned rooms with TV, telephone, room service, restaurant. Fairly expensive like everything in Labuan.

Miri

Apollo Hotel ($) 4 Jalan South Yu Seng (tel: 085 415236/33307/33418; fax: 085 419964). Fully air-conditioned hotel in central location. Rooms with bath, TV, telephone. One of Miri's best deals.

Gloria Hotel ($) 27 Jalan Brooke (tel: 085 416699). Top of budget bracket, fully air-conditioned. Rooms with TV, telephone, room service. Restaurant, parking lot. Central location.

Holiday Inn Miri ($$$) Scheduled to open in 1994. Contact Holiday Inn Kuching for information or tel: 085 418888.

Park Hotel ($$) Jalan Raja (tel: 085 414555). Well-appointed, air-conditioned hotel in good location. Restaurant, bar, health center, parking lot.

Niah National Park

c/o National Parks and Wildlife Office, Section Forest, Miri (tel: 085 36637). Wide-ranging accommodations from deluxe chalets to hostel or campsite. In delightful riverside setting.

Niah Caves Hotel ($) Batu Niah (tel: 086 737726). In village a few miles from national park. Clean, air-conditioned rooms sharing bath. Very cheap.

Pulau Sipadan

Borneo Divers Kota Kinabalu (tel: 088 222226, or Labuan (tel: 087 415867). Package diving tours only.

Sipadan Dive Center A1026, Wisma Merdeka, Jalan Tun Razak, Kota Kinabalu (tel: 088 240584/218710; fax: 088 240415). New (and more reasonably priced) competition for the above.

Sandakan

Hong Kong Hotel ($) PO Box 522 (tel: 089 212295). Right in town center. Simple 30-room hotel.

Hotel Hsiang Garden ($$) PO Box 82 (tel: 089 273122; fax: 089 273127). A 55-room hotel. Fully air-conditioned. Restaurant.

London Hotel ($) Lebuh Empat (tel: 089 216371/366). Modest, clean hotel, 17 air-conditioned rooms with bath.

Ramada Renaissance Hotel ($$$) Km 1, Jalan Utara (tel: 089 213299; fax: 089 271271). Just outside center close to rain forest. Top luxury hotel with endless amenities—golf, tennis, squash, gym, disco, business center. Spacious rooms and suites.

Santubong

Buntal Village Resort ($$) Buntal (tel: 082 841452/3; fax: 082 841454). Pretty rural village setting 6 miles inland from Santubong on Kuching road. *Kampung*-style chalets, seafood.

Camp Permai ($) Damai Beach (tel: 082 428601/2; fax: 082 244585). Well-equipped log cabins on beach with attached bathrooms, verandas, cooking facilities. Jungle backdrop.

Holiday Inn Damai Beach Resort ($$$) PO Box 2870 (tel: 082 423142/411777; fax: 082 428911). Fast-expanding resort hotel on magnificent Damai Beach next to cultural village. Spacious air-conditioned chalets in landscaped beach-front garden. All facilities, water sports, jungle trekking. Friendly service. Boat trips to Pulau Santang and Bako Park.

Sematan

Government Resthouse ($) c/o District Office (tel: 082 71101). Three-room resthouse.

Thomas Lai Bungalows ($) (tel: 082 45174). Seafront bungalows amongst coconut palms. Caters mainly to family groups.

Semporna

Dragon Inn Hotel ($$) Jalan Tastan (tel: 089 781088). Superb hotel complex on stilts in bay. Very pleasant air-conditioned rooms with bath and TV.

Government Resthouse ($) c/o District Office (tel: 089 781618). Four-room resthouse outside town center.

Semporna Hotel ($) Block 4, Peti Surat 36 (tel: 089 781378). Basic but cheerful and clean. Fan-cooled or air-conditioned rooms overlooking the only action in town. Can arrange island boat trips.

Sibu

Hoover House ($) Jalan Pulau. Methodist guesthouse with impeccably clean fan-cooled rooms plus bath at unbeatable rates. Just outside town center.

New World Hotel ($) 1–3 Jalan Wong Nai Siong (tel: 084 310313). Central location. Air-conditioned rooms with bath and TV.

Premier Hotel ($$) Jalan Kampung Nyabor (tel: 084 323222). Fairly pricey modern hotel with extensive facilities.

Tanahmas Hotel ($$$) Jalan Kampung Nyabor, PO Box 240 (tel: 084 333188; fax: 084 333288). Giant modern hotel towering over wharf and commercial center. Fully air-conditioned rooms with excellent facilities.

Tambunan

Government Resthouse ($) c/o District Office (tel: 087 74225/74331). Six-room resthouse.

Tambunan Village Resort Centre ($) Traditional bamboo constructions: longhouse, chalets or motel rooms at reasonable rates.

Tawau

Ambassador Hotel ($) 1872 Jalan Raya (tel: 089 772700/718). Just outside center. Good value for simple air-conditioned rooms with bath.

Emas Hotel ($$) Jalan Utara (tel: 089 762000). Central location. Large modern hotel, fully air-conditioned. Restaurant, disco.

Marco Polo Hotel ($$$) Jalan Klinik (tel: 089 777988/614; fax: 089 763739). High-standard accommodations at reasonable rates. Air-conditioned, restaurant, bar, pool, tennis, parking lot.

Oriental Hotel ($) 10 Jalan Dunlop (tel: 089 771500/502). Air-conditioned rooms with bath and TV.

Tenom

Government Resthouse ($) c/o District Office (tel: 087 735607). Four-room resthouse.

Hotel Tenom ($) PO Box 198 (tel: 087 735562/736378). On main street. Spacious rooms with air-conditioning, bath, TV at moderate rates.

Perkasa Hotel ($$) PO Box 225 (tel: 087 735811/2; fax: 087 736134). Modern hotel on hilltop overlooking town. Fully air-conditioned, reasonable rates.

Tuaran

Government Resthouse ($) Pantai Dalit, c/o District Office (tel: 088 788363/511/518). Six-room rest-house on beach.

Tunku Abdul Rahman National Park

c/o Sabah Parks Office, Block K, Sinsuran Kompleks, Jalan Tun Fuad Stephens, Kota Kinabalu (tel: 088 211881/652/285; fax: 088 221001. Reservations for accommodations on Pulau Mamutik and Pulau Manukan or camping permits.

Turtle Islands

c/o Regional Office East Coast Parks, 9th Floor, Wisma Khoo, PO Box 768, Sandakan (tel: 089 273453; fax: 089 214570). Bookings for chalet accommodations on Pulau Selingan. Alternatively, contact Sabah Parks Office in Kota Kinabalu (tel: 088 211881/652/285).

RESTAURANTS

The following restaurants have been divided into three price categories:

- budget ($)
- moderate ($$)
- expensive ($$$)

SINGAPORE

Alkaff Mansion ($$$) 10 Telok Blangah Green (tel: 278 6979). Beautiful 1920s colonial mansion in breezy hillside garden outside city center. The speciality is *rijstaffel*, a Dutch-influenced Indonesian buffet. Go for a drink on the veranda.

Aziza's ($$$) 36 Emerald Hill Road (tel: 235 1130). Delicious Malay cuisine aimed at Western clientele.

Ban Seng Restaurant ($) 79 New Bridge Road (tel: 533 1471). Busy at lunchtime. Steamed crayfish and stuffed sea cucumber.

Banana Leaf Apollo ($) 56 Racecourse Road (tel: 293 8682). In Little India's southern Indian food Mecca. Crowded with fish-head curry *aficionados*.

Bibi's ($) Peranakan Place, 180 Orchard Road (tel: 732 6966). In Singapore's Peranakan hub. Coffee-shop snacks and pub open until 1 am.

China Palace ($$) #02-00 Wellington Building, 20 Bideford Road (tel: 235 1378). Well-established, mainly Szechuan cuisine. Fresh fish from tanks or camphor-smoked duck.

Garden Seafood ($$) Goodwood Park Hotel, 22 Scotts Road (tel: 734 7411). Popular lunchtime *dim sum* at reasonable prices.

Hua Tuo Guan ($) 22 Tanjong Pagar Road (tel: 222 4854). Herbal teas and dishes in traditional Chinatown teahouse.

Imperial Herbal Restaurant ($$) Metropole Hotel, 41 Seah Street (tel: 337 0491). Tantalizing herbal specialties concocted by traditional resident herbalist.

Komala Villas ($) 76/78 Serangoon Road (tel: 293 6980). Good *dosai* (Indian pancakes) and southern Indian vegetarian food. Many others near by.

Lei Garden ($$$) Boulevard Hotel, 200 Orchard Boulevard (tel: 737 2911). Highly rated Cantonese restaurant exploiting every possible exotic ingredient.

Li Bai ($$$) Sheraton Towers Hotel, 39 Scotts Road (tel: 737 6888). Exquisite and inventive *nouvelle cuisine Chinoise*. Elegant setting for shark's-fin soup or suckling pig. Desserts include bird's-nest soup specialty.

Lian Heng Teochew Eating House ($) 48 Mosque Street (tel: 223 1652). Specialty is *muay*, a soupy rice porridge accompanied by savory dishes.

Madras New Woodlands Café ($) 14 Upper Dickson Road (tel: 297 1594). Excellent vegetarian *thalis* in air-conditioned setting. Popular with locals.

Nyonya and Baba Restaurant ($$) 262–4 River Valley Road (tel: 734 1382). Pleasant setting for flavorsome Nyonya cuisine. Try the chicken with black nuts.

Peranakan Inn ($) 210 East Coast Road (tel: 440 6194). Favorite local haunt for Nyonya specialties.

Prima Tower Revolving Restaurant ($$$) 201 Keppel Road (tel: 272 8822). Possibly best Peking duck in town. Fabulous harbor views.

Rang Mahal ($$$) Imperial Hotel, 1 Jalan Rumbia (tel: 737 1666). All the works in dazzling north Indian style: live music and dancing. Lunchtime buffet and excellent tandoori food.

Tai Tong Hoi Kee ($) 3 Mosque Street (tel: 223 3484). Atmospheric Chinatown teahouse serving hearty *dim sum*.

Zam Zam ($) 699 North Bridge Road (tel: 298 7011). Indian Muslim restaurant serving delicious *murtabak*, chicken *biryani* and fish curry.

KUALA LUMPUR

Bangles ($$) 60C Jalan Tuanku Abdul Rahman (tel: 03 2983780). Rather stylish first-floor restaurant serving good northern Indian cuisine.

Bilal Restaurant ($$) 33 Jalan Ampang (tel: 03 2320804). Super-hot curries from southern India in pleasant setting.

Bunga Raya Restaurant ($$) Level 2, Putra World Trade

Centre (tel: 03 4422999). Popular lunchtime spot for Malay specialities.

Coliseum Café ($) 98 Jalan Tuanku Abdul Rahman (tel: 03 2926270). Excellent steaks or fish and chips in old colonial setting.

Devi Annapurna ($) Lorong Maarof, Bangsar. Excellent southern Indian vegetarian *thalis* in popular, bustling place.

Dreamland Drink & Food Garden ($$) 14 Jalan Tun Perak (tel: 03 2482391). Popular Chinese seafood restaurant behind Equatorial Hotel.

Le Coq d'Or ($$) 121 Jalan Ampang (tel: 03 2429732). Palatial setting for sophisticated western cuisine. Bar. Also produces good-value breakfasts.

Nelayan Floating Restaurant ($$) Titiswangsa Lake Gardens (tel: 03 4228400). Picturesque water-village-style restaurant with a seemingly endless menu of Chinese and Malay dishes.

Nyonya Heritage Restoran ($$) 44, 4th Floor, Jalan Sultan Ismail (tel: 03 2433520). Upscale Nyonya restaurant.

Rasa Utara ($$) Bukit Bintang Plaza, Jalan Bukit Bintang (tel: 03 2438234). Good Malay cuisine in modern air-conditioned setting.

Restoran 123 ($$) 159 Jalan Ampang (tel: 03 2614746). Fashionable eating place offering Chinese and Malay specialities in upbeat *kampung* setting.

Satay Anika ($$) Bukit Bintang Plaza (tel: 03 2483113). *Satay* specialities.

Seri Devi ($) 9 Jalan Travers, off Jalan Brickfields (tel: 03 2744173). Popular local Indian banana-leaf specialities.

Seri Malaysia ($$) 1 Jalan Conlay (tel: 03 2414699). Traditional Malay cuisine with live cultural performances.

Shang Palace ($$$) Shangri-La Hotel, Jalan Sultan Ismail (tel: 03 2322388). Luxury setting for superb *dim sum* lunches. One of KL's top Chinese restaurants.

The Pines ($) 297 Jalan Brickfields (tel: 03 2741194). Good Cantonese food in garden setting.

The Ship ($$) 40–1 Jalan Sultan Ismail (tel: 03 2418805). Hip chain of western grilled meat and seafood restaurants; pub-style décor.

Yazmin Restaurant ($$) 6 Jalan Kia Peng (tel: 03 2415655). Delicious Malay buffets on terrace with cultural performances. Garden setting, but indoor eating also available.

WEST COAST
Alor Setar
Café de Siam ($) Jalan Kota. Pungent, spicy Thai fare in town center. Chilli crabs, prawns, shark's-fin soup.

Ipoh
Restaurant Mun Cheong Seafood ($) 511 Jalan Pasir Putih (tel: 05 212815). A popular Cantonese restaurant that specialises in steamed and fried seafood.

Restoran Cathay ($) 786 Jalan Tang Kalsom. Excellent Indian and Malay cuisine at rock-bottom prices. Try the *mee rebus* (curry noodles).

Kukup
Kukup Restaurant ($$) 1 Kukup Laut (tel: 07 890216). Right next to the jetty, a large busy restaurant specializing in steamed fish, prawns, lobsters, crabs, and chilli mussels.

Melaka
Banana Leaf Restaurant ($) 42 Jalan Munshi Abdullah (tel: 06 231607). Good southern Indian vegetarian and non-vegetarian food, plus freshly tossed *roti canai*.

De Lisbon ($) Medan Portugis (tel: 06 248067). Fresh local seafood done up in Portuguese style in open-air setting.

Gluttons' Corner ($) The Esplanade, Jalan Merdeka. Over 20 food stalls offering Malay, Indian, and Chinese specialities on what used to be the seafront.

Jonkers Melaka ($) 17 Jalan Hang Jebat (tel: 06 235578). Elegant, airy Peranakan

mansion serving European and Nyonya food. Small gallery with superb arts and crafts. Daytime only.

Restoran Nyonya Makka ($$) 123 Taman Melaka Raya (tel: 06 240737). A slightly upscale Nyonya restaurant near St Paul's Hill.

Restoran Ole Sayang ($$) 192 Taman Melaka Jaya, Jalan Parameswara (tel: 06 231966). Homely Nyonya restaurant with interesting décor. All the spicy Peranakan dishes and cool desserts.

Restoran Peranakan ($$) 317-C, Klebang Besar, 7km Melaka (tel: 06 354436). Opulent Peranakan showpiece mansion and garden serving delicious Nyonya cuisine. Go for the *udang lemak nanas* (curry with prawns, pineapple and coconut milk). Evening cultural shows with buffet every day except Saturday. The restaurant lies on the Port Dickson road.

Pulau Langkawi
Coffee Terrace ($$) Langkawi Island Resort, Pantai Syed Omar (tel: 04 788209). Upscale Malay and Western food in stunning setting overlooking bay and islands.

Seri Inai Restaurant ($) Pantai Cenang (tel: 04 712419). Good local Malay fare in small motel restaurant near Pelangi Beach Hotel.

Pulau Pinang
The Catch ($$) Teluk Bahang (tel: 04 812828). Vast place emulating *kampung* style with endless seafood menu. Choose your favorite from the tanks.

Dragon King ($) 9 Lebuh Bishop (tel: 04 618035). Delicious sampling of laboriously prepared Nyonya cuisine.

End of the World ($) Jalan Hassan Abas, Teluk Bahang (tel: 04 811189). Fabulous location by jetty at end of north coast road. The seafood includes lobsters, prawns and chilli crabs.

Green Planet ($) 63 Jalan Cintra (tel: 04 616192).

Ecologically oriented, friendly restaurant and coffee-house. Western and local dishes served all day. The newspapers are a good source of local information, as are the regulars.

Komtar Food Court ($) KOMTAR Phase 2 (tel: 04 629932). Over 60 food stalls offer tantalizing selection of Malay, Indian, Chinese, Thai, and Indonesian food. Favorite local spot open from 8 A.M. until 11 P.M.

Moghul Arch ($$) 195 Jalan Batu Feringgi (tel: 04 812891). Excellent Indian tandoori cuisine served on an outdoor terrace or in the dining room inside.

Veloo Vilas 22 Jalan Pinang (tel: 04 614169). In cluster of southern Indian banana-leaf restaurants, all the same quality and value.

CENTRAL REGION

The best places to eat in the Peninsula's central region are at the hotels and resthouses; these are listed in the accommodations section (see pages 272–273).

EAST COAST
Johor Bahru

Jaws ($$) 1D Jalan Skudai (tel: 07 236062/3). JB's most popular seafood restaurant with outdoor dining overlooking Straits of Johor. Delicious chili crab and *tom yam* soup.

Maharaad Thai ($$) 134 Jalan Serampang, Taman Pelangi (tel: 07 332730). Dine on Thai fare in the middle of a housing development! Both garden and indoor seating is available.

Kota Bharu

Malaysia Restoran($) 2527B Jalan Kebun Sultan (tel: 09 783398). Upscale but good-value seafood restaurant.

Kuala Terengganu

Nil ($), 906 Jalan Pantai Batu Buruk (tel: 09 623381). Reputable seafood restaurant on the beach near the Primula Hotel. Fabulous fresh seafood is served in a breezy garden setting. Malay, Thai, and Western cuisine is available.

Taufik ($) 18C Jalan Masjid Abidin (tel: 09 622501). Small, rather drab restaurant opposite the royal palace. Renowned for its Indian food.

Kuantan

Beserah Seafood ($) Kampung Baru Beserah, on Beserah road. Wildly popular for its excellent seafood dishes. Also has good beach views.

Hugo's Grill ($$) Hyatt Hotel, Telok Cempedak (tel: 09 525211). *The* place in town to dine on sophisticated Malay and Western cuisine.

Katong Seafood Restaurant ($) 35 Telok Cempedak (tel: 09 529947). Chili crab and claypot fish-head curry on beach.

Restoran Pattaya ($) Telok Cempedak (tel: 09 515880). Scenic beach views with Malay, Chinese, and Thai cuisine.

Marang

Marang Inn ($) On seafront road (tel: 09 681878). Popular eating place with backpackers. Both local and international food.

EAST MALAYSIA
Kota Kinabalu

Port View Seafood Restaurant ($) Jalan Haji Saman (tel: 088 221753). Late-night seafood restaurant opposite old Customs Wharf. Vast assortment of fish in tanks.

Restoran Sri Mela ($) 9 Jalan Laiman Diki, Kampung Ayer (tel: 088 55136). Traditional Nyonya food is served alongside Malay specialities.

Wind Bell Seafood Restaurant ($) 20 Jalan Selangor, Tanjung Aru Beach (tel: 088 222305). At opposite end of beach from resort hotel; a lively modern beachfront restaurant. Offers free transportation back to hotel!

Kuching

Batu Lintang ($) Jalan Market. Popular open-air food stalls near river—lots of Chinese *dim sum.*

Duffy Banana Leaf Restaurant ($), Jalan Ban Hock. Southern Indian vegetarian food.

Jubilee Restaurant ($), Jalan India. Malay food in a lively area.

Meisan Restaurant ($$), Holiday Inn, Jalan Tunku Abdul Rahman (tel: 082 423111). Szechuan cuisine.

Sri Sarawak ($$$) Riverside Majestic, Jalan Tunku Abdul Rahman (tel: 082 247777). Fabulous panoramic views over river, with exquisite international and Malay cuisine.

Toh Yuen Restaurant ($$$) Kuching Hilton, Jalan Tunku Abdul Rahman (tel: 082 248200). Top Chinese cuisine in elegant surroundings.

Miri

Apollo Seafood ($) 4 Jalan South Yu Seng (tel: 085 33077). Excellent fresh seafood and steamboat (pick and boil your own) in bustling open-air restaurant.

Bilal ($) 250 Beautiful Jade Centre (tel: 085 420471). Friendly Indian Muslim restaurant in middle of shopping district.

Sandakan

Equatorial Seafood Restaurant ($$) 6–10, Block K, Bandar Ramai-Ramai, Jalan Leila (tel: 089 272794). Good Chinese seafood restaurant in modern air-conditioned block. There is another branch at the golf course.

Supreme Garden Vegetarian Restaurant ($) Block 30, Bandar Ramai-Ramai, Jalan Leila (tel: 089 213292). Delicious Chinese vegetarian dishes.

Trig Hill ($). Trigonometry Hill. Cluster of semi-outdoor eating-places on hilltop with superb views over town. Seafood and steamboat specialities.

Sibu

Wah Hua Café ($) 4 Jalan Kampung Nyabor (tel: 084 315980). Reasonable Chinese food in stretch of equivalent restaurants.

Index

INDEX

285

INDEX

PICTURE CREDITS AND ACKNOWLEDGEMENTS

Picture credits

The Automobile Association would like to thank the following photographers, libraries and associations for their assistance in the preparation of this book:
J ALLAN CASH PHOTOLIBRARY 133b Girl in traditional costume. C K PHOTOGRAPHY 11 Mount Santubong, 182a Sunset, 226 Deer Cave entrance, 236–7 Kuching, 237 Rajah Brooke Memorial, 245 Chinese Temple. F DUNLOP 33 Man cooking over fire, 203 Making a dessert, 235 Kuching Hong San Temple, 238 Menkabong cock fighting, 251 Niah Caves. MARY EVANS PICTURE LIBRARY 30a Singapore waterfront 1910, 38c Alfonso de Albuquerque, 120–1 Somerset Maugham, 120 Joseph Conrad, 121 Somerset Maugham. A EVARD/IMPACT PHOTOS 132–3 Boys in traditional costume. FOOTPRINTS 28a Traditional drums, 211 Huts on Pulau Tioman, 214 Pennant butterfly fish, 215 Divers, 242 Coral and fish. HULTON DEUTSCH COLLECTION LTD 42b Frank Swettenham. ILLUSTRATED LONDON NEWS 30b Raffles Place 1901, 31b Bombing Singapore Harbour, 36b Representatives of the Chinese Community of the Federal Malay States, 43b Barracks Residency Banda Bahru, 44b Japanese tank, 158b Sultans. MALAYSIA TOURISM PROMOTION BOARD 206 *Songket* cloth, 212 Turtle, 225c *Tamu* market, 228 Iban boatman. MUSEUM OF MANKIND 32–3 Stone tools from Kota Tampan. NATIONAL MUSEUM OF SINGAPORE 42–3a *The Padang in Singapore* by J T Thomson. NATURE PHOTOGRAPHERS LTD 179 Great egret (P R Sterry), 180c Blue-tailed banded pitta (S C Bisserot), 212 Loggerhead turtle (J Sutherland), 244 Assam wreathed hornbill (S C Bisserot) 246a Orang-utan (E A Janes), 251 Swiftlet on nest (S C Bisserot). CHRISTINE OSBORNE/MIDDLE EAST PICTURES 240 Rafting on Padas River, 240 Poring Hot Springs. REX FEATURES LTD 12b Lee Kuan Yew, 146 Dr Mahathir Mohamad. R M COMMUNICATIONS 15c Proton. SPECTRUM COLOUR LIBRARY 38a Malacca, 39 Malacca Porta de Santiago, 40–1 Fort Margherita Kuching Sarawak, 132b Boy on horse, 141 Malacca Independence Monument, 231 Mount Kinabalu, 246b Orang-utan. THE MANSELL COLLECTION LTD 40b Sir James Brooke. ZEFA PICTURE LIBRARY (UK) LTD Cover Turtle meat drying, 229 Tattooed Iban man.

All remaining pictures are held in the Association's own picture library (AA PHOTO LIBRARY), with contributions from:
NICK HANNA 18b, 21c, 25b,32, 34–5, 126b, 133, 146–7, 175, 190, 194, 200, 213, 216, 218, 221, 222, 223, 224, 225b, 228–9, 229b, 230, 233, 239, 242, 247a, b, 248, 249, 250a, b, 252. PAUL KENWARD 6, 22b, 23, 54, 65b, 77, 79, 84, 98b, 105, 267. KEN PATERSON 3, 4, 5a, b, 7a, b, 9, 10a, b, 12–13a, 13b, 14–15a, 15b, 16a, b, 17a, b, 18–19a, 19b,c, 20–1a, 20b, 21b, 22a, 24–5a, 24b, c, 26–7a, 26b, c, 27b, 29, 34a, 36a, 37a, b, 38b, 445, 45b, 48, 49, 50a, b, 51, 52a, b, 55a, 56, 57, 58–9a, 58b, 59b, 60, 61, 62, 63, 64–5a, 64b, c, 65c, 66, 67a, b, 68, 69a, b, 70, 71, 72, 73, 74, 75, 76, 78, 80a, b, 81a, b, 82, 83a, b, 85, 87a, b, 88, 90, 91a, b, 92, 93, 94–5a, 94b, 95b, 96, 97, 98a, 99, 100a, b, 101, 102, 103, 104, 106, 107, 108, 109, 112, 113, 114, 115, 116, 117, 118, 119, 122, 123, 124, 125, 126a, 127, 128a, b, 129, 130, 131, 134, 135, 137, 138, 139a, b, 140, 142, 143, 144, 145, 146b, 147, 148, 150, 151, 152, 154–5, 156, 157, 159, 160, 161, 162, 163a, b, 164, 165, 166a, b, 167, 168–9, 170, 171, 172, 173, 174a–b, 176, 177, 178–9a, 178b, c, 180a, b, 181, 182b, 183, 184a, b, 186, 188, 191, 192, 193, 195, 196–7a, 196b, 197b, 199, 201a, 201b, c, 202, 204, 205, 206, 207, 208, 209, 211, 214–15a, 217, 225a, 226b, 235, 244a, 251a, 253, 255, 256, 257, 259, 260, 261, 262, 266. RICK STRANGE 31a.

Acknowledgements

The author would like to thank the following for their help in the production of this book: The Singapore Tourist Promotion Board in London and Singapore; the Malaysian Tourist Promotion Board in London and Paris; Karina Knight; Phillip Spencer; and Shelagh Sartin.

Contributors

Series advisor: Ingrid Morgan **Designer**: Kingfisher Design
Joint series editor: Susi Bailey **Indexer**: Marie Lorimer
Copy editor: Susi Bailey **Verifier**: Nick Hanna

288